The Secret of Secrets

Talks by

Bhagwan Shree Rajneesh

on

The Secret of the Golden Flower

Volume Two

Editor: Ma Yoga Sudha
Design: Ma Deva Arpita
Direction: Ma Yoga Pratima, MM, D. Phil., Arihanta
Copyright: ©1983 Rajneesh Foundation International
Published by: Ma Anand Sheela, MM, D.Phil., D.Litt., Acharya
                    Rajneesh Foundation International
                    P.O. Box 9, Rajneeshpuram
                    Oregon 97741 U.S.A.

First Edition September 1983 — 10,000 copies

For the sutras quoted in this book we gratefully acknowledge the use
of *The Secret of the Golden Flower—A Chinese Book of Life,* translated
and explained by Richard Wilhelm with a foreword and commentary
by C.G. Jung, translated from the German by Cary F. Baynes,
published by Harcourt Brace Jovanovich, Inc.
Reprinted with the kind permission of the publisher.

Printed in U.S.A.
ISBN 0-88050-629-6
Library of Congress Catalog Number 82-50464

CONTENTS

Introduction

Here in Oregon, U.S.A., there is a self-actualized being who guides His disciples on a path of religion as practical as a locksmith's keys. In this book, Bhagwan Shree Rajneesh speaks on Lu-tsu's *The Secret of the Golden Flower,* and unlocks one secret after another. The Tao becomes alive, the mysterious shrouds fall away from a most venerable Master of Tao. Suddenly the relevance, the sheer utility of these age old sutras lies revealed. But there's something more going on here.

To be with Bhagwan is to be with a living Lu-tsu, a living Christ, a living Kabir. He has the unique ability of not only demystifying long-gone Masters, but showing how each relates to the others. Bhagwan's penetrating vision brings Lu-tsu alive.

Bhagwan is more than just a Taoist Master—as if that in itself wasn't enough. He's a weaver as well. He weaves a cloth of exquisite beauty where each thread is a different path to God; Tao, Zen, Christianity are all just threads. The emerging cloth is the fabric of his own mystery school: a mystery school which welcomes any seeker who really hungers for awareness and love.

People arrive here as different packages. Some are wrapped in anger, some in self-loathing, others in retreat. Almost all have come well-wrapped for their journey, and tied tightly so that they will not fall apart on the way. As these people-packages become sannyasins, they slip slowly into Bhagwan's lotus pond of love. The packaging gets wet, and starts to fall away. He keeps weaving his magic cloth; loving, watching, chuckling just a bit at our foolishness. And when we finally come up for air, He hands us a towel of his magic cloth. Slowly these overwrapped packages emerge as laughing, celebrating, individual flowers of great beauty. Tears flow easily, eyes have a new sparkle.

This extraordinary Master has made religion alive for me, brought the delight of existence back and then increased it to the point where I now bow down, tears of sheer gratitude welling up.

Even as Bhagwan brings me closer to "my original face" the mystery of it all deepens. His silence contains more. Touch becomes an eloquent language. And all of it permeated by His love. His love makes me whole and thus His Buddhafield grows.

In the mystery of His very being, slowly I come to share His joy, His celebration. This book is a gift—take it and feel what Bhagwan is saying. Herein truly is *The Secret of Secrets*. Let Bhagwan show you the Tao, the Way—your life will never be the same.

Swami Anand Sugeet

Master Lu-tsu said: *Your work will gradually become concentrated and mature, but before you reach the condition in which you sit like a withered tree before a cliff, there are still many possibilities of error which I would like to bring to your special attention. These conditions are recognized only when they have been personally experienced. First I would like to speak of the mistakes and then of the confirmatory signs.*

When one begins to carry out one's decision, care must be taken so that everything can proceed in a comfortable, relaxed manner. Too much must not be demanded of the heart. One must be careful that, quite automatically, heart and energy are coordinated. Only then can a state of quietness be attained. During this quiet state the right conditions and the right space must be provided. One must not sit down (to meditate) in the midst of frivolous affairs. That is to say, the mind must be free of vain preoccupations. All entanglements must be put aside; one must be detached and independent. Nor must the thoughts be concentrated upon the right procedure. This danger arises if too much trouble is taken. I do not mean that no trouble is to be taken, but the correct way lies in keeping equal distance between being and not being. If one can attain purposelessness through purpose, then the thing has been grasped. Now one can let oneself go, detached and without confusion, in an independent way.

Furthermore, one must not fall victim to the ensnaring world. The ensnaring world is where the five kinds of dark demons disport themselves. This is the case, for example, when, after fixation, one has chiefly thoughts of dry wood and dead ashes, and few thoughts of the bright spring on the great earth. In this way one sinks into the world of the dark. The energy is cold there, breathing is rough, and many images of coldness and decay present themselves. If one tarries there long one enters the world of plants and stones.

Nor must a man be led astray by the ten thousand ensnare-ments. This happens if, after the quiet state has begun, one after another all sorts of ties suddenly appear. One wants to break through them and cannot; one follows them, and feels as if relieved by this. This means the master has become the servant. If a man tarries in this stage long he enters the world of illusory desires.

At best, one finds oneself in heaven, at the worst, among the fox-spirits. Such a fox-spirit, it is true, may be able to roam in the famous mountains enjoying the wind and the moon, the flowers and fruits, and taking his pleasure in the coral trees and jewelled grass. But after having done this, his reward is over and he is born again into the world of turmoil.

Chapter One

August 27th, 1978

A LITTLE BIT OF SKY

ONCE SOME HUNTERS went deep into a dark forest and found a hut in which a hermit was praying before a wooden cross. His face shone with happiness.

"Good afternoon, Brother. May God give us a good afternoon. You look very happy."

"I am always happy."

"You are happy living in this lonely hut doing penance? We have everything and are not happy. Where did you find happiness?"

"I found it here in this cave. Look through that hole and you will catch a glimpse of my happiness." And he showed them a small window.

"You have deceived us, for all we can see is some branches of a tree."

"Take another look."

"All we see are some branches and a little bit of sky."

"That," said the hermit, "is the reason for my happiness—just a little bit of heaven."

Bliss is man's intrinsic nature. It has not to be attained, it has only to be re-discovered. We already have it. We are it. Searching for it somewhere else is a sure way to miss it. Stop searching and look within, and the greatest surprise of your life is awaiting you there, because whatsoever you have been seeking down the ages, through so many lives, is already the case. You need not be a beggar, you are a born emperor. But the Kingdom of God is within you and your eyes go on searching without, hence you go on missing it. It is behind the eyes, not in front of the eyes.

The Kingdom of God is not an object, it is your subjectivity. It is not to be sought because it is the very nature of the seeker. And then, even in the darkest forest, utterly alone in a cave, one can be happy. Otherwise even palaces only create misery.

There are all kinds of miseries in the world: the poor suffers one kind of misery, the rich suffers another kind of misery, but there is no difference as far as misery is concerned. And sometimes it happens that the rich suffers more, because he can afford more. He has more possibilities, more alternatives, open for him. The poor cannot purchase much misery, but the rich can purchase. Hence the richest people feel the most miserable in the world. The richest people become the poorest in this sense. In fact, when you become rich, for the first time you feel the poverty of life. When you are poor you can hope that some day you will be rich, and there will be joy and there will be celebration; but when you have attained to the riches of the outside, suddenly the hope disappears and great hopelessness settles in. You are surrounded by a despair: now there is no hope and no future; now the last hope has disappeared. You had lived with the idea that "One day I will be rich and then everything will be all right." Now you are rich and nothing has changed; the inner misery continues as ever.

In fact, because of the outer riches, in contrast to the outer riches, you can see your inner poverty more clearly, more accurately, more penetratingly. The outer richness only provides a background for feeling the inner poverty. Outer possessions make you aware of the inner emptiness. Hence, it is not surprising that rich countries become religious. India was religious when India was rich, in the days of Buddha, Mahavir. India was affluent; because of that affluence India was aware of the inner poverty. And when you become aware of inner poverty, then you start searching inwards. When you become aware that no outer thing can fulfill the inner longing, that all that is outer remains out, you cannot take it in; when this becomes an absolute certainty then you start a new search, a new adventure. That adventure is religion.

India cannot be religious today. India is one of the poorest countries in the world—how can it be religious? It cannot afford to be religious. Religion is the highest kind of luxury, the ultimate in luxury. It is the ultimate music, ultimate poetry, ultimate dance. It is the ultimate drunkenness with existence itself. Hungry and starved, you cannot search for it. When a man is hungry he needs bread, he does not need meditation. When a man is ill he needs medicine, not meditation. Only a healthy person can become aware that something is missing which can be fulfilled by meditation and by nothing else.

People ask me why there are not many Indians here listening to me. It is not surprising; they are not interested in meditation. Their interest is in material things, their whole obsession is with matter. Of course they talk about spirituality but that is mere talk, a hangover from the past. It gives them a good feeling: at least they are spiritual. If they are missing in material things they can brag about their spirituality.

But to me, spiritualism is a higher stage than materialism: materialism functions as a stepping-stone. Only a rich country starts feeling spiritual poverty. And if you have started feeling spiritual poverty then there are only two possibilities: either you commit suicide or you go through an inner transformation.

Meditation is the method of inner transformation. When suicide and meditation remain the only two alternatives and nothing else is left—either destroy yourself because your whole life is meaningless, or transform yourself into a new plane of being—one has to choose between suicide and meditation.

The rich countries of the world have always been in this dilemma of choosing between suicide and meditation. Rich countries suffer more from suicide, from madness, than poor countries. A poor person has no time to think about suicide; he's so preoccupied with life. A poor person has no time to think of transforming his energies; he's so occupied with how to feed his children, how to have a shelter. He's not interested at all in anything else higher than the body, deeper than the body— and it is natural, I am not condemning it. It is absolutely natural, it is how it should be. That's why poor countries of the world are leaning more and more towards communism, and the capitalist countries of the world are leaning more and more towards spiritualism. Marx's prediction has failed. Marx has said that rich countries will become communist: it has proved nonsense. Only poor countries have become communist. Russia was one of the most poverty-stricken countries, so was China, and so is India. India can be a victim of communism any day: it is preparing, it is on the way.

America has not turned communist. Marx predicted that rich

countries would become communist. I predict that rich countries always become religious, poor countries become communist. And once, through communism, a country becomes
rich, it will start searching and seeking for religion. That's
what is happening deep down in the Russian soul now. Now
Russia has come to a point where it can again think of God
and meditation, prayer. You will be surprised to know that in
Russia people meet in secrecy to pray, because prayer is not
allowed by the government any more. To be religious is to
be a criminal.

Here, there are temples and nobody goes, and churches are
there and people have to be persuaded somehow to go to the
churches, at least on Sunday. People have to be bribed to go
to the temples, to the churches, to the mosques, to the guru-
dwaras. Can you conceive of a country where people meet in
secrecy, in their basements, to pray silently, so that nobody can
hear? Deep in the Russian soul religion is surfacing again; it
has to surface. Now Russia is rich enough to think of higher
things.

In my vision of life materialism and spiritualism are not con-
traries; materialism paves the way for religion. Hence I am
utterly materialistic and utterly spiritualistic. That is one of
the most fundamental teachings that I am delivering to you:
never create an antagonism between the body and the soul,
between the world and God. Never create any antagonism
between materialism and spiritualism—they go together,
just as body and soul. Remain materialistic and use your
materialism as a stepping-stone towards spirituality. That
creates much confusion in people's minds because they have
always been thinking that poverty is something spiritual.
That is utter nonsense. Poverty is the most unspiritual thing

in the world. A poor man cannot be spiritual. He can try, but his spirituality will remain superficial. He has not yet been disillusioned by riches—how can he be spiritual? A great disillusionment is needed, a great disillusionment with the outer world; then you turn in. The turning in comes only at a certain point when you are utterly disillusioned with the outside—when you have seen the world, you have lived the world, you have experienced and you have come to know that there is nothing in it, all soap bubbles, momentary experiences. They promise much but they deliver nothing, and in the end only emptiness is left in your hands. The outer world can only give you death and nothing else. Life has to be searched for within. The sources of life are *in* you.

The tree is in the seed. If you cut the seed open you will not find the tree, true, because that is not the way to find it. You will have to let the seed grow; then the blueprint that is hidden in the seed comes out. When a child is conceived in a mother's womb he is just a seed, but he has all the blueprint, all the possibilities—what kind of body he will have, what kind of face, what color of eyes, hair, height, age, how long he will live, healthy or unhealthy, man or woman, black or white—all is contained in the seed. Life grows out of that seed.

Meditation is turning back towards the innermost core from where all has arisen—the body has arisen, the desires have arisen, the thoughts have arisen, the mind has arisen. You have to go back to the source. Religion is a return to the source—and to know the source is to know God. To know the source is to know the goal, because they are both one. To come back to your innermost core, from where you had started, means you have come to the ultimate where you wanted to reach. The circle is full. There is a moment where the alpha becomes the omega, and then there is fulfillment. When the circle is complete there is fulfillment.

And that is the whole teaching of *The Secret of the Golden Flower* of Master Lu-tsu. He's trying to make the path clear to you: how the circle can be complete, how the light can circulate, how you can move inwards, how you can also have a little bit of sky, a little bit of heaven. And then you can be happy anywhere—even in hell you will be happy.

Right now, as you are, you would be unhappy anywhere, even in heaven. You will find ways and means of being unhappy there too, because you will carry all your jealousies, all your anger, all your greed, all your possessiveness. You will carry all your rage, all your sexuality, all your repressions; you will carry this whole luggage. The moment you reach heaven, you will create hell around yourself there too, because you will be carrying the seeds of hell.

It is said that if you are pure, if you are silent, you reach heaven. The truth is just the opposite: if you are pure, if you are silent, heaven reaches you. One never goes anywhere, one is always here, but once the inside becomes full of light the whole world outside is transformed. Buddha moves in the same world in which you move, Buddha passes through the same streets as you pass, but Buddha lives in a totally different world— Buddha lives in paradise and you live in hell. You may be sitting by the side of a Buddha, you may be holding his hand or touching his feet—so close, yet so far away, so distant, worlds apart. What is the secret of being in heaven, of being in utter bliss, of being in benediction, of being in that splendor called God?

These are the secrets:

>Master Lu-tsu said: *Your work will gradually become*
>*concentrated and mature.*

The path of Tao is not that of sudden enlightenment. It is not like Zen. Zen is sudden enlightenment, Tao is a gradual growth. Tao does not believe in sudden, abrupt changes. Tao believes in keeping pace with existence, allowing things to happen on their own, not forcing your way in any way, not pushing the river in any way. And Tao says: There is no need to be in a hurry because eternity is available to you. Sow the seeds in time and wait, and the spring comes, as it has always been coming. And when the spring comes there will be flowers. But wait, don't be in a hurry.

Don't start pulling the tree upwards so that it can grow fast. Don't be in that kind of mind which asks that everything be like instant coffee. Learn to wait, because nature is very very slow-moving. Because of that slow movement there is grace in nature. Nature is very feminine, it moves like a woman. It does not run, it is not in a hurry, there is no haste. It goes very slowly, a silent music. There is great patience in nature, and Tao believes in the way of nature. 'Tao' exactly means nature, so Tao is never in a hurry; this has to be understood.

Tao's fundamental teaching is: learn to be patient. If you can wait infinitely, it may even happen instantly. But you should not ask that it should happen instantly: if you ask, it may never happen. Your very asking will become a hindrance. Your very desire will create a distance between you and nature. Remain in tune with nature, let nature take its own course—

and whenever it comes it is good, and whenever it comes it is fast, *whenever* it comes. Even if it takes ages to come then too it is not late, it is never late. It always comes in the right moment.

Tao believes that everything happens when it is needed: when the disciple is ready the Master appears. When the disciple is ultimately ready, God appears. Your worthiness, your emptiness, your receptivity, your passivity makes it possible; not your hurry, not your haste, not your aggressive attitude. Remember, truth cannot be conquered. One has to surrender to truth, one has to be conquered by truth.

But our whole education in all the countries down the ages has been of aggressiveness, of ambition. We make people very speedy. We make them very much afraid. We tell them, "Time is money and very precious, and once gone it is gone forever, so make haste. Be in a hurry."

This has been driving people mad. They hurry from one point to another point; they never enjoy any place. They rush around the world from one intercontinental hotel to another intercontinental hotel. And they are all alike; whether you are in Tokyo or in Bombay or in New York or in Paris makes no difference. Those intercontinental hotels are all alike, and people go on rushing from one intercontinental hotel to another thinking that they are travelling around the world. They could have stayed in one intercontinental hotel and there would have been no need to go anywhere else; it is all alike. And they think they are reaching somewhere. Speed is driving people neurotic.

Tao is the way of nature, as the trees grow and rivers move, and the birds, and the children—exactly in the same way one has to grow into God.

Your work will gradually become concentrated and mature.

Don't be in a hurry and don't become desperate. If you fail today, don't feel hopeless. If you fail today it is natural. If you go on failing for a few days it is natural.

People are so afraid of failing that just because of the fear of failing they never try. There are many people who will not fall in love because they are afraid—who knows? They may be rejected—so they have decided to remain unloving, so nobody ever rejects them. People are so afraid of failing that they never try anything new—who knows? If they fail, then what?

And naturally, to move into the inner world you will have to fail many times, because you have never moved there. All your skill and efficiency is of the outer movement, of extroversion. You don't know how to move in. People listen to the words 'move in, go in', but it doesn't make much sense to them. All that they know is how to go out, all that they know is how to go to the other. They don't know any way to come to themselves. It is bound to happen; because of your past habits you will fail many times. Don't become hopeless. Maturity comes slowly. It comes sure and certain, but it takes time. And remember, to each different person it will go at a different pace, so don't compare, don't start thinking, "Somebody is becoming so silent and so joyful and I have not yet become. What is happening to me?" Don't compare with anybody, because each has lived in a different way in his past lives. Even in this life people have lived differently. For example, a poet may find it easier to go in than a scientist; their trainings are different. The whole scientific training is to be objective, to be concerned with the object, to watch the object, to forget subjectivity. The scientist, to be a scientist, has to withdraw himself completely from his experiment. He has not to be involved in the experiment, there should be no emotional involvement. He should be there completely detached, like a computer. He should not be human at all; then only is he a real scientist, and then only will he succeed in science.

Now this is a totally different skill. A poet gets involved. When he watches a flower he starts dancing around it. He participates, he's not just a detached observer. A dancer may find it even more easy because a dancer and his dance are so one, and the dance is so inner that the dancer can move into his inner space very easily. Hence, in the old, mysterious mystery schools of the world dance was one of the secret methods. Dance was evolved in the mystery schools and temples. Dance is one of the most religious phenomena, but it has lost its meaning so completely that it has almost fallen to the opposite polarity. It has become a sexual phenomenon; dance has lost the spiritual dimension. But remember, whatsoever is spiritual can become sexual if it falls, and whatsoever is sexual can become spiritual if it rises. Spirituality and sexuality are intertwined. A musician will find it easier than a mathematician to move into meditation. You have different skills, different minds, different conditionings.

For example, a Christian may find it more difficult to meditate than a Buddhist, because with twenty-five centuries of constant meditation, Buddhism has created a certain quality in its followers. So when a Buddhist comes to me he can fall into meditation very easily. When a Christian comes meditation is very alien, because Christianity has completely forgotten about meditation; it knows only about prayer.

Prayer is a totally different phenomenon. In prayer the other is needed; it can never be independent. Prayer is more like love: prayer is a dialogue. Meditation is not a dialogue; it is not like love, it is *exactly* the opposite of love. In meditation you are left all alone, nowhere to go, nobody to relate to, no dialogue because there is no other. You are simply yourself, utterly yourself. This is a totally different approach.

So it will depend on your skills, your mind, your conditioning, your education, the religion you have been brought up in, the books you have been reading, the people you have been living with, the vibe that you have created in yourself. It will depend on a thousand and one things, on how much you can take—but it comes sure and certain. All that is needed is patience, silent work, patient work and concentration happens, and maturity arrives. In fact, a mature person and a concentrated person are only two aspects of the same phenomenon. That's why children cannot be in concentration: they are constantly moving, they cannot be at one point, fixed. Everything attracts them—a car has passed by, a bird calls, somebody starts laughing, the neighbor has put the radio on, a butterfly moves— everything, the whole world is attractive. They simply jump from one thing to another thing. They cannot concentrate, they cannot live with one thing so utterly and so totally that all else disappears, becomes non-existential.

With maturity, concentration arises. Maturity and concentration are two names for the same thing. But the first thing to remember is that it comes gradually; don't compare, don't be in a hurry.

> But before you sit like a withered tree before a cliff, there are many possibilities of error, which I would like to bring to your special attention.

Master Lu-tsu says: Before the condition arises in you in which you sit like a withered tree before a cliff... This is a Taoist expression, of tremendous beauty and significance. It means alive and yet dead, dead and yet *utterly* alive. It means living in the world with great joy and celebration, but not being part of the world; being in the world but not allowing the world to be in you—"like a withered tree before a cliff." Living like a dead man...

Alexander wanted to take a sannyasin from India to his own country because his master, the great philosopher, Aristotle, had asked him, "When you come back from India, bring a sannyasin"—because India's greatest contribution to the world is the way, the lifestyle of a sannyasin. Aristotle was very interested. He wanted to see what kind of a man a sannyasin was, because it had happened only in India. This is its special contribution to world culture and humanity, a totally different way of living in the world: living in the world and yet not being of the world, remaining unattached and aloof; like a lotus flower in the pond, living in water and yet untouched by the water. When dewdrops gather on the lotus petals they look beautiful in the morning sun, like pearls, but yet they are not touching the flower at all and the flower is not touching them. So close and yet so far away...

"What kind of a man is a sannyasin?"—Aristotle was philosophically interested. He was not the man to become a sannyasin, but he had asked Alexander to bring a sannyasin: "You will be bringing many things. For me, remember to bring a sannyasin." When Alexander was leaving the country he remembered. He had looted much, then he suddenly remembered, "What about a sannyasin?" He inquired at his last station in India. He inquired about a sannyasin and the people said, "Yes, we have a beautiful sannyasin, but it is almost impossible to take him."

Alexander said, "Leave it to me. Don't be worried. You don't know me. If I order the Himalayas to come with me they will have to come with me, so what about a sannyasin? Where is he? You just give me the address"—and the address was given.

The sannyasin was a naked fakir living by the side of the river. Four strong men were sent with naked swords to bring the sannyasin to Alexander.

The sannyasin, seeing those four strong men with naked swords, started laughing. They said, "You don't understand—this is an order from the great Alexander, that you have to be brought to his court. He is waiting for you."

And the sannyasin said, "I have stopped coming and going long ago. If he wants to see me I can oblige him; he can come. But I have stopped coming and going. That coming and going disappeared with my mind. Now there is nobody to come and nobody to go. I exist no more!"

Of course, those Greeks could not have understood. The Greeks are the polar opposite of the Hindus. The Hindus are basically illogical, and the Greeks are basically logical. The Hindus are poetic, intuitive; the Greeks are intellectuals. Those four soldiers said to him, "What nonsense are you talking? We can drag you!"

The sannyasin said, "You can drag my body but not me. You can put my body in a prison, but not me. My freedom will remain intact. I am a lotus flower, the water cannot touch me."

Now this was utter nonsense to those Greeks. They said, "You wait. Let us inform Alexander, lest we do something wrong." Alexander was informed of those beautiful sentences of the sannyasin, and given the report that "He is a beautiful man, sitting naked in the sun on the riverbank. He looks like a great emperor, and there is nothing around him. He possesses nothing, not even a begging bowl. But the grandeur, the grace! You look into his eyes and it seems as if he is the emperor of the whole world. And he laughed at our foolishness—that we had come with naked swords, and he was not afraid at all. And he said, 'You can kill my body but you cannot kill me.'"

Alexander became intrigued; he went to see this naked sannyasin. He was impressed, greatly impressed, and he said, "You will have to come with me. This is my order!"

But the sannyasin said, "The day I became a sannyasin I stopped receiving any orders from anybody. I am a free man, I am not a slave. Nobody can order me. You can kill me but you cannot order me."

Alexander was angry. He took his sword out and he said, "I will immediately cut off your head!"

And the sannyasin started laughing again. And he said, "You can cut it off, because in fact I have cut it off long ago myself. I am a dead man."

Now this is the meaning of real sannyas: a dead man.

And the man said, "How can you kill a dead man? It would be utter foolishness. How can you kill a dead man? A dead man is dead, he cannot die anymore. All is already finished. You came a little late; I exist no more. Yes, you can cut off the head—you will see the head falling on the sands. I will also watch the head falling on the sands. I am a watcher, a witness."

This is the meaning of 'a withered tree before a cliff'. Alexander was the cliff, and the sannyasin was the withered tree. What can the cliff do to the withered tree? The withered tree is already dead, gone. The cliff cannot destroy the withered tree. The withered tree will not be afraid of the cliff.

> There are still many possibilities before this can happen to you—*many possibilities of error, which I would like to bring to your special attention. These conditions are recognized only when they have been personally experienced.*

Remember, all these things that Lu-tsu is saying to you in his immensely valuable message—this is one of the greatest treatises for the seeker—he's saying because he has experienced these things on his own journey. He has come across these errors, and he would like to enlighten his disciples so that they need not be hindered by these errors, so that they need not be distracted by these errors.

Those who have never meditated will not understand what these errors are. When they have been personally experienced, only then does one understand them. But those who are on the Way, they have to be prepared, they have to be told what the pitfalls on the Way are. The Way is not just simple: many other paths fork out of it at many places. You can take a path which will be a dead-end, but you will come to know that it was a dead-end after many many years, or maybe after many lives. And all the effort, and the journey, will have been wasted and you will have to come back again to the point from where you lost the main road. And there are no milestones. No fixed map is available, cannot be made, because God goes on changing. His existence is a constant change. Except for change, everything goes on changing, so no fixed map is possible. Only hints can be given; these are hints. If you understand the hints you will be able to follow the right path, and whenever there

is a possibility of going into errors your understanding will
help you.

> *First I would like to speak of the mistakes and then of
> the confirmatory signs.*

Lu-tsu says, "First I will talk about the mistakes that are possible, and then I will tell you what the confirmatory signs are
which make it certain that you are on the right path."

> *When one begins to carry out one's decision, care must be
> taken so that everything can proceed in a comfortable,
> relaxed manner.*

This is the first thing to be understood. Once you take the decision to follow the inward path, once you take the decision to
be a sannyasin, to be a meditator, once you take the decision
that now the inner has called you and you are going to seek
and search on the quest "Who am I?", then the first thing to be
remembered is: don't move in a tense way. Move in a very
relaxed manner, make sure that your inner journey is comfortable. Now this is of immense importance.

Ordinarily, this first error happens to everybody. People start
making their inner journey unnecessarily complicated, uncomfortable. It happens for a certain reason. People are angry
at others in their ordinary life. In their ordinary life they are
violent with others. In their ordinary extrovert journey they
are sadists: they enjoy torturing others, they enjoy defeat-
ing others, they enjoy competing with others, conquering
others. Their whole joy is in how to make others feel inferior to themselves. This is what your extrovert journey is.
This is what politics is. This is the political mind, constantly

trying to become superior to the other, legally, illegally, but there is constant effort to defeat the other, whatsoever the cost. Even if the other has to be destroyed, then the other has to be destroyed. But one has to win: one has to be the prime minister, one has to be the president, one has to be this and that— at any cost! And all are enemies because all are competitors. Remember this: your whole education prepares you, makes you ready to fight. It does not prepare you for friendship and love, it prepares you for conflict, enmity, war.

Whenever there is competition there is bound to be enmity. How can you be friendly with people with whom you are competing, who are dangerous to you and to whom you are dangerous? Either they will win and you will be defeated, or you will win and they have to be defeated. So all your so-called friendship is just a facade, a formality. It is a kind of lubricant that makes life move smoothly, but deep down there is nobody who is a friend. Even friends are not friends because they are comparing with each other, fighting with each other. This world has been turned into a war-camp by the education of ambition, politics.

When a man turns inwards the problem arises: what will he do with his anger, enmity, aggression, violence? Now he is alone; he will start torturing himself, he will be angry with himself. That's what your so-called *mahatmas* are. Why do they torture themselves? Why do they fast? Why do they lie down on a bed of thorns? When there is a beautiful shady tree, why do they stand in the hot sun? When it is hot, why do they sit by the side of fire? When it is cold, why do they stand naked in the rivers or in the snow? These are inverted politicians. First they were fighting with others. Now there is nobody left—they are fighting with themselves. They are schizophrenic, they have divided themselves. It is a civil war now; they are fighting with the body.

The body is a victim of your so-called *mahatmas*. The body is innocent, it has not done a single wrong thing to you, but your so-called religions go on teaching you that the body is the enemy, torture it.

The extrovert journey was the journey of sadism. The introvert journey becomes the journey of masochism—you start torturing yourself. And there is a certain glee, a perverted joy in torturing oneself. If you go into history you will be surprised, you will not believe what man has been doing to himself.

People have been wounding their bodies and keeping those wounds unhealed—because the body is the enemy. There have been Christian sects, Hindu sects, Jain sects and many others, who have become very very cunning, clever, efficient in torturing their bodies. They have developed great methods of how to torture the body.

There was a Christian sect which was not only in favor of fasting, but of beating one's body, flogging one's body, and the greatest saint was the one who was most wounded by his own beating. People would come and count their wounds. Now what kind of people were these who were counting their wounds? They must have also been enjoying, a perverted joy.

In India there are Jain *munis* who go on torturing their bodies. The Digambara Jain monks pull out their hair every year, and a great gathering happens when they pull out their hair. It is painful, and the people are joyous: "Great austerity is being done." The man is simply a perverted psychopath. He needs electro-shocks; nothing less will do.

There is a certain kind of madness in which people start pulling their hair. And you know, if you are a husband your wife sometimes tries it when she is in a rage, mad. Women try it more because they have been taught not to hit their husbands. Then what to do? They want to hit and the husband cannot be hit. The scriptures say your husband is your god, and she knows it is all bullshit but the scriptures are the scriptures. She knows the husband perfectly well—that if he is a god, then who will the devil be? But it is not to be said; she has to touch his feet. When she writes love letters to the husband she has to sign 'your slave', and she knows who the slave is! Everybody knows in fact, but it is a formality. And if she hits the husband guilt arises that she has done something irreligious, something like a sin, so she cannot hit the husband. But she *wants* to hit! Now what to do? Either she breaks plates—and that is costly, and she herself suffers that way, that is not of any use—or the easiest way, the cheapest way, economical, is to beat oneself, pull one's hair, throw oneself against the wall, hit the head against the wall; this is the cheapest. She wanted to hit the husband's head but she could not do it, it is not allowed; it is immoral. Who has taught her this idea?—the husbands and their priests and their politicians.

If you go into a madhouse you will find many people pulling their hair. There is a certain kind of madness in which people pull their hair.

Now a Jain monk pulling his hair is really pathological, but people gather together to celebrate the occasion—"Something great is happening! Look! What a great saint!" And because I call these people pathological, they are against me. That's simple, very simple; they have to be against me.

In Christian sects... In Russia there was a sect whose members used to cut their genital organs, and great gatherings would collect. There were certain days when people would do that; it was a frenzy. One person would cut his genital organs and throw them, and there was blood flowing all over the place. Then a frenzy would take over other people who had only come just to see: then somebody else would jump in and he would do it. And by the time the festival was over there would be a pile of genital organs. And these were great saints.

Now women were at a loss: they would start cutting their breasts, because how could they be defeated? They started cutting their breasts.

All kinds of stupidities became possible because of a simple error, and the error is: in life you try to make life difficult for others; when you start turning in, there is a possibility that the old mind will try to make your life difficult. Remember, the inner seeker has to be comfortable, because only in a comfortable situation, in a relaxed state can something happen. When you are tense, uncomfortable, nothing is possible. When you are tense, uncomfortable, your mind is worried, you are not in a still space. When you are hungry how can you be in a still space? And people have been teaching fasting, and they say fasting will help you to meditate.

Once in a while fasting may help you to have better health— it will take a few pounds away from your body, unnecessary pounds—but fasting cannot help meditation. When you are fasting you will constantly think of food.

I have heard...

A married couple went to the parish priest for marital counselling. In the course of the conversation which was serious at first, the priest commented on the number of good-looking girls in the parish.

"Father," said the husband, "you surprise me."
"Why?" he asked, "just because I am on a diet does not mean I can't look at the menu."

Those people who are repressing their sex will be constantly looking at the menu, and those people who are repressing their hunger will be constantly thinking of food. It's natural! How can you meditate? When you are fasting, menus upon menus will float in your mind, will come from everywhere—beautiful dishes. With all the smell of food, and the aroma, for the first time you will start feeling that your nose is alive, and for the first time you will feel that your tongue is alive. It is good to fast once in a while so that you can gather interest in food again, but it is not good for meditation. It is good to make your body a little more sensitive so you can taste again. Fast should be in the service of feast! It is good once in a while not to eat so that the appetite comes back. Healthwise it is good, but meditation has nothing to do with it. It will be more difficult to meditate when you are hungry than when you are fully satisfied. Yes, eating too much will again create trouble, because when you have eaten too much you will feel sleepy. When you have not eaten at all you will feel hungry.

To be in the middle is the right way: the Golden Mean.

Eat so that you don't feel hungry, but don't eat too much so that you feel overloaded, sleepy—and meditation will be easier. The Golden Mean has to be followed in *all* ways, in all kinds of situations.

Be comfortable, be relaxed. There is no need to torture yourself, there is no need to create unnecessary troubles. Drop that mind of anger, violence, aggression, and then only can you move inwards—because only in a relaxed consciousness does one start floating deeper and deeper inside. In utter relaxation one reaches to one's innermost core.

> *When one begins to carry out one's decision, care must be taken so that everything can proceed in a comfortable, relaxed manner. Too much must not be demanded of the heart.*

And don't demand too much, because if you demand too much you will become tense, anxiety will arise. In fact, don't demand at all. Just wait. Just put the seed in the heart and start working; wait for the spring.

> *Too much must not be demanded of the heart.*

And people start demanding too much: they want immediate *satoris*, *samadhis*. They want immediate *nirvana*.

Sometimes it happens—foolish people come to me and they say, "We have been meditating for seven days and nothing has happened yet." Seven days? And for seventy million lives they have been doing everything against meditation! And in seven days...as if they have obliged God, or me. They come with a complaint: "Nothing has happened. Seven days have passed only three days are left of the camp, and we are not yet enlightened!"

Don't demand too much, don't be too greedy. Be a little more understanding. Everything takes time.

> *One must be careful that quite automatically heart and energy are coordinated.*

Remember that you need not be worried about the result:

it is always according to your need and according to your worth. Whatsoever you are ready for is going to happen. If it is not happening that simply shows you are not ready for it. Get ready. Demanding it will not help. Just remember that you are not yet worthy, so cleanse your heart more, concentrate more, meditate more, become more silent, be relaxed, become more and more attuned with the inner. And wait. Because when the heart and energy are coordinated, the result automatically follows. If you have sown the seeds you need not dig the ground every day and look at the seeds to see what is happening. Otherwise you will destroy the seeds; nothing will ever happen. You just wait; for months nothing happens. And you have to water and you have to put manure and you have to go on caring—nothing happens for months. Then one day suddenly, one early morning, the miracle...the seeds have sprouted. Just two small leaves have come out, the miracle has happened. That which was invisible has become visible.

This is the greatest miracle in the world: a seed becoming a sprout. Now dance!

But it always happens in its own time.

> Only then can a state of quietness be attained. During this quiet state, the right conditions and the right space must be provided.

Naturally. If you are preparing a rose garden you have to change the whole soil. Stones have to be removed, old roots have to be removed, weeds have to be removed. You have to create a right condition and a right space, protected. You have to make a fence around it. When you are going to cultivate roses all these preparations will be needed. Meditation is a rose, the greatest rose, the rose of human consciousness. That's why this book is called *The Secret of the Golden Flower*...a golden rose.

What are the right conditions? And what is the right space?

> *One must not sit down (to meditate) in the midst of frivolous affairs.*

You should find a place which enhances meditation. For example, sitting under a tree will help, rather than going and sitting in front of a movie house or going to the railway station and sitting on the platform; going to nature, to the mountains, to the trees, to the rivers where Tao is still flowing, vibrating, pulsating, streaming all around. Trees are in constant meditation. Silent, unconscious, is that meditation. I'm not saying to become a tree; you have to become a buddha! But Buddha has one thing in common with the tree: he's as green as a tree, as full of juice as a tree, as celebrating as a tree, of course with a difference—he is conscious, and the tree is unconscious. The tree is unconsciously in Tao, a Buddha is consciously in Tao. And that is a great difference, the difference between the earth and the sky.

But if you sit by the side of a tree surrounded by beautiful birds singing, or a peacock dancing, or just a river flowing, and the sound of the running water, or by the side of a waterfall, and the great music of it...

Find a place where nature has not yet been disturbed, polluted. If you cannot find such a place then just close your doors and sit in your own room. If it is possible have a special room for meditation in your house. Just a small corner will do, but especially for meditation. Why especially?—because every kind of act creates its own vibration. If you simply meditate in that place, that place becomes meditative. Every day you meditate it absorbs your vibrations when you are in meditation. Next day when you come, those vibrations start falling back on you. They help, they reciprocate, they respond.

That's the idea behind temples and churches and mosques; the idea is beautiful. The idea is that it may not be possible for everybody to have a special room for prayer or meditation, but we can have a special place for the whole village—a temple surrounded by trees on the bank of a river where crowds don't gather, where mundane affairs are not done. When one wants to meditate one can go to the temple. And everybody knows that he is in the temple, he is not to be disturbed.

A sacred place is nothing but a right space for meditation and right conditions. If you are feeling very angry, that is not the time to meditate: it will be going against the flow. If you are feeling very greedy this is not the time to meditate, you will not find it easy. But there are moments when you are easily available to meditation: the sun is rising and you have seen the sun rising, and suddenly all is silent within you, you are not yet part of the marketplace—this is the moment to meditate. You have been feeling good, healthy, you have not been fighting with anybody today—this is the time to meditate. A friend has come and you are full of love—this is the time to meditate. You are with your woman and you both are feeling tremendously happy—sit together and meditate, and you will find the greatest joy of your life happening if you can meditate with your beloved, with your friend.

Find the right conditions, and they are always available. There is not a single man who cannot find right conditions. In twenty-four hours' time many moments come which can be transformed into meditation very easily, because in those moments you are naturally going inwards. The night is full of stars: lie down on the ground, look at the stars, feel in tune, and then meditate. Sometimes it is good to go for a holiday into the mountains—but don't take your radio with you, otherwise you are taking the whole nonsense with you. And when you go to the mountains don't give your address and your phone number to anybody, otherwise there is no need to go anywhere. When you go to the mountains forget all about the world for a few days. That is the meaning of a holiday: it has to be holy, only then is it a holiday. If it is not holy, if it is not in tune with the sacred, it is not a holiday. People carry their world with them.

Once I went to the Himalayas with a few friends, and then I had to ask them to leave me because they had brought their transistor sets and their newspapers and magazines, and the novels that they were reading. And they were constantly talking, talking about things that they had always been talking about. So I told them, "Why have you come to the Himalayas? You were saying these things at your home perfectly well, and again you are talking the same things, the same gossiping, the same rumors."

And whenever they would go with me to some beautiful spot they would take their cameras, they would take pictures. I told them, "You have come here to see. You have not brought your camera to see the Himalayas!"

But they said, "We shall make beautiful albums, and later on we will see what beautiful places we had visited." And right there they were not there, they were just clicking their cameras. This stupidity has to be left behind.

And it is good once in a while to go to the mountains. And

I am not saying to start living there; that is not good, because then you become addicted to the mountains and you become afraid of coming back to the world. The holiday has to be just a holiday: then come back into the world and bring all the peace and the silence and the experience of the sacred with you. Bring it with you, make an effort so that it remains with you in the marketplace.

These suggestions are for the beginners. When a person has really become a meditator, he can meditate sitting before a picture house, he can meditate on the railway platform.

For fifteen years I was continuously travelling around the country, continuously travelling—day in, day out, day in, day out, year in, year out—always on the train, on the plane, in the car. That makes no difference. Once you have become really *rooted* in your being, nothing makes a difference. But this is not for the beginner.

When the tree has become rooted, let winds come and let rains come and let clouds thunder; it is all good. It gives integrity to the tree. But when the tree is small, tender, then even a small child is dangerous enough or just a cow passing by—such a holy animal—but that is enough to destroy it.

When you are beginning, remember, Lu-tsu's suggestions are of immense importance.

> *That is to say, the mind must be free of vain preoccupations.*
> *All entanglements must be put aside. One must be detached*
> *and independent.*

When you are trying to meditate, put the phone off the hook, disengage yourself. Put a notice on the door that for one hour nobody should knock, that you are meditating. And when you move into the meditation room take your shoes off, because you are walking on sacred ground. And not only take your shoes off, but everything that you are preoccupied with. Consciously leave everything with the shoes. Go inside unoccupied. One can take one hour out of twenty-four hours. Give twenty-three hours for your occupations, desires, thoughts, ambitions, projections. Take one hour out of all this, and in the end you will find that only that one hour has been the real hour of your life; those twenty-three hours have been a sheer wastage. Only that one hour has been saved and all else has gone down the drain.

Nor must the thoughts be concentrated upon the right procedure.

And the second thing to be remembered: don't become too preoccupied with the right procedure, otherwise that becomes a preoccupation—that one should sit in a certain posture. If you can sit, good, but if it becomes an unnecessary preoccupation, drop it. For example, if you cannot sit in a full lotus posture—which is difficult for people who have been sitting for their whole lives on chairs; it is difficult because their musculature has developed in a certain way—then your legs will not feel good. They will go to sleep or they will start creating trouble for you. They will constantly hanker for attention, so there is no need to force a lotus posture. A lotus posture, if easy, is good. Otherwise any posture is a lotus posture.

If you cannot sit on the ground, if it is difficult, sit on the chair. Meditation is not afraid of chairs; it can happen anywhere.

Just the other day Renu had asked one question: "Can enlightenment happen on a rocking horse?" It can happen.

It can even happen to the rocking horse! You need not be worried about it.

So, Lu-tsu says: *Nor must the thoughts be concentrated upon the right procedure.*

Just take a little care, that's all, but don't become too worried about it—whether the spine is absolutely erect or not, whether your head is in line with the spine or not, whether your eyes are exactly as Lu-tsu wants them. Now you have a different kind of eyes than Lu-tsu; you know the Chinese and their eyes. In fact they always seem to look at the tip of the nose. Their eyes are only half-open. When I give sannyas to a Chinese, then I have much difficulty looking into their eyes.

You have different kinds of eyes. Everybody has different kinds of eyes and different kinds of noses, so don't become too occupied with these minor things. They are just indications. Understand them, absorb them, and go on your way. Find out your own way. The basic note to be remembered is: you have to be comfortable and relaxed.

This danger arises if too much trouble is taken. I do not mean that no trouble is to be taken, but the correct way lies in keeping equal distance between being and not being.

One has to be exactly in the middle. People either become too active or become too inactive. If they become too active, anxiety is created, a kind of rush, hurry, speed, restlessness; if they become too inactive, sleep, a kind of lethargy, indolence. Be in the middle. This being in the middle is a criterion to be used always. Don't eat too much, don't starve too much. Don't sleep too much, don't sleep less than needed. Remember always to be in the middle. Excess is prohibited. All kinds of extremes have to be dropped, because only in the middle is there a relaxed state of mind.

> *If one can attain purposelessness through purpose, then the thing has been grasped.*

If one can attain this kind of balance, between effort and effortlessness, between purpose and purposelessness, between being and no-being, between mind and no-mind, between action and no-action...

> *... If one can attain purposelessness through purpose effortlessness through effort, inactivity through action—then the thing has been grasped. Now one can let oneself go, detached and without confusion, in an independent way.*

This is the basic: then one can allow oneself to flow with the flow of things. One can let oneself go.

> *Furthermore, one must not fall victim to the ensnaring world. The ensnaring world is where the five kinds of dark demons disport themselves. This is the case, for example, when after fixation one has chiefly thoughts of dry wood and dead ashes and few thoughts of the bright spring on the great earth.*

Remember, the greatest problem for a religious person is not to be too serious; the greatest problem for the religious person is not to be sad; the greatest problem for the religious person is not to be negative, because ordinarily that happens—

religious persons become very sad, very serious, very life-
negative. They forget all about spring, they only think of dry
wood and dead ashes. They have lost balance. A few thoughts
of the bright spring on the great earth have to be remembered.

The really religious person is one who knows the sense of
humor. The really religious person is sincere but never serious,
utterly devoted to his work but never with that attitude of
'holier-than-thou', *never;* never feeling any superiority because
of it, but humble. The really religious person is one who can
dance with the wind and the rains, who can smile and giggle
with children, who can feel at ease with all kinds of situations
in life. That is freedom, that is freedom from the ego. Ego
makes one serious.

In this way one sinks into the world of the dark.

If you become too serious you will sink into the world of the
dark, into the negative world.

*The energy is cold there, breathing is rough, and many
images of coldness and decay present themselves.*

Remember, you are not to become cold. You will find your
so-called saints very cold: they have misunderstood the whole
point. Become cool, but never become cold—and there is a
lot of difference between the two, and a very deep paradox
is there. I call it 'cool': compared to the heated state of passion,
it is cool; it is warm compared to the coldness of death. It is
warm compared to the coldness of death and it is cool compared
to the passionate lust for life. It is warm and cool both. A really
religious person is cool because he has no lust, and he is warm
because he is not sad, he is not serious.

> *If one tarries there long, one enters the world of plants*
> *and stones.*

And if you become too cold, sooner or later you will become
a rock, you will become unconscious. You will fall from
humanity. Many of your saints, in my observation, are people
who have fallen from humanity. They have not become super-
human, they have become sub-human. They belong to the
worlds of rocks and stones.

> *Nor must a man be led astray by the ten thousand ensnare-*
> *ments. This happens if after the quiet state has begun, one*
> *after another all sorts of ties suddenly appear. One wants*
> *to break through and cannot. One follows them and feels as*
> *if relieved by this.*

This is where psychoanalysis has gone wrong. Psychoanalysis has become the method of free association of thoughts.
You can go on and on. One thought leads to another, ad infinitum. One should remain detached from the procession of
thoughts. They will come, they will surround you from everywhere. They will be like clouds; even the little bit of sky will
be lost. And when there are too many thoughts, the natural
instinct is to fight with them, because you have read that
meditation means thoughtlessness. But by fighting one never
becomes thoughtless. If you fight, you will be defeated. The
very fight becomes the cause for your defeat. You cannot fight
with shadows, otherwise you will be defeated. Try fighting
with your own shadow and you will be defeated—not that
the shadow is very powerful, but because the shadow *is not*.
And fighting with something which is not, how can you win?
Thoughts are shadows, don't fight with them.

And if you don't fight then the other alternative opens up—
that's what psychoanalysis has chosen: then move with them,
then let them move wherever they move—free association of
thoughts. Then one thought is tied with another and with
another and with another, and it goes on and on ad infinitum,
ad nauseam. This will feel like a kind of relaxation. That's
why out of psychoanalysis people feel helped, saved. They
are not saved, they are not helped; just the fight disappears.
Because you fight you become tense. When you don't fight
the tension disappears—and that disappearance of the tension
gives you the feeling as if you are saved.

Mulla Nasrudin uses very tight shoes, two sizes less than he
needs. The whole day he complains, and the whole day he is
angry with the shoes.
I asked him one day, "Why don't you change these shoes?
Why do you go on complaining? Who is forcing you to wear
these shoes? You can purchase another pair."
He said, "That I cannot do! Never!"
I said, "Why?"
"Because," he said, "this is my only solace. When after the
whole day's struggle with the shoes I come home and throw
these shoes away and lie down on my bed, it feels so good!"

It will feel good. When you fight with your thoughts and you
cannot win, then you drop fighting and you allow the thoughts
to move and you start moving with them, it feels good. That's
what the whole secret of psychoanalysis is. Psychoanalysis
does not help at all: it simply makes you feel good because it
helps you to drop fighting.

Lu-tsu says, "Both are not right. There is no need to fight,

there is no need to allow the thoughts and become a follower
of them. You remain a watcher, a witness."

This means the master has become the servant.

If you follow the thoughts, the master has become the servant.

*If a man tarries in this stage long, he enters the world of
illusory desires.*

The master has to be claimed back. You have to be the master,
not the servant. And what is mastery?—to be a witness is to be
a master. Just watch those thoughts; utterly calm and quiet,
watch. Let them come, let them go, let them arise, let them
disappear. You simply take note—the thought is arising, the
thought is there, the thought is gone—and soon you will
come to a point where they arise less and less and less; and then
one day, the gap...all thoughts have disappeared. In that gap,
the first experience of God.

*At best one finds oneself in heaven, at the worst, among
the fox-spirits. Such a fox-spirit, it is true, may be able
to roam in the famous mountains, enjoying the wind and
the moon, the flowers and fruits, and taking his pleasure in
coral trees and jewelled grass. But after having done this,
his reward is over and he is born again into the world of
turmoil.*

If you succeed in meditation you are born in heaven, in eternal
bliss. If you don't succeed, if you go astray... That going astray
in Taoism is called: "At worst, one is born among the fox-
spirits."

A fox-spirit is the spirit of a poet. The fox-spirit is the spirit of imagination. Even if you fail in your meditations something will be gained. This will be your gain: you will enjoy the trees more and the flowers more, and the world and the beauty more. But sooner or later the energy that had been created by meditation will disappear and you will have to fall back again to the old turmoil.

Remember, if you succeed in meditation the joy is eternally yours. But even if you fail you will find a few moments of beautiful joy and poetry. Those who fail in meditation become poets, those who succeed become seers. Seers are poets of the eternal, poets are the poets of the momentary.

That's why sometimes it happens: a little bit of meditation and you feel so good that you stop meditating. You think all is attained. Trees are greener, roses are rosier, love is going beautifully, things have started happening—why bother? But soon the energy that had been created will disappear: you have become a fox-spirit. That's what is happening through drugs all over the world: drugs only create fox-spirits. But meditation, if not completed, can also do the same.

Once the decision has been taken, then it is a commitment: you *have* to go to the very end of it. It is a challenge. Accept this challenge and go for this *most* beautiful journey of your inner search. And never stop in the middle anywhere unless you have arrived, unless you have arrived to the center of the cyclone.

Chapter Two

August 28th, 1978

LOVE IS THE ONLY FRIEND

The first question:

Bhagwan, while in therapy myself, I spent much time pray-
ing. Over the years I felt better. I never knew whether it was
the therapy or the prayer. As a therapist I want to urge others
to pray but feel embarrassed.

Sadananda, love is therapy, and there is no other therapy
in the world except love. It is always love that heals, because
love makes you whole. Love makes you feel welcome in the
world. Love makes you a part of existence; it destroys alien-
ation. Then you are no more an outsider here, but utterly
needed. Love makes you feel needed, and to be needed is the
greatest need. Nothing else can fulfill that great need. Unless
you feel that you are contributing something to existence,
unless you feel that without you the existence would be a
little less, that you would be missed, that you are irreplace-
able, you will not feel healthy and whole.

And prayer is the highest form of love. If love is the flower, then prayer is the fragrance. Love is visible, prayer is invisible. Love is between one person and another person, prayer is between one impersonal presence and the impersonal presence of the whole. Love is limited, prayer is unlimited.

If you can pray, no other therapy is needed.

Therapies are needed in the world because prayer has disappeared. Man was never in need of therapy when prayer was alive, flowing, when people were dancing in great gratitude, singing songs in praise of God, were ecstatic just for being, for being here, were grateful just for life. When tears were flowing from their eyes—of love, of joy—and when there were songs in their hearts, there was no need for therapy.

Therapy is a modern need, a poor substitute for prayer. Psychoanalysis is a poor substitute for religion, very poor. But when you cannot get the best, then you settle for second-best or the third-best, or whatsoever is available. Because temples have become rotten, churches have become political, religion has been contaminated by the priests, man is left alone, uncared for, with nobody to support him. The very ground on which he has been standing for centuries has disappeared. He is falling in an abyss, feeling uprooted. Psychoanalysis comes as a substitute: it gives you a little bit of rooting, it gives you a little bit of ground to hold onto, but it is nothing compared to prayer. Because the psychoanalyst himself is in need, he himself is as ill as the patient, there is not much difference between the psychoanalyst and the patient. If there is any difference, that difference is of knowledge—and that makes no difference at all. It is not a difference of being. If there is any difference it is quantitative, it is not that of quality, and quantity does not make much difference. The psychoanalyst and his patient are both in the same boat.

In the old days there was a different kind of person moving in the world, the religious person—the Buddha, the Christ. His very presence was healing. Because he was healed and whole, his wholeness was contagious. Just as diseases are contagious, so is health. Just as illnesses can be caught from others, so can you catch something of the healing energy from the other. But for that, the psychoanalyst will not be of much help. He may help a little bit to solve your problems intellectually. He may find out the causes of your problems—and when you know the cause you feel a little better, you are not in ignorance—but just by knowing the cause nothing is helped. You are suffering: the psychoanalyst will show that you are suffering because of your mother, because of your upbringing, because of your childhood. It makes you feel a little good: so it is not *you* who is the cause, it is the mother. Or, there is always something else you can put blame on. Psychoanalysis shifts the responsibility, makes you feel a little weightless, unburdened, but the problem is not solved. Just by knowing the cause, the cause does not disappear.

Religion has a totally different orientation: it does not shift the blame on others. In fact, it makes you feel responsible for the first time in your life. Hence, psychoanalysis is a kind of bribery; it is a kind of lubricant. It is a kind of help in your ego; strengthening your ego, throwing the blame on others. It is a very dangerous game because once you start throwing the blame on others you will never be transformed, because you will never feel responsible. This is one of the greatest calamities that has happened to this age.

Marx says that it is the society that is responsible for all the ills that you are suffering. You are not responsible: it is the class-divided society, it is the economic structure. Freud says it is not the economic structure but the conditioning that has been given to you by the parents, by the society, by education, by the priest, by the church. It is the conditioning: that's why you are suffering; you are not responsible.

This is the old game. In the past it was called the 'game of fate': fate is responsible, you are not responsible. This is the same game played with new names and new labels, but the trick is that you are not responsible. Of course, one feels a little bit happier, but nothing changes. Sooner or later that happiness disappears because the cause remains where it was, the wound remains. How does it matter who has wounded you? Just by knowing that your mother has wounded you—or your father or the society or the church—how does it matter? The wound is there, full of pus, growing, becoming bigger every day. You can feel a little bit good for the moment, unburdened: so you are not responsible, you are just a victim. You can sympathize with yourself. You can feel pity for yourself and you can feel anger for others, for those who have created the wound, but this is not a way of transformation: the wound is there and the wound will continue to grow. The wound does not bother about what you think about it; your thinking makes no difference to the wound.

Religion is a totally different approach: it makes you feel responsible. It is against your ego. It says, "It is *you!* It is your responsibility to have chosen a certain pattern of life. All patterns were available, no pattern has been imposed on you." Buddha was born in the same society in which others suffered, suffered hell, and he attained here-and-now the ultimate state of bliss, so society cannot be responsible. Christ was born in the same society in which Judas was born, in which everybody else was born, but he attained to God.

Religion makes you feel responsible *and* free. Freedom and

responsibility are two aspects of the same coin. If you are not ready to feel responsible, you will never be free. You will remain in bondage, in the bondage of others.

Psychoanalysis makes you feel in bondage; it can't really help. Prayer makes you free. Prayer means religion. Prayer means: you are responsible, you have chosen a certain way of life. Now there is no need to make much fuss about it. If you don't like it, drop it! It is up to you, it is *absolutely* up to you. And you can drop it in a single moment of awareness. That's what *satori* is, *samadhi* is: dropping the whole nonsense in a single moment of understanding. Seeing the point that "I am carrying it, and if I don't want, there is no need to carry it; nobody can force it on me—no fate, no society, no church", it can be dropped. Your inner essence remains free of your personality. Personality is just like clothing: you can drop it, you can be naked any moment.

Your essence can be naked any moment. And when the essence is naked, you are healed—because the essence knows no illness. The essence is always in the state of health, in the state of wholeness.

Prayer is the ultimate way of dropping all personalities— Christian, Hindu, Jain, Buddhist, Indian, German, English. Prayer is the way to put aside the whole paraphernalia of personality and just to be, pure, innocent. In that purity and innocence one starts bowing down. You may not believe in God; there is no need to believe in God. A believer is not a religious person either. But when you are utterly nude in your essence, when you have dropped all clothing—you have dropped all that has been given to you, you have disconnected yourself from the learned, from all that you have learned, the taught, the cultivated—suddenly you are in your pristine clarity, as you were before your birth. Your original face is there. It is as fresh as dewdrops in the early morning, as shiny as the stars in the night, with all the grandeur of the flowers and the trees, and with all the simplicity and innocence of children, animals, birds. In that moment you feel so joyous. Out of joy you bow down—not to a God, remember; there is no need to believe in a God. You simply bow down out of gratitude. There is no object in your bowing: you simply bow down because...to see such infinite joy showering on you for no reason at all...and you are not worthy! You don't deserve it! You have never earned it! How can you remain without giving a heartful thank-you to existence? Your head bows down, you surrender. You lie down on the earth in utter silence, your heart throbbing, pulsating with ecstasy. Your breathing has a different rhythm to it, a different melody to it. Your whole energy is dancing, streaming. You have fallen in harmony with existence. This is what I call prayer— not that which is going on in the churches and the temples: that is parrot-like, it is formal. It has nothing to do with real prayer. And this prayer heals, this prayer is real therapy.

Sadananda, you are right. This question arising in you is of tremendous significance: whether you have been healed by therapy or by prayer?

You have been healed by prayer. Therapy has not helped anybody. At the most, therapy can make you adjusted to the society. Prayer helps you to fall in tune with existence itself. Society is man-made, its values are man-made, hence they are different everywhere. In India there are different values, in the West there are different values. Something that is perfectly okay in the West is absolutely wrong in the East, and vice versa. These values are man-created.

You live in a society; you have to adjust to the society. Psychotherapy is in the service of the society you live in. When you start going out of the society, you start becoming a little rebellious, the society pounces on you and declares you ill. This is an ancient trick, one of the *most* dangerous tricks that the society has played on you: whenever you are not falling in line with the society, the society starts condemning you. In the past it used to call you 'sinners', and then it prepared hells for you. Now, that language is out of date: it calls you 'sick', 'mentally sick', 'a mental case'. That is a new condemnation.

In Soviet Russia, whenever somebody differs from communism, has his own ideas about life, existence, society, he is immediately declared a psychopath, a mental case. Once he is declared a mental case, now society is able to manipulate him. You can give him electric shocks, insulin shocks, drugs. You can force him to live in a mental asylum. And all that he has done is: he has done a little bit of thinking. His sin is that he was not obedient to the established order of the society; he was disobedient. Unless the society forces him back, gives him a mind-wash, forces him to fall in line, he will be kept in a hospital and will be treated as an ill man. This is very humiliating, degrading, dehumanizing, but that's what has been done all over the world, more or less.

Whenever a person is different from you, wants to live a different life, wants to be free from the bondage you have created in the name of the society, you declare him mad. Jesus was declared neurotic, Mansoor was declared mad, Socrates was declared dangerous to the youth of the society: "Kill them now!" Now the society can kill them without any prick of conscience. In fact, the society is doing the right thing: first condemn somebody, put a label on him; if you kill somebody without putting a label on him, you will feel guilty; to avoid guilt declare him mad, and then it is so easy to kill, so easy to destroy.

Now we have the technology too—to destroy the mind, to give the mind a complete brainwash, and to force the man to say yes to the established order, whatsoever it is: communist, capitalist, fascist.

Therapy, the so-called therapy, is in the service of the established society. It is in the service of death, of the past.

Prayer serves nobody. Prayer is freedom. Prayer is a way to commune with the whole, and to commune with the whole is to be holy.

You say, "While in therapy myself, I spent much time praying. Over the years I felt better. I never knew whether it was the therapy or the prayer."

It was *certainly* prayer.

"As a therapist I want to urge others to pray but feel embarrassed."

I can understand, Sadananda. Prayer has become a dirty word. To talk about prayer is embarrassing. To talk about God is embarrassing: people think that you are a little bit eccentric, crazy or something, but don't be afraid. Drop this embarrassment, gather courage. Talk about prayer—not only talk about prayer, fall into prayer when the patient is with you. Let the patient feel the climate of prayer.

Once Jesus' disciples asked him, "What is prayer?" He simply knelt down, started praying, with tears coming from his eyes. His eyes raised towards heaven, and he started talking to his Father—which is just a symbol. He started calling, 'Abba'. He created the climate: that is the only way to show what prayer is, there is no other way.

If somebody asks, "What is love?", be loving. Hug him, hold

his hand, let your love flow towards him. That is the only way to say what love is. This is the only way to define the indefinable.

Fall in prayer while you are helping your patient. Just kneel down. The first time the patient may feel strange, a little weird— "What is happening?"—because he has come with a certain idea that he would have to lie down on the Freudian couch and he would talk all kinds of nonsense, and the psychoanalyst would listen very attentively, as if he is delivering a gospel or a revelation. He has come with certain expectations; he will not be able to believe what is happening. But if prayer is there it is bound to have effects: it is such a potential force. Whenever there is one person praying, he creates a vibe of prayer around himself. And patients particularly are very sensitive people— that's why they have become patients. Remember it! They are more intelligent than the common lot, hence they are ill! The common lot is so insensitive, so dull, so thick-skinned. It goes on carrying all kinds of nonsenses without being disturbed by them. It goes on living this so-called, meaningless life without ever becoming aware of its meaninglessness, its utter stupidity and absurdity. Remember always that the patient is a person who is more sensitive than the common lot, more alert, has more heart to feel. Hence he finds it difficult to adjust to the society.

The society exists for the lowest because it exists for the mass, the mob, the crowd. The society is a herd-phenomenon. Whenever there is somebody who is a little more intelligent, has a slightly higher I.Q., has some more potential for love and for poetry, he will feel a little maladjusted. He will not feel at home. Seeing the beggar on the street, he will suffer; seeing all kinds of exploitations going on, he will suffer; seeing the state of humanity and its degradation, he will suffer—and all this will become too much. He will start cracking underneath this burden.

Remember that the patient is more intelligent, more sensitive, more vulnerable. Hence he is a patient. If you create the climate of prayer around him, maybe the first time he will think you a little weird, but don't be worried. Everybody knows that psychoanalysts are a little weird.

I have heard....

"I got insomnia real bad," complained a psychotherapist to his physician.
"Insomnia," said the doctor, "is insomnia. How bad can it be? What do you mean, 'real bad insomnia'?"
"Well," said the psychotherapist. "I got it real bad. I can't even sleep when it is time to get up!"

Or this story:

A young doctor who was studying to be a psychoanalyst approached his professor and asked for a special appointment. When they were alone in the professor's office, the young man revealed that he had had a considerable amount of trouble with some of his patients. It seemed that in response to his questions, these patients offered replies which he could not quite understand.
"Well," said the older man, "suppose you ask me some of these questions."
"Why, certainly," agreed the young doctor. "The first one is, what is it that wears a skirt and from whose lips comes pleasure?"

"Why," said the professor, "that's easy. A Scotsman blowing a bagpipe."

"Right," said the young doctor. "Now the second question. What is it that has smooth curves and at unexpected moments becomes uncontrollable?"

The older doctor thought for a moment, and then said, "Aha! I don't think that's too difficult to answer. It's a major league baseball pitcher."

"Right," said the young man. "Now, Professor, would you mind telling me what you think about two arms slipped around your shoulders?"

"A football tackle," replied the professor.

"Right again," said the young doctor. "But you would be surprised at the silly answers I keep getting."

So, Sadananda, don't be worried. You can pray, you can go into prayer. The first time, maybe the patient will think you a little eccentric. And in orange, and with the mala—you are eccentric! Don't be worried! You are allowed to do anything once you are a sannyasin. This is a certificate.

But if you can create a climate of prayer, soon you will find the patient participating with you. He may feel, for the first time, something of the unknown and the beyond. And if he can again feel something of the unknown, his life will start having meaning, significance. If he can have a little contact with the transcendental, just a little contact, his life will never be the same again. Just a little opening into the beyond, a little window, and the light coming in and the sky and the clouds and the stars—just a little window and you have transformed his whole being.

Use your therapy too; but the real help will come from prayer. Use therapy as a stepping-stone to prayer.

The second question:

*I am in love, and I feel like a moth dying into a candle flame.
Am I meant somehow to extricate myself and be aware and
alone, or to die into the flame. In joy, in agony, it goes on
and on...*

Madhuri, die! because to die in love is to be reborn. It is not
death, it is the beginning of true life. To die without love is
death. To live without love is death. To be in love is to know
something of God, because as Jesus says, "God is love." I have
even improved upon it: I say love is God.

Die, Madhuri, die. Utterly. Abandon yourself. Be lost.

There is no need to protect yourself against love, because love
is not the enemy. Love is the only friend. Don't protect yourself. Don't hide from love. Don't be afraid of love. When
love calls, go with it. Wherever it leads, go with it, go in trust.

Yes, there will be moments of agony, because they are always
there when there are moments of ecstasy. They come together,
it is one package; just like day and night, summer and winter,
they come together. But when there is ecstasy of love, one is
ready to pay—whatsoever agony it brings, one is happy to
pay.

And remember, nothing is free. We have to pay for everything. The more you can pay, the more you will get. If you
want to move to the higher peaks of the Himalayas, you take
the risk of falling into the valleys. Those who cannot take
the risk of falling into the deep abysses surrounding Himalayan
peaks will never know the joy of rising higher and higher.

Love is the highest peak of consciousness, the Everest of consciousness, and sometimes one slips and falls. And naturally, when you are moving on a height, you fall very deep. It hurts. When you know light and you fall into deep darkness, it hurts. But once you have known those peaks, you are ready to go into any valleys for those peaks. A single moment of ecstasy is enough: one can suffer for it in hell for eternity, then too it is worth having.

Meditate on these words of Kahlil Gibran:

When love beckons to you, follow him,
though his ways are hard and steep.
And when his wings enfold you yield to him,
though the sword hidden among his pinions may wound you.
And when he speaks to you believe in him,
though his voice may shatter your dreams
as the north wind lays waste the garden.

But if in your fear
you would seek only love's peace and love's pleasure,
then it is better for you that you cover your nakedness
and pass out of love's threshing-floor,
into the seasonless world where you shall laugh,
but not all of your laughter,
and weep,
but not all of your tears.

Love gives naught but itself
and takes naught but from itself.
Love possesses not nor would it be possessed:
for love is sufficient unto love.

When love beckons to you, follow him, follow to the very end, follow to the point where you disappear completely.

Become a moth. Yes, love is a flame...and the lover is a moth. Learn much from the moth: it has the secret, it knows how to die. And to know how to die in love, in ecstasy, dancing, is to know how to be reborn on a higher plane. And each time you die a higher plane is reached.

When you can die ultimately and utterly, not holding back even a little bit of yourself, then that very death takes you into God. That is resurrection.

The third question:

Why are you not consistent in your statements?

I cannot be. The purpose of my statements is totally different than that of ordinary statements. I am not telling the truth, because truth cannot be told.

Then what am I doing here?

If you take my statements as true or untrue, you will miss the whole point. I am using the statements to awaken you. They are neither true nor untrue. They are either useful or useless, but they have nothing to do with truth. They have a certain utility.

It is just as if you are fast asleep, and I start ringing a bell; there is nothing of truth or untruth in ringing the bell. To ask the question would be utterly irrelevant. But there is something useful in it: if it helps you wake up, it has been useful.

Buddha is reported to have said, "Truth is that which has utility." Truth is a device. It does not state anything about existence, it is just a device to provoke something which is fast asleep in you.

Now I cannot be consistent, because I have to provoke so many people—different types of minds, different types of sleeps are there. I can ring a bell: it may help somebody to wake up, to somebody else it may look like a lullaby and he may fall asleep even more deeply. To somebody it may be a provocation into awakenedness, to somebody else it may simply give a beautiful dream: that he is in a temple and bells are ringing, and he is enjoying, and the prayer is going on, and the incense is burning. He has created a dream, he has not come out of his sleep. He will need something else—maybe a hit on the head, or cold water thrown on him, or a good shaking. Different people need different approaches to be provoked, to be awakened.

My statements are not about truth. I am not a philosopher! I am not trying to give you any philosophy. I'm just trying all possible ways to wake you up. If one way fails, I try another—but I cannot leave you alone. So one day I will say one thing, another day I may say another thing. You miss the point if you don't understand the purpose of my statements.

Just the other day I had answered Habib's two questions about Carl Gustav Jung. He missed the whole point. I felt sorry for Habib: he missed the whole thing, he felt offended. And he could not even wait and meditate for a few hours: I finished at 9:45 and he wrote a letter at 9:55. He could not wait a single minute to meditate over it. He thought I am against Jung.

Why should I be against Jung?—he has not done anything wrong to me.

But poor Habib; he missed the point. He thinks I am against

Jung, so he has to defend Jung. He wrote in the letter that he would like to have a public or private discussion with me, a debate.

Now you cannot discuss with a madman! It will be utterly useless, Habib. It will be pointless, it will drive you crazy.

I have heard...

Once it happened, an Egyptian king went mad. He was a great chess player. All medicines were tried, all physicians worked on him, but nothing, no help. And he was drowning and drowning in madness.

Then one fakir came, a Sufi mystic, and he said, "Wait! If you can bring a great chess player, it will be of great help. He has to play chess with this mad king."

Now who would like to play chess with a madman? But the king was ready to offer as much money as was asked for. A chess player was ready; so much money! And the mystic was right: after one year the king was perfectly sane. But the chess player went mad.

So if you have a discussion with me, beware, you will go mad!— because I am not a consistent man. I am not logical either, I am absurd.

And Habib missed the point. If he was a Freudian I would have attacked Freud, if he was a Marxist I would have attacked Marx, and if he was a Rajneeshian, I would have attacked Rajneesh! It is not a question of Jung! Jung comes nowhere into it. The attack is on Habib's ego! Because the ego is Jungian, so poor Jung has to be attacked.

Now tomorrow somebody comes and he is a Freudian, and I will attack Freud. And I will say, "He is nothing compared to

Jung—a pygmy!" And then naturally I become inconsistent, because you miss the whole point! I have nothing to do with Freud or Jung. Who cares? My effort is to provoke you, to show you the point. It is not that Habib is feeling offended because I have criticized Jung; he is feeling offended because his ego is hurt. If he can see it, then my statements were useful. If he cannot see it, then the arrow missed the point. Then I will have to use some other device.

I have to destroy your ego-structures. Hence, don't ask me again and again why my statements are not consistent. I have only one consistency: that is of being inconsistent. I am consistently inconsistent; that's the only consistency that I have. And I have infinite freedom; a consistent man cannot have infinite freedom. I can play, I can joke, I can enjoy shattering your egos, destroying your structures. I'm not serious about these things. I dare to play, to try first one thing, then another. My statements are like the actors on the stage: let them contradict each other; they are not there to tell the truth, but to provoke it, to discover it.

And I would like to tell you too: do not do anything merely for the sake of consistency. That is the shelter for fools and philosophers—which are the same people. Never do anything just for the sake of consistency. This is undesirable since it limits experimentation and exploration. Action so as to be consistent with the past develops into a programmatic addiction. It freezes you into stasis, halting the evolutionary march of becoming. You should retain all power over current behavior. None should be yielded to the past. Acting consistent with precedent is a form of death, and destroys all potential to grow into understanding.

Remember, what is consistency? It means my today has to

be obedient to my yesterday—that is consistency. My present has to be obedient with my past—that is consistency. But then how am I going to grow? Then how am I going to move? If I remain consistent with the past, then there is no growth possible.

Growth means inconsistency. Your today has to go beyond your yesterday, has to be inconsistent with it, has to use it as a stepping-stone, has not to be confined by it. And your tomorrow has to go beyond your today. If you go on moving away from your past each day, you will be growing, you will be reaching higher peaks.

Consistent people are stupid people. Their life is stagnant. They stink of death. They are like corpses: they go on rotting, they don't live. Life is basically not a logical phenomenon but a dialectical phenomenon. Dialectics means thesis, antithesis, synthesis: your yesterday was a thesis, your today will be its antithesis and your tomorrow will be a synthesis. Again your tomorrow will create a thesis and the next day an antithesis, and then synthesis—and so on it goes. You go on in a dialectical way. Life is a dialectical process; it is not a linear, logical process. Life is a contradictory process.

That's why I cannot define myself—because today's definition won't be applicable tomorrow. I cannot define myself because it is like defining a cloud or an ocean or a growing tree or a child. I constantly change, because change is the very soul of life. Except change, nothing is eternal.

I am committed to change. Change is my God, because that is the only unchanging phenomenon in life. Hence I call it God. Everything else changes: life changes, death changes—only change remains. I worship change. I am in love with it. I cannot define myself once and forever. I have to define myself each moment of my life; and one never knows what each next moment is going to bring.

To be with me is to be in a constant flux, in a constant movement. Those who are not daring enough sooner or later have to drop out of this journey that I am taking you on. Those who are not courageous enough, who don't have guts to accept the unknown future and to remain available to the unknowable and the mysterious, and who are in a hurry to have a dogma, a belief system, a philosophy—so that they can stop growing, so that they can cling to the dogma, so that they can become fanatics about the dogma; those who are constantly in search of a certain orthodoxy in which nothing will ever change—these are the dead people, cowards. They can't become my people.

I'm bringing you a totally different kind of religion; it has never happened before in the world. All the religions in the world were believers in permanence; I believe in change. All the religions of the world were dogmatic; I am absolutely non-dogmatic, anti-dogmatic. All the religions of the world were reduced into philosophical statements. When I will be gone, I will leave you in such a mess—nobody will ever be able to reduce what I was saying, really. Nobody will be able to reduce it into a dogma.

You cannot pinpoint me. You cannot fix me. I am not a thing. I am a river, a cloud which is constantly changing its form. My idea of consistency is rooted in this continual change, this dynamic dance called life. Yes, to me God is a dancer, constant movement; that is the beauty of God. In fact I would not like to call God a dancer but dance itself—because even the word 'dancer' would be false: it gives an idea of a certain entity— just dance, just cloud.

There is an ancient Christian mystic treatise, *The Cloud of Unknowing*. No other book has such a beautiful title: 'The Cloud of Unknowing'. That is the definition of God: 'cloud' and 'of unknowing'.

You cannot make knowledge out of the experience of God. In fact, the more you experience God, the less and less you will know. The day God has happened to you totally, you will not be found there. The knower has gone, disappeared. The dewdrop has slipped into the ocean, or…the ocean has slipped into the dewdrop.

I am not burdened by my yesterday. It has already been changed by today. I live in the present because there is no other way to live. All other ways are ways of death.

So please, don't ask about consistency. You have to learn, you have to understand my inconsistency. You have to understand my contradictions. The basic thing is that my statements are not saying *anything* about truth. My statements are just provocations. I am urging you to discover, I am not delivering you the truth! Truth is not a thing to be given to you; it is not a commodity. It is untransferable. I am simply creating a desire and a longing, an intense longing in you to search and seek and explore. If I am very consistent, you will stop seeking. You will think, "What is the need? Bhagwan knows, I can believe in him." That's what Christianity has been doing, Buddhism has been doing, Jainism has been doing. "Buddha knows, so what is the need? We can believe. He is not deceiving, he cannot lie. He has stated the truth. What more truth are we going to discover? He has stated the truth; we can believe in it." You need not worry about your own exploration. And this is one of the most fundamental things about truth: that unless it is *yours*, it is not. My truth cannot be your truth; there is no way. My truth cannot be transferred to you.

Truth is absolutely individual. All the Buddhas have wanted to give it to you, I want it to be given to you, but there is no way. All that can be done is to provoke an inquiry in you, such a tremendous desire to know that you drop all your luggage, unnecessary luggage, and you start moving into the journey; that you gather courage to come out of your securities, conveniences, ideologies, philosophies, orthodoxies; that you gather courage to come out of your mind and to go into the unknown...the cloud of existence. One has to disappear into it.

So I am not going to oblige you by giving you a dogma. No, I will go on contradicting myself each day, every moment. Slowly slowly you will see there is no point in clinging to any of my ideas. And in that very moment you will become aware: there is no need to cling to *any idea whatsoever*—mine, Buddha's, Jesus', anybody's. All ideas have to be dropped.

And when there is no idea in your mind, you will find God there. When all philosophies have disappeared, then religion wells up in your being like a spring.

The fourth question:

Why is it so difficult to ask the real question? And why do I feel so stupid about this and any other question?

Bhagwato, the real question cannot be asked. Only unreal questions can be asked. That's why whenever you will ask a question you will feel a little bit stupid—because deep down you will know it is unreal. And only the unreal can be asked!

The real question cannot be asked. Why?—because to find the
real question you will have to go so deep into your being; you
will have to go to the very center of your being. Unreal questions exist on the periphery. Unreal questions are millions,
the real question is only one, but it exists at the center. If you
want to ask the real question you will have to go to the center
of your being. And the problem is when you are at the center
of your being, you know the real question, but immediately
you know the real answer too.

The real question contains the real answer in it. They are
instant, together. Simultaneously they happen. So that's why
the real question can never be asked. If you don't know the
real question, how can you ask? If you know the real question
immediately you know the real answer too. They are not
two separate things but two aspects of the same coin: on one
side the real question, on the other side the real answer.

But one has to ask many unreal questions before one becomes
aware of this, Bhagwato. You should feel blessed that you are
aware of the phenomenon: that the real question is so difficult
to ask, *impossible* to ask. This is a good sign, a milestone. Even
to ask "Why is it so difficult to ask the real question?" shows
that you are moving in the direction of the real question. It
shows that now you can detect immediately when you come
across a false question. You have become capable of knowing
the false as the false; this is the first step towards knowing the
true as the true. Before one can know truth, one will have to
know untruth utterly and absolutely.

And that's why you say, "And why do I feel so stupid about
this and any other question?"

All questions are stupid questions. But I am not saying don't
ask them; just by not asking you will not become wise. Stupid

questions have to be asked so they can be dropped. And dropping stupid questions is dropping stupidity. And slowly slowly, one becomes aware that "All my questions are useless. Why am I asking? Even if I get the answer, how is it going to change my life?"

Once I was staying in a village. Two old men came to me—one was a Hindu, another was a Jain. The Jains don't believe in the existence of God. Both were friends, almost lifelong friends. Both must have been nearabout seventy, and both had quarreled for their whole lives—whether God exists or not? The Hindu insisted that He exists and would quote the Vedas and Upanishads and Gita, and the Jain would insist that He does not exist and would quote Mahavir and Neminath and Parshwanath and his *teerthankaras*. And they argued and argued to no end, because these questions are so meaningless, so futile, you can go on arguing, ad infinitum; there is no end to it. Nobody can prove absolutely, nobody can disprove absolutely either. The questions are so utterly useless: nothing can be proved definitely this way or that, so the question goes on hanging.

Hearing that I was staying in the guesthouse outside the village, they came to see me. And they said, "Our whole lives have been a conflict. We are friends, in every way we are friendly, but about this question of God we immediately start quarreling. And we have quarreled the whole life. Now you are here: give us a definite answer so this quarrel can be stopped, and we can at least die in ease."

I asked them, "If it is proved definitely that God is, how is it going to change your life?" They shrugged their shoulders. They said, "We will live as we are living."

"Or, if it is proved," I told them, "that God definitely does not exist, how is it going to change your life?" They said, "It is not going to change our lives at all, because we both live exactly the same life. We are partners in a business. He believes in God, I don't believe in God, but as far as our lives are concerned we have the same pattern. His God does not make any difference, my no-God does not make any difference."

Then I said, "This is a futile question."

Which question is futile? One whose answer is not going to make a change in your life. It is useless. People ask, "Who created the world?" How is it going to change your life? Anybody—A, B, C, D,—anybody; how is it going to change your life? "Is there life after death?"—how is it going to change your life?

Can't you see theists and atheists all living the same kind of life, the same rotten kind of life? Can't you see the Catholic and the communist living the same kind of life, the same lies, the same falsehood, the same masks? Can't you see the Protestant and the Catholic living the same life? Can't you see the Hindu and the Mohammedan living the same life, with no difference at all? All differences are only verbal. No verbal difference makes any difference in their existence. They have been discussing about useless questions.

But why do people ask useless questions?—to avoid going in. They pretend that they are great inquirers: they are interested in God, they are interested in the after-life, they are interested in heaven and hell. And the real thing is: that they are not interested in themselves. To avoid that, to avoid seeing this fact, that "I am not interested in my own being," they have created all these questions. These questions are their strategies to avoid their central question: Who am I?

True religion consists in the inquiry: 'Who am I?' And nobody else can answer it. You will have to go digging deeper and deeper into your being. One day, when you have reached the very source of your life, you will know. That day, the real question and the real answer will have happened simultaneously.

The fifth question:

I am often able to achieve the state—or what seems like the state—which you call 'being a hollow bamboo'—silent, watching, empty. The only problem is that there is no bliss in that emptiness: it is just nothing. Can I expect something to fill it one of these days?

Mariel Strauss, it is because of this idea that you are missing the whole beauty of nothingness: this desire to fill it. You are not really a hollow bamboo, because in this hollow bamboo this desire is there, and this desire is enough to fill the hollow bamboo, to block its emptiness.

This desire to fill it one day, this expectation that "Some day, God will come and fill my emptiness", this very idea is preventing you from really becoming a hollow bamboo. Drop this desire. Forget all about filling your hollow bamboo— then you are a hollow bamboo. And when you are a hollow bamboo, it is immediately full of God. But not that you have to desire it; if you desire it you will go on missing it.

This is one of the basic paradoxes to be understood about religious inquiry. Understand it as deeply as possible, let it sink deeply into your heart, because this is not only Mariel

Strauss' problem, this is everybody's problem. Anybody who goes on in the search for truth, for being, for God, or whatsoever you call it, will have to come across it.

You can feel that you are empty, but deep down, lurking somewhere is the desire, the hope, the expectation that "Now, where is God? It is getting late and I have remained a hollow bamboo so long. What is the point? This is just nothingness."

There is condemnation when you say "This is *just* nothingness." You are not happy with this hollow bamboo-ness. You are not happy with this emptiness; there is condemnation. You have managed somehow, because you have heard me saying again and again that the moment you are a hollow bamboo God will descend in you: "Become empty, and you will become full." You want to become full, so you say "Okay, we will become empty. If that is the only way to become full, we will even try that." But this is not true emptiness. You have not understood the point.

Enjoy emptiness, cherish it, nourish it. Let your emptiness become a dance, a celebration. Forget all about God—to come or not is His business. Why should you be worried? Leave it to Him. And when you have completely forgotten about God He comes, *immediately* He comes. He always comes when you are utterly unaware of His coming, you don't even hear His footsteps. One moment He was not there, and suddenly another moment He is there. But your emptiness has to be total. And a total emptiness means no expectation, no future, no desire.

You say, "I am often able to achieve the state..."

You must be forcing it, you must be trying hard, you must

be cultivating it, you must be imagining it. It is imaginary,
it is not true.

"... or what seems like the state..."

And deep down you also know that it is not the real state.
You have managed somehow to create a kind of emptiness in
yourself. It is a forced emptiness.

"...which you call 'being a hollow bamboo'—silent, watching,
empty..."

It is not what I call the state of being a hollow bamboo; it is
not. If it were, then there would be no desire for God, because
there is no desire. It does not matter what you desire; God,
money, power, prestige, it matters not. Desire is desire, its
taste is always the same. Desire leads you away from the present,
from the herenow into the future, somewhere else. Desire
does not allow you to relax into the moment. It takes you away
from your being.

So what you desire does not matter: you can desire presidency
of a country, or you can desire money, or you can desire
sainthood, or you can desire God, you can desire truth—desire
is desire. Desire means you are torn apart between that which
you are and that which you would like to be. This is anguish,
this is anxiety. And this anxiety will not allow you to become
a hollow bamboo.

To be a hollow bamboo means: a state of desirelessness. Then
you are utterly empty, and then that emptiness has a clarity
in it. Then that emptiness has a splendor in it, a purity in it.
Then that emptiness has a holy quality to it. It is so pure, it is
so innocent that you will not call it 'just emptiness' or 'just

nothingness'. That emptiness is God itself! Once you are empty, once you are herenow, with no desire taking you away from your reality, God is. God means 'that which is'.

God is already the case; your desiring mind does not allow you to see it. Your desiring mind makes you a monkey: you go on jumping from one branch to another branch. You go on jumping, you are never in a state of rest. This desire and that desire, and one desire creates another desire, and it is a continuum.

When there is no desire where can you go? When there is no desire where is the future? When there is no desire where is time? Where is past? When there is no desire where is mind? Where is memory? Where is imagination? All gone! Just cut one single root which is the chief root of the tree of mind: cut desire and just be. In that state of being you are a hollow bamboo. And the moment you are a hollow bamboo, reality bursts upon you, as if it has been always waiting but you were not available to it. It floods you!

The last question:

Is not life stranger than fiction?

It is.

It has to be, because fiction is only a partial reflection of life, a very finite reflection of life. Life is infinitely complex. Life has no beginning, no end; it is always on and on, it is going on and on. It is a pilgrimage with no goal. Fiction is just a reflection of a small part of it.

Fiction is like a small window in your room. Yes, when the sky is full of stars, you see a part of the sky through the window, but the sky becomes framed by the window. The sky itself has no frame to it—it is infinite, it knows no boundaries—but your window gives a frame to it.

A fiction is a framed part of the sky. Howsoever strange, mysterious, unbelievable the fiction may be, it is very pale compared to real life. Real life is the mystery of mysteries... never possible to explain it. And the fiction arises out of the human mind. The mind is a mirror: it reflects a few things. If you have a good mirror, a creative mirror, you can create poetry, you can create music, you can create fiction, you can write, you can paint; but all that you will paint and all that you will create and all that you will write will remain a very tiny atomic part of reality—and not really a part but a *reflection* of the part in your mind.

To see life as it is is mind-blowing. To see life as it is is psychedelic. To see life as it is is to become expanded in consciousness.

The fiction has to begin somewhere. Of necessity, it has to begin somewhere. It will have the first page, and somewhere it has to end; it cannot go on and on. You can lengthen it, make it very long, like Tolstoy's *War and Peace*—it can go on and on and on, and it is very very tiring and lengthy. But still a moment comes when you have to put the last full stop. You cannot go on forever.

But life goes on forever. One wave turns into another wave, one tree creates other trees, one man gives birth to children—it goes on: there is no beginning and there is no end.

Art is only a poor imitation. Hence, the artist remains in imagination. The artist remains in dreams; he is a dreamer, a good dreamer—a dreamer who dreams in color, not just black and white—but still a dreamer.

A mystic is one who has dropped all dreams, who has thrown away this mirror of the mind and looks directly into life without any medium interfering. Then he sees the eternal progressing. Then in a single moment he sees all eternity, and in a single atom he can see the whole reflected.

Just think: you contain your mother, your father, your father's father, your mother's mother, and so on and so forth. You contain Adam and Eve—if there was a time when things began. I don't think there was a time when things began. Adam and Eve is again a fiction, a religious fiction. Things never began, things have always been.

You contain the whole past. All the dreams of your father and your mother are contained in your cells, and all the dreams of their fathers and their mothers, and so on and so forth; all the dreams of the whole humanity have preceded you; and not only of humanity, but all the animals that have preceded humanity; and not only all the animals, but all the trees that have preceded all the animals; and not only the trees, but all the rocks and all the mountains and rivers that have preceded trees. You contain all of that in you. You are vast!

And so is the case with the future—you contain the whole future too: the children that will be born and the poems that will be written—not only the Shakespeares of the past but the Shakespeares of the future too, the dreams that have been seen and the dreams that will be seen. All the poets and all the painters are in you, ready to be born, all the scientists, all the mystics. The whole future, the eternal future...

So you contain the whole past, you contain the whole future.

The whole converges upon this small, tiny moment. And so is the case with space, as it is with time. You contain the whole of space in you, all the trees and all the stars.

A great Indian mystic, Swami Ramateerth, started saying things which look mad when he attained to enlightenment. People started thinking that he had gone bizarre, because he started saying, "I see stars moving within me, not outside, but inside. When I see the morning sun rising, I see it rising in me, not outside."

Now this looks like a kind of madness. It is not. He was saying something tremendously significant. He was saying: I am part of the whole and the whole is part of me. So everything is within that is without, and everything is without that is within. All that has happened is in me, and all that is going to happen is in me, and all that is happening is in me.

To feel this, to see this, is to be in prayer, in awe, in wonder. Will you not be grateful to be part of this mysterious existence? Will you not feel grateful to have something to do with this splendor? Will you not feel grateful, thankful for all that surrounds you and all that is contained in you?

To see this mysterious existence, to feel it in the deepest core of your heart, and immediately a prayer arises—a prayer that has no words to it, a prayer that is silence, a prayer that doesn't say anything but feels tremendously, a prayer that is like music with no words, celestial music, or what Pythagoras used to call 'the harmony of the stars', the melody of the whole. When that music starts rising in you, that's what the *Secret of the Golden Flower* is all about. Suddenly a flower bursts open in you, a golden lotus. You have arrived, you have come home.

This is what I am provoking you towards, this is what I am trying to awake in you—this desire, this longing, this thirst, this appetite. Once you are possessed by this hunger, for the first time you will become aware of the benediction and the beautitude of existence. You will not feel meaningless, you will not feel accidental. You will not feel at all as Jean-Paul Sartre says, that "Man is a useless passion"; no, not at all. You will feel yourself tremendously significant, because you are part of an infinite significance, and you are to contribute something by your being here.

You will become creative, because that is the only way to be really thankful to God—to be creative, to make this existense a little more beautiful than you had found it. The day you leave, this will be your only contentment: if you have made the existence a little more beautiful. When a Buddha leaves he leaves in tremendous contentment because he knows he is leaving the existence behind with a little more poetry in it, with a little more awareness in it, with a little more prayer in it.

Remember that when you leave the world, you can die in contentment only if you have made this world a little more worth living in, a little more meaningful, a little more dancing, celebrating. If you have added a little festivity to it, a little laughter, a little sense of humor; if you have been able to light a small lamp of light, and you have been able to disperse a little darkness from the world, you will die in utter joy. You are fulfilled. Your life has been of fruition and flowering. Otherwise people die in misery.

Jean-Paul Sartre is right for the majority of the people, but that majority is living in ignorance, unconsciousness. That majority is not really yet able to declare its humanity. Only a Buddha or a Krishna or a Zarathustra or a Jesus can claim that they are human beings. They are human beings because they have bloomed. Their whole beings have come to flowering. Now nothing is left, all is fulfilled.

THE SECRET OF SECRETS 70

Create this longing, this thirst. You have the seed; all that you need is a thirst. That thirst will become the occasion for the seed to sprout. You have the potential; all that you need is a tremendous longing. If you become aflame with longing you will be purified. The baser metal of your life will be transformed into a higher metal, into gold. This is all that alchemy is about.

And the *Secret of the Golden Flower* is an alchemical treatise.

Master Lu-tsu said: *There are many kinds of confirmatory experiences. One must not content oneself with small demands but must rise to the thought that all living creatures have to be redeemed. One must not be trivial and irresponsible in heart, but must strive to make deeds prove one's words.*

If, when there is quiet, the spirit has continuously and uninterruptedly a sense of great joy as if intoxicated or freshly bathed, it is a sign that the light-principle is harmonious in the whole body; then the Golden Flower begins to bud. When, furthermore, all openings are quiet, and the silver moon stands in the middle of heaven, and one has the feeling that this great earth is a world of light and brightness, that is a sign that the body of the heart opens itself to clarity. It is a sign that the Golden Flower is opening.

Furthermore, the whole body feels strong and firm so that it fears neither storm nor frost. Things by which other men are displeased, when I meet them, cannot becloud the brightness of the seed of the spirit. Yellow gold fills the house; the steps are of white jade. Rotten and stinking things on earth that come in contact with one breath of the true energy will immediately live again. Red blood becomes milk. The fragile body of the flesh is sheer gold and diamonds. That is a sign that the Golden Flower is crystallized.

The brilliancy of the light gradually crystallizes. Hence a great terrace arises and upon it, in the course of time, the Buddha appears. When the golden being appears who should it be but the Buddha? For the Buddha is the golden holy man of the great enlightenment. This is a great confirmatory experience.

Chapter Three

August 29th, 1978

THE GOLDEN FLOWER IS OPENING

A PARABLE:

One day the Lord Vishnu was sitting in a deep cave within a far mountain meditating with his disciple. Upon the completion of the meditation the disciple was so moved that he prostrated himself at Vishnu's feet and begged to be able to perform some service for his Lord in gratitude. Vishnu smiled and shook his head, "It will be most difficult for you to repay me in actions for what I have just given you freely." "Please Lord," the disciple said, "allow me the grace of serving you." "Very well," Vishnu relented, "I would like a nice cool cup of water." "At once Lord," the disciple said, and he ran down the mountain singing in joy.

After a while he came to a small house at the edge of a beautiful valley and knocked at the door. "May I please have a cool cup of water for my Master," he called. "We are wandering sannyasins and have no home on this earth." A wondrous maiden answered his call, and looked at him with undisguised adoration. "Ah," she whispered, "you must serve that holy saint upon the far mountain. Please, good sir, enter my house and bestow your blessing therein." "Forgive my rudeness," he answered, "but I am in haste. I must return to my Master with his water immediately." "Surely, just your blessing won't upset him. After all he is a great holy man, and as his disciple you are obligated to help those of us who are less fortunate. Please," she repeated, "just your blessing for my humble house. It is such an honor to have you here and to be enabled to serve the Lord through you."

So the story goes, he relented, and entered the house and blessed all therein. And then it was time for dinner, and he was persuaded to stay and further the blessing by partaking of her food (thereby making it also holy), and since it was so late—and so far back to the mountain, and he might slip in the dark and spill the water—he was persuaded to sleep there that night and get an early start in the morning. But in the morning, the cows were in pain because there was no one to help her milk them, and if he could just help her this once (after all, cows are sacred to the Lord Krishna, and should not be in pain) it would be so wondrous.

And days became weeks, and still he remained. They were married, and had numerous children. He worked the land well and brought forth good harvests. He purchased more land and put it under cultivation, and soon his neighbors looked to him for advice and help, and he gave it freely. His family prospered. Temples were built through his effort, schools and hospitals replaced the jungle, and the valley became a jewel upon the earth. Harmony prevailed where only wilderness had been, and many flocked to the valley as news of its prosperity and peace spread throughout the land. There was no poverty or disease there, and all men sang their praises to God as they worked. He watched his children grow and have their own children, and it was good.

One day as an old man, as he stood upon a low hill facing the valley, he thought of all that had transpired since he had arrived: farms and happy prosperity as far as the eye could see. And he was pleased.

Suddenly there was a great tidal wave, and as he watched, it flooded the whole valley, and in an instant all was gone. Wife, children, farms, schools, neighbors—all gone. He stared, bewildered, at the holocaust that spread before him.

And then he saw riding upon the face of the waters his Master, Vishnu, who looked at him and smiled sadly, and said, "I'm still waiting for my water!"

This is the story of man. This is what has happened to everybody. We have completely forgotten why we are here, why we came in the first place, what to learn, what to earn, what to know, who we are and from whence and to where, what is our source and the cause of our journey into life, into body, in the world, and what we have attained up to now. And if a tidal wave comes—and it is going to come, it always comes; its name is death—all will be gone: children, family, name, fame, money, power, prestige. All will be gone in a single moment and you will be left alone, utterly alone. All that you had done will be undone by the tidal wave. All that you had worked for will prove nothing but a dream, and your hands and your heart will be empty. And you will have to face the Lord, you will have to face existence.

And the existence has been waiting for you; long, long it has been waiting for you to bring something for which you had been sent in the first place. But you have fallen asleep, and you are dreaming a thousand and one dreams. All that you have been doing up to now is nothing but a dream, because death comes and all is washed away.

Reality cannot be washed away by death. Reality knows no death. Reality is undying. Reality is deathless. Reality is eternal. All that dies simply proves by its death that it was unreal, that it was illusory, *maya*, a dream—maybe a nice dream, but a dream all the same. You may be dreaming of hell or you may be dreaming of heaven; it does not make much difference. The moment you will be awakened you will find yourself utterly empty—and empty in a negative sense, not in the positive sense as Buddhas know it: not empty of the ego, but empty of all that your ego has been trying to do; full of ego, but empty of any attainment, empty of any realization, empty of any knowledge. And it is not that the ego does not claim knowledge; it claims. The ego is very knowledgeable, it collects information. It is a great collector: it collects money, it collects information, it collects every kind of thing. It believes in accumulation. It is greed and nothing but greed; ego is another name for greed. It wants to possess, but all that you possess will be gone. And all that you have done, you have done in your dream. The moment you will be awakened you will be surprised at how much time has been wasted, at how many lives you have been living in a dream, at how many dreams you have lived.

To be a seeker means to come out of this dream, to come out of this dreaming state of consciousness. To be a seeker means: making an effort to wake up. To wake up is to become a Buddha—to be alert, to be conscious, to be full of light within so that all unconsciousness disappears, so that all sleep disappears, so the darkness of sleep is no more inside you and you are fully awake.

It happened:

A great astrologer saw Buddha. He could not believe his eyes— that body, that golden aura around the body, those beautiful eyes, as silent as any lake can be, and as deep and as pure as any lake can be, that crystal-clarity, that walking grace. He fell at Buddha's feet and he said, "I have studied astrology, palmistry. My whole life I have been studying types of men, but I have never come across a man like you! To what type do you belong? Are you a god who has descended on the earth?— because you don't seem to belong to this earth. I can't see any heaviness in you. You are absolutely light, weightless. I am wondering how you are walking on the earth, because I don't see any gravitation functioning on you. Are you a god who has descended from heaven just to have a look at what is happening on the earth? a messenger from God? a prophet? Who are you?"

And Buddha said, "I am not a god."

The astrologer asked, "Then are you what in Indian mythology is called a *yaksha?*"—a little bit lower than the gods.

And Buddha said, "No, I am not a *yaksha* either."

"Then who are you? What kind of man, what category to put you in?"

And Buddha said, "I am not a man or a woman."

Now the astrologer was very much puzzled, and he said, "What do you mean? Do you mean you are an animal, an animal spirit, or the spirit of a tree, or the spirit of a mountain

or the spirit of a river?"—because Indian mythology is pan-
theistic, it believes in all kinds of spirits. "So who are you, the
spirit of a rosebush? You look so beautiful, so innocent."
And Buddha said, "No, I am not an animal, nor the spirit
of a tree, nor the spirit of a mountain."
"Then who are you?" The astrologer was puzzled very much.
And Buddha said, "I am awareness and nothing else. You
cannot categorize me, because all categories are applicable to
dreams."

Somebody is dreaming he is a man, somebody else is dreaming she is a woman, and so on and so forth. Categories belong
to the world of dreams. When one becomes awakened one is
simply that principle of awakenedness, awareness. One is just
a witness and nothing else, a pure witness. All clouds have
disappeared: the cloud of a man or a woman, animal, god,
trees—all clouds, all forms have disappeared. One is just a
formless awareness, the pure sky, endless, infinite, vast. This
awareness is empty of clouds but full of the sky. This is positive
emptiness, this is *nirvana*.

Then there is a negative emptiness. You are full of clouds—
so much so that not even a bit of sky can be seen. You are
full of knowledge—so much so that not even a little space is
left for meditation.

It is said: He who knows not and yet knows that he knows,
is a fool—usually called a pundit or a scholar; shun him. He
who knows not, and knows not that he knows not, is innocent,
a child; wake him. He who knows not, and knows that he
knows not, is a Buddha; follow him.

To come to this realization: "I am nobody", is the meaning
of being a Buddha.

Buddha is not the name of somebody. Buddha is the name for 'nobody-ness'. Buddha is not an entity. Buddha is just space, open space, openness, a name for openness, for open sky.

Watch your mind: how much dreaming continues. And it is not only that you dream in the night, you are continuously in a dream. Even while you think you are awake, even in the daytime, the continuity is not broken. At any moment close your eyes and relax and you will immediately see dreams floating. They are always there, like an undercurrent. They never leave you, they are constantly present, and constantly affecting your being. Their existence is subliminal. You may not be alert about them, you may not even suspect their existence, but they are continuously there. Even when you are listening to me, there is that movie continuing, that drama of dreams. Hence you cannot hear what I am saying. First it has to pass through your dreams and your dreams distort it; you hear something else that has not been said. Your dreams distort, your dreams manipulate, your dreams project, your dreams change things.

I say one thing, you hear quite another. And those dreams are very powerful inside you, and you don't know what to do with those dreams. In fact, you have become so identified with the dreams that you don't know that you are separate, that you can watch, that you can be distant, that you can be just an onlooker. You have become too identified with the dreams.

Just the other day I was talking about poor Habib. Now he has become so identified with being a Jungian analyst that he cannot watch what is happening. I had mentioned that, just two days before, I had finished my talk at nine forty-five, and he wrote a letter at nine fifty-five, after just ten minutes. Yesterday he went even further: while I was talking he was writing the letter! While I was discussing him, he could not wait even ten minutes. And that's what I was saying: "Wait a little, be a little patient, meditate over it. You cannot understand these things immediately; you are not in that state of understanding, of clarity, of perception." But while I was talking he started writing the letter. At exactly the same time, while I was talking, he was writing the letter. Now what could he write? I had not even talked, I had not even spoken. He must have heard, he must have taken the clue from his own mind. He could not understand a single word. His dream seems to be too strong; he is burdened by his knowledge. And I was saying "Let your Jungian ego drop."

But do you know what happened? Habib died—he renounced sannyas rather than dropping the Jungian ego. That's what he heard. I was saying "Drop the Jungian ego!"; he heard something else. He heard, "Then this sannyas is not for me. I cannot drop my knowledge; that's all I have. And how can I drop it? How can one put the mind aside? It is impossible! So it is better to drop sannyas." He dropped sannyas. Now Habib no longer exists; he died a very early death. In fact, he died before he was born.

What happened? Could he not see the point? Who prevented him from seeing the point? His mind must have become too crowded. All that he has been reading, accumulating—he has become too attached to it. He had come here to seek and search. What kind of search is this if you are not ready to leave anything of your ego? What kind of inquiry is this?

People usually think they are spiritual seekers if they can add something more to their egos. Your so-called spiritual trips are nothing but subtle trips of the ego. People want more gratification for the ego, more strength for the ego, more vitality for the ego. They want a holy aura around the ego, and the holy aura arises only when the ego is gone; they cannot co-exist.

And it is very rare to come across a teaching which can awaken you. It is very rare to come across a Master who can shake you up into wakefulness, who can pull you out of your long, long deep-rooted dreams. It is a rare phenomenon to come across a Master; it is very easy to miss. It is easy to miss because the basic fundamental of being with a Master is: to put your head in front of him so that he can crush it with his sledge-hammer. A Master is a sledge-hammer. People search for a different kind of situation where the Master—they think he is the Master if he buttresses their egos—says to them, "Good! You are a great spiritual seeker."

That's what the late Habib wanted: he wanted me to say that he is a great spiritual seeker, that whatsoever he has done is perfectly beautiful, the right foundation for the temple; that he is almost ready, just a little bit has to be added to him and all would be perfect. That's what he wanted. That is not possible—because first I have to destroy you. Only through your utter destruction is the possibility of your awakening. And destruction is hard, painful.

A great Hassidic saying says: God is not nice. God is not an uncle, God is an earthquake!

So is it with a Master: a Master is not an uncle, a Master is not nice. A Master is an earthquake. Only those who are ready to risk all, in toto, who are ready to die as egos, can be born. This is what Jesus means when he says, "You will have to carry your cross on your own shoulders. If you want to follow me, you will have to carry your cross on your own shoulders."

Kabir has said, "If you really want to follow me, burn your house immediately!" What house was he talking about? The house of dreams in which you have lived has to be utterly burned so that you can be again under the open sky and the stars and the sun and the moon; so you can again be in the wind, in the rain; so you can again be available to nature—because God is nothing but the hidden-most core of nature. God is not a kind of knowledge, God is a kind of innocence. You know God not by knowledge but by becoming utterly innocent.

But it is very difficult for the ego...even to hear these words is difficult. And the ego will immediately distort them, manipulate them, change them, color them, paint them and make them in such a way that they support the ego rather than destroy it.

One story reflecting this observation concerns a man who had an obsession that he was dead. He went to a psychiatrist for help. The psychiatrist used all the known techniques at his command, but to no avail. Finally the psychiatrist tried appealing to the patient's logic.
"Do dead men bleed?" asked the doctor.
"No, of course not," answered the patient.
"All right," said the doctor. "Now let us try an experiment." The doctor took a sharp needle and pricked the man's skin, and the patient began to bleed profusely.
"There! What do you say now?" asked the psychiatrist.
"Well, I will be darned!" answered the patient. "By gosh! Dead people *do* bleed!"

That's how the ego functions, the mind functions: it turns things into proofs, supports, food for itself. The ego is very subtle and its ways are very cunning, and it can convince you that you are right. It will try in every possible way to convince you that it is right and anything that goes against it is wrong. Remember, the ego is *never* right! And anything that goes against it—don't miss the opportunity, use that occasion to destroy your ego. The moment you can destroy your ego will be the moment of great blessing, because when you are not, God is, and *when you are not, you are*. This is the greatest paradox of life and existence: when you are not, you are.

That's why Vishnu was not willing...Vishnu said to his disciple, "It will be most difficult for you to repay me in actions for what I have just given you freely." Why? Why would it be most difficult? Because the Master knows that the disciple is still in dreams, he is still in his ego. In fact, the very idea "I want to repay you, I want to do something for you because you have done so much for me," is an ego-idea. When the disciple has dropped the ego, who is there to repay? Who? Who is there even to thank? There is nobody. There is utter silence. And in that utter silence the Master is happy: the disciple has repaid through this utter silence.

A man went to Buddha. He wanted to do something for humanity; he was a very rich man. And he asked Buddha, "Just tell me what I can do for humanity? I have much money, no children, the wife has died, I am alone. I can do much."

Buddha looked at him with very sad eyes and remained silent. The man said, "Why are you silent? Why don't you speak? You always talk about compassion, and I am here ready to do something. Whatsoever you say I will do. Don't be worried— I have enough money! Just give me any task and I will do it."

Buddha said, "I understand what you are saying, but I am

feeling sad: you cannot do a thing because you still are not. Before one can do something, one has to be. It is not a question of money that you have—but that *you* are not!"

That quality of compassion is a shadow of being, and the being is missing. The ego can never be compassionate. The ego is cruel; even in its games of compassion it is cruel. And when the ego is gone, even if the egoless person looks to you to be very cruel, he is not; he cannot be. Even his cruelty must be a deep compassion.

When a Zen Master hits the disciple's head with his staff it is not cruel; it is tremendous compassion. When a Zen Master jumps on his disciple and beats him it is not cruel, because sometimes it has happened that with the hit of the Master, the disciple has become enlightened—in a single moment, in a single lightning experience.

Buddha said, "You cannot do anything. I know about your money, I have heard about you, but when I look into you I feel very sad for you. You want to do something, but the element that can do something is missing. All that you can do is dream."

That's why Vishnu says, "It will be most difficult for you to repay me in actions what I have just given you freely." That's what George Gurdjieff used to say to his disciples. The first thing that he had said to P.D. Ouspensky was this, exactly this. Ouspensky was a great seeker, a seeker of knowledge. When he had gone to see Gurdjieff for the first time, he was already a world famous mathematician, philosopher, thinker. His greatest book had already been published, *Tertium Organum*. It is a rare book—also rare because the man was not awakened. How could he manage to write such a beautiful piece? Only an awakened man can see a few faults; otherwise it is very difficult to find any fault in it. It is almost perfect, as if a Buddha has written it.

But when George Gurdjieff looked into the book, he just turned here and there and threw it out of the room. And he said, "All nonsense! You know nothing! And how can you know, because *you* are not! Before one can know one has to be!" And Ouspensky had travelled all over the East in search of a Master. It is a beautiful story, almost a parable.

He had travelled in India. He had gone to Ceylon, to Burma. He had lived in monasteries, in Himalayan caves. He had met lamas and swamis and many Hindu mystics, but nobody could satisfy him. Why?—because all that they said was nothing but a repetition of the scriptures that he had already studied. Not a single word was their own. Frustrated, he went back, back to Russia, to Petrograd where he used to live. In Petrograd, in one coffee house, he met Gurdjieff. And just the first meeting, and the Master's look at him...and the revelation: "This is the man I have been searching for. This is the town I have lived in my whole life, and this is the coffee house I have been visiting for years, and this man is sitting here in the coffee house! And I have been searching for him in Ceylon, in Nepal, in Kashmir, in faraway places."

The first thing that Gurdjieff said to Ouspensky was, "Unless you are, you cannot know a thing. Unless you are, you cannot do a thing." And the paradox is that you are only when you have disappeared, when the word 'I' is no longer relevant.

These sutras are the keys to create that state of Buddhahood— when you are just awareness, and nobody; full of light, but utter emptiness.

The sutras:

> Master Lu-tsu said: *There are many kinds of confirmatory experiences.*

A confirmatory experience means that you are coming closer to home. One has to understand, one has to be aware of confirmatory experiences because that gives courage, hope. That gives vitality. You start feeling that you are not searching in vain, that the morning is very close by. Maybe it is still night and dark, but the first confirmatory experience has started filtering in. The stars are disappearing, the East is becoming red; the sun has not risen, it is early dawn—it is confirmatory that the sun is not far away. If the East is becoming red, then soon, any moment, the sun will rise on the horizon. The birds have started singing; the birds are praising the coming morning. Trees look alive, sleep is disappearing, people are waking up. These are confirmatory experiences.

Exactly like that, on the spiritual path, there are experiences which are very confirmatory. It is as if you are moving towards a beautiful garden you cannot see, but the closer you come to the garden, the cooler the breezes are that you can feel. The farther away you go, the more coolness disappears; the closer you come, the more the coolness appears again. The more close you come, the more the breeze is not only cool, but there is fragrance too, the fragrance of many flowers. The farther away you go, the more the fragrance disappears. The closer you come the more you can hear birds singing in the trees. The trees you cannot see, but the song of the birds... a distant call of a cuckoo...there must be a mango grove: you are coming closer. These are confirmatory experiences.

Exactly the same happens when you move towards the inner garden, towards the inner source of life, of joy, of silence, of bliss. When you start moving towards the center a few things start disappearing and a few new things start appearing.

One must not content oneself with small demands but must rise to the thought that all living creatures have to be redeemed.

And remember, when confirmatory experiences start appearing, don't be satisfied too soon. The cool breeze has come, and you sit there and you think that you have arrived. The coolness is beautiful, the coolness is blissful, but you have to go far. Don't be satisfied with small things. Feel happy that they have started happening, take them as milestones, but they are not goals. Enjoy them, thank God, feel gratitude, but go on moving in the same direction from where the confirmatory experiences are coming.

And don't be contented with small demands. For example: peacefulness is a small demand, it can be easily attained. The state of a non-tense mind can easily be attained; it is not very difficult. To be happy and cheerful can easily be attained, it is not much. To be at ease, unanxious, without anxiety is not something very great. Then what is great? And what should one keep in mind as the goal?

One must rise to the thought that all living creatures have to be redeemed.

You will be surprised to know that this is the criterion, and this has always been the criterion. In Buddhism it is called 'the principle of Bodhisattvahood'. The closer you are coming to your own inner center, the more you will start feeling the suffering of all beings of the world. On the one hand you will feel very calm and quiet, and on the other hand you will start feeling a deep sympathy for all those who suffer. And there is suffering and suffering and suffering: the whole place is full of suffering. On the one hand you will feel great joy arising in you, and on the other hand a great sadness too that millions are suffering—and ridiculously suffering, suffering for no reason! This is their birthright, to attain to this blissfulness that is coming to you. And don't become satisfied that you have become blissful, so all is finished. If you become blissful, all is not finished, really. Now the journey takes a new turn. When you have attained to Buddhahood, when you have come home, now the real work starts.

Up to now it was only a dream. Now the real work starts: help others to come out of their dreams. When the disciple has attained, he has to become a Master.

This is what in Christianity is called 'the principle of Christ-consciousness'. Christians have not really been able to understand it; they have misunderstood it. They think that Jesus is the only Christ.

The word 'christ' comes from Krishna. It is a principle. The principle is that when you are redeemed, you have to redeem all. To be redeemed from misery is blissful, but nothing compared to when you start redeeming others from their misery. To redeem oneself from misery is still selfish, self-oriented. Something of the self still lingers, you are only concerned with yourself. And when the self disappears and you are redeemed, how is it possible to stop the journey? Now you have to redeem others. That's why Jesus is called 'the Redeemer'. But he is not the only Christ. There have been many before him, there have

been many after him, there will be many in the future. Who-
ever becomes a Buddha has to become, *of necessity*, a redeemer
of all.

One's joy, one's peace, one's blessings are small things; don't
be contented with them. Remember always that one day you
have to share, one day you have to help others to be awakened.
This seed must be planted deep in your heart, so that when
your Buddhahood blooms you don't disappear from the world.

Buddhists have two words; one is *arhat. Arhat* means: the
person who has become enlightened but thinks all is finished,
his work is complete. He disappears. The other is called *bodhisattva:* he has become enlightened; he does not disappear, he
insists on being here. He prolongs himself, to be here as long
as it is possible.

The story is that when Buddha reached the doors of *nirvana*
the doors were opened, celestial music was played, golden
flowers showered, angels with garlands were ready to receive
him, but he refused to enter. He turned his back to the door.
The angels were surprised, they could not believe it. They
asked him again and again, "What are you doing? Your whole
life—not only one but many lives—you have been searching
for *this* door. Now you have arrived, and you are turning your
back to the door? And we have been waiting for you, and
the whole paradise is full of joy—one more person has become
a Buddha. Come in! Let us celebrate your Buddhahood
together." But Buddha said, "Unless all those who are in
suffering are redeemed, I'm not going to enter. I will have to
wait. I am going to be the last, let others move first." And the
beautiful story says that he is still waiting at the door. The door
is open because the angels cannot close it; any moment he may
want to enter. That is his right, to enter, so the door is open.

He's keeping the door open, and the celestial music continues, and the flowers are still being showered, and the angels are waiting with garlands...and he's standing outside the door. And he's calling people forth; he's calling, challenging, he's provoking. He's telling people, "The doors are open, don't miss this opportunity. Come in! And I am going to be the last. Now the doors shall never be closed. They will be closed only when everybody is redeemed and enlightened."

This is just a parable, tremendously significant. Don't think of it as history, otherwise you will miss the point. There is no door, no angels, no garlands, no celestial music. And Buddha, the moment he became enlightened, has disappeared. How can he stand and keep his back to the door? Who is there to stand? But the principle...

The energy that Buddha released into existence is still functioning. That energy is still available to those who are *really* searching. The energy goes on and on working, and it will go on working for eternity. Jesus is no more, but his Christ-consciousness has entered into the new sphere. Mahavir is no more, but his consciousness has entered into this oceanic life. These people have become part of existence; they vibrate. That is the meaning of the parable: they still provoke you, and if you are ready to receive their message they are still ready to take you to the other shore.

The moment a Master dies he becomes part of that infinite energy which Buddha has joined, Mahavir has joined, Zarathustra, Lao Tzu, Jesus, Mohammed. Whenever a Master dies, more energy is redeemed—and it is becoming a tidal wave. So many enlightened people have existed; it is becoming a continuous tidal wave.

You are fortunate. If you really long, if you really desire, this tidal wave can take you to the other shore.

Keep it in your deepest heart: don't be satisfied with small things. Many things happen on the Way, many *miraculous* things happen on the Way, but don't be satisfied with anything. Remember, you have to become a Christ-consciousness, a bodhisattva—less than that is not going to make you contented.

This is divine discontent.

> *One must not be trivial and irresponsible in heart, but must strive to make deeds prove one's words.*

And the life of a seeker should not be that of trivia, because each small thing that you go on doing wastes time, energy, life. The seeker cannot waste. His whole life has to be devoted and dedicated to one single point. He cannot waste here and there: he cannot go and sit in the coffee-house and gossip unnecessarily. He cannot read that which is not going to help. He's not going to do a single thing which is not going to help his journey, and he's not going to collect a single thing that will become a burden later on and will have to be dropped. He remains simple. This simplicity has nothing to do with asceticism. This simplicity is simply scientific: he does not accumulate garbage because then you have to carry it. He remains unburdened. And the greatest garbage is that of knowledge, because all other garbage is outside you: knowledge gets inside. It makes your head very heavy, and the head should be very light.

Have you watched, or have you seen a Japanese doll called daruma? Daruma is the Japanese name for Bodhidharma. The doll is beautiful. It represents the enlightened man—the daruma doll. It's beauty is that you can throw it any way but it always sits back in full lotus posture. You throw it—you cannot topple it—it again comes back. Its bottom is heavy, its head is light, so you cannot put it upside-down. It is always rightside-up.

Just the opposite is the case with human beings: they are upside-down. Their heads are very heavy, they are top-heavy. They are standing on their heads. A man who is knowledgeable stands on his head. He is in a continuous *sirshasana*, a head-stand.

The man who has no knowledge in the head, whose head is empty, silent, is rightside-up. He is in a lotus posture, he is a daruma doll. You cannot topple him, there is no way; he will always come back. You cannot disturb him, there is no way; his undisturbedness remains continuous.

One must not be trivial and irresponsible in the heart...

What is responsibility? Ordinarily the meaning of the word has become associated with wrong things. The real responsibility is towards God and towards nobody else; or, the real responsibility is towards your own nature, and to nobody else. You are not responsible to the society or to the church or to the state. You are not responsible to the family, to the community. You are responsible only to one thing: that is your original face, your original being. And in that responsibility all other responsibilities are covered automatically.

Become natural. And the man who is natural is responsible—because he responds. The man who is not natural never responds, he only reacts. Reactions mean being mechanical, response is non-mechanical, spontaneous.

You see a beautiful flower and you suddenly say something: "It is beautiful." Watch whether it is a reaction or a response. Go deep into it, scrutinize it. What you have said—that "The flower is beautiful"—is it your spontaneous response this moment, herenow? Is this your experience, or are you simply repeating a cliche because you have heard others saying that flowers are beautiful. Go into it, watch: who has spoken through you? Maybe it is your mother.... You can remember the day, for the first time she had taken you to the garden, the public gardens, and she had told you, "Look at this rose. How beautiful it is!" And then the books that you have been reading, and the films that you have been seeing, the people you have been talking to—and they all have been saying "Roses are beautiful." It has become a programmed thing in you. The moment you see the rose flower your program says "It is beautiful," not you. It is just a gramophone record, it is a tape. The rose outside triggers the tape and it simply repeats. It is reaction.

What is response? Response is unprogrammed experiencing in the moment. You look at the flower, you really look at the flower, with no ideas covering your eyes. You look at *this* flower, the *thisness* of it! all knowledge put aside. Your heart responds, your mind reacts. Responsibility is of the heart. You may not say anything; in fact, there is no need to say, "This is beautiful."

I have heard...

Lao Tzu used to go for a morning walk. A neighbor wanted to be with him. Lao Tzu said, "But remember, don't be talkative. You can come along, but don't be talkative."
Many times the man wanted to say something, but knowing Lao Tzu, looking at him, he controlled himself. But when the

sun started rising and it was so beautiful, the temptation was so much that he forgot all about what Lao Tzu had said. He said, "Look! What a beautiful morning!"

And Lao Tzu said, "So, you have become talkative? You are too talkative! You are here, I am here, the sun is here, the sun is rising—so what is the point in saying to me 'The sun is beautiful'? Can't I see? Am I blind? What is the point of saying it? I am also here." In fact, the man who said "The morning is beautiful" was not there. He was repeating, it was a reaction.

When you respond words may not be needed at all, or sometimes they may be needed. It will depend on the situation, but they will not necessarily be there; they may be, they may not be.

Response is of the heart. Response is a feeling, not a thought. You are thrilled: seeing a rose flower something starts dancing in you, something is stirred at the deepest core of your being. Something starts opening inside you. The outer flower challenges the inner flower, and the inner flower responds: this is responsibility of the heart. And if you are not engaged in trivialities, you will have enough energy, abundant energy, to have this inner dance of the heart. When energy is dissipated in thoughts, your feelings are starved. Thoughts are parasites: they live on the energy which is really for the feelings, they exploit it.

Thoughts are like leakages in your being: they take your energy out. Then you are like a pot with holes—nothing can be contained in you, you remain poor. When there are no thoughts your energy is contained inside, its level starts rising higher and higher. You have a kind of fullness. In that fullness the heart responds. And then life is poetry, then life is music, and then only can you do the miracle of making deeds prove your words, not before it. Then you don't only say "I love you", your very existence proves the love. Then your words are not impotent words; they have a soul to them. And to live like that is the only life worth living: when your words and your deeds correspond, when your words and deeds are not opposites, when your words are full of your sincerity, when whatsoever you say you are.

Before that, you live in a kind of split: you say one thing, you do another. You remain schizophrenic. The whole humanity is schizophrenic unless one comes to this point where words and deeds are no more separate, but two aspects of the same phenomenon. You say what you feel, you feel what you say, you do what you say, you say what you do. One can simply watch you and will see the authenticity of your being.

> *If, when there is quiet, the spirit has continuously and uninterruptedly a sense of great joy as if intoxicated or freshly bathed, it is a sign that the light-principle is harmonious in the whole body; then the Golden Flower begins to bud.*

"When there is quiet"—a great confirmatory sign—then "the spirit has continuously and uninterruptedly a sense of great joy". For no reason at all you suddenly feel yourself joyous. In ordinary life, if there is some reason you are joyful. You have met a beautiful woman and you are joyous, or you have got the money that you always wanted and you are joyous, or you have purchased the house with a beautiful garden and you are joyous—but these joys cannot last long. They are momentary, they cannot remain continuous and uninterrupted.

I have heard...

Mulla Nasrudin was sitting, very sad, in front of his house. A neighbor asked, "Mulla, why are you looking so sad?"
And Mulla said, "Look! Fifteen days ago my uncle died and he left me fifty thousand rupees."
The neighbor said, "But this is no reason to be sad! You should be happy."
Mulla said, "First you listen to the whole story. And seven days ago my other uncle died and left me seven thousand rupees. And now, nothing.... Nobody is dying, nothing is happening. The week is passing by, and I am really sad."

If your joy is caused by something it will disappear, it will be momentary. It will soon leave you in deep sadness; all joys leave you in deep sadness. But there is a different kind of joy that is a confirmatory sign: that you are suddenly joyous for no reason at all. You cannot pinpoint why. If somebody asks, "Why are you joyous?" you cannot answer.

I cannot answer why I am joyous. There is no reason. It's simply so. Now *this* joy cannot be disturbed. Now whatsoever happens, it will continue. It is there day in, day out. You may be young, you may be old, you may be alive, you may be dying —it is always there. When you have found some joy that remains, circumstances change but it abides, then you are certainly coming closer to Buddhahood.

This is a confirmatory sign. If joy comes and goes, that is not of much value; that is a worldly phenomenon. When joy abides, remains uninterrupted and continuous—as if you are intoxicated, without any drug you are stoned; as if you have just taken a bath, fresh as morning dewdrops, fresh as new leaves in the spring, fresh as lotus leaves in the pond; as if you have just taken a bath—when you remain continuously in that freshness that remains and remains and nothing disturbs it, know well you are coming closer to home.

It is a sign that the light-principle is harmonious in the whole body.

Now your whole body is functioning as a harmonious unity, your whole body is in accord. You are no more split, you are no more fragmentary. This is individuation: you are one whole, all parts functioning and humming together, all parts functioning in an orchestra of being. Nothing is out of tune—the body, the mind, the soul, the lowest and the highest, from sex to *samadhi*—all is functioning in a tremendous harmony and an incredible unity.

...then the Golden Flower begins to bud. When, furthermore, all openings are quiet, and the silver moon stands in the middle of heaven, and one has the feeling that this great earth is a world of light and brightness, that is a sign that the body of the heart opens itself to clarity. It is a sign that the Golden Flower is opening.

Then, furthermore, when all openings, all senses are quiet, not only the mind... Mind is your inner sense; that has to be made silent first. Then there are five senses which are mind-feeders: your eyes, your ears, your nose, all the senses. They continuously bring information from the outside and they go on pooling the information inside, in the mind. When they are also quiet, not bringing anything, they are utterly silent, passive—eyes look but don't bring anything in, ears hear but don't cling to anything heard, the tongue tastes but hankers not for the taste; when all your senses are quiet and the silver moon stands in the middle of heaven—the silver moon represents the feminine principle; when the silver moon stands in the middle of heaven, when all senses are passive, mind is passive and quiet, that means you have attained to the feminine principle of passivity, awaiting. You have become a womb.

It is a full moon night. All is cool and silent and passive. Nothing stirs. The joy is infinite!

> ...and one has the feeling that this great earth is a world of light and brightness...

And it is not only that you feel it within. When it is within, you immediately start feeling it without too—that this whole earth is a world of light and brightness.

> ...that is a sign that the body of the heart opens itself to clarity.

You are becoming transparent, clear, clean, perceptive. The feminine principle brings clarity because it is a passive principle. It brings rest, utter rest. You are simply there doing nothing, all is clear, all clouds gone. You can see through and through into reality. Inwards there is silence and joy, and outwards there is silence and joy.

> It is a sign that the Golden Flower is opening.

First, it was just beginning to bud; now it is opening. One more step has been taken.

> *Furthermore, the whole body feels strong and firm so that*
> *it fears neither storm nor frost.*

As your silence and joy deepen, you start feeling that there is no death for you. In death only the persona dies, the personality; the essence never dies. When you know something abiding in you, something that never changes—the joy that continues irrespective of conditions—then you know for the first time that something is deathless in you, something in you is eternal. And that moment is the moment of strength, potentiality, fearlessness. Then one is not afraid. Then trembling disappears. For the first time you look into reality without fear. Otherwise your so-called gods are just out of fear: you have created them to console yourself, you have created them as props for your fear, as protection, as armor. You are afraid; you need somebody to cling to. These are false gods, these are not true gods. Out of fear how can you find the true God?

And the so-called religious people are known as God-fearing. The real religious person has no fear, neither of the world nor of God. In fearlessness a totally different vision of God arises.

> *Things by which other men are displeased when I meet*
> *them, cannot becloud the brightness of the seed of the spirit.*

Now nothing clouds, nothing can overwhelm you and distort your clarity. Your vision remains intact. Somebody insults you but it doesn't become a cloud. Somebody is angry, you can see through and through: you really feel compassion for the angry person because he's unnecessarily burning in a fire. You shower your bliss, your peace, your love on him. He is a fool, he needs all compassion.

Yellow gold fills the house; the steps are of white jade. Rotten and stinking things on earth that come in contact with one breath of the true energy will immediately live again.

And if you can come in contact with such a man whose inner steps are of white jade, whose inner sky is full of the moon, and whose inner house is full of yellow gold; if you can come in contact with such a man, even if you are dead, you will immediately revive. That is the meaning of the story of Lazarus: Jesus calling Lazarus forth out of his grave. All Buddhas have been calling people forth out of their graves.

I am calling you out of your graves, because the way you have lived is not the true Way. You have become concerned with trivia and you have forgotten the essential. You are just collecting seashells and colored stones on the sea beach and you have forgotten all about the diamonds which are very close by. You are collecting rubbish which will be taken away by death.

I am calling you forth to attain to treasures which no death can take away from you.

Lazarus! Come out of your grave!

And the one who listens becomes a disciple. The one who listens becomes a sannyasin. The one who listens starts moving into the inner world. His journey is totally different from other people's journey: he may live in the world, but he's no longer there. His concern is utterly different.

Red blood becomes milk.

This is the meaning of the famous parable about Mahavir.

It is said that a snake, a very dangerous snake, attacked Mahavir, bit his foot; but instead of blood, milk started flowing. Now Jains take it literally, and then they become a laughing stock. It is not a literal message, it is a parable: red blood represents violence and milk represents love.

The moment the child is born, the mother's breasts become full of milk—out of love, out of feeling for the newborn babe. Suddenly her blood starts changing to milk. Suddenly a miracle starts happening in the chemistry of the mother: up to now she had been just a woman, now she is a mother. When a child is born, two persons are born—on the one hand, the child, on the other hand, the mother. The mother has a different chemistry from the woman. The miracle has happened: out of love, blood starts turning into milk. It is symbolic: blood is violence, milk is love.

When a person reaches to this state, all violence disappears. He's all love, love and nothing else.

The fragile body of the flesh is sheer gold and diamonds.

And those who can see, those who have eyes to see, will be able to see in the body of the Buddha not fragile flesh, but sheer gold and diamonds. That's why disciples are not believed by others. Others think the disciples have become hypnotized because they start seeing things which nobody else can see, which are available only to the close disciples. They start seeing, in the ordinary physical body, something else—another body, the body of gold and diamonds, the body of eternity. This body of flesh is the body of time. Hidden behind it is the body of eternity...but for that one needs eyes to see...and only love and surrender can give you the eyes to see.

That is a sign that the Golden Flower is crystallized.

But when one is moving in this inner journey and one can see one's own body as gold and diamonds, then one can be certain that the Golden Flower is crystallized.

First it was just budding, then it was opening, now it is crystallized.

The brilliancy of the light gradually crystallizes. Hence a great terrace arises, and upon it, in the course of time, the Buddha appears.

Now you can be certain that the Buddha is not far away, the dawn is close by, the night is over. On the terrace of this vision of gold and diamonds, of the eternal body...as this brilliance crystallizes a terrace arises...in the course of time, the Buddha appears.

One cannot do anything beyond this point. When the Golden Flower has crystallized, when the lotus has crystallized, you cannot do anything beyond that point. Now one has simply to wait: sitting silently, doing nothing, and the spring comes, and the grass grows by itself.

One moment—in the course of time—when the spring comes—Buddha appears. When the golden being appears who should it be but the Buddha?

In the East we have called it Buddha, in the West you have called it Christ—it is the same principle.

For the Buddha is the golden holy man of the great enlightenment. This is a great confirmatory experience.

And when you have seen within yourself a terrace of brilliancy, a crystallized light, and on the terrace of it Buddha appearing; when you have seen the Golden Flower open, bloomed, and on the golden lotus Buddha appearing, you have come home.

This is the ultimate goal. This has to be found. This can be found. This is your birthright. If you miss, only you will be responsible, nobody else. Risk *all*, but don't miss it! Sacrifice *all*, but don't miss it!

Chapter Four

August 30th, 1978

WORDS CANNOT CONTAIN IT

The first question:

Bhagwan, I love you. I also love your jokes. I am very serious these days. This whole enlightenment game is too heavy. Please tell more jokes.

Majida, enlightenment, the very idea of enlightenment, is the greatest joke there is. It is a joke because it is trying to get something which is already there. It is trying to reach somewhere where you are already. It is trying to get rid of something which is not there at all. It is an effort which is ridiculous.

You are enlightened from the very beginning. Enlightenment is your nature. Enlightenment is not something that has to be achieved; it is not a goal, it is your source. It is your very energy.

But once you start thinking about enlightenment as a goal, you will become serious. You will be in tremendous trouble— and absolutely unnecessarily—of your own creation. And you will never succeed either, because to think of enlightenment as a goal is to already miss the whole point. It is not there to be sought, it is in the seeker. The seeker cannot seek it! If the seeker tries to seek it, he will never find it. It is as if somebody is trying to find his glasses and the glasses are on his nose; he's trying to find the glasses with the help of the glasses, and he is not aware. It is ridiculous!

You are creating a serious trip for yourself. You are making it a goal and it is your source. You are making it your ambition and it is already the case! From the very beginning, nobody is unenlightened. Then what has happened to people? Why are they searching? Why do they go on searching? Why do they make a goal out of it?

In life, everything else has to be found—except enlightenment. If you want money, it has to be a goal; otherwise you will not find it. You have to work hard for it, you have to put your whole energy into the ambition; then only will you find. Then too, it is not absolutely certain—you may find, you may not find. If you want power you will have to seek and search in every possible way, legal, illegal, right, wrong. In life, every- thing has to be found because you don't bring money with you, and you don't bring power with you, and you don't bring palaces with you. You come naked, empty-handed, and you go naked and empty-handed. You don't bring a thing of this world, and all those things are needed; and you rush and you try to achieve this and that.

Slowly, slowly the idea arises in you that all these things will be taken away from you. Death will come and will annihilate everything: you become frightened, fear arises. Out of fear, you start thinking to search for something which will not be taken away from you: God, truth, enlightenment, *nirvana*, or you can give it any name. Now you start seeking *nirvana*, enlightenment, God, *samadhi* in the same way as you have been seeking money, power, fame. Because you have learned a logic, you have learned a program; now the program says, "You cannot get money without seeking for it, how can you get enlightenment without seeking for it? So seek, search, fight, struggle." And there is the whole crux of the matter— and you become ridiculous.

Money has to be sought if you want to have more money, but enlightenment is already there. You bring it with you. It is your original face. It is your emptiness, your consciousness. It is your being. When you die, everything else will die except your enlightenment, except your consciousness. Nobody can take it away from you.

But the logic that you have learned in the world drives you crazy. It is very logical to search, seek money, power, name, fame; it is very illogical to seek enlightenment. And then it becomes a heavy trip, very serious. That's why religious people look so serious.

Religious people cannot think somebody is religious if he is not serious. Seriousness has become almost synonymous with religiousness—sad, long faces. Do you see your saints laughing? That's why the so-called Indian saints are against me: they cannot believe that an enlightened person can tell jokes. They cannot believe!

My own experience is that only an enlightened person can tell jokes. What else is left? He has seen the greatest joke of it all: he has seen the whole absurdity of searching for enlightenment. One finds enlightenment not by searching, but by one day coming to such a point of desperation that one drops all effort. In that very moment one becomes aware of it. When searching stops, desiring disappears, you are left alone with your being; nowhere to go, you are in. The inward journey is not really a journey. When all journeys disappear—nowhere to go, no interest in going, you have searched in every direction and every direction has failed you—in *utter* desperation you simply stop, you collapse, but that very collapse is the moment of the transformation. Nowhere-going, you are in. Not seeking anything, only the seeker is left. Not trying to catch anything, you suddenly become aware of the catcher. Not being interested in any object—money *or* enlightenment *or* God—only subjectivity is there. You are back home . . . and a great laughter, because you have always been there.

It is said that when Bodhidharma became enlightened he did not stop laughing for seven years.

There is another story, in Japan, of the laughing Buddha, Hotei. His whole teaching was just laughter. He would move from one place to another, from one marketplace to another marketplace. He would stand in the middle of the market and start laughing—that was his sermon. His laughter was catching, infectious; a *real* laughter, his whole belly pulsating with the laughter, shaking with laughter. He would roll on the ground with laughter. People who would collect together, they would start laughing, and then the laughter would spread, and tidal waves of laughter, and the whole village would be overwhelmed with laughter. People used to wait for Hotei to come to their village because he brought such joy, such blessings. He never uttered a single word, never. You asked about Buddha and he would laugh; you asked about enlightenment and he would laugh; you asked about truth and he would laugh.

Laughter was his only message. Now on the opposite extreme, Christians say Jesus never laughed. Christians must be mis-representing Jesus. If Christians are right, then Jesus was not enlightened—and I would rather prefer Jesus to be enlightened than Christians to be right. So I say to you, he laughed! He *must* have laughed. Only such people can laugh. Their whole energy becomes a bubbling joy. Their whole being wells up into celebration. Laughter is celebration. Jesus must have laughed.

My own feeling is that his laughter must have offended the serious so-called rabbis of his day. He must have told beautiful jokes. He was a Jew, and Jews have the best jokes in the world. And he was not a man who could be believed to be so serious that he never laughed. A wrong impression has been created by Christianity. Jesus is painted as crucified: that gives the wrong impression. He was not on the cross for his whole life. My own understanding is that on his cross also he must have laughed, because only a man of great laughter can say to God, "Father, forgive these people, because they don't know what they are doing." He was not serious, he was not sad; even the cross was a celebration.

Animals can play, at the most, but no animal can celebrate. It is given only to human beings. It is their privilege, prerogative, to celebrate. And laughter is the best celebration. To laugh is your fundamental human quality. If you came across a buffalo laughing, you would go mad. No other animal can laugh, only man; it is something special, a gift of God. And naturally, when one becomes enlightened, one will be able to have a total laugh. You need reasons to laugh; he will not need any reasons to laugh. Laughter will be just his natural quality.

That is the meaning of the story that Bodhidharma never

stopped laughing for seven years. There was no reason—just the whole ridiculousness of the thing: so many Buddhas and everybody believing that he is not a Buddha and trying to attain Buddhahood.

You are all Buddhas. Whether you know it or not, it doesn't matter—your Buddhahood is not affected by it, you still remain a Buddha. You can believe that you are not a Buddha; your belief is not going to transform your nature. You can believe anything! Your belief remains superficial. At the very core of your soul, you are a Buddha. The moment you are not in desire, you will become aware of your innermost center. Desire takes you away from yourself.

And that is the problem, Majida: you must be too desirous of enlightenment, hence you are becoming serious. Otherwise there is nothing serious about enlightenment.

The second question:

Why is truth inexpressible? Why can't it be told?

Truth is an experience of thoughtlessness. Truth is an experience of wordlessness. You come to experience truth only in utter silence. It is utter silence, hence it is impossible to reduce it to sound, to word, to thought. Its intrinsic nature is without thought. To express truth in words would be like expressing the sky through the clouds. The sky is not expressed through the clouds. The sky, covered with clouds, disappears, you cannot see it. The more clouds are there the less the sky is available; the less clouds are there the more sky is available;

no clouds, and the whole sky is available. You cannot express the sky through the clouds, they are the hindrances.

So are thoughts: truth is your consciousness, thoughts are clouds in the sky of consciousness. You cannot express through thoughts. Your thoughts can, at the most, indicate, like fingers pointing to the moon. But remember, fingers are not the moon; don't start worshipping the fingers. That's what has happened in the world. Somebody is worshipping one finger, somebody else some other finger—Christians, Mohammedans, Hindus, Buddhists. What are Buddhists doing?—worshipping Buddha. This is just a finger pointing to the moon. Where is the moon? They are sucking the finger and have completely forgotten the moon. That's why I say to you: Don't start biting *my* finger! Don't become too interested in what is said. That which is said is only pointing a finger to that which cannot be said.

So all words are, at the most, arrows. That's why they can be misunderstood, easily misunderstood: fingers you are acquainted with, the moon you have never seen. And when I show the moon with the finger it is more possible to become interested in the finger than to look away from the finger and see the moon. To see the moon you will have to look away from the finger. You will have to become completely oblivious to the finger.

"To tell the truth," said Oscar Wilde, "you have to wear a mask." All words are masks; all theories, dogmas, philosophies are masks. All religions, all theologies are masks.

He's right! To tell the truth, you have to wear a mask. You cannot tell it straight, there is no way. To bring the word in simply means: now you cannot be straight, a medium has come in. Now the expression is through the medium; the

medium will bring its own distortions into it. If you have a
colored glass before your eyes, you will see the world in the
same color. Now words will become like glasses on your eyes:
they will color your world. That's why different people look
at the world in different ways—because they have been conditioned differently.

A Hindu looks at the world differently from the Christian.
A Hindu can worship the tree and the Christian will think,
"What nonsense! Worshipping a tree?" The Christian will
think, "This man has to be brought to his senses, converted.
This man is a pagan. Make efforts to bring him to the true
religion. This man is primitive"—because the Christian has
a different upbringing, a different conditioning. Ask the
Hindu: he has a different mind. He says, "The whole existence
is divine. The tree is also divine. And the question is not what
you are worshipping, the question is that you are worshipping.
What you worship makes no difference." And the Hindu will
say, "You go on worshipping a dead cross—it is made of
wood—and I am worshipping an alive tree, and you think
I am foolish? Who is foolish? The tree is alive and life is flowing,
and the tree is green and the tree is in blossom. God is still
flowing in it as green juice. Your cross is dead. It is better to
worship the tree, the Hindu will say, than to worship the
cross."

The Hindu worships Krishna—dancing, playing on his flute—
and the Christian cannot believe it because the world is in
suffering: "And how can this man be so cruel that he is playing
on his flute? The world needs to be redeemed and he is dancing
with girls! What is he doing? What kind of religion is this?"
He has a conditioning that the man of God has to die for the
world so that the world can be redeemed. The man of God has
to become a sacrifice. He has to be a martyr; not a singer, not
a musician, not a dancer, but a martyr.

A Hindu has a different conditioning: he thinks if Jesus is crucified then he must have been suffering from bad karma from his past life—otherwise why should he be crucified? Crucifixion is not a good thing: it means he must have committed some bad things in his past life, because 'as you sow, so you reap'. "He cannot be the man of God. If he is the man of God then crucifixion is simply impossible." They have a different vision and different conditioning: the man of God has to sing the song of God, the celestial song, Bhagavad-Gita. He has to dance and sing in praise of God. The world need not be redeemed, the world has only to be enlightened, helped—to laugh, to love, to be.

Now it depends, it is according to your conditioning. Once you drop all conditionings you will be able to understand all kinds of minds very easily, and you will be able to see their benefits and their harms. You will be able to see what is beautiful in a certain conditioning and what is ugly. Yes, the Hindu has something beautiful to say: "God is there and we have to praise God." Right! But the world is suffering too, and something has to be done for the world, for its sufferings. And the Christian is not absolutely wrong: just the flute won't do. It has not done much for India. India is terribly poor, starving. Life is ugly. People are somehow pulling, dragging themselves. It has not been helped by the flute, something more is needed. Just dancing won't do: schools will be needed and hospitals will be needed and food will be needed.

Christianity is not all wrong, but again it makes only a half-statement. When the food is there, when the house is there, when the medicine is there, when the education is there, then what? Then just crucify yourself? What else is left? Where is the flute?

The West is suffering from affluence: all is there, but nobody knows what to do now. They have worked for three hundred years, hard work, to make everything right. Now everything is right: the house is ready, food is available, technology has provided for all needs. Now what to do—except commit suicide? Life seems meaningless because the flute is missing.

In the East man has lived with a half-vision: God is beautiful, and life is beautiful; but then he has been avoiding the ugly part of it and not trying to transform it at all. The East has lived in a very unrevolutionary way, an *anti*-revolutionary way. It has lived a very reactionary life, orthodox, conventional, conformist. Revolution is something Western, revolution is something Christian.

The world has to be transformed as much as the consciousness has to be transformed.

But when you put *all* conditionings aside you will be able to see that the world needs a totally different kind of vision. It needs a *total* vision—neither Christian nor Hindu nor Mohammedan. It needs a total vision. All these are aspects of that total vision: Mohammed is one door, Christ is another, Krishna is still another, and Buddha too. All are different doors to the same temple, and all the doors are needed; only then will the temple be rich. And even if all the doors are accepted, then too truth has not been told in its fullness, because it is infinite. You can put Buddha, Christ, Zarathustra, Lao Tzu, Mahavir, Mohammed together, still truth has not been told in its totality. It can never be told. It is infinite.

All words are small. All human efforts are limited. And then, it cannot be told straight. It can be communicated straight, but it cannot be told straight—and that is the difference between a thinker and a meditator. The thinker goes roundabout because he has to go through thought. He searches for the sky through the clouds and gets lost in the clouds, may never reach the sky. The thinker gets lost in thoughts. The meditator starts by dropping thoughts. He starts by dropping thinking itself, and a moment comes when there is no thought: then there is immediacy. Then there is nothing between you and that which is. Then there is nothing at all—you are bridged with reality. But that is an experience. Whenever you would like to tell that experience to somebody else you will have to use words, out of necessity, and words cannot contain it.

For certain purposes you can say the truth straight—for certain purposes. 'The cat sat on the mat': either the cat did it, he did sit there, or he did not. But there are other kinds of truths which you cannot catch hold of so easily. This is a fact, not a truth. So remember the difference: if some truth can be said through language, then it is a fact—'the cat sat on the mat' Now there is an objective way of knowing whether this is true or not. If it is true it is a fact. If it is untrue it is not a fact, it is a fiction.

But there are other kinds of truth which cannot be said so easily. You cannot catch hold of them.

Language is riddled with all kinds of ambiguity. If anyone says God, love or freedom, you need to know exactly what he means when he is saying it. These are big words—God: now a Hindu means something, a Mohammedan means something else, a Christian means something else. There are three hundred religions in the world, so there are three hundred meanings to the word 'God'. Even those three hundred meanings don't exhaust it because new religions are being created every day, and they will go on being created. There can be as many religions as there are people in the world. Each man can have his own religion.

Then what is the meaning of the word 'God'? It becomes vaguer and vaguer and vaguer. It becomes a chaos. You cannot pinpoint anything about it, and if you try to pinpoint you destroy its beauty—because you destroy its unlimitedness. If you fix it, you have killed it.

A butterfly on the wing is one thing, and a butterfly killed and pinned down in an album is a totally different thing. It is not the same butterfly. Where is the life? The moment you pin the butterfly down in an album, it is just a corpse.

When Buddha says, "God", it is a butterfly on the wing. You catch hold of the word, you pin it down in a book; you think you know, you think you have understood. All that you have got is just a corpse, the life has flown away. The life is an experience! Words cannot carry the experience. When I say something...unsaid, when it is throbbing in my heart, it is alive. The moment it has left my lips it is no more the same thing: life is left behind. It goes on throbbing there in my heart, and only the word, dead, corpse-like, moves into the air. Just a sound, a ripple, reaches to you. It is not the same thing as it was unsaid.

And then more complexities arise: the moment the sound reaches your mind you start giving your meaning to it—and your meaning may be just the opposite of my meaning because it will depend on your experience. If you meditate, then maybe your meaning will come closer and closer to me. If you have come to a point where you can stop all thinking and get in tune so deeply with yourself that there is absolute silence, then you will come closest to the meaning of what has been said to you. In fact, then there will be no need to even say it. I can just look into your eyes and you will understand. I can just sit by your side and hold your hand and you will understand.

Then understanding is a transfer, a transmission beyond words, beyond scriptures.

The higher up you go, the thicker grows the mystery. The lower kinds of facts can be relayed through words because we have all experienced them. When I say 'a tree' you understand exactly what I mean, but when I say 'nirvana' you only hear the word, you don't understand what I mean—because as far as the tree is concerned, it is a common experience, my experience, your experience. If I say 'a rock', immediately it is understood, it is a mundane fact. But when I say 'love', it is a little more difficult; and when I say 'nirvana', even more difficult—because the higher the truth, the fewer are those who will be able to understand it.

Jesus was misunderstood. Out of misunderstanding he was killed. He was talking of the Kingdom of God, and the Roman rulers became suspicious. They started thinking that he was a politician and he wanted to rule the world, he wanted to create his own kingdom. He was talking continuously and saying to people, "I have come to establish the Kingdom of God." He was saying something, the politicians were interpreting something else. He was not talking of the kingdom of this world, he was talking of the kingdom of the other world, the invisible. He was not concerned with politics at all.

It has always happened: the higher you go, the more dumb you feel. And whatsoever you say, you can *immediately* see it has been misunderstood.

Lao Tzu has said, "If I say something and people understand

it, then I know it was not worth saying. If I say something and people don't understand, then I know that there must have been some truth in it."

We must learn to live with this, this mystery of higher truths. Music is one way of doing it, far better than language. Because music has no words it cannot tell anything, truth, untruth; so it can't tell no-truth or lies. It says nothing, it simply shows—and that is the beauty of music. You don't think whether music is true or untrue; that is irrelevant. You simply listen to it. You become overwhelmed by it, you are possessed by it. You fall in tune with it. You are transported to some other realm, to some other vision of reality. You are not in the mundane world. Music takes you to the higher peaks of life and existence. It simply takes your hand and leads you, very politely, very lovingly, into the mysterious.

Music was born as part of religion: music was born in temples, music was born in the mystery schools, in the esoteric schools of seekers of truth. It was born as an effort to convey something which cannot be conveyed through words. Music can bear witness to the mystery, and that is all.

If you love a Master, you start hearing his music, the music of his being. Even through his words you start hearing the wordless message, you start hearing...listening to the gaps between the words. You start reading between the lines. Slowly slowly words become transparent; then they don't hide, they reveal. But for that, trust and love are needed. For that, disciplehood is needed.

Just the other night a new sannyasin was here, Kavio, a beautiful man with great potential. He has come here with his beloved; she's also a beautiful woman. She wants to look into my eyes, and she is not a sannyasin yet. Kavio asked me about it, and I had to say that unless she is a sannyasin, even if she looks into my eyes she will not be able to see anything. To be a sannyasin means to be ready to receive. I will be giving, but she will not be able to receive—because she is not ready to pay anything to receive it. She should take the jump into sannyas. Sannyas means surrender; surrender creates receptivity. Surrender means you become vulnerable, open, you don't defend. Surrender means now you put your arms away, now you drop your armor. Now even if the Master wants to kill you, you will be happy to be killed by the Master.

I have heard...

One day Hassan of Busra and Malik, son of Dinar, and Sakik of Bulk, came to see Rabiya el-Adawiya when she was ill.
Rabiya is one of the greatest woman mystics of the world, and these three saints came to see her because she was ill.
Hassan said, "None is sincere in his claim to the love of God unless he patiently endure the blows of his Lord."
Rabiya said, "This smells of egoism."
Sakik said, "None is sincere in his claim unless he give thanks for the blows of his Lord."
Rabiya said, "This must be still bettered. Still something of egoism is there."
Malik, son of Dinar, said, "None is sincere in his claim unless he delight in the blows of his Lord."
Rabiya said, "Good, but still needs to be improved. A very subtle ego is still hiding there like a shadow."
Then they all said, "Please do speak. You yourself say."
She said, "None is sincere in his claim unless he forgets the blows in beholding his Lord."

Let me repeat it: none is sincere in his claim unless he forgets the blows in beholding his Lord.

Even when the Master hits, you feel tremendously happy. And the Master has to hit to make openings in your being; you have grown a hard crust around yourself. That was necessary for survival, otherwise you would not have survived at all. You had to protect yourself against so many dangerous situations in life. You have become afraid, frightened; you have created a China Wall around yourself. When you come to a Master you have to drop that armor. And the armor may have gone so deep that you cannot drop it. Then the Master has to hit you, the Master has to use a sledge-hammer. He has to cut many chunks of your being because they are not really part of you. They are part of the armor which has become too much identified with your being. And when those chunks are removed and cut, it is painful, it hurts—but only then can the Master pour himself into you. One has to pay for it. And by paying I mean one has to be ready to drop all defenses. That's what sannyas is all about.

Only in a Master-disciple relationship can truth be conveyed, because only in that relationship are words not needed.

I use words to persuade you to become a disciple. Words cannot convey the truth, but words can convey this approach: that there is a possibility of being in a certain love-relationship with a Master; there is a possibility of coming closer to somebody who has seen who he is. You are also that, but you have not seen it yet. Coming closer to somebody who has known, one day his vibe starts triggering a process of knowing in your being. That is the transfer.

Kavio's woman has some longing to be connected with me, to be related with me, but still wants to be related to me as an outsider, is afraid of getting involved, is afraid of being committed. But that very fear will not allow her to receive what

I want to give. I am ready to give to anybody! It is not a condition from *my* side that you have to be a sannyasin, that only then will my energy be flowing towards you. This is my observation and experience: that only a sannyasin receives it. The others are not ready to receive.

The music of silence, the music of a loving surrender, the music of the being of a Master—that is the way to relate, to convey.

Music, in a sense, is absolutely silent. Sounds are there but those sounds only make the silence deeper. They help the silence, they are not against silence. That is the difference between noise and music: noise is just sound which does not lead you to silence, music is sound that becomes a door to silence. Modern music is not much of a music, it is noise; it does not lead you to silence. Classical music is real music. The definition of real music is: that sound which leads you into silence.

Music, in a sense, is absolutely silent. Even song is not pure music, because a song has words in it. It is a compromise with language, it is halfway to music. It is better than ordinary language. Poetry is better than prose, poetry is a little closer to music; and the closer the poetry is to music the more poetic it is. Hence the highest form of poetry comes very close to music. It does not have much meaning but it contains much silence; it provokes silence.

The being of a Master is the being of music, poetry, song. But they all lead to silence, and truth can only be conveyed in silence. Have you not observed the fact that whenever you are in love you can be silent easily? You need not talk, you can just sit together with the person you love. There is nothing to say. Just to be together is more than enough, more than one can ask. Just to be together is such a contentment. There is no need to even say that "I love you". That would be a kind of disturbance. That would be utterly superfluous, that would not say much. In love, you can be silent.

Sannyas is a love affair. And you can be silent only as the love deepens; and then the truth can be transferred. But it is a transfer of energy, of music, of love. It is not verbal, it is not a philosophy.

The third question:

Why won't you leave India? Those dim-witted politicians in New Delhi will be the last people in the world to understand what is going on here.

It is difficult for me to leave India. India has something tremendously valuable: it has the longest, deepest search for truth. Many Buddhas have walked on this land, under these trees; the very earth has become sacred. To be here is totally different than to be anywhere else, and what I am trying to bring you is more easily possible here than anywhere else.

India has fallen from its peaks. It is no longer in its past glory. It is one of the ugliest spots now on the earth, but still, because a Gautam Buddha walked, and a Mahavir and a Krishna, and millions of others...

No other country can claim this. Jesus is very alone in Jerusalem; Mohammed is very very alone in the Arabian countries; Lao Tzu has a very small company, Chuang Tzu and a few others. They tried hard to create something. But India has the longest spiritual vibe: for at least five thousand years the search has been deepening, and still the waters are flowing.

Indians themselves have forgotten about them. In fact they are no longer interested in their own heritage. They are no longer interested in those living waters, they have deserted them. But for whomsoever wants to seek and search and be, India still provides the best climate—spiritual climate, I mean.

Indians have become *very* materialistic, that is true, but with so many Buddhas the release of their energy still pulsates in spite of the Indian materialism. Indians have become *really* materialistic, far more materialistic than any country in the world. And great hypocrisy exists, because they go on claiming to be religious, and they are no more. My own observation is that now the Indian mind is more and more materialistic, more gross than any other mind. Their whole interest is in money, in power-politics, in material things.

Just a few days ago I told Laxmi to purchase the *most* costly car possible in the country. One thing good about Laxmi: she never asks why. She purchased it. It worked—it was a device. Laxmi was knocking on the doors of the banks to get money for the new commune. We need much money; near-about five crore rupees will be needed. Who is going to lend that much money to me? The day she purchased the car, seeing that we have the money, banks started coming to her office, offering, "Take as much money as you want." Now she is puzzled: from whom to take? Everybody wants to give on better terms, and they are after her.

I have been working in India for twenty years continuously. Thousands of people have been transformed, millions have listened to me and many more have been reading what I am

saying, but the Times of India, the most conventional newspaper of India, still the most British, has not published a single
article about me or my work. But the day Laxmi purchased
the car there was a big article—on the car, not on me!

Now they are all interested. The news of the car has been
published all over the country, in all the newspapers, in all the
languages. Now what kind of people are these? Their interest is
not in me, not in meditation, not in the thousands of people
who are meditating here. They are completely unaware of
what is happening here, but they became interested in the
car.

They come here. Many people come to the office not to see
me or to see you: they inquire, "Can we see the car?" Laxmi
says to them, "You can come to the early morning discourse,
and you can see the car too." And poor fellows—they have to
come and listen for ninety minutes just to see the car. What
a torture! And these are rich people, educated people. Can you
think of a more materialistic country?

And they are very worried, and editorials have been written
on the car: they ask, "Why? Why can't you live a simple life?"
My life is absolutely simple: so simple really, that I am always
satisfied with the best kinds of things. It is absolutely simple.
What more simplicity is possible? In a single sentence it can be
said: the best kinds of things. There is no complexity about it.
I like quality. I'm not interested in how much it costs but in
the quality. I like quality in people, not quantity. I like quality
in everything, not quantity. We could have purchased thirty
Indian cars instead of this one, but that would have been quantity
—and even thirty wouldn't have been of any use.

But their puzzle, why they can't understand it, is that they
pretend to be religious, but deep down their whole obsession is

materialistic. They carry a hypocrisy, and to fulfill their hypocrisy the whole Indian religious world has to compromise. If somebody wants to become a saint he has to live in utter poverty. It is almost a kind of masochism; he has to torture himself. The more he tortures himself, the more people think he is religious: "See how religiously he is living!"

To live religiously means to live joyously. To live religiously means to live meditatively. To live religiously means to live this world as a gift of God, but their minds are obsessed and they can't understand. Once the purpose of the car is served, it will be gone. The purpose is almost served, but it can show you.

I can even come in a bullock cart. It would be even more colorful, and I would enjoy the ride more.

They come here and they look, and their whole point is "Why such a beautiful ashram?" They want something dirty, shabby, a sloppy place, and then it is an ashram. They cannot believe that the ashram can be clean, beautiful, with trees and flowers, and comfortable. They cannot believe it. And not that they don't want comfort for themselves; they are hankering for it. They are, in fact, jealous. The Indian mind has become materialistic, grossly materialistic.

A spiritual mind makes no distinctions between matter and spirit; it is undivided. The whole existence is one: that is the spiritual mind. The materialist, even if he loves a woman, reduces her to a thing. Then who is a spiritualist? A spiritualist is a person who, even if he touches a thing, transforms it into a person.

You will be surprised by my definition. A spiritual person is one who, even if he drives a car, the car becomes a person. He feels for the car, he listens for its humming sound. He has all affection and care for it. Even a thing starts becoming a person, alive; he has communion with the thing too. And a materialistic person is one who, even if he loves a man or a woman, a person, immediately reduces them into a thing. The woman becomes a wife—the wife is a thing. The man becomes a husband—the husband is a thing, an institution. And all institutions are ugly, dead.

You ask me, "Why won't you leave India.....?"

This India that you see in the newspapers, this India I have already left. The India that you know, I have already left. Have you ever seen me going out of the gate? I live in my room. Whether this room is here or anywhere else, I will live in the room; it will be the same. I have left this India already. I am not concerned with this India that you come to know through radio, television, newspapers—the India of the politicians, of the hypocrites, of the masochistic mahatmas. I have left it already.

But I cannot leave. There is a hidden India too, an esoteric India too, where Buddhas are still alive, where you can contact Mahavir more easily than anywhere else, where the whole tradition of the awakened ones is like an undercurrent. I can't leave that. For me, there is no problem; I can leave, I will be the same anywhere. But for you it will not be the same.

I want to use that undercurrent for your transformation; it will be easier. Unknowingly, unawares, you will be surround-ed by the Buddha-vibe. And once the new commune is estabi-shed, you will see miracles happening, because I can make that undercurrent available to you in its totality. That would not be possible anywhere else.

Nowhere else has religion lived so tremendously as it has

lived in this country. Just as science is a western by-product, religion is an eastern by-product. If you want to learn science you have to go to the West, because the sources are there. The whole western mind is such that science comes out of it very easily. That was the case, as far as religion is concerned, in the East, and the East is synonymous with India.

You are not aware, you cannot be aware of what I am intending to do. These are all devices, so never start making a conclusion when you see something. You may not be aware of its background, you may not be aware of the intention, you may not be aware of what is going to happen through it.

Now Laxmi knows that the car has helped her tremendously. Once its work is finished it can be gone. Never take anything on its face value here, things have hidden meanings; they are devices.

The new commune is going to become a river of all the Buddhas. You will be able to use all that great energy easily. We will make a great reservoir of it. You will be able to live and breathe in it, and you can ride on those tidal waves and move to the unknown.

So I cannot leave India.

And you say: "Those dim-witted politicians in New Delhi will be the last people in the world to understand what is going on here."

Politicians are politicians. They are all alike everywhere; maybe a little bit different on the surface, but deep down they are the same people because politics is politics. I know Indian politics has become the dirtiest in the world; that too is part of Indian hypocrisy. Even Indian politicians try to prove that they are mahatmas; even Morarji Desai tries to prove that he is a super-mahatma. A politician and a mahatma? Because of this hypocrisy Indian politics has become the most dirty game.

If things are clear: if somebody says, "I am ambitious and I want to be on the top," at least he is sincere. But in India the politician says, "I am the humblest man, and I don't want to be on the top. What is there? There is nothing. My search is for God, but just to serve people I have to go. I am obliging you by becoming the Prime Minister of the country." Now this hypocrisy is making things very dirty.

Just a few days ago Indian politics took a change, and it was hoped that it would be for the better. But it is proving just the opposite: the change has been for the worse. And now it seems clear that the man who has been responsible for this change, J. Prakash Narayan, will not be forgiven by the future, because he has given power to the most reactionary section of the country. He has given power to a bunch of power-hungry wolves, and now he himself is feeling impotent and cannot do anything. Once they are in power they don't care anything about him. Now the whole Indian scene is nothing but politics: how to reach power and how to exploit, how to have more money and how to have more power, and how to remain in power longer.

But this is so everywhere, more or less. And politicians will create trouble everywhere for me and for my people, because I stand for a totally new vision of life. I stand for a revolution in human consciousness. Politics always supports the vested interest—it has to support it—so everywhere the trouble will be the same.

One thing more will be difficult: from any other country I can be thrown out immediately, here they cannot do that. And it is not that this has only been so with me, it has always been so.

Gurdjieff was not allowed to enter England; he was not allowed to settle in many countries. For his whole life he was moving from one country to another. He could not do his work. How could he do the work? The work needs a kind of settlement. He would gather his disciples and then the country had to be left and the disciples would be scattered again. Again he would gather, he would spend a few years in gathering, and by the time the disciples had gathered, the politicians were against him and he had to leave the country, and again everything was disturbed.

This continued for his whole life. He could not help; not a single person could become enlightened through him. And many would have become—he had the potential, he was a rare genius, a rare Master—but the situations wouldn't allow.

If I leave India that will be the situation again and again. Whenever my people will gather in one country, there will be trouble. And here they can create trouble for you—that can be managed easily—but they cannot create trouble for me. At least they cannot throw me out of the country. They would like me to go; they will do everything so that I leave, because my presence is becoming more and more difficult for them. The more I am here and the more my people are growing and the more the commune will become an established fact, the more I am going to shatter all their values, all their hypocrisies.

So I cannot leave India. And I know the Indian politicians will be the last people in the world to understand what is going on here. They will not even be the last—they will never understand.

The politician cannot understand religion; it is impossible. The language of politics is just the opposite of the language of religion. Religion is non-desiring, non-ambitiousness, non-possessiveness. Religion is living herenow. Politics is ambition, desire, always in the future, tomorrow. Religion is to accept oneself, to accept whatsoever one is and to relax with it.

Politics arises out of inferiority complex, out of comparison. Compare yourself with others and you are always feeling inferior: somebody is more beautiful, somebody is more knowledgeable, somebody is more intelligent—and you are suffering from an inferiority complex. You want to prove yourself. Now, if you are not intelligent, what can you do to become intelligent? It is impossible. If you don't have a musical genius, what can you do? There is no way to do anything about it. If you are not beautiful, you are not beautiful. But then only one thing is left: you can become a politician. That is the last resort of all the people who suffer from an inferiority complex: there, anybody, whosoever has violence enough, brutality enough, whosoever has the animal alive in him, can rush. No other talent is needed, no kind of genius is needed. In fact the less intelligence you have, the better will be your chances of succeeding.

I have heard...

Mulla Nasrudin suffered very much because people thought he was an idiot. Finally he decided to go to the brain surgeon and let him transplant another brain. So he went to the surgeon, and the surgeon said, "Mulla, there are brains and brains. You come in and you see." And there were many brains.
Mulla said, "What is the difference—because I see different prices written on every case? On one case the price is only

THE SECRET OF SECRETS   132

twenty-five rupees and on another it is twenty-five thousand rupees. What is the difference?"

The surgeon said, "Mulla, the first, which is priced at only twenty-five rupees, belongs to a great scientist. And the second, which is twenty-five thousand rupees, belongs to a politician."

Mulla said, "Do you mean to say that the politician's brain is far more superior to the scientist's?"

The surgeon said, "No, don't misunderstand me. It is priced more because it has never been used. It is absolutely unused, brand new. The scientist's has been used too much. It is finished, it is burnt out."

In politics you don't need brains, you don't need intelligence, you don't need sensitivity, you don't need awareness, you don't need love, you don't need compassion. These are all barriers! In politics you need just the opposite qualities. Disqualifications everywhere else are qualifications in politics. All that is needed is a mad hunger for power—and that is created by an inferiority complex.

The religious man has no inferiority complex. Only the religious man has no inferiority complex because he never compares, and without comparison you cannot be superior or inferior. So the religious man is neither superior nor inferior; he is simply himself. He accepts the way God has made him and he enjoys the way God has made him. He's utterly happy. Just because he is, he is grateful. His every moment is one of gratitude. He does not want to become anybody else, he is utterly contented. He knows he is unique—neither inferior nor superior. He knows everybody is unique, because two persons are not alike.

So politicians can never understand what religion is. They

never understood Buddha, they never understood Christ, they never understood any religious phenomenon that has happened on the earth. They were always against it. The presence of the religious person is a danger to the politician.

And I know you are right: 'Those dim-witted politicians in New Delhi' will never understand me. That's true...but we are not worried. I am not in any way concerned that they should understand me; they need not. All that I am concerned with is that they leave me and my work alone. That's enough. And sooner or later they will have to leave it alone, because they cannot argue with me. They have nothing to say. They have not answered me. I have been criticizing them for twenty years; they have not answered. They *cannot* answer. What I am saying, deep down, they also feel is right.

Politicians come to me personally and they say, "Bhagwan, whatsoever you say is absolutely right, but we cannot confess to it publicly. It is what is happening there in New Delhi."

Privately they always say, "You are right," but publicly they cannot say it, because if I am right, if they say it publicly, the crowd, the mob will go against them. They have to depend on the crowd, they have to continuously depend on it for votes. They have to go on supporting all kinds of stupid ideas and superstitions of the mob. Their dependence is tremendous.

For twenty years I have criticized Mahatma Gandhi and his philosophy. No Gandhian has answered. Many Gandhians have come to me and they say, "Whatsoever you say is right, but we cannot say it in public, because if we say that whatsoever you say about Mahatma Gandhi is right, we will lose." The public believes in Mahatma Gandhi, so utter nonsense has to be supported because Gandhi was anti-technological. Now this country will remain poor if this country remains anti-technological; this country will never be in a state of well-being. And there is no need for technology always to be anti-ecology; there is no need. A technology can be developed which can be in tune with ecology. A technology can be developed which can help people and will not destroy nature —but Gandhi was against technology.

He was against the railway, he was against the post office, he was against electricity, he was against machines of all kinds. They know this is stupid, because if this continues... But they go on saying so, and they go on paying homage to Mahatma Gandhi because they have to get the votes from the people. And the people worship the Mahatma because the Mahatma fits with their ideas of how a mahatma should be.

Mahatma Gandhi fits with the Indian mob; the Indian mob worships him. The politician has to follow the mob. Remember always: in politics the leader follows the followers. He has to! He only pretends that he is leading; deep down he has to follow the followers. Once the followers leave him, he is nowhere. He cannot stand on his own, he has no ground of his own.

Gandhi worshipped poverty. Now if you worship poverty you will remain poor. Poverty has to be hated.

I hate poverty! I cannot say to worship it; that would be a crime. And I don't see any religious quality in just being poor. But Gandhi talked much about poverty and its beauty—it helps the poor man's ego, it buttresses his ego; he feels good. It is a consolation that he is religious, simple—he is poor. He may not have riches but he has some spiritual richness. Poverty in itself is not a spiritual richness; no, not at all. Poverty is ugly and poverty has to be destroyed. And to destroy poverty, technology has to be brought in.

Mahatma Gandhi was against birth control. Now if you are against birth control this country will become poorer and poorer every day. Then there is no possibility.

One day Mulla Nasrudin was saying to me, "Bhagwan, it seems that soon everybody will be reduced to beggars. All will be begging!"
I asked him, "Nasrudin, from whom?"

The country is going to such poverty that even to exist as beggars will not be possible, because from whom will you beg? And when there is poverty there is crime. Poverty is the source of all crime—not the source of religiousness, not the source of spirituality. Richness is the source of spirituality and religiousness, because religion is the ultimate luxury. It is the highest art, the greatest music, the profoundest dance.

When you have everything else, only then do you start looking for God. When you are finished with everything else, when you have seen everything and you have found that you are not satisfied, you start searching for God. A poor man has no idea of God. His God is nothing but a support: he clings, leans upon the idea of God.

This happens every day: when a poor man comes to me he never comes with the problems which are religious. He says, "My wife is ill. Bhagwan, can you bless her? My son is not getting employment. Can you help?" Now these things have nothing to do with religion at all. But he never comes with the problem of meditation or love; those are not his problems at all. His problem is bread, shelter. Life is in such a state that he is trying to survive somehow.

When a man is drowning in the river, will he ask "What is

meditation?" or "What is love?" He wants to be helped to come out of his situation first. He is drowning, life is disappearing—who bothers about meditation? A hungry man cannot be interested in meditation. But Gandhi thinks that poverty has something spiritual in it. It is just ugly. It is the most unspiritual thing in the world, because it is the source of all crime and sin.

I have heard...

There were reports of people claiming to have seen the spirit of Diogenes stalking the streets of many capitals of the world again. The learned Greek was first spotted in Paris. Some people approached the lamp-bearing philosopher: "Diogenes, what are you doing in Paris?"

Diogenes laughed a hearty laugh, he was very very happy, and he said, "Messieurs, I am searching for truth."

There was joy, there was dance, there was hope in his eyes.

And then it was heard that he was seen walking in London. Some bobbies again found him with his lamp: "Diogenes, what are you doing in London?"

Now he was not so joyous. He tried to smile but it came only with an effort. He said, "Gentlemen, I am searching for truth."

Hope was disappearing from his eyes, sadness was settling.

And then he was seen in New York. Hope had completely disappeared, he was utterly sad, but he still repeated, almost mechanically, parrot-like, "I am searching for truth."

And then inevitably he was reported to have been seen in New Delhi. One Gandhian politician, clad in pure white khadi, approached him and asked, "Diogenes, what are you doing in New Delhi?"

And he was very angry, almost in a rage, and he said, "Netarji, I am searching for my lamp!"

In New Delhi you cannot save your lamp.

The country is falling into deeper and deeper misery every day. The misery is creating more misery—it always happens. If you have, you get more; if you don't have, even that which you have starts disappearing.

And the Indian politician is responsible for all this nonsense because he goes on preaching high ideals. The Indian politician only talks, promises—nothing is ever fulfilled. He cannot fulfill because his beliefs are stupid; or maybe he has to believe in those stupid superstitions. For example, they still talk about celibacy; not birth control but celibacy: people should be celibate so that the population can be reduced. Now this is nonsense. How many people can be celibate? And this is not a way to reduce the population. And they still think in terms of no-technology, no-machines. The whole country is becoming like a wound, a cancer.

I see all this. That's also why I don't want to leave this country. I want to create a small oasis, my commune, which will be absolutely technological and still ecological. It has to be a model so that we can say to the whole country that if this can happen with five thousand sannyasins in a small place, why can't it happen on a higher scale, a greater scale, to the whole country?

My commune can become an example. It will be simple and rich. It will be technological and not against ecology. It will be *absolutely* scientific and yet human. It will be a totally different kind of communism. It will be a commune not for something from the outside or from the top, but because people love each other, they have created a family, they want to live together.

We will be doing farming, collective farming, with all the technology possible. We will make the commune absolutely independent. There will be no need to go outside. And my effort is that we will not be bringing anything inside; we will produce everything. It can become a great oasis in this desert country. It can be of much help, it can create great inspiration.

So I am not going to leave it. The country will need me, and you too.

Master Lu-tsu said: *Now there are three confirmatory experiences which can be tested. The first is that, when one has entered the state of meditation, the gods are in the valley. Men are heard talking as though at a distance of several hundred paces, each one quite clear. But the sounds are all like an echo in a valley. One can always hear them, but never oneself. This is called: 'The presence of the gods in the valley.'*

At times the following can be experienced: as soon as one is quiet, the light of the eyes begins to blaze up, so that everything before one becomes quite bright as if one were in a cloud. If one opens one's eyes and seeks the body, it is not to be found any more. This is called: 'In the empty chamber it grows light'. Inside and outside, everything is equally light. That is a very favorable sign.

Or, when one sits in meditation, the fleshly body becomes quite shining like silk or jade. It seems difficult to remain sitting: one feels as if drawn upward. This is called: 'The spirit returns and touches heaven'. In time, one can experience it in such a way that one really floats upward.

And now, it is already possible to have all three of these experiences. But not everything can be expressed. Different things appear to each person according to his disposition. If one experiences these things, it is a sign of a good aptitude. With these things it is just as it is when one drinks water:

one can tell for oneself whether the water is warm or cold. In the same way a man must convince himself about these experiences, then only are they real.

Master Lu-tsu said: *When there is a gradual success in producing the circulation of the light, a man must not give up his ordinary occupation in doing it. The ancients said: When occupations come to us, we must accept them; when things come to us, we must understand them from the ground up. If the occupations are properly handled by correct thoughts, the light is not scattered by outside things, but circulates according to its own law. Even the still invisible circulation of the light gets started this way; how much more, then, is it the case with the true circulation of the light which has already manifested itself clearly.*

When in ordinary life one has the ability always to react to things by reflexes only, without any admixture of a thought of others or of oneself, that is a circulation of the light arising out of circumstances. This is the first secret.

If early in the morning, one can rid oneself of all entanglements and meditate from one to two double hours, and then can orientate oneself towards all activities and outside things in a purely objective, reflex way, and if this can be continued without any interruption, then after two or three months all the perfected ones come from heaven and approve such behavior.

Chapter Five

August 31st, 1978

THE SPIRIT RETURNS AND
TOUCHES HEAVEN

IT WAS A BEAUTIFUL MORNING. It must have been a morning like this. The breeze was cool and full of the sweet smell of the wet earth. The birds were singing and the sun was rising on the horizon. The dewdrops were shining on the grass leaves like pearls.

It is always beautiful; all that is needed is eyes to see it. The birds are there, singing every morning, but who is there to listen? And the trees are blooming, but who is there to appreciate? The aesthetic heart is absent, only the calculating mind is functioning. Hence you live in an ugly world.

I am relating to you an ancient story.

Gautam Buddha's sannyasins were meditating under the mango trees...

Morning is the best time to meditate. After the whole night's rest you are very close to the center of your being. It is easier to move into the center consciously early in the morning than at any other time—because for the whole night you have been there at the center, you have just left it. The world of a thousand and one things has not yet arisen. You are just on the way, moving towards things, moving into the outside world, but the inner center is very close, around the corner. Just a turning of the head, and you will be able to see that which is: truth, God, enlightenment. You will be able to see that into which you had gone when dreams had stopped and sleep was profound, but then you were unconscious.

Deep sleep rejuvenates because, although unconsciously, you enter into the core of your being—but you still enter. All the tiredness of the outside world is taken away, and all the wounds are healed, and all the dust disappears. You have taken a bath, you have dived deep into your own being.

That's why Patanjali says: Deep, dreamless sleep is almost like *samadhi*—but almost, not exactly *samadhi*. What is the difference? It is very small—or very great—but this much difference is there: in sleep you are unconscious, in *samadhi* you are conscious; but the space is the same.

So in the morning when you have just awakened and you are very close to the center... Soon the periphery will take you, will possess you; you will have to go into the world of occupations. Before you go into that external journey, have a look, so that consciously you can see who you are. This is what meditation is all about. Hence, down the ages, the morning, early morning, when the earth is awakening and the trees are awakening and the birds are awakening and the sun is awakening, when the whole atmosphere is full of awakening, you can use this situation. You can ride on this tide of awakening and you can enter into your own being, awake, alert, aware. And your whole life will be transformed. And your whole day will be transformed because then you will have a different orientation.

Then you can go into the marketplace and still you will remain in contact with your inner core. And that is the greatest secret, the Secret of the Golden Flower.

... Buddha's sannyasins were meditating under the mango trees that morning...

As you have gathered around me, thousands had gathered around Buddha. There was nothing else to learn other than to meditate.

Buddhas don't teach, they only share. They don't give you a doctrine, they certainly give you a discipline. They don't give you beliefs, they certainly give you a taste of trust. And just a drop of the taste of trust and life is transmuted. And to connect with an awakened being, the only way is to become a little bit awakened on your own part too, because the like can meet the like. To be with a Buddha is to be a little bit more alert than life generally requires you to be. Life wants you to be automatic, robot-like. When you go to a Master, he requires that you drop your automatism, that you de-automatize yourself, that you become a little more alert, that you don't go on looking at things but also remember your being.

... Buddha's disciples were meditating—such a beautiful morning is not to be missed...

And when birds are praising the morning sun, you have also to praise God. And when trees are swaying in the wind, you have also to participate in this eternal dance, you have also to celebrate. Another day is born—forget the past, die to the past, be born anew.

... Buddha had a disciple named Subhuti. Buddha was a very fortunate Master: he had *tremendously* potential disciples. A few of them were really rare beings. Subhuti is one of those rare beings who was just on the verge of Buddhahood. Just one step more and he would be a Buddha. He was coming home, every moment coming home, closer and closer to the center where ego disappears and God is born, where you die and the whole is born, when the part disappears into the whole, when the cosmos takes place and then you are no more a separate entity, trembling, afraid of death. Then you are part of this eternal play of existence. He was just on the verge. He was one of the *most* silent of Buddha's disciples. He was so silent that the scriptures say that he had almost become absent. He would come and nobody would take note of him. He would pass and nobody would become aware that he had passed. He was a very silent breeze...

Ordinarily you want to be noticed. If you are not noticed, you feel hurt. You want attention. *Who* wants attention? Attention is the requirement of the ego, the ego feeds on it. So if attention is not given to you—if you come and nobody notices you, you pass and nobody says, "Good morning. How are you?" as if you had not passed—you will feel wounded. You will start thinking, "So, I am thought to be a nobody, and I will show these people who I am."

The ego always hankers for attention.

... Subhuti was so silent: his desire for attention had disappeared. And the moment desire for attention disappears, all politics disappears from your being. Then you are religious. Then you are perfectly at home with your nobodiness. Then you live a totally different life. Then you live so silently that you don't make any fuss, that you don't make any ripples, that you come and you go as if you had never come and you had never gone. He was, and yet he was not...

In fact, the moment you *really* are, you drop all ideas of your ego. People carry the idea of the ego because they are not. Try to understand this paradox. Those who are not, they brag about themselves. They *have* to brag, they have to prove to the world, they are constantly performing. They know if they don't perform they are nobodies. They have to perform, they have to shout, they have to make noise, they have to force others to take note of them. Adolf Hitlers and Genghis Khans and Tamburlaines and all the stupid lot of politicians down the ages—all that they have been doing is to make more and more people take note of them. These are the people who are not.

The people who are are so contented with their being; who cares whether anybody takes note or not? They are so much to themselves, enough unto themselves.

So this is the paradox: the man who is not tries, pretends that he is much, somebody special, and the man who is pretends not, brags not, becomes a very silent existence.

... He existed as an absence...

And only in absence does real presence arise; the person disappears but presence arises.

... He had melted slowly and disappeared as a person...

And when that happens, when that miracle happens, the very absence becomes a radiant presence.

... Subhuti was also sitting under a tree, not even meditating. Others were meditating, he was simply sitting there doing nothing. That is the *highest* form of meditation...

To *do* meditation is to be just a beginner. The beginner has to *do* the meditation. But one who has understood meditation cannot even think in terms of doing, because the moment you do something you are stirred. The moment you do something you are tense. The moment you do something the ego enters again from the back door—because with the doing comes the doer. Meditation is a state of non-doing. Certainly in the beginning one has to do, but slowly slowly as meditation deepens, understanding arises, doing disappears. Then meditation is being, not doing.

Doing is part of the world of having. Doing is another aspect of having. You have to do if you want to have; if you want to have you will have to do. And millions of people remain in the world of doing and having.

Beyond these two there is another world: the world of being —where you don't have anything and you are not a doer either. All is utterly silent, all is absolutely passive, not even a ripple.

... So he was not doing meditation, remember. He was just sitting and doing nothing. And then suddenly, flowers began to fall around him. And those were not ordinary flowers, not of this world, not earthly. They were not falling from the trees, they were falling from the sky, from nowhere, out of the blue. He had never seen such beauty and such freshness and such fragrance. Those were the flowers of the beyond, Golden Flowers. He was naturally in awe and wonder. And then he heard the gods whispering to him, "We are praising you for your discourse on emptiness...."

Now he was really puzzled. "Discourse on emptiness? But I have not spoken of emptiness," said Subhuti.
"You have not spoken of emptiness, we have not heard emptiness," responded the gods. "This is true emptiness."
And blossoms showered upon Subhuti like rain.

This is one of the most beautiful stories I have ever come across. A great meaning is hidden there: if you are silent, if you are utterly silent, existence starts showering on you. Blessings shower on you like rain. If you are silent, if you are in the state of meditation, just being and doing nothing, the whole existence converges upon you with all its grace, with all its beauty and benediction.

This is the state Jesus calls the state of beatitude. For the first time you become aware of the splendor of existence. Each moment is an eternity then, and even to breathe is such a joy, such a celebration. Misery disappears the moment you disappear; misery is the shadow of the ego. And blessing is a natural phenomenon: it happens on its own the moment you are empty. The whole existence rushes in, explodes.

Ludwig Wittgenstein has said, "The mystical is not the 'how' of the world, but that it exists."

Just that it exists is the mystery. There is no need to go anywhere else: the mystery is not hidden, the mystery is all over the place. Just that it exists is the mystery of it! You need not dig deep to find the mystery. Mystery is everywhere, on the surface as much as in the depth. All that is needed is a heart that feels. All that is needed is a being that is available, open. All that is needed is alertness, alertness without any effort and tension. All that is needed is a state of meditation, and then favors from existence start showering like rain.

The sutras:

> Master Lu-tsu said: *Now there are three confirmatory*
> *experiences which can be tested. The first is that, when one*
> *has entered the state of meditation, the gods are in the valley.*
> *Men are heard talking as though at a distance of several*
> *hundred paces, each one quite clear. But the sounds are all*
> *like an echo in a valley: one can always hear them, but*
> *never oneself. This is called: 'The presence of the gods in the*
> *valley.'*

Lu-tsu is talking about three confirmatory signs. The first he
calls 'the gods are in the valley'. Those who are moving—
and you all are moving towards meditation—are going to
come across these strange but tremendously beautiful spaces.
The first sign that meditation has started becoming a crystallized phenomenon in you is 'the presence of the gods in the
valley'.

What does this metaphor mean? It means the moment meditation starts happening in you, the whole existence becomes
a valley and you are at the top of a hill. You start rising upwards. The whole world becomes a valley, far away, deep
down there, and you are sitting on a sunlit hilltop. Meditation
takes you upwards—not physically, but spiritually. And the
phenomenon is very clear when it happens; these will be the
signs.

When you are moving inwards in the meditation, suddenly
you will see a great distance arising between you and the
noises around you. You may be sitting in a marketplace and
suddenly you will see a gap is arising between you and the
noises. Just a moment before those noises were almost identified with you, you were in them; now you are getting away

from them. You are there physically, as you had been before; there is no need to go to the mountains—this is the way to find the real mountains of the within, this is the way to find the Himalayas within. You start moving into deep silence, and suddenly all the noises that were so close to you—and such a turmoil was there—start going far away, receding backwards. Everything is as it was before on the outside, nothing has been changed; you are sitting in the same place where you had started meditating. But as meditation deepens this will be felt: you will feel distance arising from outside things.

Men are heard talking as though at a distance of several hundred paces...

... As if suddenly the world has gone away from you or you have gone away from the world. But each thought is quite clear. Whatsoever is being said outside is quite clear, in fact, more clear than it was before.

This is the magic of meditation. You are not becoming unconscious, because in unconsciousness also you will see that noises are disappearing. For example, if you have been given chloroform you will feel this same phenomenon happening: noises start going away, away, away...and they are gone—but you have fallen unconscious. You cannot hear anything clearly.

Just the same happens in meditation, but with a difference—the noises start going away from you, but every noise becomes distinctly clear, more clear than it was before, because now a witnessing is arising.

First you were also a noise in all the noises; you were lost in it. Now you are a witness, an observer, and because you are so silent you can see everything distinctly, clearly. Although noises are far away, they are more clear than ever before. Each single note is heard.

If in meditation you are listening to music this will happen: first you will see the music is going far away; and the second thing, simultaneously will also be felt: each note is becoming so clear and so distinct as it had never been before. Before, those notes were mixed with each other, overlapping into each other. Now they are all clearcut individuals, atomic. Each single note is separate.

> *Men are heard talking as though at a distance of several*
> *hundred paces, each one quite clear, but the sounds are all like*
> *an echo in a valley.*

And the third thing will be felt: that they are not heard directly but as if indirectly, as if they are echoes of the real sounds, not the sounds themselves. They become more insubstantial, their substance is lost. They become less material, their matter disappears; they are no more heavy, they are light. You can see their weightlessness—they are like echoes. The whole existence becomes an echo.

That is why Hindu mystics call the world *maya*, illusion. Illusion does not mean unreal; it simply means shadow-like, echo-like. It does not mean non-existential, it simply means dream-like. Shadow-like, dream-like, echo-like—that will be the feeling. You cannot feel that these things are real. The whole existence becomes a dream, very clear, distinct, because you are alert; and very dream-like because you are alert. First you were lost in the dream: you were not alert, and you were thinking that this is reality. You were identified with your mind. Now you are no more identified with the mind, a separate entity has arisen in you: the watchfulness, *sakshi*.

One can always hear them, but never oneself.

And the fourth thing in it will be felt: you can hear the whole existence around you—people talking, walking, children laughing, somebody crying, a bird call, a car passes by, an aeroplane, the train. You will be able to hear everything. Just one thing: you will not be able to hear yourself, you have completely disappeared. You are an emptiness, you are becoming a Subhuti. You are just not there at all. You cannot feel yourself as an entity. All the noises are there, just your inner noises have disappeared. Ordinarily there are more noises inside you than on the outside. The real turmoil is within you, the real madness is there. And when the outer madness and inner madness both meet together, hell is created.

The outer madness is going to continue, because you have not produced it and you cannot destroy it, but you can destroy your inner madness very easily. It is within your capacity. Once the inner is not there the outer madness becomes insubstantial. It loses all reality, it becomes illusory. You cannot find your old voice; there is no thought arising in you, so no sound. This is called 'the gods are in the valley'.

You have become empty, and everything has gone deep down in the valley; only echoes are heard. And when echoes are heard, certainly you are not affected.

Just the other day a madman tried to rape Anuradha. He was caught before he could do any harm. I asked Anuradha to come to me just to see whether she's affected by it or not.

And I was tremendously happy that she is not affected at all, not at all, not even a trace. That's the beauty of growing meditation: even if you are murdered you will remain unaffected.

Now, the effort to rape her was murderous. And let Morarji Desai know that this is the true image of his India; an Indian tried it. And this is not a single case, it has been happening almost regularly. It has become so dangerous for my sannyasins to move outside. This ugly India is not my India. This ugly India belongs to Morarji Desai and Charan Singh and Advani and company. I simply disown this ugly India.

But there is another India: the India of the Buddhas, the eternal India. I am part of it, you are part of it. In fact, anywhere, wherever meditation is happening, that person becomes part of that eternal India. That eternal India is not geographical, it is a spiritual space. And to become part of that eternal India is to become a sannyasin.

And I was happy, tremendously happy, seeing Anuradha: she had remained absolutely unaffected, not a ripple of fear, nothing—as if nothing had happened, as if the attempt was made in a dream.

This is how one grows slowly slowly into meditation. All becomes insubstantial. One can see everything.

She fought back. She was courageous and brave, she did whatsoever was needed to be done, she didn't yield—but the inner consciousness remained unaffected.

This is called the presence of the gods in the valley. At times the following can be experienced: as soon as one is quiet

> *the light of the eyes begins to blaze up, so that everything*
> *before one becomes quite bright as if one were in a cloud. If*
> *one opens one's eyes and seeks the body, it is not to be found*
> *any more. This is called: 'In the empty chamber it grows*
> *light'. Inside and outside, everything is equally light. That*
> *is a very favorable sign.*

Now, the second sign is called: 'In the empty chamber it grows light'.

Unless you become empty, you will remain dark, you will remain darkness. 'In the empty chamber it grows light': when you are utterly empty, when there is nobody inside you, then light happens. The presence of the ego creates darkness. Darkness and ego are synonymous. No-ego and light are synonymous.

So *all* methods of meditations, whatsoever their orientation, finally verge in this empty chamber of your inner being. Just a silent space is left, and in that space you find great light arising, without any source. It is not like the light that you see when the sun rises, because the light that comes from the sun cannot be eternal; in the night it will disappear again. It is not like the light that needs fuel, because when the fuel is finished the light will disappear.

This light has a very mysterious quality: it has no source, no cause. It is not caused, hence once it appears it remains, it never disappears. In fact, it is already there; you are just not empty enough to see it.

And when this light starts growing in you these will be the experiences, 'as soon as one is quiet'. The moment you sit silently and you become quiet, still, unmoving within and without, 'the light of the eyes begins to blaze up'.

Suddenly you will see your light is pouring through your eyes. This is an experience that science has not yet become aware of. Science thinks that light gets into the eyes, but never otherwise. Light comes from the outside, gets into the eyes, enters you: this is only half the story. The other half is known only by the mystics and the meditators. This is only one part: the light entering you. There is another part: the light pouring out of your eyes. And when the light starts pouring out of your eyes, 'the light of the eyes begins to blaze up, so that everything before one becomes quite bright'.

Then this whole existence brightens up. Then you see that trees are more green than ever, and their greenness has a quality of luminosity in it. Then you see the roses are rosier than ever. The same roses, the same trees, but something from you is pouring into them, revealing them more clearly than ever. Then small things have such beauty: just colored stones are more beautiful to a Buddha than the Kohinoor diamond to Queen Elizabeth. To Queen Elizabeth, even the Kohinoor— the greatest diamond in the world—is not so beautiful as an ordinary stone is to a Buddha. Why?—because Buddha's eyes can pour light, and in that light ordinary stones become Kohinoors. Ordinary people become Buddhas. To a Buddha, everything is full of Buddhahood. Hence he has said, "The day I became enlightened, the whole existence became enlightened. The trees and the mountains and the rivers and the rocks—all became enlightened." The whole existence was raised to a higher plenitude.

It depends on you how much you can put into existence; only that much will you get. If you don't put anything into it you won't get anything out of it. First you have to put into it to get out of it. That's why creative people know more beauty, more love, more joy than uncreative people—because creative

people put something into existence. Existence responds...
and responds generously.

Your eyes are empty: they don't give anything, they only
take. They are hoarders, they don't share. So whenever you
will come across eyes which can share, you will see a tremendously different quality, a tremendous beauty, silence,
power, potential. If you can see those eyes which can pour
their light into you, your whole heart will be stirred.

But even to see that light you will have to be a little more alert
than you are. The sun may be rising and it may be morning,
but you may be fast asleep. But then no sun is rising for you,
and there is no morning; you may be lost in a dark night, in
a nightmare. You have to be a little more wakeful, but this
happens.

In the modern consciousness an experience of this kind has
come through psychedelics, a little bit. It is forced, it is violent.
It is not natural, you are raping your chemistry. But the
experience has happened, and many people have come to
meditation through drugs because the drug has made them
aware of something they were never aware of.

When you have taken some drug, the world looks more
beautiful. Ordinary things look extraordinary. What is happening? The drug is forcing some inner light from your eyes to
fall onto things—but it is a forced phenomenon, and dangerous.
And after each drug-trip you will fall into a deeper darkness
than before. And in the person who has been taking drugs long,
you will find his eyes *utterly* empty because he has been pouring
light out of his eyes and he does not know how to create it.
He does not know how to make his inner light circulate so that
more light is created; he simply pours. So a man who takes

drugs, by and by, loses the vitality of his eyes, the youth of his eyes. His eyes become dull, dark, black holes.

Just the opposite happens through meditation: the more quiet you become, the more light is created—and it is not a forced phenomenon. You have so much that it starts overflowing from your eyes. It simply starts overflowing. Because you have too much it has to be shared, like when the cloud is full of rain it has to rain. You are full of light and more light is coming in, streaming in every moment, and there is no end to it—now you can share. You can share with the trees and with the rocks and with people. You can give to the existence. This is a very favorable sign.

But don't be deceived by drugs. Drugs give you only false experiences, forced experiences, and any forced experience is destructive to your inner ecology, your inner harmony and finally you will be a loser, not a gainer.

At times the following can be experienced: as soon as one is quiet, the light of the eyes begins to blaze up.

You will see it! Your eyes are becoming aflame. And with the eyes becoming aflame the whole existence is taking a new color, a new depth, a new dimension, as if things are no more three-dimensional but four-dimensional. A new dimension is added: the dimension of luminosity.

. . .the light of the eyes begins to blaze up, so that everything before one becomes quite bright, as if one were in a cloud. . .

. . .as if the sun is shining on the cloud and the whole cloud is afire, and you are in the cloud and the cloud is just fire reflecting the sun. One starts living in this cloud of light. One sleeps in it, one walks in it, one sits in it; this cloud continues. This cloud has been seen as the aura. Those who have eyes to see will see around the head of the saints, around their bodies, a light. A subtle aura surrounds them.

Now even science is agreeing with it, particularly in Russia. Kirlian photography has come to very significant conclusions. One of them is: that everything is surrounded by a subtle aura—we just need eyes to see—and in different states the aura changes. Now these are scientific conclusions. When you are ill you have a different aura—dull, sad, lusterless. If you are going to die within six months your aura disappears. Then your body has no light around it. And if you are happy, joyous, fulfilled, contented, then the aura grows more and more big, becomes more and more bright.

Of course Kirlian experiments have not been done on any Buddha yet. And it is very difficult to find a Buddha in Soviet Russia, particularly now. It is unfortunate, because the whole country has fallen into a trap of utter nonsense. The whole country has fallen into the trap of materialism. Never before has any country been ruled by materialists. Materialism has always persisted, but never has a country been ruled by materialists. Never has a country been conditioned to be materialistic like Soviet Russia. Children are taught there is no God, no soul, that man is just a body. There is no question of prayer, no question of meditation, no question of becoming silent.

If Kirlian photographers come across a man like Jesus or Buddha or Subhuti, then they will know the miracle. Then they will come across the purest light, the coolest light—which is light, which is life, which is love.

If one opens one's eyes and seeks the body...

In this moment, when you are full of light inside and your eyes are afire and the whole existence is aflame with new life, if you open your eyes and try to find your body, you will not find it. In these moments matter disappears. In fact, modern physics says that there is no matter at all; it is an illusion. There is nothing solid in your body. Deep down, modern physics says, your body is constituted of electrons. Electrons mean light-atoms, atoms of light. So when this inner fire burns bright, is *really* there, and you open your eyes, you will not find your physical body. Not that it is not there; it is there, but you will not see it as you had seen it before. It will be just a cloud of light. You will see the aura; the gestalt has changed. Now you will see something which you had never seen before, and all that you had seen before has disappeared; it depends on your vision. Because you don't have a vision to see the spirit, you can only see the body, the physical. To see matter, nothing is needed—no intelligence, no meditativeness, no prayer. To see matter is very gross. To see spirit is very subtle.

Once you are capable of seeing the spirit, you will be able to see that matter has disappeared. You cannot see both together. Again let me repeat: that's why Hindu mystics have called the world illusory, because they have come to a point when they have seen that matter does not exist. And all that exists is God, all that exists is consciousness.

Matter is just a mistake. You have not seen rightly; that's how matter arises. It *is* consciousness. For example, when I see you I see you as consciousness, not as matter. When I touch you I don't touch your body, I touch you in your innermost core, I touch your energy. When I look into your eyes I'm not looking into your physical eyes, I'm trying to contact your spiritual eye. It is there. To you, it is not there yet. For me, it is already there. And if you listen to me, and if you try to understand what is being shared with you, soon it will become a reality for you too.

Either God is or the world is; both are never found together. Those who see the world never see God, and those who have seen God, for them the world has disappeared. The 'world' was just a misunderstanding. It is just like you can commit a mistake while counting or doing arithmetic: two plus two, and you can put five; then the whole thing will go wrong. When you go back and you find the mistake and you correct it and two plus two becomes four again, the whole thing changes. Exactly like this, matter is a mistake of vision.

It is just like Hindu mystics say: it is a rope seen in darkness, and you have thought it is a snake. And because you thought it is a snake you start running. And your heart is pounding, and you are out of breath, and you are trembling, and it is a cool night but you are perspiring. You may even have a heart attack, and for no reason at all! And in the morning, when it is found to have been just a rope, it will look very ridiculous.

Once I was staying in a house with a friend. There were so many mice in the house, and rats. It happened that night that a rat must have entered into the bed of my friend when we were asleep. The rat was just going to bite, just going to bite his foot, and he was awakened. He jumped out of the bed, screamed; the rat must have escaped. Nothing was harmed— he was just going to bite—but he became very much afraid. He was afraid that maybe it was a snake. And I said, "You are a fool! There is no snake, nothing"—and we looked around

—"and we know that there are so many rats in your house. It must have been a rat." So he was satisfied; we went to sleep. Everything was perfectly good.

We went to the river, we swam in the river, we came back. After lunch a snake was found in the house, and immediately my friend became unconscious—the very idea! And I tried hard, but now he was already unconscious, so what to do?

For one and a half hours he remained unconscious, in a kind of coma. Doctors were called, they checked. They said, "There is no poison, nothing. Even the rat has not done any harm, and there is no question of any snake." But still injections were given to bring him back. Just the idea...but the idea can create a reality.

When you see a rope and you start running, your running is a reality, and your heart pounding is a reality. And you may have a heart attack, you may even die—this is a reality! But the snake was not there; that was just an idea.

The mystics say the world is just an idea. You are unnecessarily afraid, unnecessarily running away, unnecessarily worried—it is just an idea, a mistake. There is no world, there is only God.

The whole consists only of consciousness.

> *If one opens one's eyes and seeks the body, it is not to be found any more. This is called: 'In the empty chamber it grows light'. Inside and outside, everything is equally light. That is a very favorable sign.*

These have to be understood because these are going to happen to you too, and the understanding will help. Otherwise one day you open your eyes and you don't find your body there, you may go crazy. You will certainly feel something has gone wrong: either you are dead or mad. And what has happened to the body? But if you understand these sutras, they will remind you in the right moment. That's why I am talking on so many scriptures: to make you aware of all that is possible, so when it happens you are not taken aback. You know, you can understand, you have maps already. You can figure out where you are and you can rest in that understanding.

> *Or when one sits in meditation, the fleshly body becomes quite shining like silk or jade. It seems difficult to remain sitting; one feels as if drawn upward. This is called: 'The spirit returns and touches heaven'. In time, one can experience it in such a way that one really floats upward.*

The third sign: 'The spirit returns and touches heaven'.

This happens very soon; it starts happening in the very early stages. Sitting silently, suddenly you feel you are a little higher than the ground, maybe six inches higher. With great surprise you open your eyes and you find you are sitting on the ground, so you must have been dreaming, you think.

No, you have not been dreaming, your physical body remained on the earth. But you have another body, the body of light hidden inside it—call it the astral body, the subtle body, the vital body, any name you want—that body starts rising higher. And from the inside you can feel only that body, because that is your inside. When you open your eyes your material body is sitting on the ground perfectly, in the same way as it was sitting before. Don't think that you have been hallucinating, not at all. It is a real fact: you had floated a little—but in your second body not in your first body.

The fleshly body becomes quite shining like silk or jade.

And simultaneously, whenever you will feel that you have risen above the ground—as if gravitation affects you no more, as if a different law has started working on you.... I call that law 'the law of grace'. One law is the law of gravitation: it pulls you down. I call the other law the law of grace; it pulls you up. And certainly, sooner or later, science has to discover it, because every law has to be complemented by its opposite. No law can exist in aloneness. Gravitation must have its complementary, just as day has night and summer has winter and man has woman and love has hate and life has death and the negative has the positive. So, exactly in the same way, there *must* be a law which has to compensate, complement from the other extreme. That law I call the law of grace; it pulls you upwards.

This experience of your fleshly body becoming quite shining like silk or jade, happens simultaneously whenever you start feeling that it is *difficult to remain sitting; one feels as if drawn upward. This is called: 'The spirit returns and touches heaven'.*

Now the upward journey is starting. And remember, the upward and inward are synonymous; outward and downward are synonymous. The more in you go, the more up you go. The deeper you reach upwards, the deeper you reach inwards. They are the same, one dimension, two aspects of the same dimension.

In time, one can experience it in such a way that one really floats upward.

And that too happens: when this inner body starts rising so high and has tremendous power, then even the physical body can start floating with it. It is possible, but there is no need to make it happen. That is foolish. If it happens one day of its own accord, enjoy it and don't take much note of it. These confirmatory signs have to be understood, not bragged about. Don't talk to anybody about them, otherwise the ego will come back and will start exploiting these experiences. And once the ego comes, experiences will disappear. Never talk about them. If they happen just understand them, take note of them, and forget all about them.

And now, it is already possible to have all three of these experiences. But not everything can be expressed.

These three experiences *are* possible, and even if you have experienced them, you will not be able to express them. And whatsoever is said here is only just symbolic, because the real experience cannot be said. All that is said becomes a lie. Say it, and you have falsified the truth. Truth cannot be said, but still we have to say something. Hence these metaphors have been developed: 'gods in the valley', 'in the empty chamber it grows light', 'the spirit returns upwards', or 'the spirit returns and touches heaven'. These are just symbols, metaphors to indicate something, but the experience is vast!

Different things appear to each person according to his disposition.

And this too has to be remembered: they all may not happen to you, or may happen in a different order, or may happen in different ways. And there are a thousand and one things too which are possible because people are so different. To somebody these experiences may not happen the way they have been described. For example, to somebody it may not happen that he is rising upward; it may happen that he is becoming bigger, becoming bigger and bigger; the whole room is full of him. And then he goes on becoming bigger and bigger; now the house is inside him. And it is very puzzling. One wants to open one's eyes and see what is happening—"Am I going mad?" And a moment is possible when one sees that "The whole existence is inside me. I am not outside it. It is not outside me, it is inside me. And the stars are moving within me."

Or to somebody it may happen that he becomes smaller and smaller, becomes a molecule, almost invisible, then an atom, and then disappears. That is possible. Patanjali has catalogued all the experiences that are possible. People have different dispositions, different talents, different potentials, so to everybody they are going to happen in a different way. These are just to indicate that things like this happen—don't think that you are going mad or something is going bizarre.

With these things it is just as it is when one drinks water. One can tell for oneself whether the water is warm or cold.

It is an experience. When you drink water, only you know whether it is cold or warm. And if you are thirsty, only you know whether it is quenching your thirst or creating more. Nobody else sitting outside watching you can know what is happening inside—if the thirst is quenched or made more, if the water is cool or warm—nobody can see from the outside. Even if they can see you drinking water, they cannot experience your experience. People can see you meditating, but they cannot see what is happening inside.

Many people come here and they ask me for permission to watch people meditating. And I say, "How will you watch?" Nobody has ever been able to watch. You can see people sitting or dancing or singing, but that is not the real thing. Meditation is happening inside them. Nobody can see except them. So if you really want to see, you will have to participate. You will have to become a meditator; that is the only way. You cannot borrow, nobody can inform you. So those who come here as spectators just waste their time. These are things which can be known only through participation.

In the same way a man must convince himself about these experiences, then only are they real.

And don't start believing because Lu-tsu is saying so. Just try to understand him, keep it stored in your memory. There is no need to believe in these things, no need to disbelieve either. Just let them be in your memory so whenever the time is ripe and something starts happening you will be able to understand. These are just giving you maps so you are not lost—because even in the inward journey there are many points from where one can be lost. One can misunderstand, one can become afraid, frightened. One can escape from the inside into the outside world.

And these experiences are *not* frightening, but your interpretation can make them frightening. Just think: one day you open your eyes and you don't see your body. Your interpretation can be frightening: "This is certainly a sign of madness." You will stop meditating, you will become afraid of meditation, because who knows now what will happen next time, and where you are moving, where you are going. You will become suspicious of the whole experience. You will think you are becoming neurotic.

Every day people come to me with their experiences. When they relate their experiences, I can see their fear, their faces, their eyes—they are afraid. When I say that these are good signs, immediately the climate changes. They start laughing, they are happy. If they can hear me saying that "This is beautiful", that "I am happy with you" that "You are growing well", *immediately* there is a great change. From sadness they jump to great joy. Nothing has changed, their experience is the same; I have just given them a different interpretation. They were frightened because they knew not.

These things have not to be believed or disbelieved, but just kept stored in the memory so if the time arises you will be able to interpret rightly—and right interpretations are of *great* significance. Otherwise the inner journey becomes very difficult. There are many points from where one wants to return and go back into the world and be normal.

One starts feeling something abnormal is happening, and 'abnormal' is a condemnatory word. And if you talk to other people who have never meditated they will say, "You go to the psychoanalyst or the psychiatrist. Better that you be checked. What nonsense are you talking?—that you become bigger! Have you lost all reason? You say that you go upward and gravitation disappears? Or you become smaller and smaller and you disappear? You are hallucinating, you have become a victim of illusions. You go to the psychiatrist—he will put you right, he will fix you."

And if you go to the psychoanalyst or the psychiatrist, they *are* going to fix you: they will hammer on your head with their so-called knowledge. They don't know a thing about meditation, meditation has not entered in their consciousness yet. They don't know anything about the experiences that happen on the Way, but they know much about mad people. And there is one thing to be taken note of: that there are many experiences which are similar, which happen to a meditator and also happen to a madman; which are so similar that the psychiatrist is *bound* to think that you are going nuts, that something has to be fixed in you. And he will treat you as a madman—he will give you drugs or injections or electro-shocks to bring you back to your normal mind. He may destroy your whole possibility for meditation.

This is now a great danger in the West: people learning meditation go back to the West, and if something happens which is not within their comprehension, and they talk to the priest—and the Christian priest knows nothing about medi-tation—he will send them to the psychiatrist. If they talk to the psychiatrist, he knows only about madmen, he knows nothing about Buddhas. And a few of their experiences are similar; he is bound to interpret that you have fallen below normality, you have to be pulled back. And whatsoever he will do will be destructive, will be harmful to your body, to your mind. The harm can be so much that never again will you be able to go into meditation—he can create *such* barriers.

So if something happens sometimes, always go to people who meditate. That's why I am insisting so much to open centers all over the world so sannyasins can meditate, and if something happens they can meet sannyasins, they can go and share their experiences. At least there will be somebody sym-pathetic. At least there will be somebody who will not condemn you, who will respect your experience, who will accept your experience, who will give you hope and inspiration, who will say, "Good, you go ahead. Much more is going to happen." A Master is needed only because of this—somebody whom you can trust and who's simply saying "It is good, and you can go ahead", and you *can* go ahead. The journey is hazardous.

Master Lu-tsu said: *When there is a gradual success in producing the circulation of the light, a man must not give up his ordinary occupation in doing it.*

That's my insistence too: that a sannyasin should not renounce the world. Your meditation *should* grow in the world. It should be part of the day-to-day existence. You should not become an escapist. Why?

The ancients said, 'When occupations come to us, we must accept them; when things come to us, we must understand them from the ground up. If the occupations are properly handled by correct thoughts, the light is not scattered by outside things, but circulates according to its own law. Even the still invisible circulation of the light gets started this way; how much more, then, is it the case with the true circulation of the light which has already manifested itself clearly.

First, whatsoever situation you are in is a God-given situation; don't reject it. It is an opportunity, an occasion to grow. If you escape from the opportunity, you will not grow. The people who go to the Himalayan caves and start living there and become very much attached to the caves remain ungrown-up. They remain childish. They have not become seasoned. If you bring them to the world they will be shattered, they will not be able to bear it.

Just a few days ago one sannyasin came after three months of living in the Himalayas, and she said, "But now it is difficult to be here. I want to go back." Now this is not gaining in maturity. Now the Himalayas will become her obsession, and whatsoever she is thinking is her meditation, her silence, is not hers; it is just a by-product of the Himalayan silence. I told her, "You be here for three weeks, and then you tell me what happens to your silence and your meditation. If it disappears, then it has nothing to do with you. And then it is better not to go to the Himalayas. Grow in meditation here! If you can be meditative here in the marketplace, and then you go to the Himalayas, your meditation will be enhanced a thousandfold. It is good as a holiday, but don't cling there; always come back to the world."

Yes, it is good once in a while to move into the mountains, it is beautiful, but to become addicted, to start thinking of renouncing the world is utterly wrong—because it is in the storms of the world that integrity arises. It is in the challenges of the world that you crystallize.

Lu-tsu says, "Accept the situation you are in. It must be the right situation for you; that's why you are in it." Existence cares for you. It is given to you not without any reason. It is not accidental; *nothing* is accidental. Whatsoever is your need is given to you. If it were your need to be in the Himalayas, you would have been in the Himalayas. And when the need arises, you will find that either you go to the Himalayas or the Himalayas come to you. It happens...when the disciple is ready, the Master arrives. And when your inner silence is ready, God arrives. And whatsoever is needed on the path is always supplied. Existence cares, mothers.

So don't be worried. Rather, use the opportunity. This challenging world, this constant turmoil on the outside, has to be used. You have to be a witness to it. Watch it. Learn how not to be affected by it. Learn to remain unaffected, untouched by it, like a lotus leaf in water. And then you will be grateful, because it is only by being watchful of all the turmoil that one day suddenly, 'the gods are in the valley'. You see the marketplace disappearing far away, becoming an echo. This is *real* growth.

And if you can rightly be meditative in the ordinary occupations of life, there is nothing which cannot happen to you. The light will start circulating; you just be watchful.

Meditate in the morning and then keep close to your center. Go into the world but keep close to your center, go on remembering yourself. Remain conscious of what you are doing.

> *When in ordinary life one has the ability always to react to things by reflexes only, without any admixture of a thought of others or of oneself, that is a circulation of the light arising out of circumstances. This is the first secret.*

And when things arise, act, but don't get identified in the act. Remain a spectator. Do whatsoever is needful just like a reflex. Do whatsoever is needful, but don't become a doer, don't get involved in it. Do it, and be finished with it—like a reflex.

> *If early in the morning, one can rid oneself of all entanglements and meditate from one to two double hours, and then can orientate oneself towards all activities and outside things in a purely objective reflex way, and if this can be continued without any interruption, then after two or three months all the perfected ones come from heaven and approve such behavior.*

Behave in an objective way. Take note of the situation, and

whatsoever is needful, do it. But don't become attached to the doing, don't become worried about it, don't think of the result. Just do the needful and remain alert and aloof and distant and faraway in your center, rooted there. But every early morning, orient yourself towards the inner center so you can remember it your whole day.

Two times are the best. The first best time is the early morning: orient yourself to the center so you can live on the circumference but yet with full remembrance of the center. And the second time is before you go to bed: orient yourself again to the center, so in your deep sleep also—even while you are dreaming, while you are unconscious—you can remain more and more, closer and closer to the center. These two times are the best. And if you can meditate these two times, you need not go anywhere else. You need not go to any monastery, to any cave, you need not renounce the world, and one day suddenly you will see blossoms showering on you and gods whispering in your ear.

The whole existence celebrates the moment when one soul arrives home. What happened to Subhuti can happen to you. Aspire to it. It is your birthright, it can be claimed.

Chapter Six

September 1st, 1978

ALONENESS IS ULTIMATE

The first question:

Master,
After the tidal wave of events and with the memory of a pro-
found experience, I face new aloneness. Efforts to share or
escape into distractions have bad results. Why do I cling to
this habit of escaping aloneness? A few comments may help
me for the task ahead.

Amrito, aloneness is ultimate. There is no way to be anything
other than alone. One can forget it, one can drown oneself
in so many things, but again and again the truth asserts. Hence,
after each profound experience you will feel alone. After a
great love experience you will feel alone, after a deep meditation you will feel alone.

That's why all great experiences make people sad. In the wake of a profound experience, sadness always settles. It is because of this phenomenon that millions of people don't hanker after profound experiences; they avoid them. They don't want to go deep in love, sex is enough. Because sex is superficial, it will not leave them alone. It will be fun, an entertainment; for a moment they will enjoy it and then they will forget all about it. It will not bring them to their own center. But love brings you to your center: love is so profound that it leaves you alone.

This will look very paradoxical, because ordinarily people think love will make you aware of togetherness. That is utter nonsense. If love is deep it will make you aware of aloneness, not togetherness. Whenever anything goes deep, what happens?—you leave the periphery of your being and you fall into your center, and the center is all alone. There only, you are; or not even you, but only a consciousness with no ego in it, with no identity in it, with no definition in it, an abyss of consciousness.

After listening to great music, or after penetrating into the meaning of great poetry, or seeing the beauty of a sunset, it always happens that in the wake of it you will feel sad. Seeing this, millions have decided not to see beauty, not to love, not to meditate, not to pray, to avoid all that is profound. But even if you avoid truth, truth bumps upon you sometimes. Unawares, it possesses you.

You can distract yourself for the moment, but no distraction is going to help. Aloneness has to be accepted because it is ultimate. It is not an accident, it is the very way things are. It is Tao. Once you accept it, the quality changes. Aloneness is not creating sadness. Your idea that you should not be alone, that is creating sadness; your idea that to be alone is to be sad is creating the problem. Aloneness is utterly beautiful because it is profoundly free. It is absolute freedom; how can it create sadness?

But your interpretation is wrong, Amrito. You will have to drop your interpretation. In fact, when you say "I face new aloneness", you really mean you face new loneliness. And you have not seen the distinction between loneliness and aloneness.

Aloneness, misinterpreted, looks like loneliness. Loneliness means you are missing the other. And who is the other?— any excuse that helps you to drown your consciousness, any intoxicant: it may be a woman, a man, a book, anything— anything that helps you to forget yourself, that takes away your self-remembrance, that unburdens you from your awareness.

You mean loneliness, really. Loneliness is a negative state: the other is missed and you start searching and seeking for the other. Aloneness is immensely beautiful. Aloneness means a moment when the other is no longer needed, you are enough unto yourself—so enough that you can share your aloneness with the whole existence. So inexhaustible is your aloneness that you can pour it unto the whole existence and it will still remain there. You are rich when you are alone, you are poor when you feel lonely.

The lonely person is a beggar; his heart is a begging bowl. The alone person is an emperor...Buddha is alone.

And, Amrito, what has happened to you has been aloneness, but your interpretation is wrong. Your interpretation is coming from your past experiences, from your past mind. It is from your memory. Your mind is giving you a wrong idea. You drop the mind. You go into your aloneness: watch it, taste it. All the aspects of it have to be looked into. Enter into it from all the possible doors; it is the greatest temple there is. And it is in this aloneness that you will find yourself— and to find oneself is to find God.

God is alone, and once you have looked into it without the mind interfering you will not want to be distracted at all. Then there is nothing to distract, then there is no need to be distracted. Then you would not like to escape from it because it is life, it is eternal life. Why should one want to escape from it? And I'm not saying that in this aloneness you will not be able to relate. In fact, for the first time you will be able to relate.

A lonely person cannot relate because his need is so much. He clings, he leans upon the other. He tries to possess the other because he is constantly afraid: "If the other goes, then what? I will be left lonely again." Hence, so much possessiveness exists in the world. It has a reason. The reason is simple: you are afraid—if the other leaves, then you will be left alone, utterly lonely. And you don't like that, and you feel miserable even with the idea of it. Possess the other! Possess the other so totally that there is no possibility of the other escaping from you. And the other is also doing the same to you: the other is trying to possess you. Hence love becomes a miserable thing. Love becomes politics; love becomes domination, exploitation. It is because lonely people cannot love.

Lonely people have nothing to give, lonely people exploit each other. Naturally, when you have nothing to give and the other starts exploiting, you feel offended. You want to exploit the other and not be exploited; that's where politics enters in. You want to give as little as possible and get as much as possible—and the other is doing the same to you, and both are creating misery for each other.

I have heard...

A man stopped his car deep down in the woods and started being very loving to the woman who was sitting by his side. But the woman said, "Stop! You don't really know who I am. I am a prostitute, and my fee is fifty dollars."

The man gave the woman fifty dollars, made love to her. When it was finished he sat silently at the steering wheel without moving.

The woman asked, "Now why are we waiting here? It is getting late and I want to go back home."

And the man said, "Sorry, but I must tell you, I am a taxi-driver... and the fare back is fifty dollars."

This is what is happening in your love-relationship: somebody is a prostitute, somebody is a taxi-driver. It is a bargain, it is tit-for-tat. It is continuous conflict. That's why couples are continuously fighting. They cannot leave each other; although they go on fighting they cannot leave. In fact that's why they are fighting—so that nobody can leave. They cannot be at ease because if they are at ease then they will be at a loss and the other will exploit more. Once you see the point you will understand the whole misery of marriage: the whole foundation of it is there.

One wonders why people don't leave each other if they are not happy with each other. They cannot leave! They cannot live together, they cannot separate either. In fact, the very idea of separation is creating the conflict. They cripple each other so the other cannot escape, even if he or she wants to escape. They burden each other with such responsibilities, such moralities, that even if the other leaves he or she will feel guilty. His own conscience will hurt, will pinch him— that he has done something wrong. And together, all that they do is fight. Together, all they do is a continuous haggling for the price. Your marriage, your so-called love, is a marketplace. It is not love.

Out of loneliness there is no possibility of love. Out of loneliness people start meditating; out of loneliness there is no possibility of meditation either. They are feeling lonely and they want something to stuff themselves with. They need a *mantra*, Transcendental Meditation or all that kind of nonsense. They would like something to stuff themselves with because they are feeling empty and lonely. Repeating "Ram, Ram, Krishna, Krishna" or "Ave Maria" or anything will help them to at least forget themselves. This is not meditation! This is just covering up loneliness, emptiness. This is just covering up a black hole in yourself.

Or, they start praying in the churches and in the temples and they start talking to God. Now God is their imagination. They cannot find the other in the world because it is too costly to find the other in the world and it takes so much trouble; so now they create 'the other' high there in heaven—they start talking to God—but they cannot live without the other, the other has to be there. They may escape into the desert, but even in the desert cave they will be looking at the sky and talking to the other. This is fantasy and nothing else. And if you go on talking for long, you may start hallucinating that the other is there.

Your need is such that you can create the other through imagination. That's why the so-called religions have tried to take you away from the others that are ordinary and available. They would like you not to get married—why?—because if you are married and you have a woman, a man, you don't need a God. It is a strategy: they will not allow you to be in the marketplace because then you are occupied and you will not feel your loneliness. Then why should you talk to God? You can talk to people. They will take you to the Himalayan caves, to the monasteries, so that you are left so lonely that out of the misery of loneliness you have to talk to God, you have to create a God to your heart's content. And then the deeper your starvation for the other is, the more is the possibility of visions of God. Those visions are nothing but illusions, dreams seen with open eyes. It is like when a person is put on a long fast, he may start imagining food, he may start seeing food.

I have heard about a poet who was lost in a forest for three days, hungry. And then came the full moon night. He looked at the moon and he was surprised, because all his life, whenever he had seen the full moon he had always remembered beautiful faces of women, his beloveds, things like that; but that day, after three days of starvation, tired, hungry, thirsty, he looked at the moon and he saw white bread, a chapati floating in the sky above the clouds. He could not believe his eyes! "What kind of poetry is this?" A great poet, and the full moon looks like a chapati!

And you all know that if you are starved of something too much, you will start substituting it with imagination. If you have lived in a forest alone for many days and you have not seen a woman, even the ugliest woman in the world will look like Cleopatra.

Mulla Nasrudin goes to a hill station. He has a bungalow

there. Sometimes he says, "I am going for three weeks," but by the second week he is back, or even after seven days or ten days.

I asked, "Nasrudin, many times you say 'I am going for three weeks and four weeks', then you come within two weeks. What is the matter?"

He said, "There is something in it. I have kept a woman there to look after the house. She is the ugliest woman—horrible she is, repulsive she is! Just to look at her and one feels like vomiting."

But I asked, "But what has she to do with it, with your coming early?"

He said, "There is a story in it. When I go to the hill station, she looks horrible. But slowly, slowly after four, five days, she is not so horrible. Then after eight, ten days, I start seeing some beauty in her. The day I start seeing beauty in her is the day I escape, because that means enough is enough! I have lived away from the world too much, away from my woman; now even this horrible woman has started looking beautiful! That simply means I have starved myself too much. So that is the criterion; whatsoever I say—three weeks, four weeks— is not the point. The real criterion is the day I see the woman is beautiful, and I start fantasizing about her, then I pack up my things and I escape. I know the woman is horrible, and if I stay one or two days more, then there is going to be danger —I may fall in love with this horrible woman!"

Loneliness cannot create love, it creates need. Love is not a need.

Then what is love? Love is luxury. It comes out of aloneness, when you are tremendously alone and happy and joyous and celebrating, and great energy goes on storing in you. You don't need anybody. In that moment the energy is so much, you would like it to be shared. Then you give, you give because you have so much, you give without asking anything in return —that is love. So very few people attain to love, and those are the people who attain first to aloneness. And when you are alone, meditation is natural, simple, spontaneous. Then just sitting silently, doing nothing, you are in meditation. You need not repeat a mantra, you need not chant any stupid sound. You simply sit, or you walk, or you do your things, and meditation is there like a climate surrounding you, like a white cloud surrounding you—you are suffused with the light. You are immersed in it, bathed in it, and that freshness goes on welling up in you. *Now* you start sharing. What else can you do? When a song is born in your heart you have to sing it. And when love is born in your heart—love is a by-product of aloneness—you have to shower it. When the cloud is full of rain, it showers, and when the flower is full of fragrance, it releases its fragrance to the winds. Unaddressed, the fragrance is released. And the flower does not wait to ask "What is coming back to me in return?" The flower is happy that the winds have been kind enough to relieve him of a burden.

This is real love; then there is no possessiveness. And this is real meditation; then there is no effort.

Amrito, what has happened to you is something immensely valuable: just your interpretation is wrong.

You say, "After the tidal wave of events and with the memory of a profound experience, I face new aloneness."

Please don't call it aloneness, or if you call it aloneness then try to understand its nature.

"Efforts to share or escape into distractions have bad results."

They are bound to have bad results—because it is aloneness, really aloneness. You will miss something if you escape from it. It is escaping from your own innermost treasure. It is escaping from your richness, from your own kingdom. The result will be disastrous. Don't escape; dig deep into it, dive deep into it. Forget all escaping. That's what, Amrito, you have been doing your whole life. This time, no! This time you have to go into it. This time you have to taste it in its totality. You have to become it. You have to see what it is, root and all. And once you have seen it and lived it, you will come out of it a totally new person, reborn.

I have been watching you since the day you came here. I have continuously been watching you, I have been around you, I have been looking into your eyes, your face: something profound *has* happened—but *much more* is going to happen! If you escape you will miss the 'much more' that is on the way. No! This time, no! Many times you have done it, for many lives you have been doing it. This time drop all fear, drop all memories. Go into the new face of aloneness. It is really aloneness, it is not loneliness. You need not escape. If you escape from loneliness you will feel good. If you escape from aloneness you will feel bad.

"Efforts to share or escape into distractions have bad results."

Don't share right now. Let it gather, let it become a cloud full of rainwater; then the sharing will happen of its own accord. There will be no effort to share. Right now, if you start sharing, it will be again just a way of finding the other in the name of sharing. It will be escape. Sharing has to be allowed to happen on its own. You just go on gathering this aloneness and one day you will see that the fragrance is released to the winds. One day you will see that the sharing has started.

You will be a witness to it; you will not be a doer, but only a witness.

"Why do I cling to this habit of escaping aloneness?"

Because you have not yet understood it as aloneness! You go on interpreting it as loneliness. And I can understand it, this is how everybody does it.

When you feel aloneness for the first time you interpret it as loneliness, because that is a known phenomenon. You have felt it all your life. The moment the child leaves the mother's womb, the first experience is of loneliness: he starts feeling lonely, he had to leave his home. The greatest trauma that happens is when the child has to leave the womb. He wants to cling to the womb, he does not want to go out of it. For nine months he has lived there, he has loved the space, the warmth, and he has been so beautifully taken care of, with no responsibility, no worry. Why should he leave? He is being thrown out, expelled. He does not want to go out. Life—we call it birth—but the child thinks it is going to be death. It is death to him, because it is the end of the life that he had known for nine months. He is shocked, he feels punished. And he cannot think yet, so the feeling goes very deep into the body. It is a feeling of his total being, not a thought, hence it permeates every cell of his body and remains there. That is the first experience of being lonely.

And then again and again many more experiences will come. One day the mother takes the breast away, and the child is again lonely. Someday the child is removed from the mother and the nurse starts taking care...again lonely. One day he is not allowed to sleep in the mother's room, he is given a separate room...again lonely. Remember the day in your childhood when you had to sleep alone in a room for the first time—the darkness, the coldness, nobody there surrounding you. And it had never been so before; the mother's warmth, her soft body, had always been available. Now the child clings to a toy—a teddy bear—but is it a substitute? Or he clings to the blanket, but is it a substitute? A poor substitute, but somehow, he manages. He feels very lonely, dark, left, thrown away, rejected. These are the wounds that go on gathering and go on making the idea of loneliness deeper and deeper. Then one day he has to leave the home and go to the hostel with strange people, unknown. Just remember all these wounds; they are there! And it goes on and on.

Your whole life is a long process of feeling lonely. Then by chance some profound experience happens, and because of that profound experience you have a glimpse of your being —but your whole mind knows only loneliness, so it transforms the experience of aloneness into loneliness. It labels it as loneliness.

The experience of solitude is defined as solitariness.

That's where, Amrito, you are missing. Forget the interpretation; this is really something new that is happening. It is new, so you cannot figure out what it is. The only way to know is to go into it, to be acquainted with it. Just as Master Lu-tsu said, "It is like when you drink water—only you know whether it is cool or warm."

Now drink this aloneness, this fresh energy that is welling up in you. Drink it, taste it, and you will be surprised: it is nothing like what you have known before. It is freedom, freedom from the other. It is what in the East we call *moksha*, utter freedom. And after this freedom, love will become possible. After this freedom, sharing will happen. After this freedom, your life will have a totally different significance, a totally different splendor to it. Your hidden splendor will be released.

The second question:

Why do revolutions fail?

First, because they are not revolutions. Revolution is possible only in the individual soul. The social revolution is a pseudo phenomenon, because the society has no soul of its own. Revolution is a spiritual phenomenon. There can be no political revolution, no social revolution, no economic revolution. The only revolution is that of the spirit; it is individual. And if millions of individuals change, then the society will change as a consequence, not vice versa. You cannot change the society first and hope that individuals will change later on.

That's why revolutions have been failing: because we have taken revolution from a very wrong direction. We have thought that if you change the society, change the structure, economic or political, then one day the individuals, the constituent elements of the society, will change. This is stupid. Who is going to do this revolution?

For example, in 1917 a great so-called revolution happened in Russia. But who is going to take charge of this revolution? Who is going to become powerful? Joseph Stalin became powerful. Now Joseph Stalin had not gone through any revolution himself; he was a by-product of the same society that he was changing or was trying to change. He proved a far more dangerous czar than the czars that he had destroyed, because he was created by those czars. He was a by-product of a feudal society. He tried to change the society, but he himself was a dictatorial mind. He imposed his dictatorship on the country, revolution became counter-revolution—and this has been the misfortune of all the revolutions that have happened in the world because the revolutionary is the same type of person. He has been created by the past, he is not new. What is he going to do?—he will repeat the past. Labels will be new—he will call it communism, socialism, fascism; that doesn't matter. You can have fancy names; fancy names only befool people.

Mulla Nasrudin went to a doctor, told him to check him and said, "Please, tell me in plain language. I don't want any of the abracadabra of medical science. You simply tell me plainly what the problem is with me. Don't use big names in Latin and Greek. Simply say in plain language what exactly is the matter with me."

The doctor checked and he said, "If you want to know exactly, in plain language—there is nothing wrong with you, you are simply lazy."

He said, "Good. Thank you. Now give it a fancy name to tell my wife. And the bigger the name, the better. Make it as difficult as you can."

We go on giving fancy names, but deep down the reality remains the same. Nothing happened in 1917. One czar was replaced by another czar, and of course more dangerous. Why more dangerous?—because Stalin had destroyed the czar, he was a stronger man, certainly more cunning. He knew how the czar had been destroyed, so he had all the ideas of how to protect himself so he did not go the same way. He created a greater slavery in Russia than there was before. Because he was afraid that sooner or later he would be thrown away, so he had to break all the bridges and he had to throw all the ladders that he had used. And he was more cautious; the czar himself was not so cautious because he was a born czar. He had got it through inheritance, he had taken it for granted. Stalin had worked his way himself: it had been a torturous way and a long journey, and he had to destroy many enemies.

After the revolution he started destroying and killing all those people who could be in some way competitors with him. Trotsky was murdered because he was the next man, very close, and in fact more influential in Russia than Joseph Stalin because he was an intellectual Jew, was a greater orator, had more mass appeal. Stalin was nothing intellectually compared to Trotsky. He had to be killed. And there are possibilities than even Lenin was poisoned by the doctors. And then the years that Stalin remained in power, he destroyed all potential competitors. One by one, all the members of the Politburo were killed. He must have been the strongest man in the whole history of humanity, and he turned the whole country into a big prison.

This is how revolutions fail. The first reason is because we try from the wrong end.

Secondly, once a revolution has succeeded we have to destroy the revolutionaries, because the revolutionaries are dangerous people. They have destroyed the first society, they will destroy the second, because they are addicted to revolution. They know only one thing, they are experts only in one thing: in throwing governments—they don't care what government. Their whole expertise and their whole power is in throwing governments. Once a revolution succeeds the first work of

the people who come in power is to destroy all the remaining
revolutionaries—and they had succeeded because of them!
So each revolution turns to counter-revolution because the
people who had brought them into power are more dangerous
people.

Try to understand. The mind of a revolutionary is a destructive
mind: he knows how to destroy, he does not know how to
create. He is very capable of provoking people into violence,
but he is absolutely incapable of helping people to become
calm and quiet and go to work and create. He does not know
that language. For his whole life he has been a revolutionary.
His whole work, his whole expertise, is to provoke people to
destroy; he knows only that language. And you cannot hope
to change his whole life pattern at the end of his life.

So those who are in power have to destroy all the remaining
revolutionaries. Each revolution kills its own fathers—it has
to be done—and once those fathers are killed, the revolution
has turned into a counter-revolution. It is no more revolutionary, it is anti-revolutionary.

It has just now happened in India. Jayaprakash Narayan led
a great upheaval, helped the country to change its government,
and the people who came into power, Morarji Desai and
others, came into power because of Jayaprakash Narayan.
But once they came into power they started getting out of the
hands of Jayaprakash Narayan. They started reducing him.
They became afraid: "This man is dangerous, and this man
has influence over the masses. Again he can prove a great
problem. The man has to be reduced, utterly reduced."

This happened also when the British government was thrown
out of this country. Mahatma Gandhi was the man who did
that. Once the power came to Indian hands, they started

neglecting Mahatma Gandhi. His last words were, "Nobody listens to me. I am the most useless person." And the people who were in power were in power because of him, but nobody listened to him. There is every suspicion that the people he had put into power were involved in his murder, directly or indirectly. Maybe they were not involved directly, but indirectly: they were fully aware that he was going to be murdered but they didn't take any precautions. This is indirect support.

Morarji Desai was in power. He was informed that some conspiracy was on, but he didn't take any notice of it—as if deep down they all wanted to get rid of the Mahatma, because now he was a continuous difficulty. He had the old idea; in the same way he continued, he had his old expertise. He had always been against the government; he was still against the government. Now the government was his but he went on saying things, criticizing. The government had been feeling very embarrassed; they all felt relieved. Although they wept, cried, and they said, "A great misfortune has happened," but deep down they all felt relieved.

The same is the situation with Jayaprakash Narayan: now he is feeling utterly left behind, nobody cares. In fact, the people who are in power will be praying that if he dies soon, it will be good. And he is very ill—half the week he is on dialysis. He cannot work, his body is getting weaker every day. And they must be feeling very happy that soon he will be gone, so there will be nobody who is more powerful than they are.

I would like to tell Jayaprakash...

I love the man. He is a good man, so good that it was not his destiny to be in politics. He is a non-politician. He is a poet, a dreamer, a utopian, a good man—as all dreamers are good men.

...I would like to tell him: Apologize to the country before you die. Tell the country that in your name a gang of power-hungry politicians has cheated you and the country both, that you have been deceived and the country has been deceived. Tell the country that the revolution has failed! But don't only tell the country that the revolution has failed, remember to tell this too: that all revolutions will go on failing in the same way, because their very foundation is wrong. Revolution cannot be imposed from above. Who will impose it? The people who impose it will be part of the past; they will continue the past. Tell the people that there is no future for political revolutions. Only one kind of revolution is possible, and that is spiritual revolution. Each individual has to change in his being, and if we can change millions of people then the society will change. There is no other way, there is no shortcut.

And this too has to be understood: It is an inherent characteristic of any developing system that heroes emerge and are heroes only in the context which stimulated their creation. As these heroes overcome and change such contexts, the heroes themselves become the context to be changed.

A certain hero is born in a certain situation. For example, Mahatma Gandhi was born because of the British Empire. He was meaningful only in the context of the British Empire. Once the British Empire died Mahatma Gandhi was meaningless. The context was not there; from where can you get the meaning? So once the context is changed, then the hero himself becomes a useless burden. Lenin became a burden to those who came into power, Gandhi became a burden to those who came into power. Jayaprakash has become a burden right now to those who are in power—and this is the history, the whole history. But there is a fundamental law working: It is an inherent characteristic of any developing system that heroes emerge and are heroes only in the context which stimulated their creation.

Political leaders are temporary leaders. They exist in a certain context; when the context is gone they are gone.

That is where Buddhas are different: their context is eternity. Their context is not a part of time. This is where Jesus, Zarathustra, Lao Tzu, remain eternally meaningful: because they are not part of time their message is eternal. Their message exists in the context of human misery, human ignorance. Unless the whole existence becomes enlightened, Buddha will not become irrelevant.

That's why I say political leaders come and go, they are on the stage just for a few moments. Only spiritual beings remain, abide.

Buddha is still meaningful and will remain meaningful, forever and forever, because enlightenment will always be a need. Politicians don't make the real history of humanity; they only create noise. The real history is something else that runs like an undercurrent. The real history has not yet been written, because we become too engrossed in the temporal things. We become too obsessed with the newspaper which is only relevant today and tomorrow will be meaningless.

If you have eyes to see, see the point: become interested in the eternal.

Old, ancient societies were not interested in the day-to-day too much. Their interest was deeper. They were not brought up on the newspaper, radio and television. They recited the Koran, they meditated on the Gita, they chanted the Vedas, they contemplated the statues of Buddha and Mahavir. These are eternal phenomena.

That's why I say the events that happen every day are almost meaningless, because the moment they happen, immediately they disappear because their context changes. Political revolutions have been happening and disappearing; they are bubbles, soap bubbles. Maybe for a moment they look very beautiful, but they are not eternal diamonds.

The eternal diamond is the inner revolution. But the inner revolution is difficult because the inner revolution needs creativity and the outer revolution needs destructiveness. Hate is easy, love is difficult. To destroy is easy. To create a Taj Mahal takes years—it took forty years and fifty thousand persons working every day—but how many days will you take to destroy it? Just take a bulldozer and within a day the land will be flat.

To destroy is very easy, so people become very interested in destruction; they think this is a shortcut. To create is very difficult.

And again I will remind you: because all political revolutions are destructive—they are capable in destroying—they can provoke people into destruction. It is very easy to provoke people into destruction because people are frustrated, people are in misery; you can provoke them into any revolt. But the moment they have destroyed, the problem arises: "Now what to do?" They don't know how to create, and your so-called revolutionaries don't know what to do now. Then everybody is at a loss. The misery continues, sometimes even becomes deeper, uglier. After a few years, again people forget and again they start thinking in terms of revolution—and the political leader is always there to lead you into destruction.

My work here is of creativity. I am not provoking you into

any destruction, I am not telling you to blame others for your misery. I am telling you you are responsible, so only those who have the guts to take this responsibility can be with me. But this is a real revolution. If you take the responsibility for your life you can start changing it. Slow will be the change, only in the course of time will you start moving into the world of light and crystallization, but once you are crystallized you will know what real revolution is. Then share your revolution with others; it has to go that way, from heart to heart.

Governments, social structures, have been changed many times, but nothing really changes. Again the same thing is repeated.

That's why I don't call my sannyasins revolutionary but rebellious—just to make the differentiation. Revolution has become too contaminated with the social idea. Rebellion is individual.

Rebel! Take responsibility for your life. Drop all that nonsense which has been put inside you. Drop all that you have been taught and start learning again from ABC. It is a hard, arduous journey.

And remember one thing more:....thus both coping systems and governments begin as useful and gradually become counter-productive. This is the nature of the evolutionary process itself.

Whatsoever happens on the outside may look in the beginning as if it is very productive; soon it becomes counter-productive —because life goes on changing. Life goes on taking jumps into the unknown and your structures always lag behind. And each structure in its own turn becomes a grave; it has to be broken again.

But I am showing you a way where there is no need for any
structure inside. Consciousness can remain unstructured. That
is the meaning of the word 'freedom'. Consciousness need
not have any structure, any character. Consciousness can live
moment-to-moment without any structure, without any
morality, without any character, because consciousness is
enough. You can respond, and your response will be good and
virtuous because you responded consciously. Live consciously,
without any structure, so you will never be caught in a counter-
productive system. Otherwise that too happens: you learn
one thing; it is beautiful, but only for a few days will it remain
beautiful. Soon it will become a habit and again you will
find yourself surrounded by a habit, encaged.

Real life has to be lived without habits. You have heard, again
and again you have been told, "Drop bad habits." I tell you:
Drop habit as such! There are not good and bad habits: all
habits are bad. Remain without habits, live without habits;
then you live moment-to-moment out of freedom—and this
is the life of a revolutionary.

And remember also: So in the light of their past service, do
not blame any program for being counter-productive as you
remove it. Housecleaning should be guiltless. You will remove
a program as it no longer fits your developing gestalt, but avoid
the temptation to be harsh with the program you remove,
because they were necessary stepping-stones to get to where
you are now. Love them for this while defusing their power
over you for upcoming phases.

Whatsoever you do will become a habit, sooner or later.
The moment you see it has become a habit, drop it. It is counter-
productive now, it is counter-revolutionary now. It will pull
you backwards, it will not allow you to move forwards. It
will keep you tethered to the known, it will not allow you

to go into the unscheduled, unmapped, unmeasured. So whenever you remove a habit don't feel guilty—'Housecleaning should be guiltless'; and it should not be harsh either. When you remove a habit, howsoever good it has been, when you remove it don't feel guilty. Don't think, "My mother taught me this. If I am removing it I am betraying her."

People write letters to me: "How can I take sannyas? My parents have taught me to be a Catholic Christian. Will it not be betraying them?" "I have been brought up as a Mohammedan. Will it not be betraying the people who have taught me with such love, with such care, to be a Mohammedan?" Guilt arises. If you are feeling flowing, free, in being a Catholic, there is no need to change. But the desire to change is there; that simply shows you are feeling confined. Yes, your mother taught you something that she knew, that she felt would be good for you, but the context has changed. You are living a totally different life than your mother lived. How can she remain a teacher to you forever?

Don't feel guilty when you drop a program, and don't feel harsh either—because these are the two extremes. Either people feel guilty or they feel very harsh, antagonistic, angry. There is no need to even feel angry, because whatsoever the poor old woman knew and thought would be good for you she taught you. It served its purpose. In fact, who knows?—if you were not a Catholic Christian you may not have come to me. It has brought you here. So whatsoever has happened in the past has been used as a stepping-stone; feel grateful to it.

No need to feel guilty, no need to feel harsh. Whenever you remove a program, remove it just like you remove your clothes. When your body grows, your clothes become small. You don't feel guilty because you are removing pyjamas your mother had given you that don't fit you anymore. You have to remove them! And you don't feel angry either. You need not first beat them and throw petrol on them and burn them and make such fuss about it. You don't do that either, because you know they have served their purpose.

Man is a growing gestalt. Every day new things are to happen. Every day you have to absorb the new and make a place for the new; the old has to be gone. The old has to be said goodbye to, with all thankfulness.

If you can remember these two things—never feel guilty when you remove an old program and never feel harsh when you remove an old program—you will be moving towards the revolution I am intending you to understand. A revolutionary is not really angry. Why should he be? There is no reason. Whatsoever your parents could do, they did, and they did it with all good wishes. It is another matter that whatsoever they were doing was not useful, was not making you free, but that was not their intention. Their intention was good. And they could not have done otherwise; they had lived in a different world.

So remember, when you bring up your own children, remember: don't give them programs, give them understanding. Don't give them fixed rules, just give them the vision to see things so they can find their own rules. Don't give them knowledge, just give them awareness. That's what I would like my sannyasins to do with their own children: give them awareness so that whenever and wherever they are...

And remember, they will not be in the same world in which you are living and you have lived. They will have their own world. You cannot dream about it, you cannot think about it. They will never repeat the same life-pattern as you. They will have their own lifestyle.

Give them awareness: wherever they are they can find a way. Give them light, give them eyes to see, to understand, and give them courage to be free. Give them enough courage so that whenever they find something is not right in their program they can put it away, they can drop it. This is love.

Don't enforce any pattern on them. They will be living in a totally different world, so give your love but don't give your knowledge. The world is changing so fast that whatsoever you give will be out of date soon and will become a burden on them, and they will feel guilty if they drop it. Or if they really want to drop it they will have to be angry with you. In both ways it is not good, so don't create that situation for your own children.

Live a life of revolution and impart revolution to your children. Live a life of revolution and impart revolution to all those you love. Only this revolution will never fail...but this revolution has not been tried yet.

Jesus was talking about this, but it has not been tried. Buddha talked about this, but it has not been tried. I am talking about this; it depends on you whether it will be tried or not. The revolution that can succeed has not been tried, and the revolutions that have been tried have all failed.

The third question:

You are known throughout the world as the Tantra Master or the sex guru, yet in the three years I have been in your ashram, not only have I had less sex than ever before in my life, but thought and heard less about it as well. Will you explain this discrepancy?

Just the other day in a magazine, *Cine Blitz*, I came across a headline, and they say I am the Hugh Heffner of the spiritual world. And what are they talking about?

Yes, I teach you how to go deep in love. I teach you how to go deep in sex too, because that is the only way to go beyond. To go through it is the only way to go beyond it—but my goal is to take you beyond. Now this is a problem, and I am going to be misunderstood again and again, all over the world.

People have become accustomed: they think religious people have to be against sex; and those who are not against sex, how can they be religious? These have become *deadly* settled categories. I am unsettling all those categories, and I don't expect the world to immediately change so much from its settled patterns of mind. So I don't expect them to understand me either. When they misunderstand, I perfectly understand their misunderstanding. I have no false hopes. It will take years or centuries for them to understand me, but this always happens.

I am creating a new vision of life. The vision is so new that they don't have any category for categorizing it. So all are angry; Mahatma Morarji Desai is angry. He is angry because he is sexually repressed, utterly repressed, with no understanding. He has just repressed his sexuality.

The story is that when Morarji Desai was young, in his young days fifty or so years ago, a man in his village raped his own sister. That shocked him very much, and he thought that it was sex that was the cause of such a great crime. In fact, repression may have been the cause; otherwise who wants to rape his own sister? In fact, sisters don't look very appealing at all. One has lived with them, one has grown up with them. Unless a person is very repressed it is very difficult to fall in love with his own sister, almost impossible.

Love always happens with the unknown, with the unacquainted. Familiarity breeds contempt. How can one love one's own sister? But the man must have been living in a deep repression—maybe he had never known any woman! He must have been desperate. But what Morarji concluded out of it was this: that sex is the root cause of all crime. If it can drive people mad and they can rape their own sisters, this is the root cause of all crime. He decided never to go into sex again—not for any religious reason, not for any spiritual reason—and since that time he has been repressing.

And the same was true about his guru, Mahatma Gandhi. It was also a trauma that created his lifelong celibacy. His father was dying and he was massaging his father's feet, and the doctors had said that this might be the last night, he might not see the morning again. But at twelve o'clock in the night when the father fell asleep, he went back and started making love to his wife. He went back to his room, and when he was just in the middle of the act, somebody knocked on the door and said, "What are you doing? Where are you? Your father is dead."

It shocked him. It was a trauma, a great trauma that transformed his whole life—not for the better, but for the worse. He felt guilty. He concluded that it was the lust, the sex, that had driven him at the last moment when his father was dying. He had committed a crime, a sin. He could never forgive himself so he renounced sex, and for his whole life he suppressed sex. Only in the end, in the last years of his life, did he become aware of the suppression because the sexual fantasy continued to the very end. Then he started trying some Tantra experiments, so that before he died he could get rid of sex—but it was too late.

These people cannot understand. They will think that I am a sex guru, that I am teaching you sex, that I am teaching you indulgence. These people cannot understand.

Hugh Heffner cannot understand either, because he will ask why am I talking about meditation, why am I talking about spirituality? Spirituality, meditation, *samadhi*—these things will look like nonsense to him.

So both Morarji Desai and Hugh Heffner will misunderstand me. I am going to be misunderstood by the so-called spiritualists and by the so-called materialists, but I understand that it is going to be my fate.

I can only be understood by a *new* kind of being who has seen this totality: that man is both body and soul, and that life matures only through experiences.

Sex can become a stepping-stone towards *samadhi*. If you understand it deeply, if you experience it deeply, you will be free of it—but that freedom will have a totally different quality! It will not be a repressed sex. A repressed sex continues underground, goes on in your unconscious, on and on, and goes on affecting your life.

I have heard...

Once a wealthy old religious woman caught a burglar ransacking her things. She had lived her whole life as a celibate, almost like a nun.
"Listen lady, keep quiet if you don't want to be hurt. Just tell me where your jewels are."
She said, "I don't keep them here. They are in the bank in the safe-deposit vault."
"Where is all your silver then?"

"I am sorry, but it is all out, being cleaned and polished."
"Give me your money then."
"I tell you," she said, "I don't keep any cash on hand."
"Listen lady, I am warning you—give me your money or I will rip it off you." And he started feeling her up and down.
"I keep telling you," she said, "I don't have any money. But if you do that again I will write you a cheque."

I have also heard another story; maybe it is about the same burglar...

In the middle of the night a phone call came through at the police station. Somebody was in need of immediate help. The voice on the phone said desperately, "Come soon! Come immediately! A burglar is trapped in an old woman's room!" The police inspector on duty said, "We will be reaching within five minutes. But who is calling?"
And the voice said, "It is the burglar."

If you repress, you will carry the wound for your whole life, unhealed. Repression is not the way.

The radical change comes through understanding, and understanding comes through experience. So I give you total freedom to experience all that your mind, your body want to experience, with just one condition: be alert, be watchful, be conscious.

If you can make love consciously, you will be surprised: love has all the keys to *samadhi*. If you go deeply into love with full consciousness, alert and aware, you will see that it is not love that attracts you; but in the highest peak of love, in the orgasmic explosion, your mind disappears, your thoughts stop, and that is from where the nectar flows into you. It is not really sex that gives you that beautiful experience. Sex simply helps you, in a natural way, to come to a point where mind is dissolved—of course, for a moment. The clouds disperse and you can see the sun. Again those clouds will be there and the sun will be lost, and again you will start fantasizing about sex. If you go unconscious, then you will miss this whole secret again and again.

It is not sex that is keeping you tethered to the world, it is unconsciousness! So the question is not how to drop sex; the question is how to drop unconsciousness. Be conscious and let your natural being have its whole flow.

And sex is a natural part. You are born of it; every cell of your body is a sexual cell. Repressing it is against nature.

But there is a transcendence which is a totally different matter. If you are alert and aware in your orgasmic moment, you will see time disappears—for a moment there is no time, no past, no future. You are utterly herenow, and that is the beauty. It is because of that that you feel such joy, so much blessing showers on you.

Now these two secrets have to be understood: one, the disappearance of the mind for a moment, and the disappearance of time for a moment. And these are two aspects of one phenomenon: one aspect is time, the other aspect is mind. When these two disappear you are in utter bliss, you are in God. And meditation is a way to let these disappear without going into sex.

When you go into meditation you will recognize one day the truth that in meditation it happens also: mind disappears, time disappears. And that day will be the day of great realization. That day you will see why you were so interested in sex, and that very day all interest in sex will disappear. Not that you will have to drop it by effort; it will simply disappear, just like dewdrops in the morning sun disappear, with no trace, with no wounds.

If you can create it through meditation, it is far easier to create it—because you do it alone. The other is not needed, you need not depend on the other.

Secondly, if you can do it meditatively, no energy is lost. On the contrary you become more vital because energy is saved.

Thirdly, if you can do it meditatively, then you can remain in it as long as you want. It is not momentary. You can by and by learn how to remain in it for twenty-four hours. A Buddha lives in the orgasmic state for twenty-four hours, day in, day out. Between the day Gautama Buddha became enlightened and the day he died there is a distance of forty-two years. For these forty-two years he was utterly in an orgasmic state. Just think! Those few moments you have are nothing compared to a Buddha's.

I am teaching you a new kind of synthesis. I am all for that transcendence that brings you to Buddhahood, but it is trans-cendence, not repression. Through repression nobody ever transcends. Through repression one goes on moving and moving in the same rut. Repressing, you have to repress every day. To the very last moment of your death, sex will haunt you. If you really want to get rid of it...and I want you to get rid of it! But I am not against sex, because those who are against sex can never get rid of it. Hence the paradox of my teachings.

Only those who are really ready to understand will be able to understand; otherwise I am going to be misunderstood. The crowd, the mass, is going to misunderstand me. But I don't expect, either, that they should understand. I feel sorry for them, but there is no expectation either, so I never feel offended.

I know that the teaching is so new that it will take centuries to create criteria on which it can be judged. Criteria are not there. It is said when a poet is really great his poetry cannot be understood, because all the old poetry is different from it. The great poet has to create his own criteria on which his poetry can be judged. So is it the case with a great painter: you cannot judge a great painter by the old painters and the old masters. He has such a new message that no old valuations will be of any help, so he has to create new values also. It takes time. And if it is so with poetry and painting and sculpture, what to say about enlightenment? That is the greatest art, the art of all the arts. It takes centuries.

The last question:

I am very much afraid that something unexpected is going to happen to me. What should I do?

It is good that something unexpected is going to happen to you. In fact, if only the expected happened, you would be utterly bored. Just think of a life in which only that which you expect always happens. What will you do with such a life? There would be no joy in it, it would be sheer boredom. You expect a friend and he knocks on the door. You expect a headache and it is there. You expect your wife to leave and she leaves. You expect, and it happens. Within twenty-four hours you would commit suicide! What will you do if all that happened, happened just by your expectation and according to your expectation?

Life is an adventure because the unexpected happens. The greater would be the adventure if more and more unexpected things happened to you. Feel blissful. The unexpected happens— be ready for it, make way for it. Don't ask for the expected. That's why I say remain empty for the future; don't project. Let the future happen on its own, and you will be continuously in joy. You will have a dance in your being, because each thing that will happen will be so unexpected, and when it is un- expected, it has a mystery in it....

I have heard about a clairvoyant little boy. It seems this boy had premonitions. Once while reciting his prayers he said, "God bless mommy, God bless daddy, God bless grandma, goodbye grandpa." The next day grandpa died of a stroke.

Then later on the little boy said, "God bless mommy, God bless daddy, goodbye grandma." Then grandma was hit while crossing the street.

Sometime later in his prayers, he said, "God bless mommy, goodbye daddy." The father was really upset. He had himself driven to the office, but he could not work there at all. Finally he decided to come home early, but he was afraid to drive back so he took a taxi home and rushed in.

He was greeted by his wife, who said, "What do you think happened today dear? The most awful thing! The milkman dropped dead on the back porch!"

Master Lu-tsu said:

> Four words crystallize the spirit
> in the space of energy.
> In the sixth month white snow
> is suddenly seen to fly.
> At the third watch the sun's disk
> sends out blinding rays.
> In the water blows the wind of the Gentle.
> Wandering in heaven, one eats the
> spirit-energy of the Receptive.
> And the still deeper secret of the secret:
> The land that is nowhere,
> that is the true home...

These verses are full of mystery. The meaning is: the most important things in the great Tao are the words: action through non-action. Non-action prevents a man from becoming entangled in form and image (materiality). Action in non-action prevents a man from sinking into numbing emptiness and dead nothingness. Heretofore we have spoken of the circulation of the light, indicating thereby the initial release which works from without upon what lies within. This is to aid one in obtaining the Master. It is for pupils in the beginning stages. They go through the two lower transitions in order to gain the upper one. After the sequence of events is clear and the nature of the release is known, heaven no longer withholds the Way, but reveals the ultimate truth. Disciples, keep it secret and redouble your efforts!

The circulation of the light is the inclusive term. The further the work advances, the more does the Golden Flower bloom. But there is a still more marvellous kind of circulation. Till now we have worked from the outside on what is within; now we stay in the center and rule what is eternal. Hitherto it was a service in aid of the Master; now it is a dissemination of the commands of the Master. The whole relationship is now reversed. If one wants to penetrate the more subtle regions by this method, one must first see to it that the body and heart are completely controlled, that one is quite free and at peace, letting go of all entanglements, untroubled by the slightest excitement, and with the heavenly heart exactly in the middle. When the rotating light shines towards what is within, it does not develop a dependence on things, the energy of the dark is fixed, and the Golden Flower shines concentratedly. This is then the collected light of polarity. Related things attract each other. Thus the polarized light-line of the Abysmal presses upward. It is not only the light in the abyss, but it is creative light which meets creative light. As soon as these two substances meet each other, they unite inseparably and there develops an unceasing life; it comes and goes, rises and falls of itself, in the house of the primal energy. One is aware of an effulgence and infinity. The whole body feels light and would like to fly. This is the state of which it is said: Clouds fill the thousand mountains. Gradually it goes to and fro quite softly; it rises and falls imperceptibly. The pulse stands still and breathing stops. This is the moment of true creative union, the state of which it is said: The moon gathers up the ten thousand waters. In the midst of this darkness, the heavenly heart suddenly begins a movement. This is the return of the one light, the time when the child comes to life.

Chapter Seven

September 2nd, 1978

THE MOON GATHERS UP THE TEN THOUSAND WATERS

THERE WAS ONCE A KING who had three sons. Desiring to determine the fitness of each of them for the prospective job of ruling the kingdom, he hit upon a strange test.

The king ordered his sons to accompany him, with bows and arrows, on a ride into the country. Pausing at a spot beside the road near an open field, the king pointed out a vulture sitting on a tree limb, within easy bow shot.

"I wish you to shoot at that vulture," said the king to his eldest son. "But tell me first, what do you see?"

Wonderingly, the prince replied, "Why, I see grass, the clouds, the sky, the river, a tree, and..."

"Enough!" said the king, and beckoned the second son to make ready to shoot. The latter was about to do so when his father again said, "Tell me first, what do you see?"

"Ah, I see the horses, the ground, a field of wheat, and an old dead tree with a vulture on it," answered the youth.

"Never mind shooting it," the king said, and turning to his youngest son, ordered him to hit the vulture, and again repeated the question, "First, what do you see?"

The youth replied deliberately, not taking his gaze for an instant from his intended victim as he drew taut the bowstring and aimed the shaft, "I see," he said, "the point where the wings join the body..." and the young man let fly the arrow and the bird tumbled to the ground.

The third son became the king.

The kingdom belongs to those who can work in a concentrated way—and with the kingdom of the within, more so. The way of moving in life with a direction, with a goal, with a clearcut vision, crystallizes your energies. The goal is just an excuse. The direction is just a device.

Ordinarily you are scattered all over the place, one part going in this direction, another part going in another direction. Ordinarily you are many, a mob, and each fragment of your being is constantly contradicting the other fragment. How can you achieve anything in life? How can you feel fulfilled? If misery becomes your whole story, and if life proves to be nothing but a tragedy, there is no need to wonder. Except you, nobody else is responsible.

You have an inexhaustible source of energy, but even that can be wasted. If your fragments are in a kind of civil war you will not achieve anything worthwhile—to say nothing about God, to say nothing about truth. You will not achieve *anything* worthwhile, because all realization, either of the without or of the within, needs one thing absolutely: that you be one—so that your whole energy can pour into your work, so that your whole energy can become a quest.

Questions you have many; that is not going to help unless all your questions are together and create a quest in you. When your life becomes a quest, when it has a direction, it starts moving towards fulfillment. Then it will have crystallization. Crystallization means slowly, slowly you become one piece, slowly, slowly individuation arises in you. And the ultimate realization of truth is nothing but the ultimate realization of unity within your being. That is the meaning of the word 'God'. God is not there somewhere in the heavens, waiting for you. God is waiting within you, but you can find Him only if you are one—because only the one can find the one. Remember the famous words of the great mystic, Plotinus: "Flight of the alone to the alone". First you have to become alone. That's what I was saying yesterday to Amrito: become alone. Alone means become all one. This aloneness, or all-oneness, this inner unity, releases immense power because all dissipation stops. You stop leaking. The ordinary man is like an earthen pot which is leaking from everywhere, has many holes in it. You can go on filling it again and again, but again and again you will find it is empty. Your effort will not bring any fruition; first the holes have to be stopped.

Think of your life as a great occasion to become one. Once you start moving in one direction, you pull yourself together. Something in you starts settling. A center arises, and that center is the door to God.

These sutras are of immense value. They are very mysterious too, because when one starts imparting truth one has to use the language of poetry, parable, mystery. There is no other way. The language of mathematics is inadequate; one has to be very metaphorical.

Before we enter into the sutras, listen to this small story.

The great Zen Master, Nansen, was getting very old and was waiting for his successor to arrive. In fact, he was ready to leave the body but was just hanging around for the successor to come so he could transfer whatsoever he had attained, so he could give the key.

Now he had many disciples, so it looks very strange; he had thousands of disciples. Why could he not give his key to one of these thousands of disciples? He had great scholars around him—very skillful, very logical, efficient, intellectual—but he had to wait. These people were able to understand logic but they were not able to understand love. And love speaks a totally different language. These people were capable of understanding mathematics but were absolutely incapable of understanding the language of metaphor. These people were perfectly able to understand prose but were not available to the mysteries of poetry—so he had to wait.

He was lying down on his bed in his chamber, sick, old, and hanging around the old body somehow, managing somehow. It was on that day that for the first time he saw his successor, Joshu, coming into the room. His very coming... not a single word had been uttered. Neither had the Master spoken nor the disciple, the future disciple. He was a stranger, but the way he entered the room was enough.

The Master asked him, "Where have you come from?"
For days the Master had not spoken: he was so sick, so old. He was preserving his energy in every way, he was not even speaking. After many days, these were his first words—to Joshu, "Where have you come from?"
Joshu said, "From Zuizo Temple." Zuizo means figure of bliss.
Nansen laughed—he had not laughed for many months— and asked, "Have you seen the figure of bliss?"

Joshu said, "The figure of bliss, I have not seen. A lying Buddha, I have seen."

At this Nansen stood up—he had not been out of his bed for almost a year. At this Nansen stood up and asked, "Do you have a Master already?"

Joshu answered, "I have."

Nansen asked, "Who is your Master?" as if all sickness had disappeared, as if he were young again. His voice was clear, youthful, vigorous, vital: "Who is your Master?!"

Joshu laughed and said, "Although winter is past its peak it is still very cold. May I suggest, my Master, that you take good care of your body?" And that was that.

And Nansen said, "Now I can die peacefully. A man has arrived who can understand my language. A man has arrived who can meet not on the surface but in the depth."

Joshu said, "My Master, take good care of your body." Just saying that, the initiation had happened. And the way Joshu said, "Although winter is past its peak, it is still very cold," he knew how to speak in metaphors. He knew the way of poetry. And he knows the way of love. That's why he said, "May I suggest, my Master, that you take good care of your body. Please lie down. You need not jump out of your bed. *You* are my Master! I have not seen bliss yet, but I have seen a Buddha."

The Master recognized the disciple, the disciple recognized the Master—in a single split moment. What transpired? That which transpired is beyond language, but still that, *even that*, has to be told in language. Even this story has to be related to you in language; there is no other way.

These words of Master Lu-tsu are very mysterious. Try to understand them through your heart in a very loving, sympathetic way.

There are two ways to listen to a thing. One is the way of the critic who is constantly inside criticizing, judging, evaluating whether it is right or wrong, whether it fits with me or not, whether it agrees with my knowledge or not? He's constantly comparing, criticizing. That is not the way to understand these beautiful sutras. These sutras are beyond the critical mind. They are available only to one who is sympathetic; or, even better, to one who is empathetic, who can fall in tune, who can become just open and listen totally so it is not only the physical heart but the deep, hidden spiritual heart that is stirred by them.

> Master Lu-tsu said,
>> *Four words crystallize the spirit*
>> *in the space of energy.*

You have the energy, you have all that you will ever need. Still you are poor, still you are a beggar. You have not used your energy, you have not opened your treasure yet. You have not even looked at what God has given to you. Without looking in you are rushing out, hence the misery. And the misery is going to remain, because you cannot find anything in the outside world that can satisfy you. Nobody has ever found anything in the outside world, not even the great Alexander. You can have the whole kingdom of the earth. You can become a *chakravartin*, the ruler of the whole earth, of all the seven continents.

You will be surprised: modern geography says there are only six continents, but the ancient Indian geography says there are seven continents. It must be Atlantis that they count in. And a person who rules over all the seven continents is called a *chakravartin*. Even if you become a *chakravartin* you will remain poor, you will not gain anything. In fact, you will have lost much, because your whole life you will have been struggling for the trivial, for the mundane, for the meaningless, for the futile—which is going to be taken away by death any moment. Unless you have something of the within, you are not going to become rich.

Only the kingdom of the within makes one rich, because even death cannot take it away. It cannot be robbed, it cannot be destroyed, it cannot be taken away. Once you have known it, it is yours forever.

You have the inner space, you have the inner energy; all is available. You have just not looked into it. You have the beautiful *veena* but you have not even touched it, you have not even seen what music it contains. You have almost become oblivious to it.

Lu-tsu says, "Four words..." only four words can crystallize your being, can create an emperor in you, can make you a Buddha or a Christ or a Krishna. What are those four words?

Now try to understand these four metaphors.

First:

> *In the sixth month white snow*
> *is suddenly seen to fly.*

Second:

> *At the third watch the sun's disk*
> *sends out blinding rays.*

Third:

> *In the water blows the wind of the Gentle.*

Fourth:

> *Wandering in heaven, one eats the*
> *spirit-energy of the Receptive.*

> *And the still deeper secret of the secrets:*
> *The land that is nowhere,*
> *that is the true home...*

Now try to decipher these mysterious words, these esoteric statements. They have great hidden beauty and great hidden meaning. Be very sympathetic, because that is the only way to understand something esoteric.

> *In the sixth month white snow...*

The sixth month is the middle of the year. It represents the middle of everything. And if you can be in the middle of everything; never leaning to any extreme, you have fulfilled the first requirement. This has immense value for the seeker, for those who are on an existential quest: be in the middle. Always remember the middle, 'The Golden Mean'. Don't eat too much and don't fast too much—neither this way nor that. Don't become too attached to things and don't renounce them either. Be with people but not too much, not so much that you cannot be alone at all. And don't start being solitary, don't become addicted to loneliness; don't avoid people. Be in the world but don't let the world enter in you. There is no need to escape from the world.

Never move to the extreme: this is one of the most fundamental things to be remembered, because the mind always moves from one extreme to another extreme. Mind lives through extremes, mind dies in the middle—this is the secret.

There are people who will eat too much, and then for a few days they will diet. And then after a few days' suffering, the so-called dieting, they will start eating too much again, with a vengeance, and again. And this is a vicious circle: from one extreme they will move to the other, from the other, again back. Back and forth, back and forth; like a pendulum of an old clock, they go on moving. And they don't know that because the pendulum moves, the clock remains alive. It is a beautiful metaphor: the clock. If the pendulum stays in the middle, the clock stops.

So is the mind: if you move from extreme to another extreme, mind continues, time continues. Mind and time are synonymous. The moment you stop in the middle time disappears, the clock stops; mind disappears, the mind stops. And in that moment, when there is no mind and no time, suddenly you become aware for the first time of who you are. All clouds have disappeared and the sky is open and the sun is shining bright.

In the sixth month white snow...

And in China, in the part where these sutras were written, it is the sixth month of the year when the snow appears. It is the middle path—when coolness appears in your being.

White snow represents a few things. First, whiteness, purity, coolness, tranquility, virgin freshness, beauty, grace. Be in the middle and you will see that your inner being is becoming like the Himalayas, Himalayan peaks covered with virgin snow, and all is cool, and all is utterly silent, and all is utterly fresh, all impurities gone.

The impurity is of the mind. When there is no mind, no thought, there is no impurity. It is thought that pollutes your being.

In the sixth month white snow
is suddenly seen to fly.

And it happens suddenly. Just be in the middle, and out of nowhere, out of the blue, the white snow starts appearing. You try it; this is an experiment. It is not a philosophy to be understood, it is an experiment to be done. Try to be in the middle of anything and you will see great coolness, calmness, collectedness arising in you.

> *At the third watch the sun's disk*
> *sends out blinding rays.*

And the second metaphor: the third watch.

Man has three layers: first is the body, second the mind, third is the soul. If you have fulfilled the first requirement, then the second will be possible. You cannot do the second before doing the first, so you will have to move methodologically. You cannot do from the middle. You cannot take any step from anywhere: there is a sequence. First attain the middle of everything, and the whole day watch whether your mind is going to extremes. Avoid the extremes and then the second thing will become possible. When you avoid the extremes you will become aware of three things in you: the body, the gross part of you, the mind, the subtle part of you, and the soul, the beyond.

Body and mind are two aspects of matter. Body is visible matter, mind is invisible matter. And when you see the body-mind both, you, the seer, are the third. That is the third watch: the watcher, the observer, the witness.

> *At the third watch the sun's disk*
> *sends out blinding rays.*

And then when you are attuned to your watching, one with

your witness, suddenly, as if in the middle of the night the sun rises and there is great light, you are full of light within and without. The whole existence becomes aflame.

And the third:
In the water blows the wind of the Gentle.

Water, in Taoism, represents the ultimate source of things. It represents the Tao itself. Lao Tzu has called his path 'The Watercourse Way' for many reasons. First, the water is soft, humble, seeks the lowest place. Just as Jesus says, "Those who are the last in this world will be the first in my kingdom of God, and those who are the first will be the last," water seeks the lowest place, the lowest level. It may rain on Everest but it doesn't remain there; it starts running towards the valley. And in the valley too, it will reach to the deepest part. It remains the last, it is non-ambition. It has no ambitions to be the first.

And to be water means to be a sannyasin. To be water-like means to be utterly happy in your being a nobody.

And secondly, water means movement. It is always moving. And whenever it is not moving it becomes dirty, impure, even poisonous. It dies. Its life is in movement, in dynamism, in flow. The whole life is a flow, nothing is static.

The scientist, Eddington, is reported to have said that the word 'rest' is utterly meaningless, because in existence, there is never anything at rest. It corresponds to no reality, to no fact. Everything is growing, moving, on the way. Life is a pilgrimage. In life, nouns are false, only verbs are true. In language we have created nouns. Those nouns give a very false impression about life; they are not right. Some day, in future, when language will become more existential, nouns will disappear and will be replaced—*all* nouns will be replaced—by verbs. There is nothing like river, but rivering; there is nothing like a tree, but treeing—because never for a moment is the tree static. It is never in a state of is-ness. It is always becoming, flowing, going somewhere. Existence is fluid, hence the metaphor of water, 'in the water'.

If you have seen the witness, then the third thing becomes possible: you will see the beauty of the flow. You will not hanker for security and you will not hanker for things to remain as they are. You will start moving with the river, you will become part of the river of existence. You will start enjoying change.

People are *really* afraid of change, *very* afraid of change. Even if the change is for the better, they are afraid. They are afraid of the new because the mind becomes very clever with the old and is always embarrassed with the new. With the new the mind has to learn again from ABC—and who wants to learn? The mind wants the world to remain static. It is because of the mind that societies are conformist, orthodox. Millions of people in the world are conventional. Why? There must be some deep investment in it. This is the investment: nobody wants to learn, nobody wants to grow, nobody wants to be acquainted with the new. People want to go on moving in the old rut, and then naturally they are bored. Then they say, "Why are we bored?" and "How to drop boredom?"—and they are creating the boredom, and they don't see the mechanism of how they create it.

Many people come to me and they say they are bored: "How to get out of boredom?" Boredom is not the problem, boredom is a by-product. Deep down the problem is: are you ready to explore the new? Are you ready to go for an adventure? Adventure means risk; one never knows—it may turn out better, it may turn out worse than you had known before. One can never be certain about it.

The only certainty in life is uncertainty. One can only be certain about uncertainty and about nothing else.

The new makes people very apprehensive. They cling to the old. Hence, the conventional people in the world—and they are the dead weight; because of them the world remains static—they will go on insisting on their old patterns.

For example, in India people have lived for almost five thousand years with the same structure that Manu created. It may have been good in those days, must have been of some significance, but five thousand years have passed and still in India the untouchable exists. There are people who cannot even be touched; they are not human beings. The really orthodox will not even touch their shadows. It used to be so. It is still so in a few villages that when an untouchable, a *sudra*, passes on the street, he has to shout "Please get out of my way. I am coming"—because if his shadow falls on somebody of the high caste, that will be a crime. He can be beaten, beaten to death! Still people are being burned for this crime, and this stupid structure has lived for five thousand years. So inhuman! So undemocratic! That's why in India it seems democracy cannot succeed: the whole Hindu mind is undemocratic. How can you succeed in creating a democratic country if the whole structure of the mind, the conditioning of the mind, is undemocratic? The basic fundamental of a democracy is that each man is equal; nobody has more value than the other— but that is not acceptable to the Hindu. In fact, the *sudra*, the untouchable, cannot be counted as a human being. He has to be counted with animals, not with man. Women cannot be counted with men; she has also been counted with the animals. Now this type of mind—how can it become democratic? So in the name of democracy there is only chaos and nothing else, because there are no foundations for democracy. But for five thousand years this country has lived with this structure and is not ready to leave the structure. What is the beauty of this structure? There is nothing like beauty in it. It is utterly ugly, horrible, repulsive, nauseating! The only thing is, because people have lived so long, they don't want to learn anything else. They want to live with it, they are at ease with it. They abhor any change.

Remember, this tendency is in every human being, more or less: you don't want change. You are afraid to change because with the change new responsibilities, new challenges will arise. And you are afraid whether you will be able to cope with them or not, so it is better to remain with the old because with the old you have become skillful, efficient. With the old you are the master. With the new, who knows? You may be the master, you may not be the master.

Only children are capable of learning. Because they don't have any past, because they don't have anything old to cling to—that's why children are ready to learn. The more they grow the less they learn. Nearabout the age of thirteen, people stop learning; that remains their mental age.

If you are a seeker you will have to learn continuously. Life is learning. Learning never stops. Even at the moment of death the seeker goes on learning; he learns death. He's always ready to change.

Water represents the changing element, the eternally changing, flux-like phenomenon. Those who are ready to change, and forget and forgive the past, and are ready to go with the moment, are the *real* human beings because they are the adventurers. They know the beauties of life and the benedictions of life. And life reveals its mysteries only to these people, and *only* to these people—because they are worthy, they have earned it. By risking, they have earned. They are courageous.

In the water blows the wind of the Gentle.

And if you become a water-like phenomenon, changing, constantly changing, moving, flowing, never clinging to the past and the old, always searching for the new and always enjoying the new, then... the wind of the Gentle blows. Then grace descends. Then beatitude descends in your being. Then, the first dance of the divinity in you... that is called 'the wind of the Gentle'.

God is very gentle. He never knocks on your doors. You never hear His footsteps. When He comes, He comes so silently, without making any noise. Unless you are water-like, the breeze of God will never dance on you. First become fluid.

That is my message too, to my sannyasins: remain fluid.

And remember, the future belongs to those who are ready to change constantly, because now the world is changing so fast that the people who cling to the old are going to suffer very much. In the past they have not suffered very much. On the contrary, the people who were ready to change have suffered very much.

In the future, just the reverse is going to be the case: the future belongs to those who will love change and who will be dancingly ready to change, who will celebrate change. And whenever there will be an occasion to change, they will never miss it. The future is going to be with them. History is taking a great turn; it is moving on another plane. That's why my insistence is always that whenever something is changing, don't prevent it.

If your relationship with your woman is changing, don't prevent it. Allow it, let it have its own course. Even if you have to separate, don't be worried. That clinging mind will keep you miserable. If it is changing, it is changing! Enjoy the change, enjoy the new. Receive the new, welcome it. And soon you will see that if you become capable of receiving the new without any fuss about the old, your life will start having an elegance, a grace, a gentleness. You will become like a soft flower.

This is the moment when a seeker starts dancing. This is the moment when celebration starts. And remember, porpoises and chimpanzees may play, but only man celebrates. Celebration is utterly human. You have heard many definitions; somebody says man is the rational animal, and somebody says something else. I say man is the celebrating animal. That is where he is different from all other animals.

But how can you celebrate if you are clinging to the old? Then you live in your grave because you live in the past, you live in the dead, and you don't allow life to reach you. It is as if a rosebush has become addicted to the old roses which are dead, dried up, and goes on collecting those petals that have fallen, and is afraid of new buds and new flowers, and is afraid of the spring.

This is the situation of millions of people, the majority of people: they remain clinging to the dead petals, dried; they go on collecting them. They live in their memories...they call it nostalgia; it is stupidity, nothing else.

A real man has no nostalgia at all. He never looks back because it is no longer there. He lives in the moment and remains open for the future. The present is his, and the present makes him capable of receiving the future. His doors are always open for the wind, for the rain, for the sun. He is an opening.

In the water blows the wind of the Gentle.

And this is the moment one becomes aware of God, not before it. First, you start balancing yourself in the center. Second, you start becoming aware of the witness, the soul. And third, you start becoming aware of the presence, some unknown mysterious presence, the wind of the Gentle.

And the fourth:
Wandering in heaven, one eats the
spirit-energy of the Receptive.

And the fourth phenomenon is: when you have started becoming aware of the presence of God, your duality, your fundamental polarity starts disappearing. Then you are neither man nor woman, neither yin nor yang. Then suddenly your man eats your woman, your woman eats your man. At this point, the Hindu concept of *ardhanarishwar* becomes significant. Then you are both and neither; you have transcended the duality of the positive and the negative.

Wandering in heaven...

... But this is possible only when you have known the gentle breeze, the subtle dance, the presence of God, and you have started wandering into the open sky. You are no more clinging to anything, you are no more crawling and creeping on the earth. You are not in your grave, you have opened your wings. You are on the wing in the sky, available to existence and all its challenges—no longer orthodox, no longer conventional, no longer conformist. You are a rebel. And only the rebellious spirit starts feeling the presence of God. This is heaven! —the presence of God.

Then the fourth miracle happens which crystallizes you absolutely: your duality disappears. Otherwise, deep down, you remain split. If you are a man you go on repressing your woman; you have to. The society teaches you, "Remember, you are a man." If you cry and weep, somebody is bound to comment, "What are you doing? It is okay for women to cry and weep, but you are a man. You are not expected to weep." And immediately your tears dry, you pull them back, you hold them back. You are a man, you are supposed to be a man, and you cannot cry.

If you cannot cry how are you going to laugh? Your laughter will be half-hearted, lukewarm, because you will be afraid that if you laugh too much you may be so relaxed that the tears that you are holding back may start flowing from your eyes.

Have you not watched this phenomenon? If somebody laughs too much, he starts crying. Why? Why do eyes become tearful when you laugh too much?—because laughter means you are allowing. And if you are allowing, you are allowing everything. You cannot allow one thing and prevent another thing; that is not possible. If you have to repress one thing you will have to repress *all* things. This is something very basic to be learned: repress one thing and your whole personality has to be repressed to the same extent. If you cannot weep, you cannot laugh. If you cannot laugh, you cannot weep. If you cannot be angry, you cannot have compassion. If you cannot be compassionate, you cannot be angry either. Life maintains a certain level: whatsoever you allow to one thing you will have to allow the same amount to other things in your life. You cannot do one thing: "I will hold my tears back but I will laugh whole-heartedly." This is impossible.

Man is taught to become more and more masculine. Small boys—we start changing their basic, fundamental balance and forcing them towards one polarity. The boy has to be forced to be a man, so a few things are not allowed to him. If he fights we say it is perfectly okay: he has to fight for his whole life. If he plays with guns and pistols and kills and reads detective novels, we say it is okay. But, to the girl we don't allow the gun. To the girl we say, "You play with dolls. Arrange marriages. Become a mother. Make a house. Cook food. Play things like that, because this is your life and this is going to be your life; prepare for it." We don't allow girls to climb on the trees, to hang on the branches upside-down. We don't allow it. We say, "You are a girl. This is not supposed to be done. This is not graceful for you."

Slowly, slowly we emphasize the polarity, one polarity, and the other polarity is repressed utterly; this is the basic schizophrenia. And everybody suffers from it because the society has not yet been able to accept your whole being. Moving towards reality you will have to accept your whole being. You are man/woman together, woman/man together. Nobody is just man and nobody is just woman. And this is beautiful that you are both, because that gives richness to your life, to your being. It gives you many colors. You are the whole spectrum, the whole rainbow. You are not a single color, all colors are yours.

At the fourth, when you start moving into the divine presence, all schizophrenia disappears—and there is no other way for the schizophrenia to disappear. Psychoanalysis is not going to help much. In fact, it goes on emphasizing your polarity. Psychology has yet to come to a point where it is not male-dominated, otherwise stupid things go on in the name of psychology.

Sigmund Freud says that women suffer from penis-envy. Utter nonsense! He never says that men suffer from breast-envy. This is male-oriented. In fact, women never suffer from any envy. On the contrary, man suffers very much because he cannot reproduce, he cannot create a child. Because he cannot create a child he moves into many other creativities as substitutes: he writes poetry, he paints, he sculpts, he makes architecture. These are substitute creations, because deep down he knows one thing: that he cannot produce life.

But Freud never talks about that; that would have been truer. He says *women* suffer from penis-envy. This is utter nonsense. Psychology is still carrying the same division between man and woman.

The human being is both, but this ultimate integration happens only at the fourth stage.

> *Wandering in heaven, one eats the*
> *spirit-energy of the Receptive.*

The receptive means the female. One eats one's opposite. And remember, eating means absorbing. That's why there are ancient sayings that each disciple has to become a cannibal— because he has to eat his Master. Don't take it literally. It is just a metaphor, but very significant, because eating means you absorb, you digest. The Master becomes part of you, is no more separate. That's what Jesus says at The Last Supper when he is taking leave of his disciples. He breaks bread and gives the bread to his disciples and says, "This is me. Eat it, this is my flesh"; pours wine and gives it to his disciples and says, "This is me. Drink it, this is my blood." Again this is a metaphor. He's saying to his disciples, "Become cannibals. Eat your Master, digest your Master, so there is no division between you and your Master."

The same is true about this fourth statement: you have to eat the other polarity in you. Lu-tsu must have been speaking to his male disciples, because down the ages it is the man who has been more adventurous, more in quest. The woman seems to be more settled, at home. So there must have been male disciples, he must have been talking to male disciples. That's why he says, "Eat your woman." But the same is true about women disciples: they have to eat their man. Inside, the other has to be absorbed so the duality disappears.

And once these four words have been fulfilled, then the greatest secret of all becomes available to you.

> *And the still deeper secret of the secrets:*
> *The land that is nowhere,*
> *that is the true home...*

And now, for the first time you will become aware that you are not, but your non-existence does not mean mere emptiness. The person in you disappears, but presence appears. Separation from existence in you disappears, but the whole starts abiding in you. You are no more an island. Now there is no way to locate where you are.

Hence,

> *The land that is nowhere,*
> *that is the true home...*

Now you cannot say where you are, who you are...and this is the true home.

This word 'nowhere' is really beautiful.

A great Indian mystic, Swami Ramateertha, used to say again and again that he had a friend who was a Supreme Court advocate, and he was utterly atheistic, continuously arguing against God. He was so atheistic that he had written on the walls in his drawing room in big letters, capital letters: God is nowhere—to provoke somebody. Whosoever would come to see him or visit him would first have to see 'God is nowhere'. And he was always ready to jump upon you if you said "God is."

Then his child was born, and the child started learning language; the child was just at the beginning. One day the child was sitting in the lap of the father and he started reading. Now 'nowhere' is a big word and the child could not read it, so he split it in two and he read: God is now-here. Nowhere can be split into two words: now, here. And the father was surprised, because he had written those words but he had never read it that way. The meaning was diametrically changed... God is now-here. He looked into the eyes of the child, those innocent eyes, and for the first time he felt something mysterious. For the first time he felt as if God had spoken through the child. His atheism, his lifelong atheism, disappeared because of the statement of the child. And Ramateertha says that when he died he was one of the most religious persons he had known in his life. But the change happened through the child, just by mistake—because the child could not read the word 'nowhere' together, as one word.

This word 'now-here', 'nowhere', is beautiful. When you know God is now-here, then you know God is nowhere;

both are the same. God is *not* somewhere, that is true, so you cannot say where He is. You cannot locate, you cannot pinpoint.

Nanak has said that to ask where God is, is utterly wrong; ask where He is not. And if He is everywhere, to say God is everywhere or to say God is nowhere means the same—because when He is everywhere, there is no point in saying where. He is.

The land that is nowhere is now-here.

Now is the only time, and here, the only space. And if you cannot find God now-here, you will not be able to find Him anywhere else. This moment, *this very moment...*

If three steps have been fulfilled and the fourth achieved, this will happen, this is the secret of the secrets: that God is not a person sitting somewhere. God will never be known as a person, has never been known as a person—and those people who have known God as a person were simply befooled by their own imaginations. If you see Christ, it is your imagination. You are creating it. If you see Krishna, it is your imagination. You can cultivate your imagination, you can practise it, but you are creating a dream, you are projecting a dream. It is your dream-mind functioning.

Truth is not a person and truth is not *there*, not outside. It is not found as an object, it is your witnessing subjectivity. And that is possible only when your man and woman have disappeared into one.

As the French say: There are three sexes—men, women, and clergymen. They say it jokingly but it has something significant in it. There *are* three sexes: men, women and the Buddhas.

The Buddha cannot be called a man or a woman. Although he has a certain body—it may be of man or woman—but a Buddha is no more identified with his body. He's just a pure witness. He's as away from his body as you are away from his body, as distant as you are distant from his body. You are standing there outside looking at his body, he's standing deep down inside looking at his body. But the distance from you to his body and from his body to himself is the same. He is no more identified with his body. You cannot call him a man or a woman; he is simply beyond.

And when this beyond has opened,

> The land that is nowhere,
> that is the true home...

You have come home.

> These verses are full of mystery. The meaning is: the
> most important things in the great Tao are the words:
> action through non-action.

Only when you have come home will you know the ultimate meaning of the words 'action through non-action'. But from the very beginning you have to keep moving in that direction; only then one day, the ultimate happens.

What is the meaning of action through non-action? It is very easy to be active, it is very easy to be inactive. There are people who are active, continuously active, restless, day in, day out. That's what has happened in the West: people have become super-active. They cannot sit in rest even for a single moment. Even sitting in their beautiful, comfortable chairs, they are fidgeting, they are changing their posture. They cannot be at rest. Their whole life is a turmoil; they need something to keep them occupied. They are driving themselves mad through activity.

In the East people have become very inactive, lazy. They are dying out of their laziness. They are poor because of their laziness. They go on condemning the whole world, as if they are poor because of the world, because of other people. They are poor because they are lazy, utterly lazy. They are poor because action has completely disappeared—how can they be productive? How can they be rich? And it is not that they are poor because they have been exploited; even if you distribute all the money that the rich people in India have, the poverty will not disappear. All those rich people will become poor, that is true, but no poor persons will become rich. Poverty is there, deep down, because of inaction. And it is very easy to choose one polarity: action is male, inaction is female.

Lu-tsu says, "One has to learn action through non-action." One has to learn this complex game. One has to do, but not become a doer. One has to do almost as if one is functioning as an instrument of God. One has to do and yet remain egoless. Act, respond, but don't become restless. When the action is complete, you have responded adequately, go into rest. Work when it is needed to work, play when it is needed to play. Rest, lie down on the beach, when you have worked and played. When you are lying down on the beach under the sun, don't think of work—don't think of the office, don't think of the files. Forget all about the world. Lying in the sun, lie in the sun. Enjoy it. This is possible only when you learn the secret of action through inaction. And then in the office, do whatsoever is needed. In the factory do whatsoever is needed, but even while you are doing remain a witness: deep down, in deep rest, utterly centered, the periphery moving like a wheel, but the center is the center of the cyclone. Nothing is moving at the center.

This man is the perfect man: his soul is at rest, his center is absolutely tranquil, his periphery in action, in doing a thousand and one things of the world. This is my concept of a sannyasin. That's why I say don't leave the world, remain in the world. Act in the world, do whatsoever is needful, and yet remain transcendental, aloof, detached, a lotus flower in the pond.

Non-action prevents a man from becoming entangled in form and image.

If you remember that your deepest core is in non-action you will not be deceived, you will not be entangled by form and image. That is materiality. You will not become worldly.

Action in non-action prevents a man from sinking into numbing emptiness and dead nothingness.

And the other danger is: you can regress into a kind of numbness, deadness, dullness, a negative kind of emptiness, nothingness. That too has to be avoided. Action in non-action will prevent this. Action will keep you positive, inaction will keep you negative. Action will keep you male, inaction will keep you female. If both are balanced then they cancel each other and the beyond opens, and suddenly you see Buddha arising in you.

Heretofore we have spoken of the circulation of the light, indicating thereby the initial release which works from without upon what lies within. This is to aid one in obtaining the Master.

The first two words: *In the sixth month white snow is suddenly seen to fly*, and the second: *At the third watch the sun's disk sends out blinding rays*—these are the lower steps; and the second two are the higher steps: *In the water blows the wind of the Gentle;* and the fourth: *Wandering in heaven, one eats the spirit-energy of the Receptive.*

The first two are the lower steps; they help you to find the Master. If you come across a Master you will recognize him only if these two steps have been taken before. Otherwise you can come across a Buddha and you can pass a Buddha without ever becoming aware of what you have missed. Someday, later in life, when you will have attained these two steps, then you will weep and cry and repent because then you will remember a Buddha had passed you on the Way. Then you will feel great guilt at how you could miss.

The first two help to find the Master. With the first two, you have to work from the without towards the within. The work is to start from without—because it is there where you are—and you have to start moving withinwards.

With the second two: you have found the Master, the Master has found you. Now the second two are to fulfill his commandments. The process is reversed: now the within starts working on the without. With the first two you were cultivating, practising, meditating. You were working, searching, groping in the dark. With the second two you have found the Master, you have heard his voice, you have seen his eyes, you have felt his heart. His presence has permeated your being. Trust has arisen. Now you simply follow, you simply fulfill his commandments—and in fulfilling those commandments is your fulfillment.

It is for pupils in the beginning stages. They go through the two lower transitions in order to gain the upper one. After the sequence of events is clear and the nature of the release is known, heaven no longer withholds the Way, but reveals the ultimate truth. Disciples, keep it secret and redouble your effort!

The first two will need great concentrated effort on your part. You will have to be consciously working, deliberately working. It is arduous. The first two steps are arduous because your eyes are closed, your heart is not beating. The second two steps are easy because now your eyes are open. You have recognized the Master, you have heard the message. Now things are clear. Now you can see. Even if the Himalayan peak is far away, you can see it. Maybe it is a thousand-mile journey yet, but you can see it. Even from far away you can see the sunlit peaks of the Himalayas, you know they are there. Now it is only a question of time. And now you know a guide is with you who has been coming down and up on those peaks again and again. Now you can listen and you can follow.

The first two steps are in great doubt: one has to struggle. Every possibility is there that one may go astray. Small things can lead people astray, very small things. When they will think later on, they will know the ridiculousness of them; very small things, of no meaning at all, but they can prevent you. The seeker has to be very alert. In the first two steps he has to be very cautious; only then can he fulfill the lower steps. The lower fulfilled, the higher becomes available.

...heaven no longer withholds the Way...

Through the Master, heaven starts opening the Way.

> ...*but reveals the ultimate truth. Disciples, keep it secret and redouble your effort!*
>
> *The circulation of the light is the inclusive term. The further the work advances, the more does the Golden Flower bloom. But there is a still more marvellous kind of circulation.*

Up to now we have talked about the circulation of the light that you do, that you have to manage, practise. But there is a still more marvellous kind of circulation that need not be practised, it happens of its own accord. It is a gift, it is a grace.

When you have fulfilled the first two steps, the Master arrives. When you have fulfilled the second two higher steps, God arrives.

And the fifth secret, the secret of the secrets is that now things start happening on their own. You need not do anything. In fact, if you do anything it will be a hindrance. Now everything is spontaneous on its own. Tao has taken possession of you—or call it God. You are possessed! You have disappeared utterly; now only God is in you. Just as He blooms in flowers and the trees, He will bloom in you in the Golden Flower. Now it is up to Him, now it is none of your concern. Now it is His will, your will has done its work.

In the first two steps, great will was needed. In the second two steps, a willing surrender was needed. And after the four steps are finished there is no need of will; there is no need of surrender either. Remember, surrender is also just to drop the will. In the first two steps you cultivate the will. In the second two steps you have to drop the will. That is surrender. And when will has been dropped by surrender, the ultimate secret of secrets is neither will nor surrender. Again, will is man, surrender is woman; with the fourth crossed, you have crossed

man and woman both. Will gone, surrender too, gone...
now you are not there, you are nowhere to be found. There
is nobody, nothingness, *nirvana*. And Tao now fulfills its
own work—just as spring comes and trees bloom and rains
come and clouds gather and morning comes and the sun rises,
and in the night the sky is full of stars—all goes on without any
effort anywhere. The sun is not making any effort to rise in the
morning, neither do the stars struggle to shine in the night,
nor do the flowers have to make great effort to bloom. You
have become part of the ultimate nature.

> *But there is still a more marvellous kind of circulation. Till
> now we have worked from the outside on what is within;
> now we stay in the center and rule what is eternal. Hitherto
> it was a service in aid of the Master; now it is a dissemination
> of the commands of the Master. The whole relationship is
> now reversed. If one wants to penetrate the more subtle regions
> by this method, one must first see to it that body and heart
> are completely controlled, that one is quite free and at peace,
> letting go of all entanglements, untroubled by the slightest
> excitement, and with the heavenly heart exactly in the
> middle. When the rotating light shines towards what is
> within, it does not develop a dependence on things, the
> energy of the dark is fixed, and the Golden Flower shines
> concentratedly. This is then the collected light of polarity.
> Related things attract each other. Thus the polarized
> light-line of the Abysmal presses upward.*

If you are divided in two, into man and woman, negative/
positive, darkness/light, mind/heart, thought/feeling—if you
are divided in two, your energy will be going downward.
Division is the way of the downward. When you are undivided,
one, you start moving upward. To be one is to move upward,

to be two is to move downward. Duality is the way to hell, non-duality is the way to heaven.

> *Thus the polarized light-line of the Abysmal presses upward. It is not only the light in the abyss, but it is creative light which meets creative light.*

And when this unity has happened within you, great creativity explodes. One never knows what potential one is carrying about. There may be a poet waiting, or a painter, or a singer, or a dancer. One never knows who is waiting inside you. When your man and woman will meet, your potential will be released; it will become actual. That's how the Upanishads were born, and the Koran, and the Bible, and Khajuraho, and Konarak, and the Taj Mahal, and Ajanta and Ellora. All this creativity is totally different from the so-called creativity that you know in the modern age. Picasso is a totally different kind of creator from the man who conceived the Taj Mahal.

The man who conceived the Taj Mahal—his polarity had disappeared. He was a Sufi mystic. It was his vision, it was out of deep meditation. Still if you meditate on the Taj Mahal on a full moon night you will be surprised: something deep inside you will start rising up, will start moving upwards. If you meditate deeply on the Taj Mahal for one hour on a full moon night, sitting there, just looking at it, something will become cool in you. Snow, coolness, freshness will appear within you. Or the statues of Buddha that were carved by the great Buddhist mystics—just meditating, looking at the statue something settles inside you.

Look at a Picasso painting and you feel it will drive you mad. If you go on looking at it for one hour, you will feel nausea. It is more like vomiting, not like creativity—as if Picasso is pouring his neurosis on the painting. Maybe it relieves him of his neurosis. That's what psychologists say too: many times it has been found that a madman was given color and canvas and was told to paint, and the moment he started painting his madness started disappearing. So now there are schools in psychoanalysis; they say: psychotherapy through painting, therapy through painting. Yes, it is possible; it releases. What has been going on inside you is poured onto the canvas, you are relieved.

It is just the same kind of relief that you feel when your stomach is disturbed, you are feeling sick, and you vomit. After vomiting you feel relieved, but what about the people who will look at the vomit? But who cares about them? And foolish people are always there: if you tell them that this is modern art—it may be just vomit—they will appreciate. They will say, "If critics are saying this is modern art, it must be."

I have heard...

There was an exhibition of a modern painter, and people were standing in front of a painting and appreciating greatly. Great critics had gathered and they were also applauding it. Then the painter came and he said, "Wait! The painting is hanging upside-down."

Nobody had seen that the painting was hanging upside-down. In fact, because it was hanging upside-down, it was looking more mysterious.

People are just stupid: in anything, they follow the fashion. This is not creativity. This is neurosis, or a neurotic kind of creativity.

There is another kind of creativity, what Gurdjieff used to call 'the objective art'.

When the inner polarity is no longer polar, when your inner divisions have disappeared and you have become one, then creativity is released. Then you do something that will be of immense help to humanity, because it will be coming out of your wholeness and out of your health. It will be a song of wholeness. It will be like the Song of Solomon—of immense beauty, of immense splendor.

Related things attract each other.

When you are one, God is attracted towards you—because the one is attracted towards the one...the flight of the alone to the alone. You start flying towards God and God starts flying towards you.

> *It is not only the light in the abyss, but it is creative light which meets creative light. As soon as these two substances meet each other, they unite inseparably, and there develops an unceasing life; it comes and goes, rises and falls of itself, in the house of the primal energy.*

And when your creativity is fully released the creativity of God descends in you, and there is a meeting between these two creators. Only a creator can meet the creator. Only the creator is worthy of meeting the creator. And when these two creativities, human and divine, meet...

Remember, there are two meetings. The first meeting is the meeting of the man and the woman within you; and the second, ultimate meeting is the meeting of you as a human being, total, whole, with the whole, the meeting of the human with the divine, the ultimate meeting. That is eternal. Once that has happened you are beyond death. It cannot be undone again.

One is aware of effulgence and infinity. The whole body
feels light and would like to fly. This is the state of which
it is said: Clouds fill the thousand mountains.

Now you are infinite like clouds filling the thousand mountains.

Gradually it goes to and fro quite softly: it rises and falls
imperceptibly. The pulse stands still and breathing stops.
This is the moment of true creative union, the state of which
it is said: The moon gathers up the ten thousand waters. In
the midst of this darkness, the heavenly heart suddenly begins
a movement. This is the return of the one light, the time
when the child comes to life.

And when it happens—this meeting of the creator within
you with the creator of the whole—when it happens, it happens
when you are so silent, so totally silent, so absent that the
pulse stands still and breathing stops.

This is the moment of true creative union, the state of which
it is said: The moon gathers up the ten thousand waters . . .

You know that when the moon is full, sea water starts rising
towards the moon, wants to go to the moon. Exactly like that,
man wants to reach to God. But unless you create this capacity
in you, this utter emptiness in you, you will rise a little and
you will fall again. But when you have become an absence—
an absence but not negative, an absence of utter positivity—
then the moon gathers up the ten thousand waters. Then you
rise and you go on rising, and the meeting with the moon! . . .

In the midst of this darkness, the heavenly heart suddenly
begins a movement.

And when your ordinary heart has stopped and your ordinary pulse has stopped, then for the first time you feel a totally different quality starting. You again breathe, but the breathing is no more the same. Your pulse again starts pulsating, but it is no more the same pulse. Now God lives in you. Now you are not there, only God is.

That's why we call Buddha 'Bhagwan': a moment came when God started living in him. The man disappeared. Then the man was just a hollow bamboo and the song of God started flowing through him. This is the ultimate goal.

Chapter Eight

September 3rd, 1978

I SURE DIG YOU, MAN

The first question:

What exactly is intelligence, and what is the relation of the intelligence of the heart to the intelligence of the mind?

Punita, intelligence is the inborn capacity to see, to perceive. Every child is born intelligent, then made stupid by the society. We educate him in stupidity. Sooner or later he graduates in stupidity.

Intelligence is a natural phenomenon—just as breathing is, just as seeing is. Intelligence is the inner seeing; it is intuitive. It has nothing to do with intellect, remember. Never confuse intellect with intelligence, they are polar opposites. Intellect is of the head; it is taught by others, it is imposed on you. You have to cultivate it. It is borrowed, it is something foreign; it is not inborn.

But intelligence is inborn. It is your very being, your very nature. All animals are intelligent. They are not intellectuals, true, but they are all intelligent. Trees are intelligent, the whole existence is intelligent, and each child born is born intelligent. Have you ever come across a child who is stupid? It is impossible! But to come across a grown-up person who is intelligent is very rare; something goes wrong in between.

I would like you to listen to this beautiful story. It may help. The story is called 'The Animal School'.

The animals got together in the forest one day and decided to start a school. There was a rabbit, a bird, a squirrel, a fish and an eel, and they formed a Board of Directors. The rabbit insisted that running be in the curriculum. The bird insisted that flying be in the curriculum. The fish insisted that swimming had to be in the curriculum, and the squirrel said that perpendicular tree-climbing was absolutely necessary to the curriculum. They put all of these things together and wrote a curriculum guide. Then they insisted that *all* of the animals take *all* of the subjects.

Although the rabbit was getting an A in running, perpendicular tree-climbing was a real problem for him. He kept falling over backwards. Pretty soon he got to be sort of brain-damaged and he could not run anymore. He found that instead of making an A in running he was making a C, and of course he always made an F in perpendicular climbing. The bird was really beautiful at flying, but when it came to burrowing in the ground he could not do so well. He kept breaking his beak and wings. Pretty soon he was making a C in flying as well as an F in burrowing, and he had a hell of a time with perpendicular tree-climbing.

The moral of the story is that the person who was valedictorian of the class was a mentally-retarded eel who did everything in a half-way fashion. But the educators were all happy because everybody was taking all of the subjects, and it was called a 'broad-based education'.

We laugh at this, but that's what it is. It is what *you* did. We really are trying to make everybody the same as everybody else, hence destroying everybody's potential for being himself.

Intelligence dies in imitating others. If you want to remain intelligent you will have to drop imitating. Intelligence commits suicide in copying, in becoming a carbon copy. The moment you start thinking how to be like that person you are falling from your intelligence, you are becoming stupid. The moment you compare yourself with somebody else you are losing your natural potential. Now you will never be happy, and you will never be clean, clear, transparent. You will lose your clarity, you will lose your vision. You will have borrowed eyes; but how can you see through somebody else's eyes? You need your own eyes, you need your own legs to walk, your own heart to beat.

People are living a borrowed life, hence their life is paralyzed. This paralysis makes them look very stupid.

A totally new kind of education is needed in the world. The person who is born to be a poet is proving himself stupid in mathematics and the person who could have been a great mathematician is just cramming history and feeling lost. Everything is topsy-turvy because education is not according to your nature. It does not pay any respect to the individual, it forces everybody into a certain pattern. Maybe by accident the pattern fits a few people but the majority is lost and the majority lives in misery.

The greatest misery in life is to feel oneself stupid, unworthy, unintelligent. And nobody is born unintelligent; nobody can be born unintelligent because we come from God. God is pure intelligence. We bring some flavor, some fragrance from God when we come into the world. But immediately the society jumps upon you, starts manipulating, teaching, changing, cutting, adding, and soon you have lost all shape, all form. The society wants you to be obedient, conformist, orthodox. This is how your intelligence is destroyed.

My whole approach is to take you out of this imposed pattern. This is a prison cell in which you are living. You can drop it. It will be difficult to drop because you have become so accustomed to it. It will be difficult to drop because it is not just like clothing; it has become almost your skin, you have lived with it so long. It will be difficult to drop because this is your whole identity—but it has to be dropped if you really want to claim your real being.

If you really want to be intelligent you have to be a rebel. Only the rebellious person is intelligent. What do I mean by rebellion?—I mean dropping all that has been enforced on you against your will. Search again for who you are, start from ABC again. Think that your time, up to now, has been a wastage because you have been following.

No person is similar to anybody else, each is unique—that is the nature of intelligence—and each is incomparable. Don't compare yourself to anybody. How can you compare? You are you and the other is other. You are not similar, so comparison is not possible.

But we have been taught to compare and we are continuously comparing. Directly, indirectly, consciously, unconsciously, we live in comparison. And if you compare you will never respect yourself: somebody is more beautiful than you, somebody is taller than you, somebody is healthier than you, and somebody is something else; somebody has such a musical voice...and you will be burdened and burdened if you go on comparing. Millions of people are there; you will be crushed by your comparisons.

And you had a beautiful soul, a beautiful being which wanted to bloom, which wanted to become a Golden Flower, but you never allowed it. Be unburdened. Put all aside. Regain, reclaim your innocence, your childhood. Jesus is right when he says, "Unless you are born again, you shall not enter into my kingdom of God."

I say the same to you: Unless you are born *again*....

Let your sannyas be a new birth! Drop all the garbage that has been put on you! Be fresh! Start from the *very* beginning, and you will be surprised—how much intelligence is immediately released.

Punita, you ask, "What exactly is intelligence?"

It is capacity to see, capacity to understand, capacity to live your own life according to your own nature. That is what intelligence is.

And what is stupidity? Following others, imitating others, obeying others, looking through their eyes, trying to imbibe their knowledge as your knowledge: that is stupidity.

That's why pundits are almost always stupid people. They are parrots, they repeat. They are gramophone records. They can repeat skillfully, but let a new situation arise, that which is not written in their books, and they are at a loss. They don't have any intelligence.

Intelligence is the capacity to respond moment-to-moment to life as it happens, not according to a program. Only unintelligent people have a program. They are afraid; they know that they don't have enough intelligence to encounter life as it is. They have to be ready, they rehearse. They prepare the answer before the question has been raised, and that's how they prove themselves stupid—because the question is never the same. The question is always new. Each day brings its own problems, its own challenges and each moment brings its own questions. And if you have ready-made answers in your head you will not be able even to listen to the question. You will be so full of your answer, you will be incapable of listening. You will not be available. And whatsoever you will do you will do according to your ready-made answer—which is irrelevant, which has no relationship with the reality as it is.

Intelligence is: to relate with reality, unprepared. And the beauty of facing life unprepared is tremendous. Then life has a newness, a youth; then life has a flow and freshness. Then life has so many surprises. And when life has so many surprises boredom never settles in you.

The stupid person is always bored. He is bored because of the answers that he has gathered from others and goes on repeating. He is bored because his eyes are so full of knowledge, he cannot see what is happening. He knows too much without knowing at all. He is not wise, he is only knowledgeable. When he looks at a roseflower, he does not look at *this* roseflower. All the roseflowers that he has read about, all the roseflowers that the poets have talked about, all the roseflowers that painters have painted and philosophers have discussed, and all the roseflowers that he had heard about, they are standing in his eyes—a great queue of memories, information. *This* roseflower that is there is lost in that queue, in that crowd. He

THE SECRET OF SECRETS 252

cannot see it. He simply repeats; he says, "This roseflower is beautiful." Those words are also not his own, not authentic, not sincere, not true. Somebody else's voice...he is just playing a tape.

Stupidity is repetition, repeating others. It is cheap, cheap because you need not learn. Learning is arduous. It needs guts to learn. Learning means one has to be humble. Learning means one has to be ready to drop the old, one has to be constantly ready to accept the new. Learning means a non-egoistic state.

And one never knows where learning will lead you. One cannot predict about the learner; his life will remain unpredictable. He himself cannot predict what is going to happen tomorrow, where he will be tomorrow. He moves in a state of no-knowledge. Only when you live in a state of no-knowledge, a *constant* state of no-knowledge, do you learn.

That's why children learn beautifully. As they grow old they stop learning, because knowledge gathers and it is cheap to repeat it. Why bother? It is cheap, simple, to follow the pattern, to move in a circle. But then boredom settles. Stupidity and boredom go together.

The intelligent person is as fresh as dewdrops in the morning sun, as fresh as the stars in the night. You can feel his newness, so new, like a breeze.

Intelligence is the capacity to be reborn again and again. To die to the past is intelligence, and to live in the present is intelligence.

And, Punita, you also ask, "What is the relationship of intelligence of the heart to the intelligence of the mind?"

They are diametrically opposite. The intelligence of the head is not intelligence at all; it is knowledgeability. The intelligence of the heart is the intelligence, the only intelligence there is. The head is simply an accumulator. It is always old, it is never new, it is never original. It is good for certain purposes: for filing it is perfectly good. And in life one needs this—many things have to be remembered. The mind, the head, is a bio-computer. You can go on accumulating knowledge in it and whenever you need you can take it out. It is good for mathematics, good for calculation, good for the day-to-day life, the marketplace; but if you think this is your whole life then you will remain stupid. You will never know the beauty of feeling and you will never know the blessing of the heart. And you will never know the grace that descends only through the heart, the God that enters only through the heart. You will never know prayer, you will never know poetry, you will never know love.

The intelligence of the heart creates poetry in your life, gives dance to your steps, makes your life a joy, a celebration, a festivity, a laughter. It gives you a sense of humor. It makes you capable of love, of sharing. That is true life. The life that is lived from the head is a mechanical life. You become a robot—maybe very efficient; robots are very efficient, machines are more efficient than man. You can earn much through the head, but you will not live much. You may have a better standard of living but you won't have any life.

Life is of the heart. Life can only grow through the heart. It is the soil of the heart where love grows, life grows, God grows. All that is beautiful, all that is really valuable, all that is meaningful, significant, comes through the heart. The heart is your very center, the head is just your periphery. To live in the head is to live on the circumference without ever becoming aware of the beauties and the treasures of the center. To live on the periphery is stupidity.

You ask, "What is stupidity?"

To live in the head is stupidity. To live in the heart and *use* the head whenever needed is intelligence. But the center, the Master, is at the very core of your being. The Master is the heart, and the head is just a servant: this is intelligence. When the head becomes the Master and forgets all about the heart, that is stupidity.

It is up to you to choose. Remember, the head as a slave is a beautiful slave, of much utility, but as a master is a dangerous master and will destroy your whole life, will poison your whole life. Look around! People's lives are absolutely poisoned, poisoned by the head. They cannot feel, they are no more sensitive, nothing thrills them. The sun rises but nothing rises in them; they look at the sun empty-eyed. The sky becomes full of the stars—the marvel, the mystery!—but nothing stirs in their hearts, no song arises. Birds sing, man has forgotten to sing. Clouds come in the sky and the peacocks dance, and man does not know how to dance. He has become a cripple. Trees bloom.... Man thinks, never feels, and without feeling there is no flowering possible.

The Golden Flower that we have been talking about this whole month is there in you, waiting—waiting for centuries, for lives. When are you going to give attention to it so that it can bloom? And unless a man becomes a Golden Flower— what the yogis have called the 'one-thousand-petalled lotus', *sahasrar*—unless your life becomes an opening, one thousand petals open and the fragrance is released, you will have lived in vain, "a tale told by an idiot, full of fury and noise, signifying nothing".

Watch, scrutinize, observe, have another look at your life. Nobody else is going to help you. You have depended on others so long; that's why you have become stupid. Now, take care; it is your own responsibility. You *owe* it to yourself to have a deep penetrating look at what you are doing with your life. Is there any poetry in your heart? If it is not there, then don't waste time. Help your heart to weave and spin poetry. Is there any romance in your life or not? If there is not, then you are dead, then you are already in your grave.

Come *out* of it! Let life have something of the romantic in it, something like adventure. Explore! Millions of beauties and splendors are waiting for you. You go on moving around and around, never entering into the temple of life. The door is the heart.

So I say: the real intelligence is of the heart. It is not intellectual, it is emotional. It is not like thinking, it is like feeling. It is not logic, it is love.

The second question:

What is it in the make-up of someone like Eva Renzi that makes her tell such outrageous lies about a community like ours?

I feel sorry for Eva Renzi. She was really in great need. She has missed an opportunity. She must be suffering from a split personality. She is not one, she is two. She is schizophrenic. That's why she had come in search, to find some clarity, some integration.

She has been in psychotherapy, she has been psychoanalyzed, but the psychoanalysis has not been of much help. That's why her husband suggested that she come here. The husband also has not been able to live with her, they are separated.

And just the other day I was reading a statement by one of the directors—she is a film actress—and the director remembers that ten or twelve years ago he was directing a film and she was the heroine in the film. They had booked a beautiful castle somewhere in Germany for only one day. And the whole crew waited and all the actors waited, and Eva Renzi never turned up! Almost in tears, everybody left. And in the evening she turned up, laughing, smiling. And the director says he became so crazy that he hit her with a chair! And then he felt bad too. He had a heart attack; for three, four months he had to rest. He says that anybody who can live for one hour with Eva Renzi will hit her!

Now the poor woman must have been in deep suffering. She is crazy! She would have been immensely helped if she had been a little patient, if she had been here a little longer.

But these patterns go very deep. These patterns go so deep that it is almost impossible to help such people.

She was in one group, Centering; she created trouble there —and she was creating so much trouble that the whole group was disturbed. And you cannot allow one hundred and twenty-five people to be disturbed for one person. So Prasad, the group leader, had to tell her that if she was so angry, in a rage, so much in violence, that it would be better that she should participate in the Encounter group where she could release her anger, her rage, cathart, but the Centering group was not for her.

She immediately left and entered into the Encounter group, and within hours she was gone—because there also she created much trouble, provoked everybody to fight. The Encounter group is meant for release, and when people started fighting with her she left the group.

Now the other personality must have taken possession of her. She did not report to the police here in Poona. If there had been something wrong with her she should have gone to the police. She went to police in Bombay and reported that she had been beaten—so much so that the room was full of blood—her clothes had been torn apart and she had to go out of the ashram naked to the hotel! Now, do you think a beautiful woman like Eva Renzi walking naked on the Poona streets would have survived? Nobody remembers a naked woman in the 'Blue Diamond', bleeding and going there; nobody had seen her. There are thousands of people here the whole day: nobody had seen her going and leaving, naked, bleeding, shouting, crying; nobody had seen her. She reported to the police in Bombay, not here. And the police came and searched and found the whole thing was a lie.

But I don't think that she is lying; it is her other personality, her other self. The other person had taken possession of her, not that she was lying knowingly. When the other person takes possession, it becomes impossible—you don't know what you are saying, why you are saying it.

The people who are split function almost like two persons. When they are in one personality they are one person, when they are in another personality they are a different person, and both personalities never meet.

Now she has created much fuss in Germany, in the newspapers, but I feel real compassion for her. I invite her again. I have not seen her. All this just happened within a day, I have not seen her. I would like to see her and help her; she needs help. And she has gone so deeply into this schizophrenia that I don't think she can be helped anywhere else. If she comes back it will be good: those two personalities can be welded again. But it will need patience. If she had come with her husband or some friends it would have been better. They would have prevented her from escaping so soon.

A little time will be needed. A lifelong pattern can't be changed in one day. And the schizophrenics have their own ideas about things. They are so full of their own madness that they think everybody else is mad. Their projections are such, they feel that they are being persecuted, everybody is going to murder them or kill them.

Once it happened: I had to live in the same room with a professor for a few months. He was a schizophrenic. When he was good he was utterly good, a really nice fellow, but when he was bad he was really bad. And it was very difficult to know when he was going to be good, when he was going to be bad. In the middle of the night he would start shouting or would start provoking me to fight with him. If you didn't fight, you didn't honor him. If you didn't start fighting, then he would be angry. If you fought him you unnecessarily got into trouble with him. And then the neighbors would come, and he would shout and he would make such fuss. And by the morning he would have forgotten everything! If you reminded him he would say, "No, you must have dreamt it." If you called the neighbors he would say, "They must have been dreaming, because I have slept so well the whole night." It was so difficult. I would go to the university to teach; when I would come home all my things would be gone!

He had two personalities. The other personality was really something! He would store everything in his suitcases and lock them. When he was good he would be very generous, he would give his things to me. I enjoyed living with him for a few months because it was such a surprise—you never knew what was going to happen today. And when he was in his bad personality, in the neurotic, he was so afraid, that *anything*... and he would think the murderer was coming or the police were coming to catch hold of him. And he would imagine: just a jeep passing by in the middle of the night—he would wake me up. He would say, "Look, the police are reaching, the jeep has come. Now I will be caught. And I tell you that I am innocent! And I have not done anything wrong—you are my witness!" Just the whistle of the police in the night and he would be alerted.

These people are in deep suffering. They have their own ideas, and they are so clouded in their ideas that they don't see the reality.

Now I don't think she is aware at all of what she is saying, of what she is reporting to the newspapers. She says one man, an old man, a Dutchman—he is none other than the famous author, Amrito—tried to rape her. Now he will be the last man to think of rape; she is just like a daughter to him. And such a nice, loving person. But somehow she had got the idea that there was an old Dutchman in the Encounter group who wanted to rape her. Now she is going around telling people, the newspapers. But the idea had got into her, and newspapers are always ready to exploit anything.

A man came home to find his wife having a nervous break-down, screaming and banging her head on the wall.
"What is the matter, darling?" said the worried husband.
"I am homesick!" sobbed the distraught woman.

"But you are at home, darling," said the husband.
"Exactly!" said the wife, "I am sick of home!"

When you have your ideas, your own interpretations, things start appearing like that. And you can always find explanations, excuses; you can always find arguments. And remember, neurotic people are very argumentative because they are hung-up in the head.

So don't feel angry with Eva Renzi, not at all. And don't be worried about what is happening in Germany. It is going to help my work tremendously! I know my business and how to do it; don't be worried about it.

Now it is all over Germany. *Everybody* knows my name— this is something great—and everybody is asking about me, "Who is this man?" Sannyasins who have come from Germany just a few days ago report that even taxi-drivers ask, "Are you going to Poona? I am also thinking of going! What is happening there?"

Now many people will be coming because of Eva Renzi. And remember, there is always a balance, otherwise life would collapse. Her negative statements started creating positive statements. That's how it always happens. That's what I mean when I say I know my business. Now this director has come to defend me. He does not know me, but he says that if it has happened to Eva Renzi it is perfectly good; she needed it, she deserved it! He says all the people who knew her will be happy—particularly her husband. Now more and more positive statements will be coming.

Just create the negative and the positive starts coming. Create the positive and the negative starts coming. They always balance, otherwise life would collapse. So never be worried about negative things; it is always like that.

Do you know who created Christianity?—not Christ, but the people who crucified him. If they had not crucified him there would have been no Christianity, you would never have even heard of Jesus. It is the people who crucified him. Now crucifixion is such a negativity that the positive is bound to happen. Now somebody is bound to start worshipping; then the balance. Life always balances.

So the poor woman is in suffering but it is good for my work. Nothing is wrong in it. Those lies that she is telling will be refuted from many unknown quarters. People will come up on their own, and many people will come just out of curiosity. Many more lies will follow, and many more truths to balance them. Now, because she started the thing, many newspapers have come to Poona. Since she started the ball rolling, many newspapers, many journalists have come. A few have written against, a few have written for.

One journalist seems to be really very inventive. He writes that he reached to the ashram-gate door at five thirty, early in the morning. He knocked on the door. A great beauty, a blonde, opened the door—at five thirty!—and welcomed him with an apple, or something like an apple. He said, "I don't know what fruit it was. She gave the fruit to me and she said, 'You are welcome in the Garden of the Master. Come in!' And I asked, 'What is this apple?' and she said, 'You eat it. It will give you sexual energy.'"

Now the taxi-drivers are asking, "Are there such types of fruits in the garden? We would like to come." Who would not like to come!

Let these people work. They are helping my work; nothing to be worried about. I always rejoice!

The third question:

What is your message, Bhagwan? I don't understand you.

My message is that there is no message. I am not here to give you a message, because a message will become knowledge. I am here to impart something of my being. It is not a message, it is a gift. It is not a theory, it is not a philosophy. I want you to partake of my being. It cannot be reduced into a dogma. You cannot go back and tell people what you have learned here; you will not be able to. If you have learned anything you will not be able to relate it to anybody, although your whole being will show it. You will not be able to say it but only to show it. Your eyes will show it, your face will beam, your whole energy will have a different vibe.

I am not functioning here as a teacher. This is not a school. I don't teach you a thing. I simply want you to participate with me, in this mystery that has happened to me. Fall in tune with my energy, vibrate with me, pulsate with me—and you will know something which is beyond words, which no message can contain.

Once the great Master Joshu was asked for his word.
Joshu said, "There is not even half a word."
When he was asked further, "Master, but are you not here?" he said, "I am not a word."

He is right. A Master is not a word, a Master is a door. A Master is not a message but a medium. A Master is a link, a bridge. Pass through the door, pass through the bridge, and you will come to know exactly what life is all about. If you can dive deep into the Master you will start feeling the presence of God— but it is not a message.

And you say you don't understand me. I know why you can't understand me: because whatsoever I am saying is so simple, that is why. Had it been complex you would have understood it. You are accustomed to complexity: the more complex a thing is, the more your intellect starts working on it. The challenge to the ego...

My communion with you is so simple, so utterly simple that there is no challenge for the ego; that is the reason why you can't understand me. What I say is simple and absolutely clear. I don't use any jargon. I am simply using the language that you use in your day-to-day work, in your day-to-day life. Maybe that is the reason for your not understanding me. The obvious is what I say and teach—yes, the obvious—but the obvious sounds bizarre because you have become so accustomed to the complexities that the mad mind goes on spinning and weaving around you.

And moreover, always keep in mind that what I say is said for no particular reason. There is no motive behind it. Just as they say 'art for art's sake', what I am saying to you has no particular reason behind it, no motive, but a sheer joy of being together with you, a sheer response to your questions. Not that my answers will solve your questions; no, not at all. If my answers can solve your questions, then it becomes a message. My answers will only help you to understand your questions— and when a question is understood, it dissolves. No question is ever solved. If you understand a question rightly it dissolves, it is not solved. It becomes insignificant, trivial and false, like a dry leaf from the tree. It loses all meaning. I am not going to give you answers, I am going to take away your questions.

And when the mind has no question to ask, in that utter silence where no question is present, you come to know that which is—call it God, call it Tao, truth, *nirvana*, or what you will.

That's why I say there is no particular reason in my saying whatsoever I say to you. There is no particular motive behind it, it is a simple response to your being. I am only being a mirror, hence there is no particular need to understand me. Don't try to understand me. There is nothing to understand. Just be with me and understanding will come on its own. And these are two different types of understandings.

When you try to understand me you will miss, because while I am imparting something to you, you are engaged and occupied in understanding it. You will miss it. Don't try to understand it, just listen! Just as I am talking to you without any motive, listen on your part without any motive—and the meeting is bound to happen. When I am without motive and you are without motive, what can hinder, what can obstruct the meeting? Then the meeting is going to happen. And in that communion is understanding; in that communion is light, clarity, transparency.

So rather than trying to understand me, celebrate me, rejoice in me—and you will understand, and without any effort to understand.

Nobody ever understands through effort. What effort do you make when you listen to music? Do you try to understand it? If you try to understand it, you will miss the whole joy of it. The music has to be rejoiced in. Do you try to understand a dance?

Then you will miss it. The dance has to be celebrated. Do you try to understand the roseflowers and the songs of the birds in the morning? There is no need! Just be with the roseflower, just see the bird on the wing. Don't let anything hinder, and suddenly, understanding arises. That understanding arises from the heart, from your intelligence. It is not of the head.

And then the understanding has a totally different flavor, a totally different fragrance to it. Then it has beauty—because it comes out of effortlessness, it comes out of love. If you try to understand me, logic will be there, mind will be there. If you don't try to understand me, if you just listen for the sake of listening, then slowly, slowly something starts opening in you, arising in you, awakening in you.

Let me be a provocation, not a message. Let me be an alarm to wake you up, not a message. If you think in terms of a message you will create a wall between me and you. Just be here. Just as I am with you, you be with me—for no particular reason, just for the sheer joy of this silence, this presence that surrounds me and you, that joins me and you, this meditativeness, this grace, this moment of sheer beauty and benediction.

And your heart will understand. Whether your mind understands or not is of no significance.

The fifth question:

Morarji Desai says that students should not take part in politics. What do you say about it?

Remember always: whatsoever the politicians say, it is always politics. Whenever a politician reaches to power he always starts telling the students not to participate in politics—but only when he is in power. When he is not in power he is all in favor—students *should* participate in politics.

How has Morarji reached to power? Basically, it was a students' movement in Gujarat and Bihar; on that tidal wave of the youth movement he has reached to power. Now he must be afraid; now if students continue to participate in politics he can be toppled.

This is something beautiful to be understood: whenever politicians are out of power they provoke the students. The same politicians, when they reach to power, they start telling the students, "Please, this is not your work. You should go to the colleges, to the universities. Politics has to be avoided. Don't be distracted by politics!" Because that is the bridge, that bridge has to be broken. Otherwise others will be coming. And students cannot be befooled so easily as others can be befooled. Youth cannot be befooled as easily as others can be befooled because youth is still not involved in the vested interests of the society. The older you grow the more your investment is in the status quo; you cannot go against it. You are married, you have children, you have a job, you have to look after the family, and there are a thousand and one responsibilities on you. You would like everything to remain as it is, you will be afraid of any change. Who knows?—your job is lost, and what is going to happen to your children?

Students prove to be the most revolutionary part of the society for the simple reason that they have no investment; for the simple reason that they can ask for, demand, change. And of course they are young; their eyes can still see a little bit. They can still feel. And of course they are going to live in the future. The past is not their world, but the future. The older you grow the less future you have and the more past. A man of seventy has very little future and a very long past. And the man who is only twenty has very little past and a long future; his orientation is the future. And whenever the future is the orientation there is rebellion, revolution.

And the people who are in power are always afraid of any kind of rebellion, of any kind of revolution.

So remember, when politicians say, "Participate in politics," then too it is politics. When they say, "Don't participate in politics," then too it is politics. They always speak politics, whatsoever they say. Even in their sleep, if they start saying something, it is politics—don't believe them! Even in their dreams they remain politicians.

But they are cunning people, shrewd people: whenever there is a revolution, whenever there is some change, some movement, and the youth is stirred, the shrewd politicians simply ride on the wave.

Now this revolution that happened just one and a half years ago was created by the youth, and the power went into the hands of the very rotten old. This is strange—that the stir was of the youth but the people who came into power are all above seventy, and a few are even above eighty. One sometimes wonders why dead people can't get out of their graves and become prime ministers and presidents...they will prove to be even better!

I was reading a story:

Three old friends met for lunch one day. Well advanced in years, they met periodically to keep up to date on each other. The youngest of the three told his news first. His wife had just given him a baby girl—and he was almost seventy-nine years old!

The second man spoke. He was eighty-three years of age and his wife had just had a son. The two fathers were proud as peacocks.

Then the third man offered some food for thought. "My friends," he said, "let me tell you a story. I am eighty-eight. Used to hunt a lot, but I am too old for that nonsense now. But last week I was strolling in the park and a cottontail came bounding out of the bushes. True to an old instinct, I raised my walking cane to shooting position, cried, 'Bang! Bang!' and the rabbit rolled over dead!

"A few minutes later I spied another cottontail. Again I simulated a rifle with my cane and cried 'Bang!' Again the rabbit dropped dead!

"What necromancy, what strange spell is this? I wondered aloud. Then, gentlemen, I glanced behind—ten paces to the rear was a young boy shooting with a real rifle!"

Morarji Desai should ponder over it: your 'bang! bang!' has not done anything; just the youth of the country have been shooting behind you.

But now, naturally, once you have reached to power you become afraid.

But you ask me, "What do you say about it?"

I also say to you to avoid politics, don't take part in politics—not for the same reason, of course. First, I am not a politician. Second, I am not in power. I have nothing to be afraid of in your taking part in politics. So, the reason why Morarji Desai —says, "Don't participate in politics," is something else. The reason why I say to you, "Don't participate in politics," is totally different. The reason is: leave politics for the stupid people, the utterly stupid who cannot do anything else. First try to be a scientist, a poet, a painter, an architect, a musician, a novelist, a potter, a weaver, a carpenter—something intelligent, something creative. If you find that you cannot create anything; when you have looked around and tried everywhere, and everywhere you get 'F', then go into politics—that is the last resort of the stupid and the scoundrels—never before. First try; there are beautiful experiences in life. Politics is destructive. It is the most ugly phenomenon. Leave it to others who cannot do anything else. And remember, if you don't leave it to others who cannot do anything else, those others will become criminals.

The criminal and the politician are the same type of people. If the criminal becomes politically successful he is a great leader. If the politician cannot succeed in being in power he becomes a criminal. They are destructive people: their whole effort is to dominate others.

The really creative person is not interested in dominating anybody. He is so utterly rejoicing in life—he wants to create, he wants to participate with God. Creativity is prayer. And whenever you create something, in those moments you are with God, you walk with God, you live in God. The more creative you are the more divine you are. To me, creativity is religion. Art is just the entrance to the temple of religion.

Create something! When you fail everywhere, then politics. It is not for the intelligent people, it is for the utterly unintelligent and stupid. And of course, they also need somewhere, some place to do some nonsense of their own. They need parliaments to quarrel in and go mad. Leave it to them!

I also say to students: Don't participate in politics unless you have failed everywhere else. First try other dimensions of life, far richer. But my reason is totally different.

And if you become interested in politics too early you will remain retarded for your whole life. When are you going to read Kalidas and Shakespeare and Milton and Tennyson and Eliot and Pound? When are you going to see the great painters, learn their art? When are you going to meditate in Khajuraho, Konarak? When are you going to dream great dreams of creating a Taj Mahal or a painting or poetry? When? There is great literature, great painting, great poetry. Watch your steps.

Politics seems to be attractive for only one single reason, and that has to be understood.

The English word 'self-consciousness' has to be understood; that will help you. It has two meanings. One is the meaning which Buddha preaches and Gurdjieff preaches and I preach: it means to become conscious of yourself, become alert. Gurdjieff used the word 'self-remembering', and Buddha uses the words *sama smrati*, mindfulness, consciousness. Krishna-murti uses the word 'awareness'—become fully alert and aware. This is the one meaning of the word 'self-conscious'. The word is very ambiguous.

The other meaning is when you stand on a stage and you become self-conscious, and you start trembling. The other meaning is pathological. The first meaning means you are conscious of yourself—you are not a robot, you function out of awareness. The second means that you are aware that *others* are conscious of you, that others are watching you, that you are an object of others' consciousness—and you become afraid. So many people watching...if something goes wrong ...and they will laugh and they will think you are a fool or ridiculous—and you become afraid. Others are watching you; you are an object. You become conscious of this phenomenon—conscious that others are conscious of you—then fear arises. But joy too arises—"So many people watching me"—so you repress your fear. You stand there on the stage without trembling: "So many people watching me..." The fear is: if something goes wrong they will think you are a fool. The joy is: "If nothing goes wrong, and I can perform well, then so many people will think, 'Look! What a great man! What a great artist, actor, speaker, orator!' If I can succeed in performing something, so many people will look towards me, upwards at me, and will enhance my ego."

The politician lives in this. He wants many people to look up to him so his ego is enhanced. He is afraid of going within because he knows there is nothing, emptiness. He does not know who he is. He collects his information about himself from others' eyes, from what they say. If they say "You are a great man" he believes he is a great man. He rides on the winds. If they say "You are a mahatma" he feels greatly happy, his ego is fulfilled. He is attaining a kind of identity—now he knows who he is. But this is not true self-knowledge; others can take it away any moment. And they always take, because sooner or later they can see that you have not fulfilled your promises, that your performance has been bogus.

You can see Morarji Desai's great ego eroding by and by. You can see the same with Jimmy Carter—the smile becoming smaller and smaller, disappearing—because you cannot fulfill the promises that you have made to the people. And you always make big promises. Without making big promises you will not reach to power, so you give fantastic promises that you know you cannot fulfill—but who cares! Once you are in power, then we will see. Then we will see how they can take you out of power; you will cling, and you will have all the powers to cling and the whole bureaucracy and the whole government machinery will be with you. Once you are in power who cares about the promises? The leaders forget all about their promises. And don't remind them! They feel very hurt and very annoyed.

But people start seeing that the promises are not being fulfilled: "These people have cheated us!" The image starts falling, the person becomes smaller. That hurts.

The politician is continuously in search of enhancing his ego. He needs others' attention. Millions of people have to feed his ego. The artist, the mystic, the musician, the dancer—if they are also asking for others' attention, then they are politicians. Then they are not real artists, not real mystics.

The real mystic, the real artist, is one who knows the other meaning of self-consciousness: he is simply conscious of himself. He does not need anybody else's attention, he is enough unto himself. He can be silently sitting and enjoying himself; he does not need anybody. His life is of awareness, he moves with awareness, his each step is full of light. Hence he never repents, he never feels guilty. Whatsoever he does, he does with full awareness. All that he can do he does, and whatsoever happens he accepts—because that is the only thing that could have happened. He never looks back. He moves ahead and he lives in the present, but he lives in a very conscious way.

Self-consciousness in the meaning Buddha gives the word makes you a creator, and self-consciousness the way a politician needs it makes you just an egoist.

I say to you: Don't participate in politics because that is searching for the ego. And to search for the ego is to search for something poisonous that will destroy your whole life. The politician is the poorest man in the world, the most empty man, the most hollow, stuffed with straw and nothing else.

The last question:

When can a therapy be called 'finished'?

Therapy is the need of the divided person. Therapy is the need of the person who has fallen into fragments. Therapy is complete when you have become a whole, when you are one piece.

But no therapy, as it is known in the modern world, brings you to wholeness. Therapy is, at the most, nothing but a rearrangement—maybe a little better than before, but you remain fragmentary. It is the same furniture rearranged in the same room—maybe a little bit more conveniently—but it doesn't make you whole, because when a person becomes whole his life becomes prayer.

Prayer is the by-product of wholeness. Wholeness makes you holy. Unless your therapy brings prayer to your heart it is not complete yet. The basic need is that of prayer.

Jung is reported to have said—and his observation is absolutely right—that one half of his patients were in need not of therapy but of religion. He is also reported to have said—and again he is right—that all the patients that went to him who were above forty-two didn't need therapy, but needed prayer.

The real need is to have a context in this infinite existence.

The ego makes you separate; prayer dissolves the ego and you become one with existence again. To become one with existence is to attain to bliss. To remain separate, there is conflict. To remain separate means you are fighting with existence, you are not flowing with the river. You may even be trying to go upstream—and going upstream you are going to be frustrated, you are going to fail. Flowing with the river—so much so that you become one with the river, just a part of the river, you don't have any will of your own, you are surrendered to the will of the total—this is prayer. And a therapy is complete, finished, when prayer is born in your heart.

But the prayer has to be true. It should not be a formality, it should not be a repetition, parrot-like. It should arise, it should have roots in your being.

Anutosh has sent me a beautiful joke. Meditate over it.

Every day for six months the kneeling figure, hands clasped in prayer, had intoned the same pitiful story in the shadow of the back pews in his local Catholic church.

"Oh Lord, sure I am only a poor simple fellow. Not even the price of a glass of wine do I have for after mass on Sunday, and I know I am a terribly wicked fellow. I give the missus a clout now and then, and when the kids get too much I have to rebuke them with the back of my hand.

"But I am not asking for much, just a couple of quid in the old wage packet—not for myself, mind, just for the house-keeping to keep the old lady off my back and some sweets for the kids. Maybe the odd drink for me. I would not abuse it though, Lord. Can you help me? It would make an awful lot of difference, and I will ask for nothing more, to be sure. God bless, Hail Mary, Amen!"

Suddenly the door of the church burst open and a smartly dressed West Indian swaggered down the aisle and took a defiant stance in front of the altar, and raising his fist shouted, "Hey dere, Lord. Now you listen here! I dun just got to dis country. I dun got nuttin, and dey ain't about to give me no credit, so I dun come to you. I needs a li'l sugar-mama first. I dun need furs and jewels to dress her in, I needs a big car to drive her in, and I needs money to spend. So I want a big win on de horses and den a good investment, and I needs it double quick. So quit messing around and just get at it. I know you'se can do it Lord, I just knows. . . ." ·

Turning and striding out, he added, "I sure dig you man, I sure dig you."

Some weeks later the kneeling Catholic is still there, mumbling into his hands, when suddenly the doors burst open and the same West Indian, arms around a gorgeous girl, bops straight down to the altar and grinning from ear to ear, laughs, "I knews you could do it, Lord! I done got a Rolls Royce. I owns de racecourse now. Talk about winning hard, I got my pants full of money here. Say 'thank you' to the Lord, honey."

"Thank you, Lord," said the little honey.

As they walked out he said, "And Lord, any time you want a favour you just come to me, 'cause I just dig you, man!"

Shocked and angry, the little Irishman watched them go, then rushed to the altar and prostrated himself, sobbing. "What have I done that you don't hear my suffering and anguish? How come you don't answer my prayers? I have been asking for months. I don't ask much—he is a foreigner too, and the color of the devil himself! How come you give to him and not so much as answer me? Ah, Holy Mary, have pity and tell me what I'm doing so wrong!"

Suddenly the church went dark, a deathly rush descended all

around, a steely blue light appeared above the altar and a voice boomed out: (three finger-clicks) "I guess I just don't dig you, man!!"

Prayer has to be of the heart. It has to arise from your total being. It has to be true. Only then, and *only* then, has something happened. God and you should not be on formal terms. You should dig Him—only then does He dig you.

Formality has killed all religion. Be informal, be friendly, be relaxed with God. And the moment you are relaxed with God, therapy is finished; you have entered into the world of religion. Therapy is needed only because people have forgotten how to be religious. Therapy was not needed in the Buddha's time; people naturally knew how to be religious. Therapy is a modern need—people have completely forgotten the ways of being religious. They are Christians, they are Hindus, they are Mohammedans, but not religious.

In my commune I have made it a must that everybody should pass through therapies, because unless you pass through therapies you will not be able to connect yourself with prayer. Therapies will help you to unburden the garbage that has been forced on you by the society. Therapies will help you to cathart all the rubbish that you have repressed within yourself. Therapies will clean you. And only in a clean, clear heart is prayer possible. And when prayer arises, the miracle has happened. Prayer is the greatest miracle there is.

Master Lu-tsu said: *When the silence comes, not a single thought arises; he who is looking inward suddenly forgets that he is looking. At this time, body and heart must be left completely released. All entanglements have disappeared without trace. Then I no longer know at what place the house of my spirit and my crucible are. If a man wants to make certain of his body, he cannot get at it. This condition is the penetration of heaven into earth, the time when all wonders return to their roots.*

When one is so far advanced that every shadow and every echo has disappeared, so that one is entirely quiet and firm, this is refuge within the cave of energy, where all that is miraculous returns to its roots. One does not alter the place, but the place alters itself. This is incorporeal space where a thousand and ten thousand places are one place. One does not alter the time, but the time alters itself. This is immeasurable time when all the aeons are like a moment.

As long as the heart has not attained absolute tranquility, it cannot move itself. One moves the movement and forgets the movement; this is not movement in itself. Therefore it is said: If, when stimulated by external things, one moves, it is the impulse of the being. If, when not stimulated by external things, one moves, it is the movement of heaven. But when no idea arises, the right ideas come. That is the true idea. When things are quiet and one is quite firm, and the release of heaven suddenly moves, is this not a movement without purpose? Action through non-action has just this meaning.

The deepest secret cannot be dispensed with from the beginning to the end. This is the washing of the heart and the purification of the thoughts; this is the bath. Its beginning is beyond polarity and it empties again beyond polarity.

The Buddha speaks of the transient, the creator of consciousness, as being the fundamental truth of religion. And the whole work of completing life and human nature lies in the expression 'to bring about emptiness'. All religions agree in the one proposition, the finding of the spiritual Elixir in order to pass from death to life. In what does this spiritual Elixir consist? It means forever dwelling in purposelessness. The deepest secret of the bath that is to be found in our teaching is thus confined to the work of making the heart empty. Therewith the matter is settled.

Chapter Nine

September 4th, 1978

WITH EMPTINESS, THE MATTER
IS SETTLED

IT WAS A FULL-MOON NIGHT. The earth was looking like a bride. Light was showering like rain, and there was great delight in the sky, in the ocean, in the wind. The trees were swaying in the wind as if drunk, intoxicated, lost, and the faraway mountains with their snow-covered peaks looked like Buddhas in deep meditation. The wind passing through the ancient pines was pure music, and the quality of a dancing universe was so solid and so tangible that one could have almost touched it. And on such a night of sheer joy and benediction, something of the beyond descended on the earth. A rare woman, Chiyono, became enlightened. She regained paradise. She came home. What a moment to die in time, and to time, and be born in eternity, as eternity! What a moment to disappear utterly, and be for the first time.

The nun Chiyono studied for years, but was unable to find enlightenment. One night she was carrying an old pail filled with water. As she was walking along, she was watching the full moon reflected in the pail of water. Suddenly, the bamboo strips that held the pail together broke and the pail fell apart. The water rushed out, the moon's reflection disappeared, and Chiyono became enlightened.

She wrote this verse:

> This way and that way
> I tried to keep the pail together,
> Hoping the weak bamboo would never break.
> Suddenly the bottom fell out....
> No more water,
> No more moon in the water,
> Emptiness in my hand.

Enlightenment happens when it happens: you cannot order it, you cannot cause it to happen. Still, you can do much for it to happen, but whatsoever you do is not going to function as a cause. Whatsoever you do is not going to bring enlightenment to you, but it prepares you to receive it. It comes when it comes. Whatsoever you do simply prepares you to receive it, to see it when it comes, to recognize it when it comes.

It happens...but if you are not ready you go on missing it. It is happening every moment. Every breath that goes in and comes out brings enlightenment to you, because enlightenment is the very stuff the existence is made of. But to recognize it is the problem, to see that it is there is the problem.

God is. There is no question of God's being. The question is: we cannot see Him, we don't have eyes. All the meditations and the prayers and the purifications only help you, make you

capable of seeing. Once you can see, you will be surprised—
it has always been there. Day in, day out, year in, year out,
it was showering on you, but you were not sensitive enough
to catch hold of it, you were not empty enough to be filled
by it. You were too much full of your own ego.

If one comes to fundamentals then this is the most fundamental
thing: the moment you are not, enlightenment is. With emptiness, the matter is settled.

If you continue you will remain ignorant and full of darkness.
You are darkness. Your presence is the 'dark night of the soul'.
When you are, you are separate from existence. That's what
darkness consists of: the idea of separation, that there is a gap
between me and the whole. Then I am left alone. Then there
is misery because fear surrounds me. I am so alone, and I am
so tiny, and sooner or later death will come and destroy me.
And I have no way to protect myself against death. Hence
one lives in trembling and fear.

But we create the trembling and the fear. We cause it by the
very idea of being separate from existence. The moment you
drop this separation, the moment you see that you are not
separate, that you *cannot* be separate, that there is *no way* to
be separate, that you are part of the whole, intrinsic to the
whole, that you are in the whole and the whole is in you, the
matter is settled and settled forever. Death disappears, fear
disappears, anguish disappears. And the whole energy that
is involved in fear, in anxiety, in anguish, is released. That
same energy becomes the celebration of the soul.

What is enlightenment?—the capacity to see oneself *as one
really is*. We are utterly empty of the ego. The ego is just a
make-believe. We have created it, we have projected it; it
is our illusion, our dream. It exists not; in itself it is not there,

so the more one becomes aware and looks within, the more one finds oneself not.

The more you become aware, the less you are. And the moment awareness is full, you have disappeared—no more water, no more reflection of the moon in the water, emptiness in your hands. And it is emptiness...therewith the matter is settled.

This happened to Chiyono. She had studied for years, she had practiced all kinds of meditations, she had cultivated all kinds of techniques but was unable to find enlightenment.

You cannot cause it, it is beyond you. If you could cause it, it would be below you. If you could cause it, then it would be again nothing but a new decoration for your ego. You cannot cause it. You cannot make it happen. You have to disappear for it to be.

So you can study all the scriptures of the world: you will become very learned, knowledgeable, but you will remain unenlightened. In fact you will become more unenlightened than you were before because the more knowledge you have the more ego you have; the more you practice ascetic techniques the more your ego is strengthened: "I am doing this and I am doing that, and I have done so much—so many fasts, so many bows." The more you do, the more you feel that now you are worthy and you can claim enlightenment.

Enlightenment cannot be claimed. One has to utterly disappear for it to be. The mind has to cease for God to be. Call it God or enlightenment—it is the same thing.

"Chiyono studied for years but was unable to find enlightenment."

Enlightenment is not something that you can find by searching;

it comes to you when all search proves futile. And remember, I am not saying don't search, because unless you search you will never come to know that search is futile. And I am not saying don't meditate; if you don't meditate you will never come to understand that there is a meditation which you cannot do but which comes to you.

Your meditations will simply cleanse your eyes, will make you more perceptive. Your heart will become more alert, aware, loving, sensitive. Your being will start seeing things you had not seen before. You will start exploring new spaces within your being. Something new will happen every day, every moment. Your meditations are like a bath: they will give you a freshness—but that freshness is not enlightenment. That only prepares the way. You never reach to enlightenment; it is always the other way round—enlightenment reaches to you.

Prepare the way for God so that He can reach you. You cannot find Him; you can only wait, in deep trust, so that He can find you.

That's how Chiyono was missing: she was searching, seeking, she was *too much* involved in this enquiry. But this enquiry will also feed your ego, that "I am a seeker", that "I am no ordinary man", that "I am spiritual", that "I am religious", that "I am holy". And if that attitude of 'holier than thou' arises, you are lost forever. That is the greatest sin you can commit in your life, the greatest fall. If the idea arises in you that you are holier than others, that you are a saint and others are sinners, "Look at my virtuous life"; if you become righteous you are lost, because this righteous ego will be the most subtle ego, and it will be very difficult for you to drop it. It is easier to drop iron chains. But if you can have golden chains studded with diamonds, it will become more and more difficult to drop them because they will not look like chains, they will look like valuable ornaments.

It is easy to get out of a dirty prison cell, but if it is a palace, who wants to get out of it? Really one wants to get into it, not out of it. The sinner is closer to God than the saint, because the sinner wants to get out of his bondage and the saint is enjoying an ego-trip.

Chiyono was a nun. She must have been enjoying subtle, righteous attitudes—knowledgeability, virtue. Her renunciation was great. It is said that she was one of the most beautiful women, so beautiful that when she went to one monastery they refused her, because to have such a beautiful woman in the monastery would create trouble for the monks. Then she had to disfigure her face to enter into another monastery. She must have been a very beautiful woman, but just think...she disfigured her face, made it ugly, but deep down she must have been thinking, "Look at my renunciation. I was one of the most beautiful women. I have disfigured my face—nobody has done this before, or since. Look at my renunciation, look at my detachment from the body: I don't care a bit about beauty. I am bent upon finding enlightenment, whatsoever the cost." And she continued missing.

But one full-moon night it happened. It happened out of the blue, suddenly. It always happens out of the blue. It always happens suddenly.

But I am not saying that it could have happened to anybody else; it happened to Chiyono. All that she had done had not caused it, but all that she had done had caused one thing in her: the understanding that whatsoever you do, you fail, that man cannot succeed.

She must have come to a state of *utter* hopelessness. That hopelessness can be felt only when you have done all that you can do. And when that hopelessness comes, hope has arrived— because in that hopelessness the ego is shattered to the ground. One no longer claims.

The ego disappears only from the peak, when it has come to its crescendo. You cannot drop a lukewarm ego. No, that is not possible, because it still hopes. It says, "Who knows?— a few efforts more, a few more practices, a little more renunciation...who knows? We have not looked in all the directions yet, there is still a possibility"—and the ego lingers. But when you have explored, searched in all possible directions and you have always failed; when nothing but failure has been your experience, how long can you continue searching, seeking? One day, searching and seeking drop.

So remember this paradox: enlightenment is possible only to those who stop seeking. But who can stop seeking?—only one who has searched deeply enough. This is the paradox. This is one of the great secrets to be understood; let it sink into your heart.

There is every possibility of choosing one. There are people who say, "Seek, and ye shall find." That is only half the truth: just by seeking nobody has ever found. Then there are people who say, "If by seeking, God cannot be found, then why seek at all? Wait. It will happen through His grace." It never happens that way either. You have been waiting for centuries, for lives, and it has not happened: it is enough to prove that it doesn't happen that way.

Then how does it happen? It happens to a seeker when he drops his seeking. It happens to one who has searched with his total potential and has failed, utterly failed. In that failure, the first ray of light, and then it takes you by surprise! When you are completely feeling hopeless, when you are thinking to forget all about enlightenment, when the search has stopped, when even the desire to be enlightened has left you, suddenly it is there...and therewith the matter is settled.

That's how it happened to Chiyono, that's how it happened to Buddha; that's how it always happens.

Buddha worked for six years—hard work. I think nobody else has done such hard work. He did whatsoever he was told, whatsoever he heard could be done, whatsoever he could gather from anywhere. He went to every kind of Master and he did real, arduous work, sincere, serious. But then one day, after six years of wastage, he realized the fact that it was not going to happen that way, that "The more I work for it, the more I am."

That day he relaxed; he dropped the whole search. And that very night.... And again it was a full-moon night. The full moon has something to do with it: the full moon affects your heart as deeply as it affects the ocean. The full moon stirs you towards beauty and beatitude. It creates something in you...an elixir. It makes you so sensitive that you can see things you had never seen before.

It was a full-moon night. Buddha relaxed, utterly relaxed, slept for the first time—because when you are searching for something how can you sleep? Even in sleep the search continues, the desire goes on creating dreams. Now all had failed. He had seen the world, the kingdom, the joys and the miseries of love and relationship, the agony and the ecstasy of the body, of the mind; and then he had been an ascetic, a monk, followed many paths—that too he had seen. He had seen the so-called world and he had seen the so-called other-worldly world, and both had failed. Now there was nowhere to go, not even a single inch to move. All desire disappeared. When one is so hopeless, how can one desire? Desire means hope. Desire means that still something can be done.

That night Buddha came to know that *nothing* can be done, nothing at all. Just see the point, it is of tremendous beauty... nothing can be done, nothing at all. He relaxed. His body must have been in a let-go, his heart in a let-go, no desire, no future. This moment was all.

And it was a full-moon night, and he slept deeply, and in the morning when he woke up he not only woke up from his ordinary sleep, he woke up from the metaphysical sleep we all are living in. He became awakened.

He used to say to his disciples, "I worked hard and could not attain, and when I had dropped the very idea of work, then I attained."

That's why I call my work 'the play'. You have to be in a paradoxical state. That is the meaning of the word 'play'. You work very seriously, as if through work something is going to happen, but it never happens through work. It happens only when work disappears and playfulness arises, relaxation arises; and not a cultivated relaxation either, but a relaxation that comes out of the understanding that: "In all that I can do, my 'I' will go on persisting; all that I can do will go on feeding my ego. And the ego is the barrier, so my doing is really my undoing." Seeing this, doing evaporates. And when there is no doing, how can the doer exist? Doing gone, the doer follows it just like a shadow. And then you are left—total, whole, in the whole, part of this cosmic play. That is enlightenment.

These sutras are of tremendous value. Meditate over them.

Master Lu-tsu said: *When the silence comes, not a single thought arises; he who is looking inward suddenly forgets that he is looking.*

There are two kinds of silences: one is that which you cultivate, the other is that which arrives. Your cultivated silence is nothing but repressed noise. You can sit silently, and if you sit long and you continue the practice for months and years together, slowly slowly you will become capable of repressing all noise inside. But still you will be sitting on a volcano—it can erupt any moment, any small excuse will do. This is not real silence, this is just imposed silence.

This is what is happening all around the world. The people who try to meditate, the people who try to become silent, are only imposing a silence upon themselves. It can be imposed. You can have a layer of silence around yourself, but that is just deceiving yourself and nothing else. That layer is not going to help.

Unless silence arises from your very being, is not imposed from the without on the within but comes just the other way round—it comes, wells up from the within towards the without, rises from the center towards the circumference... That is a totally different phenomenon.

Lu-tsu said, "When the silence comes"—remember, it is not brought, not forced, but when it comes—"not a single thought arises." Then you are not sitting on a volcano. That's why my whole approach is in catharting your inner noise, throwing it out rather than cultivating silence.

People become very puzzled when they come to me for the first time. If they have been with some Buddhist Master, then they were doing vipassana, sitting, forcing themselves into a certain static posture. Why the static posture?—because when the body is forced to remain in one posture, mind also is forced to remain in one posture.

Body and mind function together. Mind is the inner aspect of the body; it is a material phenomenon. It has nothing to do with your being. It is as much matter as your body, so if you do something with the body that automatically happens to the mind. Hence down the ages people have been cultivating postures—sit in a lotus posture, force your body to be like a statue, a marble statue. If your body is *really* still, forced, you will see your mind falls into a kind of silence, which is false, which is not true. He has just been forced to be silent by the body posture. You try it: just make the posture of anger with your fists, your face, your teeth; just go into the posture of anger and you will be surprised, you start feeling angry. That's what the actor does: he moves the body into the posture, and following it, mind comes in.

Two great psychologists, James and Lange, discovered a very strange theory at the beginning of this century. It is known as the James-Lange theory. They said something very uncommon which goes against the old commonsense of the ages. Ordinarily we think that when a man is afraid he runs away; in fear, he starts running. James and Lange said it is not true—because he runs, that's why he feels fear.

It looks absurd, but it has some truth in it—half. The commonsense truth was half; this too is another half of the same whole. If you start laughing, you will find yourself feeling a little less sad than you were before. You just go and sit with a few friends who are laughing and telling jokes, and you forget your sadness, your misery. You start laughing, and once you start laughing you are feeling good. You start with the body.

Try it! If you are feeling sad, start running, go running around the block seven times, breathing deep breaths, in the sun, in the wind; and after seven rounds, stand and see whether your mind is the same. No, it can't be the same. The bodily change has changed the mind. The body chemistry changes the mind. Hence the yoga postures. They are all postures to force the mind into a certain pattern. That is not real silence.

The real silence has to be a silence that comes on its own. My suggestion is: don't force your body. Rather, dance, sing, move, run, jog, swim. Let the body have all kinds of movements so your mind also has all kinds of movements, and through all those kinds of inner movements, the mind starts catharting, releasing its poisons.

Shout, be angry, beat a pillow and you will be surprised— after beating a pillow you feel very good. Something in the mind has been released. It does not matter whether you were beating your wife, your husband, or the pillow. The pillow will do perfectly as well as beating the wife or the husband, because the body does not know whom you are beating. Just the very posture of beating and the mind starts releasing its anger. Mind and body collaborate.

Start with catharsis, so that you become empty of all the rubbish that has been accumulating in you from your very childhood. You were angry but you could not be angry because the mother becomes mad if you become angry—so you repressed it. You were angry, you wanted to shout, but you could not shout; rather, on the contrary, you smiled. *All* that is accumulated in you—it has to be thrown out. And then wait... and a silence starts descending in you. That silence has a beauty of its own. It is totally different; its quality is different, its depth is different.

THE SECRET OF SECRETS

"When the silence comes, not a single thought arises"—
not that you force your thinking not to arise, not that you
keep watch, not that you become very tight and you won't
allow a single thought to pass. You are not struggling, you
are in a let-go, but nothing arises. That is beautiful—when
no thought arises, when thoughts disappear of their own accord.
Then you are utterly silent, and this silence is positive. The
forced silence is negative.

> *He who is looking inward suddenly forgets that he is
> looking.*

> And in this experience this will happen: *He who is
> looking inward suddenly forgets that he is looking.*

This is *real* inward looking—when you forget that you are
looking inwards. If you remember that you are looking inward,
that again is a thought and nothing else. First you were looking
outward, now you are looking inward, but the ego is there.
First it was extrovert, now it is introvert, but the ego is there.
First you were looking at the trees, now you are looking at
the thoughts. First you were looking at the objects, now you
are looking at the subject, but the whole thing remains the
same. You are still divided in two—the looker and the looked
upon, the observer and the observed, the subject and the object.
The duality persists.

This is not real silence, because when there are two there is
bound to be conflict. Two cannot be silent. When you are
one then you are silent because there is no possibility of any
conflict.

Allow silence to descend on you rather than forcing it. The
forced silence is artificial, arbitrary.

That is one of the great changes that I am trying to make here with you, with my people. All the old methods are basically of enforcing something. My own understanding is: never enforce anything. Rather, throw out all junk that you have been carrying. Become more and more empty, become more roomy. Create a little more space in you, and in that space the silence comes.

Nature abhors emptiness, and if you can throw all the junk out and you are empty, you will see something from the beyond start descending in you. A dancing energy enters in you, in your every cell. You are full of song—wordless, soundless— a divine music. In this music there is nobody who is looking. In this music there is nobody who is looked at. The observer is the observed. The dancer has become the dance, and all duality has disappeared.

This non-duality is the only real silence.

At this time, body and heart must be left completely released...

And in such moments you should remain in a let-go. Forget all your postures. Forget everything that you try to do; don't try to do anything. Be in a state of non-doing. Just relax, relax utterly, doing nothing, because the more relaxed you are the more silence can penetrate into your being—just open, vulnerable, relaxed.

All entanglements have disappeared without trace.

And then you will be surprised—all those desires that you have been trying to drop and were unable to drop have disappeared on their own. All entanglements, all occupations of the mind, all those thoughts, all that traffic of the mind is no more there. You will be surprised—where have all those people gone? You were trying hard, and not even a single thought can be forced out when you try. You can do it: if you want to throw out a single thought, you will be an utter failure. You will not be able to throw it out. The more you will throw it out, the more it will bump in, rebound in.

Just sit silently and try not to think of a monkey, and you will see; it is a simple experiment. Not one, but many monkeys will start coming, and they will make faces at you, and the more you push them away the more they will knock on your doors, and they will say, "We want to come in." And monkeys are not so polite: they may not even ask, they may simply jump in; you will be surrounded by monkeys and monkeys. The more you try to forget them the more they will be there, because to try to forget something is nothing but remembering it. It is another way of remembering. You cannot forget by making efforts.

When silence descends, then suddenly all entanglements disappear—and without trace! They don't even leave a trace behind. You cannot believe that all that noise...where has it gone? You cannot believe that it ever existed in you. You cannot believe that it still exists in others.

This is one of the basic problems every realized person has to face. When you come to me with all your problems you don't understand my difficulty. My difficulty basically is: how can you manage so many problems, how do you go on managing? You are doing something really incredible, something impossible!—because even if I try to hold to a thought, it slips away. I cannot hold it, it wants to get out. And you say that you want to stop your thoughts and you cannot stop, and you are tired and you are weary and you are fed up and bored. You are really doing something impossible! And the day silence will descend on you, you will understand...not even a trace. You cannot believe that they had ever existed in you; they have simply disappeared. They were just shadows.

Thoughts are not substantial, just shadows. When a shadow disappears it doesn't leave a trace. You cannot find the footprints of a shadow, because in the first place it was non-substantial—so are your thoughts, so is your mind.

> *Then I no longer know at what place the house of my spirit and my crucible are.*

And when this state happens, silence descends in you and you are overwhelmed by it, and you don't know whether you are looking in or out. You don't know who is the looker and who is the looked upon.

> *Then I no longer know at what place the house of my spirit and my crucible are.*

Then you cannot say who you are. You are. In fact for the first time you are—but who? what? No answer will be coming.

When the Emperor Wu asked Bodhidharma, in China... Bodhidharma had annoyed the Emperor very much. Bodhidharma was an outrageous man, blunt, would call a spade a spade and nothing else. The Emperor had asked, "I have done many virtuous deeds. What will be my reward in heaven?" Bodhidharma looked with great contempt at the Emperor and said, "Reward? You will fall into hell! What heaven are you talking about?" The Emperor said, "For my virtuous deeds I will fall into hell? And I have made so many temples and thousands of Buddha-statues, and thousands of Buddhist monks are maintained, monasteries are maintained by the treasury, and I am doing so much service to Buddha's *dharma*, his message. The whole country is becoming Buddhist. People are meditating, worshipping. Scriptures are being translated, thousands of scholars are working on the translations, and you think there will be no reward? Are not my acts holy?"

And Bodhidharma said, "Holy? There is nothing holy in the world. There is nothing holy, nothing unholy. But mind you," he said, "drop this idea of being a virtuous man. Drop this idea of doing great things, otherwise you will fall into the seventh hell."

Naturally the Emperor was annoyed, irritated...must have been a very polished and cultured man. Otherwise he would have been violent with Bodhidharma. But even he could not resist the temptation: annoyed, angry, he asked, "Then who are you standing before me? Nothing holy, nothing unholy, no virtue? Who are you standing before me?"

Bodhidharma laughed and said, "I don't know, sir."

But the Emperor could not understand. You also would have missed.

Ordinarily people think that a man who has arrived knows who he is; we call him the man of self-knowledge. And Bodhidharma says, "I don't know." This is the highest peak of self-knowledge, this is *real* self-knowledge. One has disappeared; who is there to know? Knowing means the knower and the known. There is no duality anymore. Who is there to know? There is just silence, *tremendous* silence, no division, indivisibility. How could Bodhidharma say "I know"? If he had said, "Yes, I know that I am an eternal soul," that would have been very ordinary. Maybe Wu would have been more convinced, but

Bodhidharma would have lost face. He was true. He said, "I don't know."

Who follows a man who says "I don't know who I am"? Wu dropped the idea of following this man. And when Emperor Wu could not understand Bodhidharma, Bodhidharma said, "If even the Emperor cannot understand me, then what about others?"

So he went into the mountains and sat for nine years, facing a wall. When people would come and ask, "Why do you go on facing a wall?" he would say, "Because if I face people they also look like walls. It is better to face the wall. I will face a person only when I see that he is not a wall, that he can respond, that he can understand."

His statement that "I don't know" is of immense beauty, grandeur.

> Then I no longer know at what place the house of my
> spirit and my crucible are. If a man wants to make certain
> of his body, he cannot get at it.

In this moment, when silence overwhelms you, encompasses you, if you want to make sure about your body you will not be able to get at it. There is no body anymore, or, the whole existence is your body because you are not separated anymore. You cannot define, you cannot draw a line that "This is my body." The whole existence is your body, or there is no body at all.

This sometimes can drive you crazy. Beware. Don't be worried if sometimes it happens that you open your eyes and you cannot find your body, you cannot see it.

Just the other night a sannyasin was asking me, "When I stand before a mirror I feel very puzzled, because I cannot see that this reflection is mine." Now it is puzzling. He avoids the mirror because whenever he looks into the mirror this problem arises: "Who is this fellow?" He cannot feel that "This is me." Now it can drive you crazy, and he was very disturbed because of it.

But this is a beneficial sign, a confirmatory sign. Something really good is happening: he is becoming de-identified with the body. It is good; he is on the right way. I told him to look into the mirror as much as possible, whenever he had time to just sit before the mirror, see the body reflected in the mirror and go on feeling that "This is not me." There is no need to repeat "This is not me" because that would be false. Just feel! And it is happening to him of its own accord, so there is no problem. This will be his natural meditation. This is enough. Slowly slowly, one day, the moment will arrive when he will not be able to see the reflection in the mirror. That is even more disorienting.

It happened to Swabhava. I had given this meditation to him. For months he did it, and then one day he was standing before the mirror and the reflection disappeared. He rubbed his eyes... "What is happening?" Had he gone mad? The mirror was there, he was standing before the mirror, and the reflection had disappeared. And that day became a great day of transformation for his being.

Now Swabhava is a totally different person, utterly different. When he had come to me for the first time, he was just ego and nothing else—and a Punjabi ego, which is the most dangerous in India. In fact he was trapped because of his Punjabi ego. He wanted to know about truth, and I asked him "Are you ready to risk?" Now that was a challenge to his ego:

"Are you courageous enough to risk all?" He could not say no, he could not withdraw. He said, "Yes." He looked a little frightened—"Who knows what will be expected of me?"—but he took the jump. And the day it happened in the mirror—that his reflection disappeared—something very deep inside him changed, moved.

Now you can see Swabhava in a totally different way. He has become so simple, so humble, goes on working in the Vipassana godown. He is a rich man, a millionaire. He was a boss in a big factory, his own factory; hundreds of people were working under him. Now he is working like a laborer in the Ashram but has never been so happy as he is now, has never been so blissful as he is now.

This moment may come to you one day: that meditating, silence descends and you cannot find your body. If you want to look in the mirror, you cannot see your face. Don't be worried, take it as a very confirmatory sign. Something beautiful is on the way: your old identity is eroding, your old idea of yourself is disappearing. And you have to disappear totally before God can take possession of you.

> If a man wants to make certain of his body, he cannot get at it. This condition is the penetration of heaven into earth. . . .

When you cannot see your body, when you cannot feel your body, you cannot touch your body—this is the penetration of heaven into earth. Paradise is descending, God is coming to you. God has reached. His heart is with your heart, His hand is in your hand. That's why you have disappeared. The part has become the whole.

...the time when all wonders return to their roots.

And now your whole life will be nothing but wonder. Each moment will be a unique moment. Each experience will be incredible, just far out. Your life from then onwards will be sheer poetry. From then onwards you will never be bored; because each moment life is so new, how can one be bored? People are bored because they go on carrying their old, dead, dull ego; that's why they are bored. When there is no ego there is no boredom. Then life is delight! Then each single thing that happens is a gift from God. One feels constantly like bowing down, one feels constantly in gratitude...

...the time when all wonders return to their roots.

When one is so far advanced that every shadow and every echo has disappeared...

You must remember that first Lu-tsu says: A moment comes when gods are in the valley. You feel yourself sitting on a hilltop and the whole world is in the valley. You can hear the sounds, and very clearly, and very distinctly, but they are faraway, distant, like echoes in the valley. Now even those echoes disappear. All shadows are gone.

Remember Chiyono? She wrote these words in celebration of her enlightenment:

> This way and that way
> I tried to keep the pail together,
> Hoping the weak bamboo would never break.
> Suddenly the bottom fell out....
> No more water,
> No more moon in the water,
> Emptiness in my hand.

All reflections, shadows, echoes are gone. Only that which is remains, and the utter beauty of it.

> ...so that one is entirely quiet and firm, this is refuge within the cave of energy, where all that is miraculous returns to its roots.

The whole life outside becomes a constant wonder. You are again a child on the seabeach, running in the wind and in the sun, and collecting seashells and colored stones as if you have found a mine of diamonds. The whole existence outside takes the quality of wonder. And what happens inside?

> ...that is miraculous returns to its roots.

And in the deep insight, parallel to the outside wonder, the miraculous returns to its roots.

What is the miracle? To be is the greatest miracle, just to be. You need not be rich to feel it; you need not be educated to feel it; you need not be famous to feel it. Just to be... That you are is the greatest miracle there is, the greatest mystery. Why are you? There is no reason. You have not earned it, you had not even asked for it. It has simply happened.

So outside there is wonder, inside the world of miracles— this is how the enlightened person lives. And now these things start happening.

> One does not alter the place, but the place alters itself.

Now you need not go to the Himalayas, you need not renounce the marketplace. You can be in the marketplace, but the place is no more the same—the place alters itself. Even the market- place becomes so beautiful that the Himalayas are nothing compared to it. The ordinary reality becomes suffused with *extraordinary* beauty. The same trees that you had been passing every day and had never looked at, were always oblivious to, suddenly burst forth in bloom, suddenly burst forth on your consciousness with all their flowers and fragrance. Life becomes very colorful, psychedelic, and things change themselves—just because you have come to this inner silence, this egolessness.

One does not alter the place, but the place alters itself.

That's why I insist again and again that my sannyasins are not to leave the world. Let this be the criterion for your enlightenment: that the world has to change itself when you are enlightened; it *has* to change. And by escaping from the world you will not be going anywhere. Wherever you go you will create the same world again, because the blueprint for creating it is within you. You can leave one woman thinking that because of this woman the problems arise—the children are there, and the house, and the responsibilities. You can leave this woman and these poor children and you can escape— many have done that down the ages—but you had fallen in love with this woman; that possibility to fall in love again is within you. You will fall in love again with some other woman. And sooner or later—and it is going to be sooner than later— another family will arise, another man, another woman, children, responsibilities.

You cannot change life so easily, so cheaply. You only change the context, but deep down you carry the blueprint. The context was created by the blueprint; the blueprint will again create it. It is like a seed: you destroy the tree but you carry the seed. Wherever the seed will fall into the soil again, the tree will be back. The seed has to be burned.

Then wherever you are this miracle will be felt.

One does not alter the place, but the place alters itself.

This very world becomes paradise, this very world *nirvana*, this very body the body of Buddha.

This is incorporeal space where a thousand and ten thousand places are one place. One does not alter the time, but the time alters itself. This is immeasurable time when all the aeons are like a moment.

You don't alter anything. And these two are the constituents of the world. Just see, what Lu-tsu is saying is now perfectly collaborated by modern physics. Albert Einstein says that the world consists only of two things, time and space. And in fact they are not two, but one, so he has to coin a new word. He does not call it time and space, he calls it 'spatiotime', one word with not even a hyphen needed between the two, because time is the fourth dimension of space. You need not change space, you need not change time. They change of their own accord. *Just change yourself.* With the change in the heart, the whole existence changes.

Heaven is not somewhere else, neither is hell somewhere else. It is within you, both are within you; you create them. But people go on doing stupid things.

Just a few days ago a man wrote me a letter: "What is happening?" He has changed wives four times. This is now the fourth time he has got married, this is the fourth woman he is living with. And now he says, "What always happens? In the beginning everything seems to be beautiful, and within six months it is the same all over again." It will happen the same all over again, because you are the same.

And there are complexities. For example, you are fed up with your wife—mind is always hankering for the new, something new, sensational. You have seen the woman, you are acquainted with her whole topography. Now you know her geography, nothing more is left to explore; you become interested in some other woman. When you become interested in some other woman, your woman will start creating more trouble for you. Seeing that you are not interested in her but in somebody else, jealousy will arise. She will create much trouble: she will nag you, she will become nasty, and the more she will nag the more you will be repelled by her.

Now see the vicious circle: she wants you to be with her, but whatsoever she is doing is repelling you away. She will become more and more possessive and more and more jealous, and life in the home will become impossible to live. It will be hell. You will avoid her as much as you can. You will work late in the office; even if there is no work you will go on sitting in the office, because to go home means to face your woman, and again the same misery. And what does she actually want?— she wants you to be with her. But whatsoever she is doing is just the opposite: she is driving you away. And the more she will drive you away, the more the other woman will look beautiful, fantastic. The more the other woman will look fantastic and beautiful, the more you would like to be with her and she would like to be with you. And soon she will start saying, "Leave the other woman if you want to be with me."

Now she does not know that the beauty that the man is finding in her will disappear the moment he leaves the other woman, because ninety percent of the beauty that he is seeing in this woman depends on the other woman. She thinks the other woman is her enemy; she is not. In fact it is because of the other woman that this man has fallen in love with her. These are unconscious ways. See it! You don't see, and they go on working. And she will feel very happy. And the more she will feel happy and the more you would like to be with her, the more your woman will look ugly in comparison. Soon you would like to live with this woman forever. You leave the other woman, you start living with this woman. The day you leave the other woman the whole context has changed: now you will be with this new woman but she will not look so beautiful, so alluring. The hypnosis will start disappearing because there is nobody else to repel you.

Within six months the hypnosis has disappeared: this woman is as the other was. Now, the geography explored, you are finished. And the woman cannot believe what has happened—"This man was so much in love. What happened?" She destroyed it herself. And this man cannot believe what happened —"This woman was so incredible, and has proved so ordinary." Again the movement, the same movement, the same vicious circle with the same seed deep in the unconscious: he will start falling in love with somebody else. People fall in love and fall out of love unconsciously. They go on changing partners but they don't change themselves. They go on changing the outside but they remain the same.

You can go on changing—that's what you have been doing for many many lives, the same repetition. It is a vicious circle that goes on moving; it is a wheel. The same spokes come on the top and go down, and again come on the top and go down. It is the wheel that goes on moving, and you are caught in the wheel.

Become aware. You need not change the place, you need not change time, you need not change anything on the outside. The outside is as perfect as it can be. There is just one thing you have to do—you have to become more conscious, more alert, more aware, more empty, so there is nothing to project on the outside. You have to burn all the seeds inside, you have to burn the whole blueprint inside. Once that blueprint is burnt, seeds are burnt, and you have thrown all that was inside and you are just empty, something from the beyond enters in you. Paradise penetrates into the earth. And that is the moment of transformation.

With this change, the whole existence is totally different. The same woman, the same children, the same people, the same office, the same marketplace, but it is no more the same because you are no more the same. This is the right way of transformation: never start from the without, start from the within.

> *As long as the heart has not attained absolute tranquility, it cannot move itself. One moves the movement and forgets the movement; this is not movement in itself. Therefore it is said: If, when stimulated by external things, one moves, it is the impulse of the being. If, when not stimulated by external things, one moves, it is the movement of heaven.*

Remember, let heaven move you, allow God to move you. Surrender to the total. Otherwise you will go on reacting to situations, and the situations will go on functioning on you, on your unconscious, and you will remain the same. You can change women, you can change men, you can change jobs, you can change houses; you can go on changing things but nothing will really ever change. Unless the whole takes possession of you and your heart is no more moved by outer things, but is moved by the innermost core of your being— call it God, heaven, Tao—when you are not moving it, when you are just an instrument in the hands of the total, this is what Jesus means when he says, "Thy kingdom come, thy will be done." That is his way of saying it, a Jewish way of saying the same truth. This is a Chinese way of saying it: Let heaven move your heart.

But when no idea arises, the right ideas come.

And this is the miracle: when *no* ideas arise then whatsoever you do is the right thing. There is no question of deciding what is right and what is wrong. When the mind is silent and the heart is moved by God, whatsoever happens is right.

It is not that if you do right things you will become a saint; if you are a saint, then whatsoever you do is right. If you are trying to become a saint by doing right you will simply become repressed and nothing else. You will go on repressing the wrong and you will go on pretending the right. You will be a hypocrite.

Don't try to become a saint. Let God take possession of you. You just be empty, surrendered, in a state of let-go. Let Him move your heart, and then all is beautiful. Then whatsoever happens is virtuous, then wrong is not possible. In short, whatsoever comes out of the ego is wrong. That's why Bodhidharma said, "You will go into hell. Although you have been doing things which look *apparently* virtuous, religious, deep down you are feeling very deep gratification in the ego." Whatsoever comes out of the ego is going to take you into hell, into misery.

Drop the ego, and then let things happen—just as when the wind comes and the trees sway and the sun rises and the birds sing. Let the whole possess you. You don't live a private life on your own. Let God live through you, then all is good. All that is out of God is good.

That is the true idea. When things are quiet and one is quite firm, and the release of heaven suddenly moves, is this not a movement without purpose?

Now there is no purpose in your life because there is no private goal.

Action through non-action has just this meaning.

One lives because God wants to live through one. One does because God wants to do something through one; but one is not interested this way or that. Whatsoever role is given to you, you go on playing it. It is His drama; He is the author of it and the director of it—you do your act as perfectly as you can. Whatsoever act is given to you, you perform it.

If you are a householder then be a householder; if you are a businessman then remain a businessman. There is no need to change these things. All that is needed is to drop the idea that you are the doer, drop the idea that you have to attain to some goal, drop the idea that you have to reach somewhere. Let Him take you wherever He wants. You be just a dry leaf in the wind—and then all is good, and then life is blissful.

There can't be any tension now, can't be any anxiety. You cannot fail. You can never feel frustrated, because in the first place you were not expecting anything. This is living a purposeless life.

Action through non-action has just this meaning.

The deepest secret cannot be dispensed with from the beginning to the end. This is the washing of the heart and the purification of the thoughts; this is the bath.

Lu-tsu says: This we call 'the bath'—God showers on you and you are cleansed, utterly cleansed. God floods you, and you are not left anywhere, not even in a corner somewhere in the unconscious. No nook or corner is left without God; He fills you totally. God is light, and when He fills you totally this is called enlightenment. You are full of light.

> *Its beginning is beyond polarity and it empties again*
> *beyond polarity.*

And now you have come home. Now again you are one as you were before you were born, as you were before the beginning. Zen people call it 'the original face'. The original face is one, single, neither man nor woman, neither positive nor negative. The moment you are born, the moment you enter into the manifested world, you become two.

When you enter meditation again deep silence descends. Suddenly the two have disappeared; you have become one again. In the beginning you are beyond polarity, in the end you are again beyond polarity. Only in between the two are you divided. In the middle is the world; in the beginning is God, in the end is God. The source is the goal. Either fall back into the source or disappear in the goal; it is saying the same thing in different ways.

> *The Buddha speaks of the transient, the creator of conscious-*
> *ness, as being the fundamental truth of religion. And the*
> *whole work of completing life and human nature lies in the*
> *expression 'to bring about emptiness'.*

The whole of religion can be reduced to a simple phenomenon, 'to bring about emptiness'. Be empty and you will be full.

Remain full and you will remain empty. Be utterly absent and the presence of the beyond will penetrate you. Go on holding yourself, clinging to yourself, and you will remain just an emptiness, a shadow, a reflection, not a reality.

> *All the religions agree in the one proposition, the finding*
> *of the spiritual Elixir in order to pass from death to life.*

And this is the Elixir all the religions have been searching for: the secret of being utterly empty. Then you cannot die because there is nobody to die; you have already disappeared. Now there is no possibility of death, you have already died! The man who has died as an ego has attained eternal life.

> *In what does this spiritual Elixir consist? It means forever*
> *dwelling in purposelessness.*

Now when the ego is no more there and you are empty, and the silence has descended in you, how will you live? You will live eternally in purposelessness.

Is there any purpose when a rosebush blooms? Is there any purpose when a bird starts singing in the morning? Is there any purpose when the sun rises? Is there any purpose in this existence at all? This existence is not a business, hence there is no purpose. It is sheer joy, playfulness, what the Hindus call *leela*. It is just delight in energy. Energy is there and energy is dancing and delighting. When you have energy you delight in it. You run, you sing, you dance, you swim, you play.

Energy delights in expression. You become creative—you paint, you write poetry, you compose music—out of sheer energy. Existence is energy and the energy wants to dance, for no purpose at all. Dance for dance's sake, art for art's sake, love for love's sake...existence for existence's sake.

It means forever dwelling in purposelessness. The deepest secret of the bath that is to be found in our teaching is thus confined to the work of making the heart empty.

Do only one thing: pour out all that you are carrying in the heart, throw it out—and you have done the only fundamental thing that is needed to be done.

Therewith the matter is settled.

A tremendously beautiful statement: "Therewith the matter is settled." Nothing else is needed. No scriptures are needed, no temples are needed, no priests are needed—therewith the matter is settled. Only one thing is needed—become empty so God can flow in you. Make space for Him. Be a hollow bamboo so He can make a flute out of you. And when He sings there is beauty. When He sings there is ecstasy, when He sings there is laughter.

When you sing there is only misery, and tears, and agony, because the ego is a very small thing. It cannot contain esctasy, it can only contain agony. To contain ecstasy you will have to become infinite because ecstasy is infinite. If you want to contain the ocean you will have to become vast.

By being empty one becomes vast, by being empty one becomes spacious, by being empty you become ready. You can become a host. God can become a guest if the host is ready. By being empty you become the host.

Become a host; God has been waiting at your door for long,

knocking, but you don't listen. There is so much noise within you—how can you listen to the knock? You are so preoccupied with your own foolish things, how can you see the sheer beauty of purposelessness? You are worried about how to have a bigger bank balance, you are worried about how to succeed in politics, you are worried about how to become a little more famous, and God goes on knocking on your door. He is ready to pour Himself into you but you are not ready to receive Him.

Yes, Lu-tsu is right: the most fundamental thing of all the religions is to bring about emptiness. The whole work of all the yogas, tantras, of all the alchemical systems—Tao, Sufi, Hassidic—consists in only one thing: making the heart empty...

...Therewith the matter is settled.

I will repeat this beautiful story:

The nun Chiyono studied for years but was unable to find enlightenment. One night, carrying an old pail of water, as she was walking along, she was watching the full moon reflected in the pail of water. Suddenly the bamboo strips that held the pail together broke and the pail fell apart. The water rushed out, the moon's reflection disappeared, and Chiyono became enlightened.

She wrote this verse:

> This way and that way
> I tried to keep the pail together,
> Hoping the weak bamboo would never break.
> Suddenly the bottom fell out.

No more water,
No more moon in the water,
Emptiness in my hand.

And therewith, the matter is settled....

Chapter Ten

September 5th, 1978

BECAUSE OF LOVE,
WE ARE TOGETHER

The first question:

Can you give me a message to take to the Western world so that people there might understand you and your followers?

Joey Simons, my message is very simple. That's why it is difficult to understand. I teach the obvious; it is not complex at all. Because it is not complex there is nothing much to understand in it. It has to be lived, experienced. My message is not verbal, logical, rational. It is existential, so those who want to understand it intellectually will only misunderstand it.

Still, there are a few fundamentals I would like to tell you. One: up to now man has lived only half-heartedly. In the East, in the West, man has remained lopsided. Neither has the Eastern man been whole nor has the Western man been whole. The West has chosen the body, is body-oriented; the East has chosen the soul, is soul-oriented; and man is both, a great harmony of both. Man is both and a transcendence. Neither in the East nor in the West has man been accepted totally. We have not yet dared to accept man in his totality.

That is one of the most fundamental things I want everybody to understand about my teaching: I teach the whole man. The very idea of East and West is nonsense; that too is because of the ancient division. All divisions have to be dissolved.

I teach one world. East and West have to disappear; both are schizophrenic. The West is right-handed, the East is left-handed; the West is active, the East is passive; the West is extrovert, the East is introvert—but man is both and beyond both.

To be total, one has to be as capable of being extrovert as of being introvert. To be total, one has to be capable of breathing out and breathing in. Inhalation is as much needed as exhalation. In fact, they are not two; exhalation-inhalation is *one* process.

The West has chosen the outside world, matter, has become very scientific, has created great technology; but man is crushed underneath that technology because man has not grown simultaneously. Man is lagging far behind. Science has gone far ahead, and the science that man has created is now destroying man himself.

Man's inner world has remained poor in the West, man is

spiritually starved in the West. And the same has happened in the East from the other extreme: man has completely denied his body, his world. The East has insisted on denying all that is outside you, renouncing the manifested world and just going in, remaining at your center. The East is spiritually rich but materially very poor and starved. The East has suffered, the West has suffered.

My message is: now it is time that we should drop this division of the outer and the inner, of the lower and the higher, of the left-handed and the right-handed. We should drop this division between man and woman, between East and West. We should create a whole man who is capable of both.

That's why I am going to be misunderstood everywhere. The Eastern religious person is angry with me because he thinks I am teaching materialism, and the Western rational thinker is angry with me because he thinks I am teaching spiritual mumbo-jumbo. *Everybody* is angry at me, and that is natural; I can understand it.

I am teaching the whole man—from the lowest rung of the ladder to the highest rung, from sex to samadhi, from the body to the soul, from matter to God. My trust is total.

I would like to tell you that up to now man has not trusted. Not even in the East has man trusted. In the East man has doubted the world; hence in the East the world is called illusory, *maya*. In the West man has doubted God, soul; they are thought to be just hallucinations, pathologies. To the really Western mind Jesus looks like a neurotic, psychologically ill, needs psychiatric treatment. To the East the West looks animalistic. "Eat, drink, and be merry"—that seems to be the understanding of the East about the West, that that is the only Western philosophy: be like animals, gross.

The West has doubted the inner world, the East has doubted the outer world. Both have lived in doubt and their trust has been half-hearted.

My trust is total. I trust the outer, I trust the inner—because outer and inner are both together. They cannot be separated. There is *no* God without this world; there is *no* world without God. God is the innermost core of this world. The juice flowing in the trees is God, the blood circulating in your body is God, the consciousness residing in you is God. God and the world are mixed together just like a dancer and his dance; they cannot be separated, they are inseparable. So I don't say the world is illusion; that is nonsense. The world is as real as consciousness. Neither do I say that the inner world is neurosis, madness, hallucination; it is not. It is the very foundation of reality.

I teach the whole man. I am not a materialist or a spiritualist. My approach is wholistic—and the whole man can only be holy.

Because of this there is going to be great misunderstanding about me, and anybody can pick things, find faults with me, and it is very easy. The spiritualist can call me Epicurean, a follower of Charvaka—and he is not absolutely wrong because half of me is Epicurean. I accept Epicurus and Charvaka because they teach the body and the joys of the body and the exhilaration of the body. And there *is* exhilaration in the body, and the moment you drop that, you become serious and sad.

That's why the Eastern saint looks so sad, no joy. They talk about bliss but it doesn't show on their faces. They look utterly miserable. They look utterly dead—because they are afraid of the outer, and one who is afraid of the outer will be afraid of love because love is an outgoing process. Love means the other, love means relating, love means communicating with the other. Love means the relationship between I and thou. The East denies the other, hence the East is against love. And if you are against love you will lose dance.

Without love, there is no dance in life and no song. Without love there is no poetry. Life becomes dull, a drag. Without love you can live, but only at the minimum. It will be almost like vegetating.

And that's what is happening to the Eastern spirituality; go into the monasteries, go into the ashrams.

That's why my ashram looks so utterly different—because people are dancing, singing, holding hands, hugging, loving, joyous; this is not the Eastern concept of an ashram. An ashram has to be absolutely joyless; it has to be more like a cemetery than like a garden. But the moment you stop love, all that is flowing in you stops, becomes stagnant.

You cannot celebrate without love. How can you celebrate without love? And what will you celebrate, and with what?

Mulla Nasrudin was saying to me one day, "I have lived a hundred years. I have celebrated my hundredth birthday, and I have never chased a woman in my life, and I have not ever been drinking. I have never played cards, gambled. I don't smoke. I eat simple, vegetarian food."

I asked him, "But then how did you celebrate your hundredth birthday? How can you celebrate? With what? And for what? Just living for a hundred years can't be a celebration."

You have not lived if you have not loved.

The East is against love. That's why Eastern spirituality is sad, dull, dead. No juice flows through the Eastern saint. He is afraid of *any* flow, any vibration, any pulsation, any streaming of his energy. He is constantly controlling himself, repressing himself. He is sitting upon himself, on guard. He is against himself and against the world. He is simply waiting to die, he is committing a slow suicide.

That's why my ashram is going to be misunderstood. This will look like the Ashram of a Charvaka, this will look like the garden of Epicurus.

The Western man has loved—there is laughter and there is dancing and there is song—but the Western man has lost *all* idea of who he is. He has lost track of consciousness, he is not aware. He has become more and more mechanical because he denies the inner. So laughter is there but laughter cannot go deep, because there is no depth. The depth is not accepted. So the West lives in a shallow laughter and East lives in a deep sadness. This is the misery, the agony that has happened to man.

My message is: it is time now, man is mature enough to come out of these half-hearted, lopsided patterns. These programs have to be dropped and changed. One should accept the outer and the inner both, and totally, and with no conditions at all. Then there will be consciousness and there will be love, and they will not be contradictory to each other but complementary. Love will give you joy, consciousness will give you crystallization. Consciousness will make you aware of who you are, and love will make you aware of what this world is. And between these two banks, the river of life flows.

I teach the whole man. This is one of the most fundamental things to be understood—then all else will become easy, then things will be simple. This is the base. I teach the world and I teach God, and I teach them in the same breath. I want to bring Epicurus and Buddha as close as possible. Buddha is sitting under his tree; you cannot conceive of Buddha dancing. Epicurus is dancing in his garden; you cannot conceive of Epicurus sitting silently under a tree, meditating.

I would like Epicurus and Buddha to become one. Life should be a rhythm of dance and silence, of music and sound and silence. Life should be a rhythm of going out as far as possible and going in as far as possible, because God is both.

Close your eyes and you see God, open your eyes and you see God, because God is all there is.

Joey, you ask me, "Can you give me a message to take to the Western world so that people there might understand you and your followers?"

The people who are with me are not my followers. They are my lovers, but not my followers. They are my friends, but not my followers. They are my disciples, but not my followers.

And what is the difference between a disciple and a follower? A follower believes; whatsoever is said, he makes a dogma out of it. The disciple learns, experiments, and unless he finds the truth himself he remains open.

I am not giving any dogma to my friends here, to my sannyasins. All that I am doing here is helping them to understand themselves. All I am doing here is helping them to be themselves.

A follower imitates. A Christian has to imitate Christ and a Buddhist has to imitate Buddha—and all imitators are pseudo.

I want my friends to be authentic. How can you follow me? I am so different from you and you are so different from me. You are so unique. There has never been a person like you and there will never be again. God only creates one person once. He is very innovative, He does not repeat, He does not make man on an assembly line. It is not like Fiat cars or Ford cars: you can see thousands and thousands alike, exactly alike. God always creates the unique.

Go into the garden: you will not find two grass leaves the same. Not even identical twins are the same.

So how can you follow anybody? All following is wrong.

So my second message: man has not to follow anybody. Understand certainly, learn certainly, listen certainly, remain open, but follow your own inner spontaneity. Follow your own being. I help people here to be themselves. Just as in my garden I help the roses to be roses and the lotus to be a lotus. I don't try so that the lotus be a rose. The world is rich because there is variety. The world would be ugly if only roses grew and no other flower. Thousands of flowers grow, and the world is beautiful. Each person has to be authentically himself, utterly himself.

So the sannyasins who are here with me are not my followers. They love me. Through their love they have come close to me. Their love has brought me here, their love has brought them here; because of love we are together. But I am not the leader and they are not the followers. And I am not creating a cult, I am not creating a church. The sannyasins are just a commune of friends, not a church. We don't have any dogma that everybody has to believe in. There is nothing to be believed in, but millions of things to be experimented with. My ashram is a lab; we experiment here.

That too is creating great trouble, because man has forgotten to experiment. We are experimenting in a multi-dimensional way. We are experimenting with Tao, we are experimenting with Sufism, we are experimenting with Jainism, Hinduism, Islam, Christianity; we are experimenting with Tantra, Yoga, alchemy. We are experimenting with all the possibilities that can make the human consciousness rich and a human being whole. That is creating trouble, because when the follower of Yoga comes he cannot understand why Tantra should be experimented with; he is against Tantra. When the follower of Tantra comes he cannot see why Yoga should be experimented with; he is against Yoga.

I am not against anything. I am for all. I am *utterly* for all. I claim the whole human heritage, and whatsoever is good in any tradition is mine, and whatsoever can make man richer is mine. I don't belong to any tradition, all traditions belong to me.

So this is a new experiment; it has never been done before in such a way. This is the synthesis of all the paths. So I am teaching a synthesis. And my feeling is that the man who has only been experimenting with Yoga will remain partial, will grow only in part—as if a man's hand has become too big and the whole body remains small; he will be a monster...unless he can experiment with Tantra also, because Tantra is complementary to Yoga.

Remember, this is one of my basic insights: that in life there are no contradictions. All contradictions are complementaries. Night is complementary to the day, so is summer to winter, so is death to life. They are not against each other. There is nothing against, because there is only one energy, it is one God.

My left hand and my right hand are not against each other, they are complementary. Opposites are just like wings of a bird, two wings—they look opposite to each other but they support each other. The bird cannot fly with one wing.

Tantra and Tao have to be experimented with together.

Now Yoga has a great insight into discipline, and Tao has a great insight into spontaneity. They are opposite on the surface, but unless your discipline makes you more spontaneous and unless your spontaneity makes you more disciplined, you will not be whole. Yoga is control, Tantra is uncontrol; and both are needed. A man has to be so capable of order that if the need arises he can function in utter order. But order should not become a fixation, otherwise he will become a robot. He should be able to come out of his system, his discipline, whenever the need arises. And he can be spontaneous, floating, in a let-go. That he can get only through Tantra, from nowhere else.

I am bringing all the opposites into my sannyasins' lives as complementaries. Yogis will be against me because they cannot see how sex and love can be a part of a seeker's life. They are afraid. They are afraid of sex because sex is the most spontaneous thing in your life. It has to be controlled. They know that once sex is controlled, everything else is controlled, so their basic attack is on sex.

Tantra says if your sex is not spontaneous your whole life will become robot-like. It has to be in freedom. And both are right, and both are right together!—this is my approach. I will look absurd because my approach is very illogical. Logic will always insist: either be a Yogi or be a Tantrika. I believe in life, I don't believe in logic; and life is both together.

A great discipline is needed in life, because you have to live in a world with so many people. You have to live in discipline; otherwise life would become a chaos. Life would become impossible if you couldn't live in a discipline. But if you only live in discipline and you forget spontaneity and you become the discipline and you are not capable of getting out of it, then again life is lost. You have become a machine. Now, these are the two alternatives that have been available to man up to now: either become a chaos—which is not good—or become a machine—which is not good either.

I want you to be alert, conscious, aware, disciplined, and yet capable of spontaneity. When you are working, be disciplined. But work is not all. When you are playing, forget all discipline.

I used to stay in a Calcutta house with a High Court judge. His wife told me, "My husband only listens to you. You are the only person who can bring something into his life. Our whole family is tired with his attitude. He remains the magistrate even in the house." She said, "Even in bed he remains the judge of the High Court. He expects me to call him, 'My Lord'. He is never spontaneous, and in everything he makes rules and laws. The children are tired. When he enters into the house the whole house falls silent, all joy disappears. We all wait for him to go to the court."

Now I know that man: he is a good judge, a very conscientious magistrate, very sincere, honest—and these are good qualities— but he has become a machine. If he comes home and remains the magistrate, that is not good. One has to relax too. One has to play with children, but he cannot play with children; that would be coming down too much. Even with his wife he remains on the high pedestal, far away; he still remains the magistrate.

This is what has happened to the followers of Yoga: they cannot be playful, they cannot rejoice in anything, they cannot participate in celebration—because they cannot relax.

And Tantra alone creates chaos. Tantra alone makes you very, very selfish. You don't care about anybody. You forget that you are part of a great whole, that you belong to a society, that you belong to existence and you are committed to this existence; without it you will be nowhere. You have to fulfill some demands from the side of existence, from the side of society. If you become utterly chaotic, then you cannot exist. Then nobody can exist.

So there has to be a great understanding between chaos and mechanicalness. Exactly in the middle there is a point where I would like my sannyasins to be, exactly in the middle; capable of going to both the extremes when needed, and always capable of moving away from there. I teach this fluidity, I teach this liquidity.

I don't teach fixed life patterns, dead gestalts. I teach growing life syntheses, growing patterns, growing gestalts, and always capable of comprehending the other, the opposite. Then life is beautiful.

And one can know truth only when one has been able to transform the opposites into complementaries. Then only is one's life symmetrical. There is balance—positive and negative are both equally balanced. In that balancing is transcendence. In that balancing one knows the beyond, one opens up to the beyond. The Golden Flower blooms.

The second question:

What should I do?—follow the path of action, the path of knowledge, or the path of devotion?

Follow all three. Act with love and awareness. Love with awareness, and let your love be creative. Bring awareness not against love, but full of the juice of love. And let your awareness participate in existence, let it be creative.

These three are part of your being. This is the real trinity. And if you avoid one then something in you will be denied and will remain stuck. And remember that you can grow only as a total being. If you want to come to me you can come only if your whole being comes here. Your one hand cannot come, your one leg cannot come.

I have heard about a villager. He went to the capital city of his country for the first time and he asked the taxi-driver to take him to a certain place. Now it was a big place. The taxi-driver asked, "Which part?" And the villager said, "Part? I want to go whole."

You cannot go in parts. You can go only when you are whole. Now action is a must; so is awareness, so is love. Why should you choose?—there is no need. All choosing will be committing suicide. Let all the three mix and meet and merge and become one. Be this trinity, be this *trimurti*. These are the three faces of God.

Mulla Nasrudin's mother-in-law died far away in Brazil. Telegraphically he was asked how the remains should be disposed of. He replied, "Embalm, cremate, bury. Take no chances."

The third question:

As you call yourself 'God', what is the meaning of this word? And are there more Gods? Who are they?

Joey, I am God because I am not. And the moment you are not, you are also a God. God is not something special; God is our very being, God is our very existence. When I say I am God I am simply saying I exist. Existence and God are synonymous in my language. I say the trees are also God, and so are the rocks, and so are you.

Yes, Joey, even a journalist is a God! He may not know. You may not be aware of your godliness. I am aware of it! And the moment I became aware of my godliness I became aware of everybody else's godliness. So it will be difficult for me to tell you how many Gods there are. Infinity...

All beings are Gods at different stages of recognition, realization, awareness.

But I can understand your problem. Joey is a Dutch journalist. People coming from the West cannot understand a few things, because their idea of God is the very limited idea that Christianity has given to them. Their idea of God is a very limited idea.

In India we have three words for God; no other language has such richness. And certainly, because we have been working on the inward for centuries, thousands of years have been devoted to it, naturally we have followed all the possibilities of God's existence. It is just like I have heard that Eskimos have nine names for snow because they know different kinds of snow. Now no other language can have nine names for snow; we never come across it so much. Now the West has all the words for science. In the East we have to coin words for scientific terminology; we don't have it. But as far as religion is concerned the whole world will have to follow the East, because we have worked deep down into the interiormost being.

We have three words for God. The first is 'Brahma'. It means the one, the undivided one, when the creator and the creation were asleep in each other. Now Christianity has no word for it. God created the world, Christianity says, so one day—it must have been Monday—God created the world...just that the working week starts on Monday...and He rested on Sunday, just a holiday. Theologians have even been searching for an exact date, and they have found one: four thousand and four years before Jesus, on a certain Monday, God created the world. Before that, where was the world? And before that, who was God?—because He had not created, so He was not a creator. God means 'the creator'. But before creation, how could He be a creator? So creation was latent, potential, unmanifest in the creator. The creator and the creation were together, one. Christianity has no word for it.

We have; we call it Brahma. It is the state when the dancer has not started dancing; the dance and the dancer are one. When the dancer has started dancing, now there is a division. The singer has not sung his song yet, the song is fast asleep in the singer; the moment he sings the division starts. The painter, once he paints, is separate from the painting.

The second word in India is 'Ishwar'. Ishwar means the creator. The unity has broken in two, the duality has arisen. Now the world is separate and the creator is separate. Now Brahma, the one absolute, has become two.

The third word is 'Bhagwan'. It means *anybody* who has again seen the unity—of the dancer and the dance, of the painter and the painting, of the poet and the poetry, of the creator and the creation. One who has seen the unity again, one who has comprehended the unity again in his being, he is called Bhagwan. Literally, the word means 'the blessed one'. It does not mean God, but because of the poverty of Western languages there is a problem. You have to translate 'Brahma' also as 'God'; you have to translate 'Ishwar' also as 'God'; you have to translate 'Bhagwan' also as 'God'. This is simply a poor language, nothing else. Bhagwan literally means 'the blessed one'.

Who is the blessed one?—one who has known the unity again, one who has reached to the original source again; he is called Bhagwan. That's why we call Krishna 'Bhagwan', and Buddha 'Bhagwan'.

And you will be surprised to know: Buddha never believed in any God; certainly Bhagwan cannot mean God. Buddha never believed in any God, he never believed in any creation or any creator. Still, Buddhists call him Bhagwan, the blessed one, because he understood whatsoever the truth is. You call it God, creator, truth, *nirvana*, enlightenment; that is not the point. He understood, and in that understanding blessings showered on him. He became Bhagwan, the blessed one.

Now this is going to be a constant problem. I declare myself to be the blessed one. I have seen. Those flowers have showered on me. By declaring myself Bhagwan I am not saying that I have created the world. I don't take that responsibility!

By declaring myself Bhagwan I am simply saying that I have been blessed by existence. The grace has descended into me. I have seen. And the moment seeing happens you disappear, you are no more. The blessed one is one who is no more. I am not, God is: this is the *experience* that makes one blessed.

Now the paradox has to be understood. Man never meets God. Man can only dissolve, disappear; then God is. In your absence God's presence descends. The whole work of religion is nothing but helping you to disappear as an ego. The moment you look into yourself and there is no I, no ego to be found, but utter silence, utter emptiness, therewith the matter is settled...you are God.

You are God not against others—not that others are not God and you are God. You are God because then only God is! So I am not saying I am God and you are not God. In declaring myself, I am also declaring you divine; and not only you—the animals, the birds, the trees, the rocks, the whole existence consists of God and nothing else.

I am not saying I am holier than you. I am not saying I am more special than you. All that I am saying is that I have disappeared, and in that disappearance grace has showered, ecstasy has arisen.

I am utterly gone, and gone forever.

And in this space that is left behind there is nothing else but God.

In fact, when you say "I am" you are uttering a falsehood, because you are not. The moment you say "I am" you are separating yourself from existence, and this is absolutely false, a lie. You are not separate from existence. You are not capable of being yourself apart from existence; not even for a single moment can you exist. No man is an island. The moment you see it, separation disappears. Suddenly you are one with the trees and with the stars, and that moment is the moment of blessings. You have come home.

That's all that is meant by 'Bhagwan': the word simply means 'the blessed one'.

The fourth question:

Why am I so afraid of women? And why am I so bored with my wife?

All men are afraid of women, and all women are afraid of men. They have good reasons to mistrust each other, since they have been trained from early years to be enemies of each other. They are not born to be enemies, but they achieve enmity. And after about twenty years of such training in being afraid of each other they are supposed to marry one day and find complete trust in each other. All this for a five rupee marriage license? Twenty years training of being afraid of each other... In a sixty, seventy-year life, one third of your life, and the most delicate and sensitive part of your life...

Psychologists say a man learns fifty percent of his whole life's learning by the time he is seven. In the remaining sixty-three years he will learn only fifty percent more. Fifty percent is learned by the time you are seven. By the time you are twenty almost eighty percent is learned. You have become fixed, hard. Distrust has been taught to you.

The boys have been told, "Avoid girls, they are dangerous." The girls have been told, "Avoid boys, they are nasty, they will do something evil to you." And then after this complete conditioning of twenty years—just think, twenty years of constantly being taught by the parents, by the school, by the college, by the university, by the church, by the priest—one day suddenly how can you drop this twenty years of conditioning?

This question arises again and again. So many people come and tell me that they are afraid of women. Women tell me they are afraid of men. You were not born afraid. Otherwise no man would enter into a woman's womb. If he was really afraid then no woman would be conceived, because she can be conceived only through a man.

You were not afraid in your beginnings. A child is born simply unafraid. Then we teach him fear and we condition his mind.

This has to be dropped. This has driven people almost neurotic. Then people fight, then they are constantly fighting—husbands and wives constantly fighting. And they are worried about why they go on fighting. And all relationships turn sour. Why does it happen? You have been poisoned, and you have to consciously drop that conditioning. Otherwise you will remain afraid.

There is nothing to be afraid of in a man or a woman. They are just like you—just as much in need of love as you are, hankering just as much to join hands with you as you are hankering. They want to participate in your life. They want others to participate in their lives—because the more people participate in each other's lives, the more joy arises. People are looking very sad. They have become very lonely. Even in crowds people are lonely because everybody is afraid of everybody else. Even if people are sitting close to each other, they are holding themselves, holding so much so that their whole being becomes hard. A hard crust surrounds them, an armor arises around their being. So even when they meet there is no real meeting. People hold hands but those hands are cold, no love is flowing. They hug each other, yes, bones clash with each other, but the heart remains far away.

People have to love. Love is a great need, just as food is a need. Food is a lower need, love is a higher need, a much higher-order value.

Now psychologists have been doing much research work on children who were brought up without any love. Almost fifty percent of children die if they are brought up without love; within two years they die. They are given good food, nourishment, every scientific care, but mechanically. The nurse comes, gives them a bath, feeds them; *every* care is taken, but no human love. The nurse will not hug them close to her heart. The nurse will not give her warm body to the child; warmth is not given. Within two years fifty percent of those children die. And this is strange, because there is no visible reason why they die. They were perfectly healthy, the body was going perfectly well, they were not ill or anything, but suddenly, for no reason at all, they start dying.

And the remaining fifty percent are in more trouble than those who die. Those who die are more intelligent. Those who survive become neurotic, schizophrenic, psychotic, because no love has showered on them. Love makes you one piece. It is like glue—it glues you together. They start falling into fragments. There is nothing to hold them together, no vision of life, no experience of love—nothing to hold them together. Their lives seem meaningless, so many of them turn neurotic, many of them become criminals. Because love makes a person creative, if love is missing then a person becomes destructive.

Had Adolf Hitler's mother loved him more, the world would have been totally different.

If there is no love the person forgets the language of creativity, becomes destructive; so criminals, politicians are born—they are the same types of people. There is no difference in them, no qualitative difference. Their faces differ, their masks are different, but deep down they are all criminals. In fact, you have been reading the history of human crimes and nothing else. You have not yet been taught the real history of human- ity, because the real history consists of Buddhas, Christs, Lao Tzus.

That's what I am trying to do here! Now talking about Lu-tsu— you may not even have heard his name—now talking on this tremendously beautiful book, *The Secret of the Golden Flower*, I am trying to make you aware that a totally different human history exists which has been kept out of the schools. History takes note only of crimes, history takes note only of destruc- tion. If you kill somebody on the streets you will be in the newspapers, and if you give a roseflower to somebody you will never be heard of again. Nobody will know about it.

If love is missing in childhood the person will become either a politician or a criminal, or will go mad, or will find some destructive way because he will not know how to create. His life will be meaningless. He will not feel any significance. He will feel very very condemned, because unless you have been loved you cannot feel your worth. The moment some- body loves you, you become worthy. You start feeling you are needed, existence would be a little less without you. When a woman loves you, you know that if you are gone somebody is going to be sad. When a man loves you, you know that you are making somebody's life happy, and because you are making somebody's life happy, great joy arises in you. Joy arises only in creating joy for others; there is no other way. The more people you can make happy, the more you will feel happy.

This is the real meaning of service. This is the real meaning of religion: help people become happy, help people become warm, help people become loving; create a little beauty in the world, create a little joy, create a little corner where people can celebrate and sing and dance and be. And you will be happy. Immense will be your reward. But the man who has never been loved does not know it.

So the fifty percent that survive prove to be very dangerous people.

Love is such a basic need; it is exactly the food for the soul. The body needs food, the soul also needs food. The body lives on material food, the soul lives on spiritual food. Love is spiritual food, spiritual nourishment.

In my vision of a better world children will be taught to love each other. Boys and girls will not be put apart. No division, no disgust with each other should be created. But why has this disgust been created?—because there has been a great fear of sex. Sex is not accepted; that is the problem. Because sex is not accepted children have to be kept apart. And humanity is going to suffer unless it accepts sex as a natural phenomenon. This whole problem of man/woman arises because sex is condemned.

This condemnation has to go—and now it can go. In the past I can understand there were reasons for it. For example, if a girl became pregnant, then there would have been problems. Parents were very much afraid, the society was very much afraid, people lived in fear. The boys and girls had to be kept apart, great walls had to be raised between them. And then one day, after twenty years, suddenly you open the door and you say, "She is not your enemy, she is your wife. Love her!" and, "He is not your enemy, he is your husband. Love him!" And what about those twenty years when he was the enemy? And what about those twenty years' experiences? Can you suddenly drop them so easily? You cannot drop them. They linger on, they hang around you your whole life.

But now there is no need. In my understanding, the greatest revolution in the world has been that which is created by 'the pill'. Lenin and Mao Tse Tung are nothing compared to the pill. The pill is the greatest revolutionary. This is going to create a totally different world because fear can be dropped; now there is no need to be afraid. The fear of pregnancy has been the cause of condemning sex. Now there is no need to condemn it at all, it can be accepted.

Science has prepared the ground for a new culture, and I am heralding that future! That's why all those who are burdened with their pasts are going to be against me. They *cannot* understand me, because I *see* into the future, what is going to happen in the future, and I am preparing the way for it. Man and woman have to be brought as close as possible. And now there is no fear.

In the past, I understand the fear was there. I can forgive those people in the past, because they were helpless. But now you cannot be forgiven if you teach your children to be separate and antagonize them against each other. There is no need. Now boys and girls can mix and meet and be together, and all fear about sex can be dropped. And the beauty is that because of the fear and because of the condemnation and because of the denial sex has become so important; otherwise it is not so important.

Try to understand a simple psychological law: if you deny something too much it becomes very important. The very denial makes it important. You become *obsessed* with it. Now boys and girls have to be kept apart for twenty years—they become *obsessed* with each other. They only think of the other, they cannot think of anything else.

I have heard of an incident that happened to former Ambassador Ellis while he was an envoy to Greece. Both he and his secretary had been preoccupied by an approaching deadline. He had to fly to Rome to give a report before a European security conference. She, a healthy, buxom lass of twenty-three, was two days away from her wedding to a handsome Marine guard after a six-month engagement. Naturally, her mind was on the state of her trousseau rather than on the state of the Greek government. Ambassador Ellis was trying to finish up his paper on Greece before rushing to the airport. He had entitled his study—a report saying that the political situation was more shaky than the economic—'Man Shall Not Live by Bread Alone'. Before he had a chance to really go over the copy, he had to race to the Athens airport. He left word that the speech should be teletyped to the Rome Embassy so they could type in for distribution for the next day's conference. When he arrived in Rome he was met by a group of foreign service officers who were to take him to the hotel to deliver the speech. They were a bit puzzled by the printed title of the report; Ambassador Ellis looked at one of the mimeographed copies. The bride-to-be's rendition of the Ambassador's dictated

Biblical saying came out not 'Man Shall Not Live by Bread Alone' but 'Man Shall Not Love in Bed Alone'.

The mind can become preoccupied. Twenty years' training in anti-sexual teachings makes the mind preoccupied, and all kinds of perversions arise. Homosexuality arises, lesbianism arises, people start living in fantasies, pornography arises, dirty films, 'blue films' arise—and this whole thing goes on because of the nonsense that you do.

Now you want pornography to stop; it cannot stop. You are creating the situation for it. If boys and girls could be together, who would bother to look at a nude picture?

You go and meet some aboriginal tribe in India who live naked and you show your *Playboy* magazine to them and they will all laugh. I have lived with them, and I have talked with them, and they all laugh. They cannot believe: "What is there?" They live naked, so they know what a woman looks like and they know what a man looks like.

Pornography is created by your priests; they are the foundation of it—and then all kinds of perversions...because when you cannot actually meet the other pole for which the attraction is natural, you start fantasizing. Then a greater problem arises: twenty years of fantasies and dreams, and then you meet a real woman and she falls very low, very low in your expectations—because all those fantasies! You were completely free to fantasize; no real woman is going to satisfy you. Because of your fantasies and dreams you have created such ideas about a woman—which no woman can fulfill, and you have created such ideas about men—which no man can fulfill. Hence the frustration. Hence the bitterness that arises between couples. The man feels cheated—"This is not the woman." He was thinking, dreaming, and he was free to create whatsoever he wanted in his dream, and this woman looks very poor compared to his fantasy.

In your fantasy women don't perspire—or do they?—and they don't quarrel with you, and they don't nag you, and they are just golden, just sweet flowers, and they always remain young. They never become old. And they don't get grumpy. Because they are your creations, if you want them laughing, they laugh. Their bodies are made not of this world.

But when you meet a real women she perspires, her breath smells, and sometimes it is natural to be grumpy. And she nags, and she fights, and she throws pillows and breaks things, and she won't allow you a thousand and one things. She starts curbing your freedom. Your fantasy women never curbed your freedom. Now this woman seems to be like a trap. And, she is not as beautiful as you had been thinking; she is not a Cleopatra. She is an ordinary woman, just as you are an ordinary man. Neither you are fulfilling her desire nor she is fulfilling your desire. Nobody has the obligation to fulfill your fantasies! People are *real* people. And because this twenty years' starvation creates fantasy, it creates trouble for your future life.

You ask me, "Why am I afraid of women? And why am I bored with my wife?"

You must have fantasized too much. You will have to drop your fantasies. You will have to learn to live with reality. You will have to learn to see the extraordinary in the ordinary. That needs great art. A woman is not just her skin, not just her face, not just her body proportion. A woman is a soul! You have to be intimate with her, you have to get involved in her life, in her inner life. You have to merge and meet with her energies. And people don't know how to meet and how to merge; they have never been taught. The art of love has not been taught to you, and everybody thinks that they know what love is. You don't know. You come only with the potential of love but not with the art of it.

Fifty years ago, near Calcutta, in a jungle, two girls were found, Kamala and Vimala. They were brought up by wolves. Maybe they were unwanted children and the mother had left them in the forest. It has happened many times: almost in every part of the world, once in a while, a child has been found who has grown up with the animals.

Those two girls were absolutely inhuman. They walked on all fours, they could not stand on two feet. They learned from the wolves to walk on all fours. They howled like wolves. They could not speak Bengali. And they were very dangerous— they ran like wolves. No Olympic champion would have defeated them, they were so quick and fast. And if they jumped, if they became angry, they would tear you in parts. They looked human, but their whole training had been that of the wolves.

You are born with a capacity to learn language, but you are not born with a language itself. Exactly like this, you are born with the capacity to love, but you are not born with the art of love. That art of love has to be taught, has to be imbibed.

And just the opposite is happening: you have been taught the art of hate and hatred, not of love. You have been taught how to hate people. Christians have been taught to hate the Mohammedans, Mohammedans have been taught to hate the Hindus, Indians have been taught to hate the Pakistanis. Hate has been taught in many ways. Man has been taught to hate the woman, the woman has been taught to hate the man, and now suddenly one day you decide to get married...and you get married...to your *enemy!* And then the whole turmoil starts; then the life becomes just a nightmare.

You are bored with your wife because you don't know how to enter into her soul. You may be able to enter her body, but that is going to become boring very soon because that will be the repetition. The body is a very superficial thing. You can make love to the body once, twice, thrice, and then you become perfectly acquainted with the body, its contours. Then there is nothing new. Then you start becoming interested in other women: you think they must be having something different from your wife—at least behind the clothes it appears they must be having something different. You can still fantasize about them.

Clothes have been invented to help your sexual desire. A naked woman leaves nothing to your fantasy. That's why naked women are not so attractive; neither are naked men. But when a woman or a man is hidden behind clothes, they leave much to your fantasy. You can fantasize about what is behind it, you can imagine again.

Now you cannot imagine about your wife; that is the trouble. You can imagine about your neighbor's wife, she looks attractive.

I have heard...

A man had a severe coronary and was told that if he wanted to live he had to completely cut out drinking, smoking and all forms of physical exertion. After six months he went into the doctor's office for a check-up. After he was told he was progressing fine, he said to the doctor, "You know, sometimes I want a drink so much—not a lot, just a taste of it. Could I not have just one drink or two? Maybe once a week on a Friday or Saturday night?"

"No," the doctor said, "but I will tell you what. I will allow you one glass of wine with your evening meal."

Some months later he was back for another physical. This time he told the doctor, "You know, doctor, sometimes I just crave for a cigarette. If I could just puff one when I wake up and another after each meal."

"No," said the doctor. "You would soon be smoking a pack a day. But if you want you can smoke one cigar a week, perhaps after your Sunday dinner."

Months went by, and our friend's health as well as state of mind improved. There was only one thing that gnawed at him. When he went to the doctor again he came out with it very bluntly. "Doctor, it is not normal to go without sexual relations. Surely I am healthy enough to be able to resume that."

"No," said the doctor. "The physical exertion as well as excitement could just be too much. But I will tell you what: I will allow you once a week to have sex—but only with your wife."

People feel bored with their wives and with their husbands. The reason is they have not been able to contact the other's real soul. They have been able to contact the body, but they have missed the contact that happens heart to heart, center to center, soul to soul. Once you know how to contact soul to soul, when you have become soulmates, then there is no boredom at all. Then there is always something to discover in the other because each being is an infinity, and each being contains God Himself. There is no end to exploring.

That's why I say Tantra should become a compulsory phenomenon for all human beings. Each school, each college, each university, should teach Tantra. Tantra is the science of contacting souls, of going to the deepest core of the other. Only in a world which knows the art of Tantra will this boredom disappear; otherwise it cannot disappear. You can tolerate it, you can suffer it, you can be a martyr to it. That's how people have been in the past—martyrs. They say, "What to do? This is fate. This life is finished. Next life we will choose some other woman or some other man, but this life is gone, and nothing can be done. And the children are there, and a thousand and one problems"...and the prestige and the society and the respectability—so they have suffered and they have remained martyrs.

Now they are no longer ready to suffer so they have moved to the other extreme: now they are indulging in all kinds of sex, but that too is not giving any contentment.

Neither the Indian is contented nor is the American. Nobody is contented, because the basic thing is missed by both. The basic thing is unless you become capable of decoding the inner mystery of your woman or your man, you will sooner or later get fed up, bored. Then either you become a martyr—remain with it, suffer it, wait for death to deliver you—or you start indulging with other women. But whatsoever you have done with *this* woman will be done with the other, and you will get fed up with the other, and with the other, and your whole life will be just changing partners. That is not going to satisfy either.

Unless you learn the secret art of Tantra...

Tantra is one of the most important secrets ever discovered. But it is very delicate because it is the *greatest* art. To paint is easy, to create poetry is easy, but to create a communion with the energy of the other, a dancing communion, is the greatest and the most difficult art to learn.

People are against me because I am telling people how to love. I am telling people how to make love a prayer. I am telling people how to love so deeply that love itself becomes your religion—that your woman one day disappears and you find God there, that your man one day disappears and you find God there; that one day, in deep communion, in deep orgasmic experience, in that ecstasy, for a moment you both disappear and there is only God and nothing else.

You have been taught down the ages to be against sex, and that has made you very sexual. Now this paradox has to be understood. If you want to understand me, this paradox has to be understood very very deeply, clearly: you have been made sexual by all the condemnation of sex.

Just the other day one government officer came to look around the Ashram...because the government is very worried: "What is going on here?"—what am I teaching people? And he kept a very haughty posture. Sheela took him around the Ashram, Sheela was walking with him. He started moving closer and closer to Sheela, he started touching her body; so she would keep aloof, but he would come close again. And Sheela was worried, "What to do with this man?" She was worried; she could have hit him. And I have told her that next time it happens, give him a good beating. He needs it, he deserves it.

He had come to find out what was going on here—particularly about sex. And when he found Sheela alone—she was taking him around—he came close, perspiring, and asked, "Can I kiss you?" Now this man is sent here to inquire about what is happening here.

Remember it: next time you find a government official here, give him a kiss of death!

And in the office he again became very holier-than-thou.

This repressed sexuality...

I have heard of the visit of J.P. Morgan to the home of Dwight Morrow. The great American financier was noted, among other things, for a bulbous red nose of unsurpassing ugliness.
"Remember, Anne," Mrs. Morrow kept saying to her daughter, "you must not say one word about Mr. Morgan's red nose. You must not even look at it very much."
Anne promised, but when Morgan arrived her mother watched and waited tensely. Anne was as good as gold, but Mrs. Morrow dared not relax. Turning to the financier with a gracious smile, she prepared to pour tea and said, "Mr. Morgan, will you have one or two lumps in your nose?"

That's what has happened to the whole humanity: repressed sex has become the obsession.

People think I am teaching sexuality? I am teaching transcendence. Soon this will be the only place where nobody will be obsessed with sex. It is already the experience of hundreds of sannyasins. Every day I receive letters: "What is happening, Bhagwan? My sex is disappearing, I no longer find much interest in it"—men and women both.

That interest is a pathological interest that has been created by repression. Once repression is taken away that interest will disappear. And then there is a natural feel—which is not obsessive, which is not pathological. And whatsoever is natural is good. This interest in sex is unnatural. And the problem is: this is being created by the priest and by the politician, by the so-called *mahatmas*. They are the culprits. And they go on creating it, and they think they are helping humanity to go beyond sex. They are not! They are throwing humanity into this whole mess.

If you understand me rightly, then you will be surprised by the experience that you will go through in this commune. Soon you will find sex has become a natural phenomenon. And finally, as your meditations will deepen, as you will start meeting with each other's souls more and more, the body contact will become less and less. A moment comes when there is no need for sexuality to be there, it has taken a new turn. The energy has started moving upwards. It is the same energy— at the lowest rung it is sex, at the highest rung it is *samadhi*.

I have written one book—not written, my discourses have been collected in it—it is called *From Sex to Superconsciousness*. Now fifteen years have passed. Since then nearabout two hundred books have been published, but nobody seems to read any other book—not in India. They all read *From Sex to Superconsciousness*. They all criticize it also, they are all against it. Articles are still being written, books are written against it, and *mahatmas* go on objecting to it. And I have written two hundred books, and no other book is mentioned, no other book is looked at.

Do you understand?

"Mr Morgan, will you have one or two lumps in your nose?" —as if I have written only one book.

People are suffering from a wound. Sex has become a wound. It needs to be healed.

Remember, there is no need to be afraid of women, no need to be afraid of men. We are all alike, the same God. We have to learn how to love each other. We have to come closer to each other because that is the only way to come close to God. Love is one of the greatest doors to God, just as awareness is another.

The East has followed the way of awareness and become lopsided. The West has followed the way of love and has become lopsided. I teach you both: a loving awareness, a conscious love. And with this you will become integrated, you will attain individuation.

Master Lu-tsu said: *If you are not yet clear, I will make it clear to you through the threefold Buddhist contemplation of emptiness, delusion, and the center.*

Emptiness comes as the first of the three contemplations. All things are looked upon as empty. Then follows delusion. Although it is known that they are empty, things are not destroyed, but one attends to one's affairs in the midst of emptiness. But although one does not destroy things, neither does one pay attention to them; this is contemplation of the center. While practicing contemplation of the empty, one also knows that one cannot destroy the ten thousand things, and still one does not notice them. In this way the three contemplations fall together. But, after all, strength is in envisioning the empty. Therefore, when one practices contemplation of emptiness, emptiness is certainly empty, but delusion is empty too, and the center is empty. It needs great strength to practice contemplation of delusion; then delusion is really delusion, but emptiness is also delusion, and the center is delusion too. Being on the way of the center, one also creates images of the emptiness; they are not called empty, but are called central. One practices also contemplation of delusion, but one does not call it delusion, one calls it central. As to what has to do with the center, more need not be said.

Chapter Eleven

September 6th, 1978

THE CONTEMPLATION
OF EMPTINESS

A ZEN STORY...

Just before the Zen Master, Ninakawa, passed away another
Zen Master, Ikkyu, visited him. "Shall I lead you on?" Ikkyu
asked.

Ninakawa replied, "I came here alone and I go alone. What
help could you be to me?"

Ikkyu answered, "If you think you really came and you are
really going, if you think that you come and go, that is your
delusion. Let me show you the path on which there is no coming and no going."

With his words Ikkyu had revealed the path so clearly that
Ninakawa smiled, and without saying a single word, nodded
and passed away.

This is a beautiful story. A few things have to be understood about it; they will help you to enter into the sutras of Lu-tsu.

First: to a man who is in search of truth, even death is an occasion. To the man who is not in search, even life is not an occasion to learn. People live their lives without learning a thing at all. They pass through life but without gaining any maturity through it. They remain almost asleep. People live like sleepwalkers. They remain drunk—they don't know what they are doing, they don't know why they are doing, they don't know from where they come, they don't know to where they are going. They are simply like driftwood, at the mercy of the winds. Their lives are accidental; remember that word 'accidental'.

Millions of people live only accidental lives, and unless you take hold of your life and start changing it from the accidental to the existential, there is going to be no transformation.

That's what sannyas is all about: an effort to change the accidental into the existential, an effort to change the unconscious life into a conscious life, the effort to wake up. And then life is learning, and so is death. Then one goes on learning. Then each moment, each situation, comes as a gift. Yes, even suffering is a gift from God, but only for those who know how to learn, how to receive the gift. Ordinarily even blessings are not gifts for you because you don't know how to receive them, you don't know how to absorb them. Your life is lived in a robot-like way.

I have heard...

A man came home very late in the night. The excuse that he gave to his wife for coming home too late was this...

In fact, the poor man had imbibed a bit too freely and told his angry wife that he had taken the wrong bus.

His wife said, "That's easy to understand—considering the shape you are in—but how did you know you were on the wrong bus?"

The husband said, "Well, it seemed strange when I stood on one corner for a couple of hours, but what finally convinced me was the fact that people kept coming in and ordering hamburgers and coffee."

It was not even a bus!

The life that you are living is not even a life; it can't be. How can it be life if there is no light in you? How can it be life if there is no love in you? How can it be life if you function mechanically? Only with consciousness does life arrive—not by birth but by consciousness. Only a meditator starts beginning to live. Others are befooling themselves; they are not really living. They may be doing a thousand and one things. They go on doing; to the very end they go on doing: accumulating wealth, achieving power, fulfilling this ambition and that. They go on and on, but still the total, the sum-total of their lives is nil.

Interviewing the sixty-year-old rodeo champion in Austin, Texas, the New York newspaperman remarked, "You are really an extraordinary man to be a rodeo champion at your age."

"Shucks," said the cowboy, "I am not nearly the man my Pa is. He is still place-kicking for a football team and he is eighty-six."

"Amazing!" gasped the journalist. "I'd like to meet your father."

"Can't right now. He's in El Paso standing up for Grandpa. Grandpa is getting married tomorrow. He's a hundred and fourteen."

"Your family is simply unbelievable," said the newspaperman. "Here you are, a rodeo champion at sixty. Your father is a football player at eighty-six. And now your grandfather wants to get married at a hundred and fourteen."

"Hell, mister, you got that wrong," said the Texan. "Grandpa does not want to get married. He *has* to."

This way life goes on and on to the very end. This is not real life. You are just a victim—a victim of your unconscious instincts, a victim of biology, a victim of physiology, a victim of nature. This is the bondage. To be free of all this unconsciousness is liberation. To be free of the bondage of your body chemistry, to be free of the bondage of the program that nature has put in your body cells, to be free of all that is unconscious in you, to be on your own, to be a conscious light—that is the beginning of real life. Count your age only from the moment when you start living consciously, fully alert, meditatively. When each act has the flavor of consciousness, then you are coming closer to home. Otherwise you are going farther and farther away.

And life gives you many opportunities to wake up. But rather than waking up, rather than using those opportunities, you start searching for even deeper drugs to drown you in unconsciousness. When suffering comes that is an occasion to wake up, but then you start searching for a drug. The drug may be sex, may be alcohol, may be LSD; the drug may be money, may be power-politics; the drug can be anything. Anything that keeps you unconscious is a drug. Anything that keeps you engaged in the non-essential is a drug. Drugs are not only sold at the chemist, drugs are available every-where. Your schools, your colleges, your universities sell drugs because they create ambition, and ambition keeps peo-ple unconscious. Ambition keeps them running, chasing shadows, illusions, dreams. Your politicians are the greatest drug-peddlers: they continuously go on creating a power-lust in you, a hunger, a greed for power; that keeps you occupied.

To be ambitious, to be competitive, is to be alcoholic. And this is a deeper alcohol. The ordinary alcohol can be prohibited. This alcohol is so tremendously available from every nook and corner—from parents, from priests, from politicians, from professors. Your whole society lives in this drugged state. If you have something to run after, you feel good. The moment you have nothing to run after, you feel lost. You immediately create some new occupation.

The observation of the Buddhas down the ages is that when suffering comes it is a hint from God that it is time—"Wake up". But you drown the suffering in a drug.

Your wife dies—you start drinking too much, or you start gambling. It was an opportunity to see that this life is not going to last forever. This house is made on the sands, this life is a paper boat; it will be drowned any moment. Any whim of the winds and the life will be gone. Wake up! Your wife is dead, you are going to be dead because you are standing in the same queue, and the queue is coming closer and closer to the window called death.

But you don't wake up; you start searching for another wife. You go bankrupt but you don't wake up. You are defeated but you don't wake up; you start searching with more vigor, with more vengeance.

A woman went to one of those health clinics where they have
about seven doctors. After twenty minutes in one doctor's
office she ran screaming down the hall. Another doctor who
finally got the story out of her called the first doctor. "What is
the idea of telling that patient she is pregnant? She is not! You
nearly frightened her to death."

"I know," the first doctor said, "but I cured her hiccups,
didn't I?"

If you listen, if you watch, you will see that every suffering
that happens in your life is a blessing in disguise. It can cure
you of your hiccups. It is a shock...and you need shocks!
—because you have grown many buffers around yourself,
you have grown many shock absorbers around yourself. They
have to be broken. Unless they are broken you will live in a
dream. And remember, in a dream the dream looks real. And
you know it perfectly well; you dream every night: in a dream
the dream looks absolutely real. And you can always find
reasons and logic to support your dreams. Even when the
dream is broken you can find reasons to support the dream
which was absolutely false.

I have heard...

A man woke up one morning in a state of shock. He woke
his wife and said, "Darling, I had a terrible dream last night.
I dreamt I was eating a ten kilo marshmallow, and on top of
that, I can't find my pillow anywhere."

Even when you wake up you may find some support. You
may look around, and you can *always* find support. Your
mind is very cunning. Your mind plays many games upon
you, many tricks upon you, and it can look very logical. It
can appear very convincing.

A Frenchman came home and was startled to find his son in bed with his grandmother...

Now it can happen only in France!

..."Son," he said, "how can you do this?"
"Well," said his son, "You sleep with my mama, I sleep with your mama. C'est logique."

You can prove things are logical, even absurd things. Be alert. Your mind is all in favor of dreams. Your mind is the source of dreaming, hence your mind has a duty, an obligation, to support those dreams. If you are not very alert you will be deceived and tricked and trapped by your own mind again and again, in the same stupidities that you have come across many times and you have repented for many times and you have decided many times, taken a vow, "Never again!" But the mind will come with subtle allurements.

The mind is the greatest salesman. The mind is very persuasive. And because the mind is always helping your unconscious desires, the body also supports the mind.

The effort to wake up is really arduous. This is the greatest challenge that a man can encounter in life—and only a *man* can encounter it, a courageous man. It needs guts to accept the challenge to wake up. This is the greatest adventure there is. It is easier to go to the moon, it is easier to go to Everest, it is easier to go to the depths of the Pacific Ocean. The real problem arises when you go into your own self. The real problem arises when you start waking up; then your whole past is against it. Your whole past then hangs around your neck like mountains—it pulls you down, it does not allow you to fly into the sky, into the infinite, into eternity, into God, into *nirvana*.

This is a beautiful parable, that one Master is dying and another Master comes to say goodbye to him—but what a way to say goodbye! The opportunity of death is used. Yes, only very conscious people can use the opportunity that death makes available. Death looked at unconsciously is the enemy, death looked at consciously is the greatest friend. Death looked at unconsciously is just a shattering of all your dreams, of all your life patterns, of all the structures that you have been raising, of all that you have invested in—an utter collapse. But death looked at consciously is the beginning of a new life, a door to the divine.

Ninakawa is dying and Ikkyu asks, "Shall I lead you on?" He is saying that death is a beginning, not an end. "Shall I lead you on? Do you need my help in any way? You are going to learn a new way of being, a new vision is going to arise; you are entering into a new dimension, a new plenitude— shall I lead you on? Is my help in any way needed?"

Ninakawa replied, "I came here alone and I go alone. What help could you be to me?"

Yes, we come alone and we go alone. And between these two alonenesses we create all the dreams of togetherness, relationship, love, family, friends, clubs, societies, nations, churches, organizations. Alone we come, alone we go. Aloneness is our ultimate nature. But in between these two, how many dreams we dream! One becomes a husband or a wife, a father or a mother. One accumulates money, power, prestige, respectability, and knowing perfectly well that you come empty-handed and you go empty-handed. You cannot take a thing from here—still one goes on accumulating, still one goes on becoming attached, more and more attached, more and more rooted in this world from where we have to leave. Use this world as a caravanserai, don't make a home in it. Use it, certainly, but don't be used by it. There is no point in possessing anything because the moment you start possessing something you are possessed by it. The more you possess the more you are possessed. Use!—but remember to be watchful that death is coming, it is always on the way. Any moment it may knock on the door and you will have to leave *everything* as it is. And it is *always* in the middle that you have to leave. One cannot complete anything in life.

Ninakawa replied perfectly well: "I came here alone and I go alone. What help could you be to me? How can you help me in death? Maybe in life we can have the illusion of being helped, of being helpers, but how in death?"

He's telling a great truth, but there are truths and truths and greater truths.

Ikkyu answered with an even higher truth.

Remember this: the conflict is not between the untrue and the true. The real conflict is between the lower truth and the higher truth. The untrue is untrue; what can it do, what harm can it do to truth? The problem is never of a choice between the untrue and the true. The problem is always between a lower truth and a higher truth.

What Ninakawa said is a *great* truth—that we come alone and we go alone. But there is still a higher truth.

Ikkyu answered, "If you think you really come and go, that is your illusion."

Who comes? Who goes? All is as it is. Coming and going is also a dream.

For example, in the night you fall asleep, a dream arises. In the morning the dream disappears. Do you think you had gone somewhere and you have come back? You find yourself in the same room, on the same bed, and all that dreaming! You may have travelled to faraway places—you may have visited the moon, the planets, the stars—but in the morning when you wake up you don't wake up on a star. You wake up in the same place where you had slept.

Life is a dream! We are where we are. We are that which we are. Not for a single moment have we moved, and not a single inch have we moved from our true nature! This is the ultimate statement of truth.

Yes, Ninakawa was saying something significant, very significant—"Alone we come, alone we go"—but Ikkyu is stating something even far more profound. He says, "What going? What coming? You are talking nonsense! Who comes? Who goes?"

Waves arise in the ocean and then disappear in the ocean. When the wave arises in the ocean it is still the ocean, as much as it was before it had risen. And then it disappears back into the ocean. Forms arise and disappear, the reality remains as it is. All changes are only appearances. Deep, at the deepest core, nothing ever changes; there it is all the same. Time is a peripheral phenomenon. At the center there is no time, no change, no movement. All is eternal there.

Just see the point of this dialogue happening at the moment when Ninakawa was dying. These are not the things to be discussed at the time of death. At the time of death people try to help the person, console him, "You are not dying. Who says you are dying? You are going to live." Even when they know—the doctor has said, "Now all is finished and nothing can be done anymore"—then too the family goes on pretending that you are not going to die. The family goes on helping the dream to remain a little longer, and the family goes on hoping some miracle will happen and the person will be saved.

This dialogue is immensely beautiful. When somebody is dying, it is better to make him aware that death has come. In fact it is better to make everybody aware, whether the death has come today or not. Whether it is going to come tomorrow or the day after tomorrow doesn't matter; it is going to come. One thing is certain: that it is going to come. In life only one thing is certain, and that is death, so it is better to talk of it from the very beginning.

In the ancient cultures every child was made aware of death. Your very foundation should be made on that awareness of death. The man who is aware of death will certainly become aware of life, and the man who is unaware of death will remain unaware of life too—because life and death are two aspects of the same coin.

Ikkyu said, "If you think..."

But remember, he uses the word 'if' because he knows; he knows this man, Ninakawa. He can see through and through, the man is transparent. He knows that he has arrived. Maybe he is just provoking Ikkyu to say something beautiful, to say something of truth. Maybe his provocation is just a trick, he is playing a game. That's why he says, "*If* you think you really come and go, that is your delusion. Let me show you the path on which there is no coming and no going."

What is that path on which there is no coming and no going? Yes, there is a place inside you; that is your eternal home, where nothing ever happens, where nothing ever changes—no birth, no death, no coming, no going, no arising, no disappearing. All is always the same.

With his words Ikkyu had revealed the path so clearly that Ninakawa smiled, nodded and passed away.

It can't be said in a better way—that's why Ninakawa didn't utter a single word anymore. But he smiled...because that which cannot be said can be smiled, that which cannot be said can be nodded, that which cannot be said can be shown. He showed it with his face. He recognized, he nodded, he said to Ikkyu, "Right, absolutely right. So you have also come home."

The dialogue between two Masters is very rare, because when two Masters meet, ordinarily they remain silent. There is nothing to say. But whenever it happens that two Masters say something to each other, it is a great play. There is a playfulness. It is not an argument, remember; it is a dialogue. They are provoking each other to say it in a better way. And Ikkyu has said it. Ninakawa is satisfied, utterly satisfied.

What has Ikkyu said?—that the life that we think is, is not, and we have not looked at that which is at all. We have become too occupied with the illusory, and we go on remaining occupied with the illusory to the very end.

I have heard...

A man was very worried about his widowed mother-in-law. The widow was eighty-two years old and in much agony. One night, just to get her out of the house, the man arranged a date for her with a man who was eighty-five years old. She returned home from the date very late that evening and more than a little upset.
"What happened?" the man asked.
"Are you kidding?" she snapped, "I had to slap his face three times!"
"You mean," asked the man, "he got fresh?"
"No!" she replied. "I thought he was dead!"

But even up to that point people go on making dates. If there are really ghosts, they must be doing the same things you are doing...the same things. And it continues life after life.

I have heard about a couple. They were in deep love with each other and they were both spiritualists; they believed in Christian Science. Just one day, talking to each other about death and profound subjects like that, they decided that if one of them died he had to contact the other on the thirtieth day after death, and the other would be open, receptive and would call on the thirtieth day at a particular time.

As it happened, the man died in a car accident. The woman was eagerly awaiting. The thirtieth day came, the right fixed time came. She closed the doors, put the light off, and asked, "John, are you there?" half believing, half not-believing. But she could not believe it when she heard John's voice.

John said, "Yes, darling. I am here."

The woman asked, "How are you? Are you happy there?"

And he said, "I am very, very happy. Look at this cow—how beautiful she looks."

"Cow?" the woman said, "What are you talking about?"

"Yes," he said, "such a beautiful cow. Such big tits, such a beautiful, young body, such proportion."

The woman said, "Have you gone mad?! I am dying to hear something more about heaven and you are talking about a foolish cow!"

And he said, "What heaven are you talking about? I have become a bull in Koregaon Park, Poona!"

It continues—the same stupidity, life after life. Unless you become conscious you will go on moving in this wheel, and this wheel goes on mercilessly repeating itself. It is very boring, and it is utterly stupid to continue it.

But to become aware needs great effort. To become aware, you will have to go into a long struggle with your own sleep, with your own unconscious states. You will have to fight your way. The struggle is hard and arduous and the path is uphill.

Now the sutras...these sutras can immensely help you to awaken.

> Master Lu-tsu said: *If you are not yet clear, I will make it clear to you through the threefold Buddhist contemplation of emptiness, delusion, and the center.*

The compassion of the Master is infinite. He makes things clear again and again, knowing perfectly well that your sleep is deep. You may not have heard the first time; he says it again. You may not have heard the second time; he says it again.

Buddha lived for forty-two years after his enlightenment, saying the same thing morning, evening, day in, day out, for forty-two years, the same thing continuously—because one never knows in what moment you will be able to understand. One never knows when you may be receptive. One never knows when a small window will open in your heart and the guest will be able to enter and the ray of light will penetrate you.

In twenty-four hours' time you are not always the same. Sometimes you are very hard and it is very difficult to penetrate. Sometimes you are very deaf—you hear and yet you hear not. But sometimes you are a little more open, more vulnerable, more loving, more capable of listening, less argumentative. Sometimes you are soft, feminine; sometimes you are masculine and hard. It is a rhythm that goes on changing. You can watch it, and you will soon become aware that there are moments when you are more understanding and there are moments when you are less understanding. You are not the same for twenty-four hours. You are constantly changing, you are in a flux, hence the Master has to go on speaking. One never knows when the right moment for you is, so he goes on repeating. Whenever the right moment comes the transformation will happen. A single hit in the heart and you will be a totally different person after that. You will never be the same again.

Lu-tsu has been speaking...

We are coming closer and closer to the end of this beautiful book, *The Secret of the Golden Flower*.

Again he says, "If you are not *yet* clear..."

He has made everything clear, but,

> *If you are not yet clear, I will make it clear to you through the threefold Buddhist contemplation of emptiness, delusion, and the center.*

And what is clarity?

Clarity is a state of mind when there are no thoughts. Thoughts are like clouds in the sky. And when the sky is full of clouds you cannot see the sun. When there are no clouds in your sky, in your inner sky, in your consciousness, there is clarity.

Clarity does not mean cleverness, remember. Clever people are not clear people. To be clever is easy because to be clever is nothing but another name for being cunning, a good name for being cunning. Clever people are cunning people but they are not clear people. To be an intellectual is not to be intelligent, remember. To be intellectual is easy: you can gather information, you can acquire knowledge and you can become a great intellectual, a scholar, a *pundit*—but that is not clarity and that is not intelligence. Intelligence is just the opposite. When there is no knowledge moving in the head, when there is no cloud passing in the inner sky, when there is no calculation, no cleverness, no cunningness; when you are not thinking at all but you are just there like a mirror reflecting whatsoever is—that is clarity. Clarity means a mirror-like quality. And to be clear is to face God.

God cannot be known by knowledge, God is known by clarity. God is not known by cleverness, not by cunningness, but by innocence. Innocence is clarity. That's why Jesus says, "Unless you are like small children, you will not enter into my kingdom of God." What does he mean? He simply means that unless you are as clear as a small child whose inner sky is yet unclouded, whose mirror is still without any dust on it, whose perception is absolutely pure... He can see things as they are. He does not distort them, he has no investment in distorting them. He does not project, he simply sees whatsoever is the case; he is a passive mirror—that is clarity.

> Lu-tsu said: *If you are not yet clear, I will make it clear to you through the threefold Buddhist contemplation...*

This threefold Buddhist contemplation is one of the greatest devices of meditation. Remember, it is a device, it is not a philosophy. If you think it is a philosophy you have missed the point totally.

And that's what has happened: down the ages great treatises have been written on Buddhist philosophy, and that is just nonsense because Buddha is not a philosopher. He has not taught any philosophy at all. He was really very anti-philosophical.

It was his usual procedure, whenever he would enter into a town, that his disciples would go in front of him declaring to the people, "Please don't ask philosophical questions of the Buddha." He had made a list of eleven questions; in those eleven questions the whole of philosophy is contained: about God, about creation, about reincarnation, about life after death and all that. In those eleven questions the whole possible philosophy is contained. You cannot ask any question if you look at that list of eleven questions. That list was declared in the town: "Please don't ask those questions of the Buddha, because he is not a philosopher, he is not a metaphysician, he is not a thinker! He has come here as a physician, not as a philosopher. If your eyes are blind, he has some medicine. If your ears are deaf, he's a surgeon."

Buddha has said again and again, "I am a physician", but great philosophy has arisen in his name, and the words that he used as devices have become philosophical tenets. For example, emptiness: now there are Buddhist schools which say that this is a fundamental principle—that all is empty. It is simply a device. It says nothing about existence, it simply says something about your mind. It helps you to become clear, that's all. Buddha is not concerned about existence, Buddha is concerned about your clarity. He says, "If you are clear you will know what existence is." And what is the point in talking about existence? It is utterly futile. It is as if you are talking about light and colors and the rainbows and the flowers to a blind man. It is utterly absurd. You cannot talk about the sunrise to the blind man and you cannot talk about the silver light of the moon in the night to a blind man. You cannot tell him that trees are green, because green will make no sense to him. He will hear the word—just the way you hear the word 'God', he will hear the word 'green'. Neither you understand nor does he understand. Just by hearing the word again and again don't get the idea, the stupid idea, that you understand what God is. God has to be seen to be understood; there is no other way. And green has to be seen to be understood; there is no other way.

Ramakrishna used to tell:

A blind man was invited by his friends. They prepared *kihr*, a delicacy made out of milk. The blind man loved the *kihr* very much and he asked, "What exactly is it? And how does it look?"

Sitting by his side was a great philosopher, and as philosophers are prone to—they cannot miss an opportunity to teach, to philosophize—he immediately started telling the blind man how the *kihr* was made, how it looked. And when he said, "It is pure white", the blind man said, "Wait! That word does not make any sense to me. What do you mean by 'pure white'? Will you be kind enough to explain it to me?"

And as philosophers go, without ever seeing that the man was blind, he started explaining what pure white was. He said, "Have you seen white swans, white cranes? Yes, it is just like a pure white crane, or a white swan, or a white flower."

"Crane?" the poor blind man said, "You are making it more and more mysterious. I don't understand what white is. Now the problem arises: What is this crane? I have never seen it."

And still the philosopher was not aware that this man could not see, so whatsoever he said was going to be irrelevant. And he started explaining what a white crane was. And then he invented a device: he gave his hand to the blind man and told him to touch it. And he said, "Look, the way my hand is bent, this is how the neck of the crane is."

And the blind man laughed joyously and was very happy. He thanked him from the very bottom of his heart and said, "Now I understand what *kihr* is—like a bent hand? Now I understand. I'm so grateful to you."

Then the philosopher became aware of what he had done.

You cannot explain whiteness to a blind man; there is no way at all. Yes, you can help him, you can treat his eyes. You can send him to Dr. Modi's eye camp—Dr. Modi sometimes comes here—he needs surgery. The day he's able to see, no explanation will be needed; he will know what white is, what green is— so is the case with God, so is the case with existence.

So remember, the first thing is that this is just a device: emptiness, delusion, and the center. This is not a philosophical statement. Buddha is not saying that "I am proposing a system of thought." He is simply saying that "I am creating a device."

Another story so it becomes clear to you:

A man came home from the market. Suddenly he saw his house on fire. His children were playing inside, small children. He shouted from the outside because he was afraid to go in himself. He shouted, "Children, come out! The house is on fire!" But the children were so engrossed in their games, they wouldn't listen. Then he devised: he shouted loudly, "Do you hear me or not? I have brought many toys for you from the market!" and they all rushed out. He had not brought a single toy, but those children had told him, "You are going to the market, so bring some toys for us." Outside, seeing no toys, they said, "Where are the toys?" The man started laughing and he said, "It was a device to bring you out of the house which is on fire. Tomorrow I will bring toys for you."

These are devices. Remember, a device is neither true nor untrue. A device is either useful or useless, but never true or untrue. Those words are not relevant to a device. The meditations that you are doing here are all devices—neither true nor untrue. They are useful or useless, certainly, but there is no question of truth. I'm giving you toys so that you can come out of the house which is on fire. When you are out you will understand. Even those children understood: when they saw the house on fire they forgot all about toys and they understood the love of the father. He must have loved those children immensely; that's why he could even lie. It was a lie.

You will be surprised to know that Zen Masters have been saying down the ages that Buddha was the greatest liar. But his compassion was such that he lied. He created devices. This is a device—three things to be contemplated: emptiness, delusion, and the center.

Emptiness means: this whole world outside, the objective world, is utterly empty. Think of it as empty. Contemplate on it as empty and you will be surprised—the moment you start getting into this idea of the emptiness of the whole world, many things will start changing of their own accord. You will not be greedy—who can be greedy when things are empty? You will not be ambitious—how can you be ambitious when things are empty? If you know that the president's chair is just empty, who bothers? Because you give it too much substance, you make it too real, you become ambitious. When you know money is empty, who bothers? One can use it, but there is no question of worrying about it.

Start thinking that all this world that surrounds you is empty ...forms and forms, like dreams.

Gurdjieff used to say to his disciples, "Walking on the street, remember that you are in a dream, and the people that are passing you are just dream phenomena. The shops are dreams." And meditating on this for three months it starts happening. A *great* explosion happens: suddenly everything becomes empty. Shops are there, people are walking, people are purchasing and the people who are passing you by are there. Nothing has changed on the surface, but suddenly you see just empty forms.

You go to a movie house and you know perfectly well that on the screen there is nothing but empty forms, but you are befooled by those empty forms. Sitting in a movie house you pass through all kinds of emotions. Some tragedy is happening and you start crying. Maybe that's why a movie house has to be kept in darkness, otherwise it would look so stupid and silly. If somebody—your wife, your friend sitting by your side—comes to know that you are crying, they will laugh. They will say, "What are you doing? There is just an empty screen, nothing else, and a projected film, just a game of white and black"—or maybe it is technicolor—"but it is all shadows." But one can become so involved in the shadows that the shadows start looking substantial.

Just the other way round is the device of the Buddha. Buddha says: These people who are looking so substantial to you, just think that they are a dream, empty. And one day you will be surprised: the whole world has become a white screen and only shadows are passing. And when only shadows are passing you will find a great detachment arising in you. You will be aloof, far away. Then nothing matters.

The second is delusion.

When you see, when you meditate, contemplate continuously that the whole world is empty, just a dream, the second phenomenon will start happening. Just by thinking that it is a dream it is not going to disappear, remember. Don't fall into that fallacy. Don't think, "If I think for long that the world is a dream, it will disappear." It is not going to disappear. You can go on knowing perfectly well that the film on the movie screen is just a projection, but still it continues. Just by your thinking, it will not disappear. It is not possible for the meditator sitting in the movie house that the film will disappear, that others will be able to see and he will not see, that he will see only the white screen, no. He will also see the film but with a difference: knowing that it is a dream. The world does not disappear; the world remains but its significance is gone, its substance is gone.

It is like when you put a straight stick into water. The moment it enters into the water it looks bent. You take it out, you know it is not bent. You put it in again, but in the water it looks bent. Now you know perfectly well that this is a delusion—it only appears bent, it is not bent. But just by understanding that it is a delusion, the bentness will not disappear.

So the first thing is to meditate that the world is empty. Then the second thing will arise: the world still remains but now it is a delusion. Now it has no substance in it, it is the same stuff dreams are made of. The first unconscious perception of the world looked very substantial—it was very objective, it was *there*. After meditating on emptiness, it is still there but it is no longer substantial, it is only a mind game. It is like a dream.

That's what Hindus mean when they say, "The world is maya." It does not mean that for the saint it disappears. It simply means: now there is no value in it; it has become valueless, *utterly* valueless.

And the third thing is the center.

When the world is no longer substantial, the objective world disappears and becomes subjective delusion, then a new experience arises in you. For the first time *you* become substantial. Ordinarily you are projecting substance in the objective world. When you take it away from there, you become substantial. When the world is real, you are unreal. When the world becomes unreal, you become real. Let me explain it again through the movie.

If you become aware that there is only screen and shadows passing by, you will suddenly become aware that you are. Those shadows are false but you are real. When you become completely lost in the shadows you become unreal, you forget yourself completely. In a dream, you forget yourself completely; the dream becomes real. Your whole reality is exploited by the dream. The dream takes all the reality and leaves you just hollow. When you have taken away the reality from the dream, you become real; a center arises in you, you become integrated. This is what is called individuation, crystallization. Either the world can be real or you can be real; both cannot be real together. Remember it... both cannot be real together. It is a change of gestalt. When you take reality out of the world, you start becoming real—you attain to being. And there are only two types of people: the people who are interested in having and the people who are interested in being.

The people who are interested in having believe that the world is real—have more money, have more power, have more name, fame. They are unreal people. They have lost their center completely, they don't know who they are, the self has become a shadow. And the other kind of people, whom I call the religious people, are those who take the reality from the outside world and put it back where it belongs. They start gaining substance, they start gaining being. They have *more* being. And whenever you come across a person who has more being, you will feel a magnetic force. If Buddha attracted thousands of people it is because of this substantial being.

You can see it. If you look into the person who has political power you will find him just hollow, stuffed with straw and nothing else. The man who has much money and thinks that he has something—look into him and you will find just a black hole. A poor man is hiding behind, a beggar.

When a man has being then he may be an emperor or he may be a beggar—he's always an emperor. He may be a beggar like Buddha or he may be an emperor like Janak, it makes no difference; he's always an emperor *wherever* he is. His kingdom is of the within, he has become substantial. He *is!* You are not. You have things, you don't have being. And you are using things as a substitute. The more things you have, the more you can believe that you are; hence, the hunger, the greed, the ambition. Have more and more and more, because that is the only way you can deceive yourself that "I am somebody."

But the person who has being is unconcerned. Having is not his game. That does not mean that he leaves the world and renounces the world. If somebody renounces the world that simply shows that he still thinks the world is very real. Otherwise why should you renounce? You don't go shouting around the neighbourhood in the morning after you get up, saying "I have renounced my dreams. I was a king in the dream, and I have renounced the kingdom." People will think you have gone mad; they will inform the police. They will tell you to go to a psychiatrist, that you need some psychological treatment: "Are you mad? If it is a dream, how can you renounce it?"

Buddha renounced because he was living in a dream, thinking it very substantial. He became enlightened in the forest. Remember, when he renounced he was ignorant. Had he become enlightened before renouncing the world, he would never have renounced; there would have been no point. Janak became enlightened when he was a king in the palace, hence he never renounced it; there was no point. Krishna never renounced; there was no point. How to renounce something which is a shadow? Buddha renounced, Mahavira renounced —because they were not yet enlightened.

What I am trying to say is this: people have renounced the world only in ignorance. Even a Buddha, when he was ignorant, renounced the world. When he became enlightened he came back into the world. He had to come, because he knew that there were many other people who were fast asleep and thinking that their dreams were real. He had to wake them up.

The center arises only when you have taken all the reality from the outside world. You have given your reality to things, you have poured your reality into things. You can watch it— people are in deep love with things. They have poured their souls into things and they have completely forgotten who they are. They are lost in their things.

Come back home. Take your reality back. Things are only as real as you make them, it is your projection. Otherwise they are empty, just white screens, of no significance at all, neither to be indulged in nor to be renounced. Both are irrelevant.

Emptiness comes as the first of the three contemplations.
All things are looked upon as empty. And then follows de-
lusion. Although it is known that they are empty, things
are not destroyed, but one attends to one's affairs in the midst
of the emptiness.

Listen to it deeply, because the people who are miserable in
the world almost always start thinking or renouncing the
world—as if the world is the problem! The world is never
the problem, *you* are the problem, and wherever you go you
will create the problem. You are the projector. You can renounce the world, the world is just a white screen; but the
projector is within you. You can go anywhere and you will
start projecting your film there, onto something else. It may not
be a palace; then it may be a small hut—but that hut will
become your kingdom. It may not even be a hut.

Wandering in the Himalayas I have come across many people.
Once I came across a saint—a so-called saint—who had lived
for at least thirty years in a cave. I liked the cave and I had two
or three friends with me, so we stayed overnight in the cave.
He was very angry. He said, "What do you mean? This is
my cave!"
I said, "But you have renounced the world. How can this cave
be yours?"
He said, "This is *mine!* I have lived for thirty years here."
"You may have lived here for thirty lives. But what is the
meaning of renunciation? Why did you leave your wife?
Why did you leave your house? What was the problem there?
The problem was 'mine'. Now this cave is yours. Now the
problem has come with the cave, now the possessiveness has
become attached to the cave."

It doesn't matter where you go; it is not so simple to change your life. You have to change your perception, your gestalt, your very being. You have to change the inner mechanism.

> Lu-tsu said: *Things are not destroyed, but one attends to one's affairs in the midst of the emptiness.*

One knows that all is empty but one continues to attend to one's affairs. There is no need to go anywhere. Where can you go? The whole world is empty! The Himalayas are as empty as the shops on MG Road. And the trees and the animals in the Himalayas are as much shadows as the people that live in Poona. It does not make any difference. The difference has to happen in your center, in your inner being.

> *But although one does not destroy things, neither does one pay attention to them. . . .*

This is the change: one does not destroy, renounce; but one does not pay attention to them, one takes away one's attention. Attention is food; that's how you become attached to things. If a woman attracts you, you want to look at her again and again and again. You are feeding, you are projecting. If you love a thing, you pay attention to it. By paying attention you become attached to it. Attachment is through the bridge of attention. There is no need to renounce anything, just cut the bridge. Live in the world without paying attention to things. Go on moving as if you are moving in emptiness.

> *. . .this is contemplation of the center.*

And if you can do this, a center will arise in you. If you can live in the world as if you are not in it, if you can live in the world as if the world is just a dream, then suddenly a great energy will crystallize in you—the whole energy that was being dissipated. In a thousand ways you have been dissipating your energy. In every direction, you are leaking. Your attention is a leaking point. When you are not leaking anymore, when your attention is no more moving, when your attention is gathering inside, accumulating inside, crystallizing inside, the center arises.

> *While practicing contemplation of the empty, one also knows that one cannot destroy the ten thousand things, and still one does not notice them.*

One knows that this dream has to continue. This is a beautiful dream too; there is nothing to be worried about in it. No need to renounce, no need to destroy, no need to fight with it. You don't fight with your shadow—you know it is a shadow. You don't want to destroy it either because you know it is a shadow. You are not worried about it because it goes on following you, it never leaves you alone, because you know it is a shadow. To know that the world is a shadow...a reflection of the real but not the real itself...the moon seen in the lake but not the moon itself—then one is at home even in the world. Without taking any notice of the world one goes on doing one's duties, goes on doing one's work, goes on living in a very detached way.

> *In this way the three contemplations fall together.*

Then the three contemplations are no longer three; it becomes one single contemplation. You are gathering at the center and you become aware of the center. This is what Gurdjieff calls self-remembering and Buddha calls *sammasati*, mindfulness, and Mahavira calls *vivek*, discrimination. Now you have seen what is unreal, you have discriminated the unreal from the real. Now you have seen what is shadow and what is substance.

You have seen the real moon and you have seen the reflection in the water. Now...the reflection continues! Just by knowing that it is a reflection it is not going to disappear; it continues. And there is no problem—it is beautiful! You can sit by the side of the lake and see the reflection—it is beautiful, there is no problem out of it, but you know it is not real.

But, after all, strength is in envisioning the empty.

But remember, the whole integration, crystallization, arises out of envisioning the empty. That is the beginning of meditation.

Therefore, when one practices contemplation of emptiness, emptiness is certainly empty...

Now you will have to go into a little more depth. When you know that all is empty, there is a problem. You may start thinking that emptiness is something very real—that is the problem, because the mind always gets caught in words.

There is a small story in the beautiful book *Alice in Wonderland*:

Alice reaches to the king. The king is waiting eagerly for some love-letter to arrive. He's asking everybody, "Have you seen the messenger?" He asks Alice also, "Did you see some messenger coming towards me?"
Alice says, "Nobody, sir," and the king thinks she has seen somebody whose name is Nobody.
The king says, "But it seems Nobody walks slower than you, otherwise he would have reached. Because I have been hearing the news again and again: many people have arrived and they all say 'Nobody, sir,' and Nobody has not reached yet! So it

seems Nobody walks slower than you."
And naturally Alice thought, "What is he saying?—nobody walks slower than me?" She retorted back. She said, "Nobody walks faster than me!" She felt offended.
And the king said, "Nobody walks faster than you? Then why has he not arrived yet?"
Now Alice became aware of what the problem was. She said, "Sir, Nobody is nobody."
And the king said, "Of course. I know Nobody has to be Nobody. But where is he?"
And in this way it went on.

Even emptiness can become a thing. That's what happened in Buddhist philosophy. Philosophers started talking about emptiness as if emptiness were God, as if emptiness were the very substance of life. They started talking of nothing as if nothing were something. Nothing is only a word. In nature, no does not exist. No is man's invention. In nature, everything is yes. In nature, only the positive exists, the negative is man's invention.

For example, this chair is just a chair. In nature the chair is just a chair—it is what it is—but in language we can say, "This is not a table. This is not a horse. This is not a man"—and all those statements are right, because the chair is not the table, and the chair is not the horse, and the chair is not the man. But these are just linguistic negatives. In nature, in existence, the chair is simply the chair. In nature the negative does not exist, but only the positive. But in language the negative exists, and because of the negative great philosophies have arisen. Nothingness becomes a thing in itself. Absence is talked about as if it were some kind of presence, so beware of it.

To make you alert, Master Lu-tsu says:

> ... Remember, *emptiness is certainly empty, but delusion is empty too!* ...

Don't start thinking that delusion is real at least as a delusion. The delusion is also empty, just nothing in itself. For example, you see a snake in a rope: when you look, it is there, when you bring the light it is not there. Now the question can arise, "Where has the snake gone? From where had it come?" It never came, it never went away, it never existed; in nature the rope was always a rope. It was your illusion. You created, you projected the snake; it was just a mind phenomenon.

> Remember, emptiness is empty, *delusion is empty too and the center is also empty.*

This is the greatest contribution of Buddha.

The Hindus say: The world is illusion. The Jainas say: The world is illusion, the mind is also illusion. Buddha says: The world is illusion, the mind is illusion, and the center too. His insight is tremendous. He says if the seen is illusion, how can the seer be a reality? This is the profoundest statement of *nirvana*: if the dream is illusion then the dreamer is illusion too. If the dance is illusion, then the dancer is illusion too.

What is he trying to say? He's trying to say: first leave the world, then leave the illusion of the mind, and then leave the idea of the center too, of the self too. Otherwise ego will persist. In a new name, in a subtle way, ego will persist. Let that too be gone. Let everything be gone. Let there be simply emptiness, nothingness, and in that nothingness is all. In that utter absence is the presence.

Buddha never talks about that presence, because he says that has to be known. That should not be talked about because mind is so cunning—if you talk about that presence it starts becoming greedy for that presence. If you talk about God, the mind starts thinking how to attain to God. Buddha never talks about God; not that God is not—who else can know that God is other than a Buddha? But he never talks for a very certain reason: the talk of God can create desire for God, and if desire is there you will never attain God. All desire has to disappear. Only in a state of desirelessness, God arrives.

It needs great strength to practice contemplation of delusion;
then delusion is really delusion, but emptiness is also delusion,
and the center is delusion too. Being on the way of the center,
one also creates images of the emptiness.

These images of emptiness are just helps. First, to take you out of the world Buddha says the world is empty. Now the delusion becomes true. Then he says the delusion is also empty. Now the center becomes true. Now he says the center is also empty. All has disappeared with no trace, utter silence—and in that utter silence is benediction, is God.

One practices also contemplation of delusion, but one does
not call it delusion, one calls it central. As to what has to do
with the center, more need not be said.

And what will happen when all has gone—the world, the mind, the self? Master Lu-tsu is right. He says, "More need not be said"—because to say more will be dangerous. To say more will be giving you an object to desire. And the desire comes, and the whole world comes in.

This is a great device. If you can meditate over it, you will attain to the infinity, to the eternity, to the timeless, to the real life.

Chapter Twelve

September 7th, 1978

TAO IS ALREADY HAPPENING

The first question:

Yes! Yes! Wake me up! This silly, multi-schizophrenic, leaking, watering can has been deeply affected by these lectures —but one thing lately is, I am feeling more and more gross. Bhagwan, I want my lotuses to bloom, to feel Tao, be worthy of Tao, to be Tao.
I want to fall into love! Will it, can it really happen? Can this real, beautiful soul inside burst into being?

Tao, that's why I have given you the name Tao: there is a message for you in it. Tao means spontaneity, nature. Tao is not a practice, it is not effort, it is not cultivation. It is patience, it is trust, it is waiting for things to happen, even if one has to wait for eternity.

Tao needs no work on your part. All that you can do will be
an undoing, because the moment the doer comes, nature disappears. The moment the doer takes hold of you, you are
possessed by the idea of the ego. And then there is a wall between you and Tao—or call it God.

The doer has to dissolve, and you cannot do anything to dissolve it. How can you do anything to dissolve the doer? Whatsoever you do will go on feeding it. Just a simple understanding
that all is taken care of... Trees are growing—not that they
are making any effort to grow; birds are singing—not that
they go to some music school; rivers are flowing—nobody
has taught them how to reach to the ocean, they don't carry
any map, they don't know any path, they don't have any
scriptures: still, every river reaches to the ocean.

Just look around! This immense universe is functioning so
perfectly well that nothing can be added to it. It needs no
improvement. Seeing this, one relaxes. If stars can go on dancing and flowers can go on blooming and birds can go on
singing, why not you? You also belong to this universe. You
are part of it. In fact, you are the most valuable part of it—the
greatest flowering is going to happen in you, the flowering of
consciousness, the Golden Flower of being. You are not neg-
lected, you are taken care of.

To understand life is to relax.

Yes, only understanding is needed, not cultivation, not practicing. You don't need to become virtuous, religious. The people
who try to become virtuous and religious become simply
egoistic and nothing more.

Drop this hankering, Tao, to be something other than you are.
This is the moment! Just be in it! Be *utterly* one with the whole.

And it need not be practiced because it is already the case. All that is needed is a little bit of understanding, a vision, and then all starts happening of its own accord.

That's why I have given you the name Tao. The message is that you are not to create a character around you, that you are not to manufacture a certain personality in you, that you are not to think of future, of *nirvana*, of enlightenment, of God. God is not in the future, neither is God in the past. God is herenow, always herenow. God is *this* very condition.

People always think of God as the source, the original cause. They miss the point. God is not the original cause somewhere back, far, far away. God is not the original cause. Or, there are people who think of God as the ultimate goal, again far, far away in the future. Either in the past or in the future—and that's how you go on missing. And God knows only one tense, and that is present. The now is another name for God. He is *this* very condition! *This moment*, within and without, God is.

And God is not something sacred, holy, far away again in heaven. God is all the conditions—and when I say all, I mean all: the sacred/the profane, the body/the soul, matter/consciousness. The lowest of the low is God, and the holiest of the holy is God, and there is not *any* difference between the two. Judas is as much God as Jesus, because there cannot be anything else. These are just roles, just acts played on the stage in a drama.

To understand it is to relax. Then there is nowhere to go, then there is nothing to do. Then what is left is celebration, then what is left is to live joyously. Rejoice moment-to-moment, and don't divide things. Don't say "I am going to the temple"; don't say that this is something sacred, holy. Drinking tea is as sacred as doing yoga. Sleeping silently, relaxed, is as sacred as prayer. Looking at a tree, talking to a friend, walking early in the morning, working in the factory or in the office, is as holy as anything else. This is the understanding that is needed for Tao to happen.

Tao is already happening; just your misunderstanding... Tao is already showering—in the sunrays, on the green trees. But you just think, "This is just the sun and they are just the trees— where is God? These are just people—where is God?" You want God to be something specific, and that's why you miss. God is not something special, not something specific. God is all these conditions, God is this totality. This moment—my talking to you, your listening to me, this communion, this silence, this bridging—yes, this is God, this is Tao.

So forget all about achieving. Don't become an achiever. My sannyasins have to drop all kinds of ambitions—material, worldly and spiritual—all. To be ambitious is to be stupid. That's why I say politicians are stupid, because they are the most ambitious people in the world. The more ambitious you are the more stupid you will be.

Ambition makes you stupid. Why?—because intelligence is of the herenow and ambition is of the future. Intelligence blooms *this* moment, and ambition always thinks of faraway lands. Ambition is of the tomorrow, and because of ambition you go on missing the intelligence that is just now showering, welling up within you.

I have heard...

It was decided to send a monkey and a politician to the moon. Their instructions on what to do after landing were sealed into pockets in their suits. As soon as they had touched down on the lunar landscape, the monkey opened his set of instructions.

It read:
>   Check all fuel tanks.
>   Check computer and re-program the same.
>   Take samples of rock, sand and air.
>   Check oxygen levels and density.
>   Check landing craft for damage.
>   Check stabilizers and anti-gravity devices.
>   Then send radio message down to earth reporting
>   position.

Then the politician opened his sealed instructions. It said in big letters:

>   Feed the monkey!!!

Ambition makes a person *really* stupid—even a monkey is more intelligent. Don't be ambitious!

And remember, mind is very cunning: you drop ambition in one direction and the mind starts creating the same ambitious trap in another direction. Running after money, one day you understand that it is futile—even if you attain it, death will take it away. You start dropping that ambition. But then you start thinking "How to have more virtue?" It is the *same* game —"How to have more money"; now you say "How to have more virtue, more *punya*."

Do you know, the name of this town, Poona, comes from the Sanskrit root *punya? Punya* means virtue. Do you see any virtuous people in Poona?

In fact, the virtuous person cannot be religious, because he has allowed ambition to enter from the back door. Again he has started accumulating, acquiring. Somebody is on a power-trip in the world, and then one day, seeing the futility of it... And one day everybody comes to see the futility of it; even the mediocre mind comes to see the futility of it. It is so futile!

If you fail you fail, if you succeed you fail—it is so futile! If you fail, certainly you fail, and there is frustration. If you succeed, then too deep down you fail, because you see you have succeeded and nothing has happened through your success. You remain the same kind of empty, hollow, ugly beggar. Nothing has happened. All the money has accumulated around you, you are sitting on the throne of a president, and deep down the same beggar, the same ugly face, the same monster, the same horrible mind. So failing you fail, succeeding you fail—this is the futility.

Then the mind starts thinking of having something in paradise, but that is again the same game, played with different names, in different times, in different spaces—but the same mind projecting.

My teaching to you is: live herenow! Drop *all* kinds of ambitions. This is sannyas: drop *all* kinds of ambitions, and see the miracle happening. Once you drop all ambitions you will have so much energy left that there will be no way other than to celebrate. You will have so much energy in you—all the energy that is involved in ambitions is released because ambitions have been dropped—and that energy becomes an oceanic experience within your soul. That is paradise, that is God.

God is not a goal, but an experience of a non-ambitious mind. Tao has not to be achieved! The achievers go on missing it. The non-achievers suddenly realize that they have always lived in paradise, but because of their ambitions they were not able to see it.

So Tao, just try to understand what I am sharing with you. I am sharing with you this moment, this space. I am not giving you any goals. I am not driving you crazy for some achievement in the future. I am not inspiring you to run and chase some shadows. I am simply imparting to you what has happened to me. I want it to be shared with you. Dropping all ambition, I have arrived.

Drop all ambitions and just be, and see the beauty and the benediction of existence. It is incredible, it is simply far-out! You have never dreamt about it, how beautiful it is. You *could not* have dreamt about it, it surpasses all your imaginations and fantasies. Its beauty is unbelievable, and the grace that is showering on you is just showering for no reason at all. It is *very* unreasonable! God does not give you because you are worthy. God gives you because He has so much, He cannot contain it!

Try to see my vision; it is totally different from your so-called religions. Your so-called religions are very miserly and very economical. Your so-called religions believe in the laws of economics: you do this and God will do this to you; be worthy, and He will make you happy; do something wrong, and you go to hell—a very simple mathematics, as if your God is nothing but a magistrate who goes on looking into the books of laws and goes on sending people to hell or heaven.

God does not believe in your economics; God believes in love. God is love, not economics. He does not give you because you are worthy, He gives because He has. Remember the famous Jesus parable?—and Jesus has told the most beautiful parables ever told in the world. Nobody has ever been able to surpass him.

The parable is: A man, a very rich man, has a great garden. The grapes are ripe. He sends his manager to the marketplace to bring a few laborers. Those grapes have to be collected, otherwise they will start falling, they will start rotting. A few laborers come and they start working. By the afternoon it is realized that these people are not enough, so more are called. When the sun is almost setting it is realized that even this will not do, so more laborers are called. And then the sun sets and the darkness descends and they all gather, and the owner of the garden gives everybody the same amount of money—to those who had come in the morning and to those who had come in the afternoon, and even to those who had just come and had only worked not more than half an hour. Naturally, the people who had come in the morning became annoyed, irritated, angry. They said, "What is this? This is unfair! We worked the whole day and we get the same amount of money for our work. And these people have just come, they have not even worked at all—they are also getting the same amount of money? This is unfair!"

And the master started laughing and he said, "Just think of one thing: is whatsoever you have got not enough for your labor?"

They said, "It is enough. It is in fact double what we ordinarily get from somebody else."

The master said, "Then why are you worried about others? This is my money. You have got double what you would have got anywhere else, but you are not happy. You are being miserable because I have given to others. This is my money and I have so much to give. My treasures are full, I am burdened. I give to these laborers not because they have worked, but because I have so much that I don't know what to do with it. Why are you angry?"

Jesus tells this parable in reference to God. And he says, "When you are facing God He will give you not because you have done this or you have done that—not because of your worth— but because He has so much. He is burdened, He is burdened like a cloud full of rain. It has to rain not because the earth is worthy. Have you not watched the clouds come?—and they rain on all kinds of soil. They rain on stones, rocks, they rain on fertile soil; they rain also on wastelands where nothing grows and nothing will ever grow.

Exactly like that, when a flower opens up, its fragrance is released to the winds, in all the directions. To whomsoever passes by the road, it is available; it makes no distinction between the worthy and the unworthy. That's what I want to relate to you.

Somebody else has asked one question: "Bhagwan, I have listened this whole month. You have not even mentioned once the law of karma."

I cannot mention it because it is part of economics. It is part of human cunningness and cleverness. It has nothing to do with real religion.

The law of karma says you will get only that which you earn. And I want to say to you: you don't get according to your worth, you get according to God's abundance—sinners and saints, all; good and bad, all. The only thing that is needed is ...are you ready to receive it? I am not talking about worthiness. I am simply saying: are you open to receiving it? Are you ready, available, vulnerable, so when it showers on you you can let it soak in?

Who is available? One who lives in the present, moment-to-moment, is available to God. And this I am saying to you because this has been *my* experience. I am not talking philosophy to you, but simply stating what I have experienced. God gives out of His abundance. But you are not available, you are in the past or in the future. The future is not yet, the past is no more. You move in shadows.

Come to the real! And the real is always herenow. God knows only one time and that is now, and only one space, that is here.

The second question:

You said meditation is 'non-doing'. But to lose oneself in an activity, is it not required to focus, choose, will?

Kavido, if you focus, you will remain. If you choose, the chooser will be there. If you will, the ego cannot disappear. If you really want to get lost in any kind of activity you have to be a non-chooser, you have to drop your will.

Your will simply means you don't trust God's will yet. Your will simply means you are still fighting, struggling, with God. Your will simply means you are trying to push the river, you are not ready to go with the river. Your will simply means you are trying to conquer something; you are violent, you are aggressive.

To be lost in any activity—it may be cleaning the floor or dancing or painting or loving; it may be anything—to be lost in it, you have to drop your will. You have to simply be like a dead leaf in the wind, so wherever the wind blows the dead leaf moves with it; to the south, it says yes, to the north, it says yes. If the wind leaves it on the ground, it says yes. It knows only yes, it knows no no. It is a yes-saying. And that is the moment of benediction, of bliss. Then you will never be frustrated because there is nobody to be frustrated. Frustration comes out of expectations. Out of will is your defeat.

And see people's faces: they are all looking defeated, sooner or later. Except for small children, you will find everybody defeated. And small children are still laughing and smiling because they don't know what is going to happen. Soon their laughter will disappear, soon their smiles will be gone, soon they will become dry, desert-like, just as everybody else has become. Look at the old people—how they are living. Disillusioned they are. They had great dreams, and all dreams have failed. All gods have failed. They are utterly frustrated, root and all. Now they have only one climate around them—that of frustration.

That is why old people are so chronically irritated: life has been cheating them. With what great fantasies they had started the journey, with what beautiful dreams! And slowly, slowly all dreams have turned into dust, and they have only one taste in their mouths—that of dust and nothing else. How can they avoid not being irritated? They are annoyed—not towards somebody in particular; they are simply in rage! They lived in vain. Seventy years, eighty years have passed, and they passed through all kinds of turmoil. They suffered all kinds of anxieties and nightmares, and for what?—"a tale told by an idiot, full of fury and noise, signifying nothing"?

And when a man comes to see that this whole affair of life has been a kind of idiocy, he really feels frustrated: "What kind of joke is this?" God does not look to be benevolent, seems to be a kind of sadist, torturing people, giving them great ideas and then frustrating them continuously. As you grow up you grow deeper and deeper into frustration. Soon your life is nothing but a tragedy.

This happens because of your dreams, expectations, ambitions, your will. You wanted to do something in the world and you could not, hence the impotence.

My teaching is: please, don't try to do anything in the world. Let things happen and you will never be frustrated, and your life will remain fresh, as fresh as ever. And you will be able to smile even at the very last moment; you will die smiling. You will be a conqueror without any effort to conquer, because all efforts to conquer lead to defeat. The real conquerors are those who never try to conquer. This is the paradox to be understood: the real gainers are those who had never thought of gaining anything, who simply lived moment-to-moment, enjoyed the morning and the afternoon and the evening.

When the great Zen Master, Joshu, was asked, "What is your fundamental teaching?" he said, "When it is hot it is hot, and when it is cold it is cold."
The man who was asking was a great philosopher. He said, "Are you kidding me? This is your philosophy—'When it is hot it is hot, when it is cold it is cold'? What kind of philosophy is this?"
Joshu said, "This is the whole of what I have been teaching to my disciples. Just live in the moment, whatsoever it is—if it is hot it is hot. Don't desire the opposite."

That is what will is—it is hot and you want it to be cool, it is cool and you want it to be hot. That is will. Will means desiring something which is not. Desiring against reality is will. When young be young, when old be old.

Another Zen Master was asked, "How do you live? What is the secret of your constant joy?"

He said, "Not much of a secret, a simple phenomenon: when I feel hungry I eat and when I feel tired I sleep."

This is living will-lessly—when hungry one eats, when tired one sleeps. This is living moment-to-moment with no plan, with no program, with no desire to impose your will upon existence. The very effort to impose your will on existence is *violent*. The really non-violent person is one who does not impose his will upon existence. He takes things as they come and he is always surprised that whatsoever comes brings a treasure with it.

But you are constantly desiring something else, so whatsoever comes never fulfills you. And what you desire is not going to come because this whole, this immense whole has no obligation to fulfill your desires. You can be with it, you can be against it. If you are against it you will live in hell, if you are with it you will live in heaven. That's my definition of heaven and hell: to be with the whole is heaven, to be against the whole is hell.

Kavido, you ask, "You said meditation is 'non-doing'."

Yes. I am not saying that a meditator will become lazy, indolent. No! He will do a thousand and one things but he will not be the doer of it; that is to be remembered.

It happened: a Zen Master was chopping wood. A man had come to enquire. He had heard the name of the Zen Master. It had been a long journey to come to the mountains where the Master lived with his disciples. He asked this woodcutter—because he could not think that the Master would be chopping wood—he asked this woodcutter, "I have heard about a great Zen Master who is enlightened. Where is he?"
And the Master said, "Look at me! I am that!"

The seeker thought this man to be mad. Still, to be polite
with him—and it is better to be polite with a madman....
And he had a great axe in his hand, and who knows? And he
looked so ferocious....

And he said, "I am that! What do you want?"

He said, "So you are that great Master. What did you do before
your enlightenment?"

He said, "I used to chop wood and carry water from the well."

"And now what do you do?"

He said, "I chop wood and carry water from the well."

And the man said, "Then what is the difference? Then what
is the point of your enlightenment if you still chop wood and
carry the water from the well?"

And the Master laughed...and the mountains must have
laughed with him, and the trees. It is said that around that
monastery, still, after thousands of years, sometimes that
laughter is heard. He laughed and said, "You fool! Before
enlightenment *I* used to chop wood, *I* used to carry water.
Now water is carried, wood is chopped. I am not the doer;
that is the difference."

I am not saying that a meditator has to become lazy. I am not
saying that a meditator has to become dull and dead. In fact
the meditator will have more energy than the non-meditator
can ever have, and the energy will have its own dance. It will
chop wood, it will carry water from the well.

A meditator is bound to become very creative. Only a meditator
can be creative, because all the energies converge on the moment. He has so much that it starts overflowing. His cup is
small and his energy is so much that it starts overflowing.
But he is a non-doer; his action has no will in it. He dances
because he finds dance happening, he loves because he finds
love happening.

Observe the fact: can you will love? If you are ordered "Love this woman!" or "Love this man!" can you will it? You can only go through empty gestures of loving. You may hug the woman, you may kiss the woman, but can you love? It is impossible to will love; there is no way. You can be forced, you can be ordered: "See the beauty of the roseflower!" and if somebody is standing behind you with a gun and he says, "Look at the beauty of the flower, otherwise you will be killed," you will look and you will say, "Yes, so beautiful, so tremendously beautiful."

It happened...an ancient Sufi story...

Tamburlaine conquered the town of Mulla Nasrudin. He had heard many stories about Mulla, many mysterious stories of his occult powers, esoteric powers, and all that.

The first thing he did was, he asked Mulla to come to the court. He told Mulla, "I have heard many stories of your occult power, esoteric experiences. Are they true? And don't try to lie to me. And you know that I am a dangerous man. If you lie your head will be cut off immediately." And he took his sword out of the sheath—a naked sword in the hands of Tamburlaine, who used to cut people as if there was no life in them. And he used to enjoy cutting people.

Mulla looked down and said, "See, I can see hell there, deep down in the earth. And devils are torturing people and great fire is burning." And then he looked up and he said, "Look, I can see heaven, God sitting on a great golden throne and angels dancing and singing and praising Him."

Tamburlaine said, "How do you manage to do these miracles? How can you see? I don't see anything! What is your secret?" Mulla said, "No secret; it is just fear. I don't see anything either. You put your sword back into the sheath and then all these visions will disappear. It is just fear, nothing else."

You go on living a life of fear, desire, ambition, greed. And out of your fear you create heaven and hell, and out of your greed you create heaven and hell. Out of your ambition you create heaven and hell, but these are all your creations. Out of your greed you create great philosophies. Your God is nothing but your fear personified, and your prayers are nothing but your tremblings. You are afraid.

What I am saying to you is: no other prayer is needed, no hell and heaven are needed; all is available right this very moment. You just drop all this nonsense of willing. Let God will through you, let God *live* through you. And it is not that you will become lazy; you will become very, very creative. Great poetry will be born out of you and great music will arise in your being. But one thing is certain: you will not look at it as if it is your creation, you will know it is God's. He has spoken through you, He has painted through you, He has loved through you.

You cannot will love. You can be ordered to love, and that is what is happening: millions of couples in the world have been ordered to love, because "She is your wife—love her!" and "He is your husband—love him!" And now what can you do?—because the police are there and the court is there and the government is there, and if you don't love you will be in trouble. Out of fear you try to manage—you pretend. And naturally, pretensions cannot make you happy.

And the same way, you go to the church and to the temple and to the mosque to pray because you have been ordered to pray. If you don't pray you will fall in hell. And who wants to suffer in hell? Is this life not enough of a suffering? Who wants to go to hell? Enough is enough! One wants to avoid hell, so it is better to go and pray. But it is out of fear, and anything that is out of fear is false. You cannot will prayer and you cannot will love and you cannot will the experience of beauty. It is not possible.

Nothing that is of any value is possible through willing. All that is beautiful and great happens when your will disappears.

Kavido, focusing is not needed, because focusing means concentration, concentration means tension. Non-focusing is needed. A state of utter un-concentration is needed so that you are open and available to all the sides, to the whole existence. And the difference is great: when you concentrate you are focused on one thing, but closed to everything else.

For example, if you are listening to me you can listen in two ways. One is the way of concentration that has been taught to you in the schools, colleges, universities. If you concentrate on me, then you will be sitting here very tense and you will feel tired. Then you cannot listen to this aeroplane passing by, and the birds chirping, and the wind blowing through the trees. No, all that has to be excluded from your consciousness. You have to narrow down your consciousness, and narrowing down your consciousness is great effort, tiring.

There is another way of listening, and that is my way of listening. You are simply open, available. I am speaking, the aeroplane passes by—you hear that noise too. The birds sing, you hear that noise too. And this is not a distraction; in fact, what I am saying becomes more beautiful because it partakes of many other things too. The birds singing around add something to what I am saying: it becomes more total, it is not taken apart from life. It represents the whole life then. Then the trees are a part of it, and the wind and the rain and the sun— all are a part of it. And then you are not tired. After one hour you will feel refreshed, relaxed. You may not be able to remember exactly what I have said, but that is not needed at all; you will have absorbed it. It will have its impact on your being forever. It will have become part of you, you will have digested it.

One needs to memorize something if one does not understand it. If one understands it, it is finished; there is no need to carry it as a memory. You need to memorize something because you don't understand it—out of fear: maybe sometimes in future it will be needed, so you have to program your mind. But it is a tiring business. Focusing is concentration; concentration is tiring.

I teach you meditation, not concentration. And this is the difference: meditation is just an open, relaxed being, availability to all that is happening. And then suddenly silence descends, the beyond penetrates you, the heaven penetrates the earth. Then God is very close by, He is hand in hand. You breathe Him.

I want you to experience God with me. I don't want you to practice experiencing God later on. That is nonsense! If you cannot experience it here with me, where are you going to experience it? Sitting in your room in a lotus posture, looking silly, you will experience God? Experience it this very moment! *This* is a state of non-doing—I am not doing anything. Talking to you is not an act for me; it is just a response, it is natural. Your presence provokes it. And I am not there willing it, it is happening. And your listening to me need not be in any kind of will; you also let it happen. Then there will be meeting, communion.

Kavido, there is no need to focus, no need to choose, no need to will. These are the ways of the ego, and the ego has to be utterly dropped. Then you live in a totally different way, an egoless way. And that is the way of Tao.

The third question:

Bhagwan, why do I always fall asleep during the discourse?

This is a very ancient religious practice, this is not new. You are not doing something special. Religious people have always been doing it. So take it as a confirmatory sign! You must be becoming religious.

I have heard...

During the Second World War the pastor at a church was asked how many persons could sleep in the church-building in the event of an attack.
"I don't know," replied the pastor, "but we sleep four hundred every Sunday morning."

This is perfectly good. You enjoy your sleep! Don't feel guilty about it. Sleep is as much a spiritual activity as anything else. Let it happen. Don't be worried about it, otherwise you will start fighting with your sleep. What will you do?—you start feeling sleepy and you have not to sleep.

I don't give you any commandment. I don't give you any orders. I don't say, "Don't sleep. This is bad-mannered, this is a sin." No! What can you do? If sleep comes, sleep comes. Let it come. Fall into it easily, totally, and you will be sur-prised—soon it will disappear. Or, a new phenomenon will arise in you: that you will become able to sleep and yet absorb me.

We have a special term for it in India—no other language of the world has such a term because no other people have gone so deeply into these spaces. We have a special term; we call it *yoga nidra*, a meditative sleep. If you listen to me totally, you can relax. And the relaxation will take you into a kind of sleep which is not ordinary sleep. You will not hear exactly what I am saying, but still you will find that something has been constantly happening to you. So nothing to be worried about.

And there can be many reasons. Maybe your sleep is not deep enough in the night. And remember, I am not against sleep at all, no. I am not against anything. If your sleep is not good in the night, maybe in the morning, feeling love for me, feeling warmth for me, being together with me, you start almost feeling like you are cuddled, and you go into sleep. It is perfectly good, it is healthy. And if you can sleep deeply here, soon you will be able to sleep deeply in the night too. Then it will disappear. If it is an ordinary sleep it will disappear. If it is *yoga nidra*, a meditative sleep, it will become deeper and deeper. But you will not be missing anything.

And one thing is very good about it—don't feel guilty, because I say this is a very ancient religious tradition. In fact doctors have been known to send people to religious discourses when they suffer from insomnia.

It reminds me of an atheist who often got into discussions with the minister. After much urging the atheist finally agreed to attend a church service the following Sunday. The minister prepared a masterly discourse to appeal specially to his friend's appreciation of logic.
When the two met the next day, the atheist conceded, "I will say this for your Sunday sermon—it kept me awake until the early hours of the morning."
The clergyman beamed. "I am happy that I succeeded in making you doubt the wisdom of your convictions."

"Ah," said the other, "it was not that. You see, when I nap in the daytime I can't sleep at night."

Remember perfectly well that with me all is allowed. Never feel guilty. If there is anything I want you to get rid of, that is guilt. Otherwise small things start becoming wounds in you. You feel guilty—"What will others think? You have fallen asleep!" This has nothing to do with anybody else. Fall asleep! Waking also, you are not very awake, so I don't think you will be losing anything. What is your wakefulness? Just your eyes are open, that's all. And one can sleep perfectly well with open eyes—just a little practice is needed.

That's what happens in many car accidents. Many car accidents happen somewhere in the night nearabout between two and four, and the reason is that the driver is trying hard to keep his eyes open; by and by, he becomes capable of keeping his eyes open, and still he falls asleep. He keeps his eyes open and falls asleep with open eyes. Now this is a scientific finding. And that makes the whole problem: because he thinks he is awake he goes on driving because his eyes are open, but the sleep has taken possession of him, he is no longer aware.

When you are awake, there is not much wakefulness; just a small part of you is awake. So you are not a loser, don't be worried. Whenever sannyasins come and ask me, "What should we do?" I tell them: Don't fight, otherwise you will miss me and you will miss the sleep too. That will be really unnecessary trouble. If you fight with your sleep you cannot understand what I am saying and you cannot sleep either. At least save one—sleep. If it is physical sleep it will help you. Soon you will be able to sleep deeply in the night, because you will learn the art of sleeping. If you can sleep here while I am shouting at you, then who can keep you awake in the night? Or, if it is *yoga nidra*, then it is a tremendously beautiful space.

There are a few people who fall into *yoga nidra*: Sheela is one, Mukta is one, Arup is one. These people fall into *yoga nidra*. That is good! They become so utterly silent that it *looks* like sleep. They also feel asleep, but something starts entering into them. *Yoga nidra* is more like a hypnotic sleep.

You can go to Santosh, our hypnotist; he will tell you more about it. In a hypnotic sleep something tremendously beautiful is possible. What happens in a hypnotic sleep? The person becomes asleep to the whole world, but not to the hypnotist's voice. He goes on listening to it, one window remains open. That is why the hypnotist can order. He can tell the hypnotized person, "Stand up!" and he immediately stands up. If somebody else orders him he will not listen, he will remain asleep. In *yoga nidra* that happens.

Being with the Master you become so relaxed—where else can you be so relaxed? Where else are you so accepted and so welcomed, so loved, so cherished? You start falling into a kind of sleep.

In fact, the word *hypnos* means nothing but sleep. The meaning of the word *hypnos* is sleep. You start falling into a kind of relaxed state, deep relaxation, but still my voice is being heard. Your intellect may not understand but your heart goes on absorbing it. And then it goes very deep, sometimes deeper than you can hear it while awake.

I have heard...

Herb McGlinchey, a Philadelphia ward leader, was once followed around by a reporter who was trying to write a feature story on how a busy politician spends his day. Now

McGlinchey's drinking abilities were legendary. By the end of the day McGlinchey was still fresh and dapper, but the reporter who followed McGlinchey back to the bar at the forty-second ward clubhouse was soaked to the gills and was taking a nap sitting at the bar with his head resting on his folded arms.

McGlinchey was whispering into his ear, "McGlinchey is the greatest. McGlinchey is terrific."

"What are you doing, Herb?" an aide asked.

"Shut up!" McGlinchey is reported to have said. "I am talking to his subconscious. We are going to own this guy!"

When you fall into *yoga nidra*, your conscious mind goes into sleep, but your unconscious is very alert and goes on absorbing. And that absorption is very deep, it goes to your very roots.

So don't be worried about it. If you fall asleep, fall asleep. Hungry, eat; tired, sleep. And when it is hot, it is hot, and when it is cold, it is cold. This acceptance is trust.

The fourth question:

Bhagwan, how do you feel when somebody leaves sannyas?

I feel great!—because unless I leave you, you cannot leave sannyas. When I see that it is almost impossible to work upon you, when I see that you are not going to be available to me— in this life at least—I start taking myself away from you. You can't be aware of it, because you are not even aware that I had got involved with you. If you were aware of my involvement with you, then there would be no need for me to drop you. I start taking away, because the same energy can be used by somebody else. The same time can be used by somebody else who will be more potential, more receptive.

And you will need another Buddha in some other time, in some other life. This is not the time for you, this is not the life for you. But because you are not aware of anything, one day you think you are leaving sannyas. Before you leave, I have left you—in fact, long before. Sometimes it has happened that I have left the man two years before, and after two years' time he leaves sannyas. It takes him two years because people go on postponing, postponing, postponing. But I always give him the feeling—so that he feels good—that it is he who is leaving sannyas. I don't expel anybody from sannyas, at least not directly. I always give the feeling to the person that he is leaving it; at least he will feel good that he has done something.

But I always feel great, because I feel unburdened. If a person is rock-like, to carry him is a burden. And if he is non-cooperative, then it is utterly useless to go on working on him. There is a certain time limit. I work, I do whatsoever can be done, but if I see it is an impossible case—and there are impossible cases—then he has to be left for somebody else in some future life.

And certainly, many more Buddhas will be coming in future and they will need disciples, so I cannot finish all! Gautama the Buddha took care of me; I have to take care of other Buddhas who will be coming.

It reminds me of what happened to a Presbyterian minister. One summer the Baptists and the Methodists agreed to stage an evangelical revival week. The Presbyterians reluctantly

THE SECRET OF SECRETS

agreed to go along with it. At the end of the week the ministers got together to discuss the results of the camp Bible session.

The Methodist said, "We won four new members."

The Baptist said, "We did even better. Six people became converts to the Baptist faith."

They both turned to the Presbyterian and asked him how he did.

The parson answered, "We did best of all. We did not add any but we got rid of ten."

The work consists of two things: I have to help people to become sannyasins—seeing their possibilities, potentialities, hoping for them; but when I see that a person is impossible, that the more I give to him the less he receives, the more I give to him the more closed he becomes—as if he is obliging me... When this feeling becomes settled—and it is not that I take a hasty decision about it, I give all the opportunities and occasions for the person; but if it is impossible, then it is impossible—then I withdraw myself from his being. Once I have withdrawn, sooner or later he will have to drop sannyas.

It functions both ways. The moment you take sannyas, you think *you* are taking sannyas. In the majority of cases I have chosen you—that's why you take sannyas. Otherwise you would not have been able to take such a risk. And it also works the second way: when you drop sannyas, I have chosen you and I help you to drop it, because left to yourself you may go on postponing for your whole life. When you take sannyas, then you postpone for a long, long time. When you want to drop it, then too you postpone for a long, long time. You cannot do anything immediately. You cannot live the moment in its totality.

And this too I have felt: once you have left sannyas there is a possibility you may come back—because then you will miss me, and then you will understand what was being showered on you. Then you will miss the nourishment, then you will miss the contact. When you are getting it you start taking it for granted. Sometimes it is good to take it away so real thirst and an appetite arises in you and you start seeing.

But next time, when you come for sannyas, it is not going to be that easy. I will not initiate you so easily. Then you will have to earn it. Once you drop sannyas, coming back is going to be difficult. I will create all kinds of barriers. Unless you transcend those barriers you will not be accepted again.

That too is to help you, because there are people who can enjoy things only if they are difficult. If things are very simple and easy they cannot enjoy them. They need long, hard, arduous ways.

Sannyas is a simple phenomenon because the whole foundation of it is to relax and live in Tao, relax and let God take care of you. It has to be very simple; it is simple, but your mind understands difficult things more easily. If you have barriers to cross you become challenged. When Hillary reached the Everest peak, do you know what he said? He was asked, "Why? Why did you take such a risk?—because there is nothing. You went there and you came back; there is nothing to get! Why did you take such a risk? And many people have died before: for almost seventy years people have been trying to reach Everest."

And do you know what Hillary said? He said, "It was such a challenge! Just the presence of Everest, unconquered, was a great challenge. It had to be conquered! There is nothing, I know, but that is not the point. Unconquered, and Everest is standing there, proud? Man has to conquer it!"

This is how man's mind functions.

So next time when a person comes back—and many want to come back—then it is going to be difficult. Then I am going to create all kinds of difficulties for you, for your sake. That too is a help for you.

The last question:

Bhagwan, I wonder why you don't hit me on the head as you hit the others.

I will tell you a small story.

The question reminds me of the flies that those expert Japanese Samurai wielders can cut in mid-air. An American tourist heard of the incredible swordsmanship of the cultists of the ancient rite. While in Tokyo he made inquiries as to where the best swordsman was. The best was not available. Neither was the second best. But the American got a chance to see Japan's number-three Samurai wielder. The swordsman let a fly out of the bottle. While it was in flight he struck with the sword. Swish!—the fly was cut in half.

The American was impressed. He could not see that anyone could do better than that. But a little later he wangled an invitation to the number-two man. Again a fly was released from the bottle. The Japanese expert made two swishes with the sword. Incredibly the fly was hacked and quartered in mid-air.

Now he could not see how number-one could do better than that. Finally his place on the waiting list went to the top. He was ushered into the presence of the best swordsman in Japan. Once again there was the ritual of opening the bottle with the fly. While it was buzzing above, the swordsman wielded a great chop. To the American's surprise the fly kept in flight. The American said, "I don't see why you are number-one. The number-three sliced the fly in two, and then I saw the number-two cut it to quarters in two passes. But you missed completely."

"Miss, did I?" said the number-one swordsman. "I assure you, that fly will never propagate again!"

The Tao, the undivided, great One, gives rise to two opposite reality principles, the dark and the light, yin and yang. From yin comes the receptive feminine principle; from yang comes the creative masculine principle; from yin comes ming, life; from yang, hsing or human nature.

Each individual contains a central monad, which, at the moment of conception, splits into life and human nature, ming and hsing.

In the personal bodily existence of the individual they are represented by two other polarities, anima and animus. All during the life of the individual these two are in conflict, each striving for mastery.

If the life-energy flows downward, that is, without let or hindrance into the outer world, the anima is victorious over the animus; no Golden Flower is developed. If the life-energy is led through the 'backward-flowing' process, that is, conserved, and made to 'rise' instead of allowed to dissipate, the animus has been victorious. A man who holds to the way of conservation all through life may reach the stage of the Golden Flower, which then frees the ego from the conflict of the opposites, and it again becomes part of the Tao, the undivided, great One.

Chapter Thirteen

September 8th, 1978

WHERE THE POSITIVE AND NEGATIVE MEET

The old pond
Frog jumps in
The sound of water

THIS IS ONE of the most famous haiku by Matsuo Baso. It has that special flavor that only awakened people are aware of. Its beauty is not only aesthetic but existential. Its fragrance is that of Buddhahood.

Tao simply means that which is, with no qualification, with no adjective. Tao means: just so.

The old pond
Frog jumps in
The sound of water

Haiku is not ordinary poetry. The ordinary poetry is of imagination. The ordinary poetry is a creation of the mind. Haiku simply reflects that which is. Consciousness becomes a mirror and reflects that which confronts it. The mirror remains untouched by what it reflects. An ugly person passes before a mirror—the mirror does not become ugly, the mirror remains in its sameness. A beautiful person passes by, the mirror does not become beautiful either. And when there is nobody to reflect, the mirror is still the same. Reflecting, not reflecting, reflecting good, reflecting bad, the mirror remains virgin.

So is the consciousness of one who has awakened.

Baso was a disciple of the Zen Master, Buko. The time this incredibly beautiful haiku was born, he was living in a small hut by the side of an old pond. One day, after a brief rain, Master Buko visited Baso and asked, "How is your understanding these days?"

Remember, the Master has not asked, "How is your knowledge?" He has asked, "How is your understanding?"

Understanding is totally different from knowledge. Knowledge is borrowed, understanding is one's own. Knowledge comes from without, understanding wells up within. Knowledge is ugly, because it is secondhand. And knowledge can never become part of your being. It will remain alien, it will remain foreign, it cannot get roots into you. Understanding grows out of you, it is your own flowering. It is authentically yours, hence it has beauty, and it liberates.

Truth can never be borrowed from anybody, and the borrowed truth is no longer truth. A borrowed truth is already a lie. The moment truth is said, it becomes a lie. Truth has to be experienced, not to be heard, not to be read. Truth is not just going to be a part of your accumulation, part of your memory. Truth has to be existential: each pore of your being should feel it. Yes, it has to be a feeling. Each breath should be full of it. It should pulsate in you, it should circulate in you like your blood. When truth is understood, you become it.

Hence the Master Buko asked his disciple, "Baso, how is your understanding these days?" And don't forget those two beautiful words, 'these days'.

Truth is always growing. Truth is a movement. It is not static, it is dynamic. It is a dance. It is like growing trees and flowing rivers and moving stars. Truth is never, at any point, a static phenomenon. It is not stasis; it is utterly dynamic, it is movement. To be alive it has to be moving.

Only death is static, only death is stagnant. Hence the people who are dead may look alive on the surface, but if their truth is no longer growing they are dead. Their soul is no longer growing. Truth is not an idea but your very being, your very soul.

Hence the Master asked, "How is your understanding *these* days?" He is not asking about the past. Knowledge is always about the past, imagination is always about the future. He is asking about the present, he is asking about the immediate.

Baso responded,

Rain has passed
Green moss moistened.

Just a few moments before, it was raining: the rain has passed, green moss moistened. It is good, but not *very* good. It is already past. It is no longer immediate. It is a memory already, it is no longer experiencing. Buko was not contented—the answer was good but not great. And a Master is never contented unless the answer is absolute, unless the answer is really as it should be—and certainly not with the potential of a man like Baso.

Now nobody knows about Buko, his Master. He is known only because of Baso. The disciple had infinite potential; the Master cannot be contented so easily. Remember it!—the more potential you have, the more you will be put to hard tasks. The Master will be severe with you. He is going to be very hard on you.

The answer was good if it had come from somebody of lesser potential than Baso; the Master might have nodded his head in consent—but not to Baso. Even a few minutes' gap is gap enough. The rain is no more there, the clouds have dispersed, it is already sunny, the sun is shining all around, on the old pond, on the hut....
He said, "Say something more!"
And when the Master says, "Say something more," he does not mean talk a little more about it. He does not mean 'more' in a quantitative sense. He means: say something deeper, say something more intense, say something more existential, say something more, qualitatively!

At that instant Baso heard the plop of a frog jumping into the pond.

He said,

Frog jumps in
The sound of water

Now, this is Tao: the immediate, that which is, alive, throbbing, this very moment. Tao knows no past, no future. Tao knows only one kind of time, that is present. Tao knows only herenow. Just let your mind disappear and then there is no past and no future. Past and future are mind creations. In reality, there is only present. And when there is no past, no future, how can you even call it present?—because present has meaning only in reference to past and future.

The present is sandwiched between past and future. If you have taken away past and future, the present also disappears. That is the moment of Tao: when time disappears, when one is in utter immediacy, when one is utterly herenow, neither roaming somewhere in the ghosts of the past or in the unborn images of the future. This is the moment of enlightenment: when time is not, and when you are utterly here and nowhere else. And when there is no time, there is no mind. Mind and time are synonymous. The more mind you have, the more you are conscious of time. That's why in the Western world a great time-consciousness has arisen: it is because of the cultivation of the mind.

Go to the primitive people living in the mountains or in the jungles. Go to the aboriginals and there is no time-consciousness, because the mind has not been cultivated yet. And it again happens—when through understanding one drops all the nostalgia for the past and all the fancies for the future, time disappears again. And with the disappearance of time, suddenly mind is no more found. And when there is no mind there is silence. In that silence the beyond penetrates the earth. In that silence the unknown descends into you. In that silence, the meeting with God. In that silence, the benediction, the blessing. In that silence is the Kingdom of God.

Baso said,

> Frog jumps in
> The sound of water.

This is a statement of Tao. This is Tao—simple, pure, nude.

At this response the Master was immensely delighted. The Master is always delighted whenever a disciple comes back home. The delight of the Master knows no bounds, as if he becomes enlightened again! More perfection is added to his already perfect being. He needed nothing to be added to him, but each time a disciple flares up into awareness, becomes aflame, the Master feels as if he has again become enlightened.

The Master was immensely delighted, and the very delight of the Master became the occasion of Baso's enlightenment. Seeing the delighted face of the Master, seeing the aura of his joy, the nod of his consent—or maybe he said nothing—his silence showering on the disciple as grace, Baso became enlightened! What a moment to become enlightened! Thousands of people have become enlightened in the past, but the way Baso became enlightened is simply unique. Because the Master was delighted, the very delight of the Master penetrated his heart like a sword. Flowers showered on him, because the Master must have smiled. . . . The unheard music was heard because the Master must have looked at him with joy, with blessing.

I don't know, but Buko must have danced or done something crazy like that. The enlightenment of a disciple is no small matter.

Later on, Baso continued to polish the haiku like a diamond.

For his whole life he continued to polish it—because this is a rare phenomenon, this small haiku:

> The old pond
> Frog jumps in
> The sound of water.

It was because of this that his own process of enlightenment was triggered. He continued to polish it like a diamond. He continued to cut it and give it more and more depth.

He added: The old pond. The first statement was only:

> Frog jumps in
> The sound of water.

Later on he added: the old pond. My feeling is that the old pond must have insisted on being included. And the old pond had every right to be included—without the old pond there would have been no frog, no jumping in, no sound of water. Baso owed much to the old pond; he included it.

Now the haiku was:

> The old pond
> Frog jumps in
> The sound of water.

And still later on, he dropped the words 'of water'.

Now the haiku was not so perfect as before, but more complete than before. Now it was:

> The old pond
> Frog jumps in
> The sound

It is not so perfect as before, but it is more complete. What do I mean when I say it is more complete?

Now it is a growing phenomenon, it does not put a full stop. Before there was a full stop, it was a finished product; you could not have added anything to it. It didn't leave anything for you to meditate upon. But just 'the sound', and it opens a door. There is no full stop anymore. It becomes a quest. So now it is more complete but less perfect. Now it is utterly complete, complete in the sense that it is growing. Now it is a tree growing, unpredictable. Now each one has to meditate over it. And this became one of the great meditations for the seekers who were to follow Baso. Now it has more beauty than before.

Always remember, anything complete, anything absolutely complete, loses something from it—it becomes dead. All the great painters know this. And the greatest paintings are those which have been left a little bit incomplete, the last touch has not been given to them. And the greatest poems are those which have been left incomplete—so a door remains open for you to enter, so your being can have a communion with the incomplete poetry, so your being can complete it, so it can be completed in your existence.

Now it was,

> The old pond
> Frog jumps in
> The sound

Still later, he dropped a few more things. Now it became,

> The old pond
> Frog jumps in
> Plop!

Now this is getting to the crescendo: just 'plop!' This is truer—truer to the frog, truer to the pond, truer to reality. The reality knows only 'plop!' and it simply leaves you there—to wonder, to inquire, to meditate.

Somebody asked Baso, "Why have you dropped the words 'of water' and finally even 'the sound'?"

Baso said, "I want you to hear what kind of sound it is. I don't want to say, I want you to hear what kind of sound it is."

> The old pond
> Frog jumps in
> Plop!

You are left in a new kind of meditative space. Suddenly the old pond becomes a reality very close by. You can feel it, it is here. And the frog jumps in. It is not a frog of the past... "Plop!" you can hear it again. It becomes a reality. This is great art, that what the artist lived through, he can create again in somebody who is receptive, who is available, who is ready to go on the journey of exploration.

This is the way of all the Buddhas. Their statements are nothing but triggering points of a certain process in you called meditation. This is the way of Tao: to bring you to that which is. This is my way too: to help you to fall utterly in the moment. *This* moment! *This* is it!

Tao is not a doctrine. It is a special way of becoming aware. It is the way of awakening, the way of enlightenment, the way of coming back home. Tao simply means 'the Way'. And remember, it does not mean it in the ordinary sense of the word. Whenever you hear the words 'the way' you start thinking of a goal somewhere faraway, of where the way leads you. No,

Tao means 'the Way', but not in reference to a goal. Then what does it mean? It means 'the way things are'. It simply means the way things are, already are, just so.

Nothing has to be achieved, all is showering on you. Just be herenow and celebrate.

My definition of religion is celebration.

But there are people who would not like such a simple phenomenon as Tao: their egos do not feel challenged enough, they are always interested in the hard way. They are always interested in difficulties. If there are not difficulties, they will create them. They cannot do things in a simple way. They are almost incapable of being simple, and to be simple is the only way to be in God. God is simplicity, innocence.

God is as simple as the rosebush and the call of the cuckoo from the mango grove. God is as simple as the giggle of a girl. God is as simple as a leaf falling from the tree. God is as simple as the breeze passing through the ancient pine trees.

But there are people who would not like God to be so simple. These are the people who create theologies, these are the people who create difficult, abstract speculations about God, who make the whole thing so difficult that it becomes almost incomprehensible. And God is very simple.

> The old pond
> Frog jumps in
> Plop!

Yes, God is like that....

It has to be remembered again and again by you, because your ego will play tricks on you. That is how people go on missing the simple way of Tao. Christianity has so much of a following, Buddhism has a great following, Islam has a great following, but Tao is still not a church. It never has been a church, it never became an organization. Individuals have existed, individuals have followed it, individuals have attained through it, but it never became the way of the masses. Why?—because it is available only to those who are ready to drop the ways of the ego, who are ready to be simple, innocent, childlike.

There are some people who always look for the difficult side of the problem. To them the easy solution never appears, they always have to think of the most complicated one.

I recall a young man who was applying for admission to one of the most exclusive country clubs in Newport. The rather reserved, unimpressive-looking young man was notified that he must play a round of golf with the club officers as a pre-requisite to his acceptance.
On the appointed afternoon he met them on the first tee equipped with a hockey stick, a croquet mallet and a billiard cue. The officers looked him over incredulously but nevertheless proceeded to tee off. To their dismay the young man coolly drove off 275 yards with the hockey stick, gracefully arched his second shot to the green with the croquet mallet and sank a twenty-foot putt with a billiard cue.
After soundly drubbing the baffled officers with a subpar 68, the applicant retired with them to the club bar. There he ordered a Scotch and soda, and when it arrived he mixed the drink himself by tossing the contents of the shot glass over his shoulder into the waiting soda behind him on the bar. This further display of the young man's incredible physical coordination was too much for the officers of the club.
"You are miraculous!" they exclaimed. "What is the story behind these fantastic talents of yours?"

"All my life," the man explained, "physical activity of any sort has been child's play for me. To overcome the boredom that has resulted from my monotonous mastery of everything, I try to do almost everything the most difficult way possible. Thus I play tennis with a ping-pong paddle, ping-pong with a tennis racket, and so on."

"Wait a minute," interrupted one of the club officers. "If it is true, as you say, that you do everything physical in the most difficult manner possible, I have one question..."

"I know," said the young man, smiling. "Everyone asks me the same thing, and I don't mind telling you—standing up, in a hammock."

This is the way of the ego.

Tao is simple, utterly simple. You don't have to stand up in a hammock. The most fundamental thing about Tao is that it is a child's play. But to be a child seems to be almost impossible for people. Who wants to be a child? Jesus says, "Unless you are like small children, you will not enter into my Kingdom of God." But it seems nobody wants to be a child; that is where our misery lies.

All these days we have been going deeper and deeper into the world of Tao. Today are the last sutras, the concluding remarks by Master Lu-tsu. They are simple. You have to be simple to understand them. There is not much knowledge in them, but certainly much insight. They will not make you knowledgeable. In fact, they will take all knowledge away, they will make you ignorant. But if a man can be ignorant, can be courageous enough to drop all his knowledge and can live in a state of not-knowing, then there is no barrier between him and God, no barrier between him and existence. Knowledge creates the barrier.

Adam has been expelled from the Garden of Eden because he has eaten the fruit of the Tree of Knowledge. That fruit has to be vomited. Once knowledge is vomited out, you are clean. And in that cleanness, all is available. All is already available; just because you are not clean and stuffed with knowledge, you cannot see it.

The sutras:

> *The Tao, the undivided, great One, gives rise to two opposite reality principles, the dark and the light, yin and yang. From yin comes the receptive feminine principle; from yang comes the creative masculine principle; from yin comes ming, life; from yang, hsing or human nature.*

This is the concluding part of *The Secret of the Golden Flower*. This is a summary of the whole treatise, so that you can remember.

> *The Tao, the undivided, great One, gives rise to two opposite reality principles...*

First, what is Tao?—that which is, unnamed, unqualified, simply that which is. It contains all. It contains the trees and the stars, it contains you and me and the animals and the birds. It contains all that is. And that which is contains all that has ever been, and that which is contains all that is ever going to be.

Tao cannot be said just because it contains all—and no word can contain all. The very purpose of a word is to denote. The very purpose of a word is to classify. A table is a table and not a chair, and a chair is a chair and not a dog, and a dog is a dog and not a man. The word is meaningful only because it has a definite boundary around it. It excludes everything out of it. It includes only something tiny and excludes the whole existence.

Tao includes all, excludes nothing. That's why Tao cannot be said. It can be shown but not said. The man of Tao can give you a taste of it if you are ready to go into him and let him come into you. The man of Tao can give you a glimpse, a lightning glimpse of the totality of existence...but you may become frightened.

That's what happened in the great song, Bhagavad-Gita. The disciple Arjuna asked Krishna his Master, his friend, his guide, "You say great things. You argue well. Your proofs are very convincing, yet doubt persists deep down within me. The doubt is because I have not experienced what you are saying to me. Why don't you give me a little experience of it? Just a little taste on the tip of the tongue will do. There is no need to go on arguing about it so long, there is no need to produce so many proofs for it. Just a little taste and I will be convinced and my doubts will disappear."

Krishna said, "Okay."

And then it happened, one of the most beautiful stories that has ever happened between a Master and a disciple: Krishna became huge and Krishna became infinite and worlds started rotating within him, and Arjuna was frightened. Krishna had millions of hands and all the stars and all the planets within him, and life and death within him, all polarities meeting and merging in him. It was a chaos. Arjuna thought he must be going mad. He closed his eyes in fear, and he cried and shouted, "Come back! Come back to your ordinary form with two hands. Be my old friend again. This is too much!"

Krishna came back and he said, "I knew it. You are not yet ready to have the taste of the totality."

Totality will frighten you. Its sheer vastness is such, it is going to frighten you out of your wits. It is abysmal, and you will start disappearing into it like a soap-bubble. It is so vast that you will lose all orientation of who you are.

That's what happened to Arjuna. And he said, "Yes, I was feeling as if I was going to die, or as if I was going to be mad, or as if I had already gone mad. Thank you for coming back to your original form."

And Krishna said, "This is not my original form. That was my original form."

Tao is infinity. Tao is totality. Tao is all that is, hence it cannot be said. But in the deep intimacy of a Master and a disciple, something of it starts pulsating. There are moments when you become available to the whole, when you don't function as a separate entity, when you lose the idea of separation for a few moments, when you are one and united. When the drop disappears into the ocean—even for a single moment—then you know what Tao is.

So Tao cannot be said but can be showed. That's what I have been doing here.

This is not a school of philosophy. I'm not teaching you any philosophy at all. This is an existential school. I am teaching you existence as it is. And existence is already here; you just have to become a little more courageous to open up, to allow it in. It is knocking on your doors!

Jesus says, "Knock and the door shall be opened unto you. Ask and it shall be given. Seek and ye shall find."

I would like to say just the opposite to you. God is knocking on your doors, has been knocking for millenia. Hear! He's knocking on the door...open your doors. Listen! He's asking you to come out of your self-imposed prison. He's seeking you! Let him seek you! Help him seek you! He's searching for you and you are escaping, and you have been escaping for lives together. You are miserable, and still you go on escaping. And whenever His hand comes close to you, you become frightened. And I understand, the fear is natural. What is the fear? The fear is: if God is, then you cannot be.

Friedrich Nietzsche has said, "If God is, then how can I be? So, I *decide* that there is no God; then only can *I* be." And that's how millions of people have decided: they have denied God in order to be. If there is no God, ego is possible. If there is God how can the ego be supported? By what? Then you are no more there; that is the fear. God is the death of the ego.

Tao can be tasted, Tao can be experienced, but one condition has to be fulfilled: you have to be so simple that you don't have any ego. You have to be so silent that there is no idea of 'I'.

> *The Tao, the undivided, great One, gives rise to two*
> *opposite reality principles...*

This is the very fundamental of the Taoist approach: that the one becomes two—because then only is the play possible. The one has to become two, and the two have to be opposites to each other; then the game starts.

The ancient Hindu scriptures say God was alone and was feeling really very very lonely. He decided to create the other. That's why Hindus say the existence is *leela*, a play. God created the other just to have a little fun.

Tao is one, but the moment it becomes manifested it has to become two. Manifestation has to be dual: it cannot be one, it has to be two, it has to split into two. It has to become matter and consciousness, it has to become man and woman, it has to become day and night, it has to become life and death. You will find these two principles everywhere. The whole of life consists of these two principles, and behind these two principles is hidden the One. If you continue to remain involved between these two dualities and the polar opposites, you will remain in the world. If you are intelligent, if you are a little more alert, and if you start looking deeper, into the depths of things, you will be surprised—these opposites are not really opposites but complementaries. And behind both is one single energy: that is Tao.

> *Tao...gives rise to two opposite reality principles, the dark and the light, yin and yang. From yin comes the receptive feminine principle; from yang comes the creative masculine principle; from yin comes ming, life; from yang, hsing or human nature.*

Basically, the polarities can be named man/woman: the masculine, the feminine. And it is closer to our human reality to understand it that way. We can call it negative and positive, but that would be a little far away. To call it yin and yang, Shiva and Shakti, man and woman, brings it very close to our heart—we know this duality.

Man is attracted towards the woman, the woman is attracted towards the man, and yet when they are together they constantly fight. They cannot live separately and they cannot live together either. Attraction is tremendous, repulsion too. When you are with your woman or with your man you start thinking of how to be alone. You start thinking of freedom, of being alone, and the beauty and the silence and all that. When you are alone you simply start feeling lonely and you start hankering for the other, and you start thinking of those loving spaces, warmth and all that. When alone you want to be together, when together you want to be alone.

Watch it, it has a great message for you. It simply says: you are half and the woman is half. Together you become one. But then a problem arises. In that moment of oneness you are ecstatic, you rejoice, but then the problem arises: this oneness, is it man or woman? Which is the dominating factor? That is the conflict. Man and woman want to be one, but man wants to remain the dominating factor in that oneness; the woman should surrender, submit. And the same is the desire from the woman's side, that the man should surrender and submit.

Both want to be one, but that oneness has to be 'mine'. If I am man then that oneness has to be man's; the woman has to disappear into the man. If I am a woman then it has to be that of woman; the man has to disappear into the woman. Hence the conflict, the attraction and the repulsion, and the whole comedy and tragedy of life.

The feminine principle is receptive and the masculine principle is creative, and both can only go together. Separate, they both suffer. Then the woman has nothing to receive and feels empty. And if there is nobody to receive, the man's creativity is lost because there is nobody to appreciate, inspire. The woman receives, inspires and helps the man to flow in his creativity. Man's creativity helps the woman to flow into her receptivity. This receptivity of the woman is not only biological, it is spiritual too. Behind all great poets you will find the inspiration of a woman. The women have not themselves been great poets —they need not be—but no great poetry is ever born without a woman. She functions as a lighthouse. Men have been great poets, but without a woman the poetry simply dies and withers away.

Receptivity and creativity are two wings of the bird. This flight towards the unknown can be completed only with both wings. With one wing the bird is not going to go anywhere. And remember, creativity is not more valuable than receptivity —they are equal, they are utterly equal. No wing, right or left, is greater than the other; cannot be. They are equal. They are not similar but they are equal.

Now there is a great desire in women's hearts to be creative —for a certain reason: because creativity is praised. Nobel Prizes are given only to creators, not to those who show tremendous receptivity. Now this is an ugly situation which creates an obsessive desire to be creative, because the receptive person is not appreciated at all, is not valued at all, is not talked about at all. So all over the world the woman wants to be creative, but the moment she wants to be creative she starts losing her femininity, her grace. She starts becoming more and more masculine, because the creative is the masculine principle. She starts becoming more and more hard. She loses softness and roundness, starts growing corners, starts fighting. You can see the shouting Lib Movement women—their shouts are ugly. And I know their fight is right, but fighting is not the way of woman!—the very fight will destroy their womanhood. It has to be done in some other way. In fact, man should fight for woman's equality.

The people who can understand, the people who can think, the people who are intelligent, should create a man's movement for women's liberation. They should fight! It is their imposed slavery on woman—they should feel guilty, they should undo whatsoever they have done. But if the woman starts fighting— and then naturally she starts thinking to be creative, paint, dance, sing, sculpt, compose—very unconsciously she is imitating man. And remember, woman imitating man will always be a second-rate man. And that is ugly. The very effort of being equal is lost. The woman can only be a first-rate woman. If she wants to be a man, she will only be a second-rate man. It is just the same way if a man wants to be receptive: he can't have that natural receptivity of a woman. He will become a second-rate woman. To be first-rate you have to follow your nature.

Never imitate. Follow your own intrinsic nature. Follow your own built-in nature, because only from the fulfillment of that nature does one arrive to a state of bliss, fulfillment, contentment.

Woman creates life, life in general, life as a universal phenomenon. Man, or the male element, creates human nature. Man is particular, woman is universal. Man goes into details of things. Man becomes a specialist. That's why male-dominated fields all become fields of specialization sooner or later. That's what is happening in science. Everything slowly, slowly becomes a specialization, and new branches arise, branches out of branches and now the whole thing seems to be a very absurd situation.

Man has created much knowledge and has gone into deep detail, but now there is nobody to make a whole out of that knowledge. Nobody knows how to create a synthesis. That synthesis is possible only through a woman, not through a man, because woman is a universalizing principle.

Man dissects, woman unites. That's why a woman feels closer

to religion than a man, and has always felt closer to religion than a man. You may not have observed the fact. The fundamental fact is: that religion thinks in terms of one, wholeness, totality. That's what Tao is, or God, or whatsoever you will. Science dissects and goes on splitting and has reached to the electron, to the smallest particle. These are polar-opposite ways. Religion goes on joining things together, together, together, and comes to the ultimate Tao which contains all. It is the ultimate unity. Science goes on splitting and splitting, specializing and more specializing. They say specialization means to know more and more about less and less.

I have heard...

It is the twenty-first century, and a man goes to a doctor. He is troubled by his eyes; he is getting old. And the doctor asks, "Which of your eyes is in trouble?"
And he says, "My right eye."
The doctor says, "Sorry, you will have to go to somebody else, because I only specialize in left eyes."

It is going to happen. It is already happening.

Man is no longer one unity; there are so many specialists. Nobody thinks about the man as a whole, as a totality. That is one of the greatest problems that medical science is facing and has to face and find a solution for—because the patient is not thought to be one unity. If his head is in trouble, then the head has to be taken as a separate part. Just give some medicine—aspirin or something. Nobody bothers about the whole system. The aspirin will first go to the stomach, it can't go directly to the head. What is going to happen to the stomach? —that is nobody's concern.

Man is a unity. You cannot treat him like a machine.

If something is wrong with your car you go to the garage; he changes the part. Because the machine has no soul, it is only the sum total of its parts. And what is a soul? Soul means that something more is there than the sum total of its parts. There is a unity behind. Modern medical science is facing it tremendously, and the reason is because all of these sciences have been developed by men. The impact of the woman is missing.

The woman always universalizes. She thinks in terms of unities, she never thinks in terms of parts. A woman is never mathematical; she cannot be. Her whole approach is wholistic. That is the meaning of this statement made twenty-five centuries ago; it is yet contemporary.

> *The Tao...undivided, great One, gives rise to two opposite reality principles, the dark and the light, yin and yang. From yin comes the receptive feminine principle; from yang comes the creative masculine principle; from yin comes ming, life; from yang, hsing or human nature.*
>
> *Each individual contains a central monad, which, at the moment of conception, splits into life and human nature, ming and hsing.*

Each individual comes as a single unit, unitary, and then is split. It is just like a ray passing through a prism is split into seven colors. Conception functions like a prism: the one white ray splits into seven colors. The one Tao splits into two opposite polarities: man and woman. Remember that no man is man alone, the woman is behind, hidden in him; and so is it with the woman. Both are bisexual.

If the conscious mind is man, then the unconscious is woman.

If the conscious mind is woman, then the unconscious is man. It has to be so. And the desire to meet with the woman or with the man on the outside is not going to fulfill you—unless you know how to meet the inner man and the inner woman. The outer woman can give you only a few glimpses of meeting, beautiful moments, but at a great cost. And all lovers know that yes, there are a few ecstatic moments, but one has to pay a great price for them: one has to lose one's freedom, one has to lose one's own being, and one has to become dependent. One has to compromise in a thousand and one ways, which hurts and wounds. The meeting with the outer woman or the outer man is going to be only momentary.

But there is another meeting, and that is one of the secret messages of Tao: that you can find your inner woman—where your conscious and unconscious meet, where your light and darkness meet, where your earth and sky meet, where your positive and negative meet. And once that meeting has happened within you, you are whole. This is what is called the man of Tao.

The man of Tao is neither man nor woman. He has come back to his oneness. He is alone...all one. You cannot call Lao Tzu a man or a woman, or Buddha a man or a woman, or Jesus a man or a woman. Biologically they are, spiritually they are not. Spiritually they have gone beyond. Buddha has no unconscious in him, no division. He's undivided. And when you are undivided all conflict within you ceases. Otherwise you are in a *constant* civil war: you are not only fighting with the outer woman, you are fighting continuously with the inner woman too. And you know those moments.

A moment comes when you want to cry, your inner woman is ready to shed tears, but your man stops it. Your man says,

"What are you doing, man? Are you mad? People will think that you are being very feminine. Stop your tears! This is not right for a man like you. It is okay for women, let them cry and weep, but you have to keep a face, hard, strong, invulnerable. Hold your tears back!" And the fight has started.

And the same happens to the woman. You would like to climb a tree, and it is so beautiful, and the highest branches of the tree are playing with the clouds. Who would not like to climb? But your inner woman says, "Wait! This is allowed only to men, not to you. You are a woman. You have to think of what is right for a woman and what is not right. You have to follow certain manners, etiquette." And you repress it.

This goes on continuously: man represses his woman, woman represses her man, and the repressed part starts taking revenge in subtle ways. It starts coming from the backdoor, it starts poisoning you. So there are moments when the woman becomes very hard, cruel, nagging, fighting, ugly; that is the man taking revenge. Climbing on a tree would have been beautiful, but that you denied. Now the man comes through the backdoor and you start screaming at your husband or at your children, and you start throwing things. Now this is ugly, this is pathological. It was good to cry. Tears are beautiful because they are part of life. It was good to cry, there was no need to hide those tears. If you hide your tears, you will not be able to laugh either. You will always be afraid—if you laugh too much, you may feel so relaxed with the laughter that the repressed tears may start coming up.

Nietzsche has said, "I laugh just to keep my tears hidden, because I am afraid if I don't laugh I may start crying."

Now this is one aspect. One can go on smiling, this is not real laughter. One can go on smiling—this is diplomatic—so that nobody can see tears ready to come from your eyes. People become engaged in your smile and don't look at your eyes; this is one way. The other way is to keep a very hard face— don't even laugh, don't even smile. Let people know that you are a man of steel. That is the meaning of the word 'stalin': man of steel. It is said that Stalin never used to laugh. How could he laugh?—a man of steel. Steel men cannot laugh.

But this is ugly, this is becoming mechanical. This is dehumanizing. Either one becomes false, pseudo, or one becomes very hard, has to grow a hard crust to keep oneself in constant control.

Tao says there is no need to deny the opposite polarity of your being. Accept it, it is you! Both these rays are you. Let them meet and merge! Let them dance together! Let them become one so deeply that again you can have the vision of one— Tao, the great One, undivided.

> In the personal bodily existence of the individual they are
> represented by two other polarities, anima and animus. All
> during the life of the individual these two are in conflict,
> each striving for mastery.

Drop fighting for mastery! That is your inner politics. Both are equal and nobody can ever be the master. Both are needed and equally needed. Accept both, although it is very difficult, logically very difficult to accept both, because they are diametrically opposite. But logic is not true to life itself. More true to life is what is known as dialectics.

Logic is not true to life. Logic is linear; it does not contain the opposite. Tao says the opposite is always there, running parallel to it. The process is not logical but dialectical. Thesis is opposed by antithesis: man is opposed by woman, and out of this opposition, out of this conflict, out of this challenge, energy is released. And that energy can either be dissipated—if you are foolish—or can be accumulated—if you are wise. If dissipated you will remain in constant conflict, a civil war. Your life will become schizophrenic. Or, if you are wise, intelligent, and you know how to contain the opposites together in a deep friendly embrace, then thesis opposed by antithesis will create a new phenomenon in your being: synthesis. On a higher plane you will arise. In a deeper way you will be united. And then again the synthesis functions as a thesis, creates its antithesis, and again, on a higher plane, synthesis. It goes on and on, waves upon waves, higher and higher. There are planes upon planes, and one can go on reaching. The ultimate plane is the total synthesis of your life. All conflict disappears—is not dropped, but disappears of its own accord.

This is Tao, the Tao, the undivided, the great One.

> *If the life-energy flows downward, that is, without let or*
> *hindrance into the outer world, the anima is victorious over*
> *the animus; no Golden Flower is developed.*

If energy flows downward and outward, your energy becomes reproductive, sexually reproductive. A great phenomenon! That's how you were born, that's how everybody else was born—a Buddha, a Jesus, a Krishna. If energy flows downward, it creates new people, new forms for God to embody. But the Golden Flower does not bloom. You produce somebody else— a child, a beautiful child; life continues, life goes on moving, remains flowing, but the Golden Flower cannot bloom this way.

How does the Golden Flower bloom?

If the life-energy is led through the 'backward-flowing'
process, that is, conserved, and made to 'rise' instead of
allowed to dissipate, the animus has been victorious.

These are the two possibilities: energy flowing downward
becomes sexuality, energy flowing upward becomes spirituality.
Energy flowing downward is reproductive, energy flowing
upward is creative. Energy flowing downward creates new
life, energy flowing upward gives *you* a new birth. That's
what Jesus means when he says, "Unless you are born again"
—not from a father and mother, but by your own upward
movement; unless you become a *dwija*, a twice-born—"you
will not enter into my kingdom of God."

The Golden Flower is waiting at the highest peak of your
being. In the yoga map it is called *sahasrar*, one-thousand-
petalled lotus. It is the seventh chakra—in your head. The
lowest is the sex chakra, *muladhar*, and the highest is the seventh
chakra, *sahasrar*. From the lowest chakra, energy moves downward, creates new life. If the energy is conserved, helped to
move upwards, it reaches one day to the *sahasrar*—and the
Golden Flower blooms.

Of course, it needs energy. It is there only as a potential, as a
possibility. Unless energy becomes available for it, it will not
become actual.

It is like when you don't give water to a tree: the tree is waiting,
the water is not coming. The green juice is not flowing upwards. How can it bloom into a thousand and one flowers?—
impossible. It will remain sad, it will almost remain dying. It
will be a slow suicide. By and by the leaves will also wither
away, by and by the branches will die, and ultimately, the
roots. It needs a constant upward flow of energy.

Just as the green sap moves in a tree, man is also a tree. And this is not a new symbol that I am using—of man as a tree— it is one of the most ancient symbols. It has been used in the Jewish mystical schools: it is called the Tree of Life. Just as Buddhism has reached to its crescendo in Zen, and Islam in Sufism, Judaism has reached its ultimate peaks in the Kabbala. The Kabbala says that man is a tree, and it needs great energy for the flowers to bloom.

But remember, to conserve energy does not mean to repress energy; that's where many people become misguided. To conserve energy does not mean to repress. The processes are absolutely different.

Repression means you are continuously repressing at the lowest center. If it becomes too much at the lowest center it will create perverted sexuality. If you don't allow it a natural let-go and the energy accumulates at the lowest center too much, it will find some way or other; it can become perverted. It *will* become perverted! It will create pathology. Ask the psychiatrists, psychologists, psychoanalysts: they say, "Out of a hundred percent, ninety-five percent of the psychological cases are because of sexuality. Somewhere or other, sex is involved." This is too big a number, ninety-five percent. And the people who never go to the psychiatrists and the psychoanalysts are not in a better position either. Everybody is suppressed.

Suppression is not transformation. Let it be understood once and for all!—repression can never become a transformation.

Then what is transformation? And what is conservation of energy?

Conservation of energy is a meditative process. It is not

moralistic. I will suggest a small method to you that will be of immense help. It has been used by Taoists down the ages. It is given only from the Masters to the disciples; that's why it has not been written in the books. But now the time has come that it should be given, because now millions of people are working on their spiritual search *through* books. Masters are not so available either.

This is a simple method of transforming your energy and leading it upwards. And always remember, Taoist methods are very simple, so don't think, "How can such a simple thing be of such great importance?" Practice it, experiment with it and you will know.

The process is:

At least twice a day—the best times are early in the morning, just before you get out of your bed. The moment you feel you are alert, awake, do it for twenty minutes. Do it *first* thing in the morning!—don't get out of the bed. Do it there, then and there, immediately!—because when you are coming out of sleep you are very very delicate, receptive. When you are coming out of sleep you are very fresh, and the impact will go very deep. When you are just coming out of your sleep you are less in the mind than ever. Hence some gaps are there through which the method will penetrate into your innermost core. And early in the morning, when you are awakening, and when the whole earth is awakening, there is a great tide of awakening energy all over the world. Use that tide; don't miss that opportunity.

All ancient religions used to pray early in the morning when the sun rose, because the rising of the sun is the rising of all the energies in existence. In that moment you can simply ride on the rising energy wave; it will be easier. By the evening it will be difficult, energies will be falling back; then you will be fighting against the current. In the morning you will be going with the current.

So the best time to begin is in the early morning, *immediately*, just when you are half-asleep, half-awake. And the process is so simple. It needs no posture, no *yogasana*, no bath is needed, nothing.

You simply lie down, as you are lying down in your bed, on your back. Keep your eyes closed.

When you breathe in, just visualize great light entering from your head into your body, as if a sun has risen just close to your head—golden light pouring into your head. You are just hollow and the golden light is pouring into your head, and going, going, going, deep, deep, and going out through your toes. When you breathe in, do it with this visualization.

And when you breathe out, visualize another thing: darkness entering through your toes, a great dark river entering through your toes, coming up, and going out through the head. Do slow, deep breathing so you can visualize. Go very slowly. And just out of sleep you can have very deep and slow breaths because the body is rested, relaxed.

Let me repeat: breathing in, let golden light come into you through your head, because it is there that the Golden Flower is waiting. That golden light will help. It will cleanse your whole body and will make it absolutely full of creativity. This is male energy.

Then when you exhale, let darkness, the darkest you can conceive, like a dark night, river-like, come from your toes upwards—this is feminine energy: it will soothe you, it will

make you receptive, it will calm you, it will give you rest—
and let it go out of the head. Then inhale again, and golden
light enters in.

Do it for twenty minutes early in the morning.

And then the second best time is when you are going back to
sleep, in the night.

Lie down on the bed, relax for a few minutes. When you start
feeling that now you are wavering between sleep and waking,
just in that middle, start the process again, and continue for
twenty minutes. If you fall asleep doing it, it is the best, because
the impact will remain in the subconscious and will go on
working.

And after a three-month period you will be surprised: the
energy that was constantly gathering at the *muladhar*, at the
lowest, the sex center, is no more gathering there. It is going
upwards.

Just the other day somebody had asked a question. He said
that he has seen the most beautiful women around here that he
has ever seen anywhere else, but they are non-erotic.

Why is it so? It is so, his observation is right. If you meditate
deeply you will become non-erotic. You will have a different
kind of beauty, but it will not be erotic. It will start having the
flavor of spirituality. It will start having the subtleness of grace,
not the grossness of sexuality.

Sex is gross because it is the lowest rung of your ladder. As
energies move upwards a totally different kind of beauty and
grace arises in you, which is divine. You become less and less of
the body and more and more of the spirit.

If you do this simple method for three months, you will be surprised: there is no need to repress. Transformation has started happening.

> *A man who holds to the way of conservation all through life may reach the stage of the Golden Flower...*

And if you can go on doing this for your whole life, one day it is going to happen.

The Master Lu-tsu says 'your whole life' so that you remain patient. It can happen any day, it can happen today, or tomorrow, or the day after tomorrow. It depends with what intensity, with what sincerity you work for it, with what longing, what totality you go into it. And the day the Golden Flower blooms in you is the day of Buddhahood. You have attained the greatest treasure there is.

> *A man who holds to the way of conservation all through life may reach the stage of the Golden Flower, which then frees the ego from the conflict of the opposites, and it again becomes part of the Tao, the undivided great One.*

From Tao to Tao, from One to One—as Plotinus says, "The flight of the alone to the alone."

Chapter Fourteen

September 9th, 1978

THIS VERY WORLD THE PARADISE

The first question:

Your dancing meditations seem to be bringing forth an over-whelming sensuousness. All that has not been taken, all that has not been given is revealed then.... The play of nature on my whole being, all the beauty that I behold, all the music that enchants my ears and my soul, all seem to be expressed in voluptuousness. Even when I close my eyes in silent sitting, this tangible presence is felt.

I welcome and enjoy this growing sensitivity and 'orgasmic' affair with life. I cannot imagine God descending upon me but as the ultimate lover when I will be turned inside out, totally open and as readable as the glorious moon.

Can I trust this feeling? And is it of any meaning with regard to being with you and growing through you?

I have not been blessed with transcendental experiences. All I know and all that seems to be my lot to know is this joy, ever-increasing and fresh, to be part of the cosmic play and to be able to transmute it in my daily living—in all kinds of creative fashions, from cooking to dancing and praying. Can you please advise me.

Tanmaya, this is what I am teaching here. I don't teach the transcendental, I teach the immanent—because the immanent is the transcendental. I don't teach the ultimate, I teach the immediate—because the immediate is the body of the ultimate. If you enter into the immediate you will find the ultimate pulsating there. The ultimate is the heartbeat of the immediate.

This is my fundamental teaching: that there is no division between this and that. That is contained in this, the other shore is contained in this shore. You need not go anywhere. If you can be joyous, flowing, alive, sensitive, orgasmic, *this* very shore immediately is transformed into the other shore...*this* very world the paradise, *this* very body the Buddha.

Remember it, because down the ages religions have been teaching a dichotomy between this and that. Religions have been teaching a kind of schizophrenia, a split, between the body and the soul, between the lower and the higher, between the outer and the inner, and so on and so forth.

All divisions are false; reality is one. There is nothing lower and nothing higher, and there is nothing outer, nothing inner. There is no body, no soul. It is all one. The body is the soul visible, and the soul is the body invisible. There is no creator other than this very creation. The creator and the creation are not separated, they are as one as the dancer and the dance. They cannot exist apart, they can only exist as one. You cannot take the dancer apart from his dance; if you take him, he is no more a dancer. You cannot take the dance apart from the dancer, there is no possibility. They are utterly one, expressions of the same energy, the same phenomenon.

So what is happening to you, Tanmaya, is *exactly* what should happen. This is what I am desiring, longing, praying for you. This is the way you are coming closer and closer to me. Forget all about transcendental experiences. All those so-called transcendental experiences are nothing but bullshit. These are the real experiences: this sensitivity that is growing in you, this receptivity that is becoming deeper and deeper every moment, this joy of existence, of life, of being, of love.

Don't think of seeing some spiritual visions—God sitting on a golden throne. Those are all fantasies of starved minds, of mediocre minds. Don't think about something extraordinary, because the extraordinary is desired only by the very ordinary. That is the desire of the inferior. If you are intelligent, if you are alert, the ordinary becomes the extraordinary. And that is the magic I teach you.

I am giving you an alchemy. Yes, cooking can become prayer; only then are you religious. If cooking can become prayer, only then...if cleaning the floor can become meditation, only then....

This ordinary life is ordinary only because you are dull, because you are asleep, because you are thick. It is ordinary only because you don't have perception to see its depth. You can't see the colors of life and the beautiful forms of life and the eternal benediction that goes on showering each moment of it. It is a continuum. Because you can't see the beauty of a rising sun and you can't see the beauty of the stars in the night, and because you can't see the beauty of human eyes, hence out of this poverty arises the desire for some transcendental experience—experiencing God, heaven, paradise, experiencing the arousal of the serpent power in your spine. Experiencing these things or desiring to experience these things is all mind-games. The true religion is always of the here and the now.

Yes, that's what I want you to become, sensuous, because if you are not sensuous you can never be spiritual. If you cannot enjoy the small things of life, if you cannot sip your tea with celebration, you are not religious at all. You can go to Kaaba or to Jerusalem or you can go to Kashi; you will never be religious anywhere if you cannot sip tea with utter gratitude. And the aroma of the tea, and the beautiful smell that is arising— if you cannot feel it, if you are not sensuous enough to feel it, you will not be able to feel God....

...Because God is the center of everything.

God is not the original cause and God is not the ultimate goal; God is the center of every condition that you come across every moment of your life. God is the center of the woman you have fallen in love with, God is the center of the man you have become friendly with. God is the center of everything that you come across. God means the center, and the world means the periphery, the circumference. And they are never separate. And the center is hidden in the circumference.

To be sensuous means to become aware of the circumference, and to be spiritual means to become aware of the center. Sensuousness is the beginning of spirituality.

Become more and more sensuous; that is the way of being alive.

But your old religions have been teaching you just the opposite: they teach you a kind of bodily death, they teach you to make your body more and more insensitive. That is a cheap trick: make your body more and more cold so that you can pretend a kind of aloofness, so that you can say, "Nothing affects me." Because you are carrying a dull and dead body around yourself, naturally nothing affects you, but this is not growth.

Real growth is: you are open, vulnerable, you are affected by everything *and yet* nothing affects you. You are in the midst of situations and yet not part of them. You are on the circumference of everything and yet the center is never forgotten.

You say, "Your dancing meditation seems to be bringing forth an overwhelming sensuousness."

Tanmaya, you are blessed. Allow it, don't become afraid, and don't let your old conditionings interfere.

That's why I teach dance, I teach music, I teach singing. I want your body to vibrate at the optimum, I want your body to become a pulsating, streaming phenomenon; not a stagnant pool, but a running, rushing river to the ocean.

"All that has not been taken, all that has not been given is revealed then...."

Yes, when you are sensuous God is available. All the mysteries are close by, because that is the only way to know the mysterious.

Sensuousness means you are open, your doors are open, you are ready to throb with existence. If a bird starts singing, the sensuous person immediately feels the song echoed in his deepest core of being. The non-sensuous person does not hear it at all, or maybe it is just a noise somewhere. It does not penetrate his heart. A cuckoo starts calling—a sensuous person starts feeling as if the cuckoo is not calling from some faraway mango grove, but from deep down within his own soul. It becomes his own call, it becomes his own longing for the divine, his own longing for the beloved. In that moment the observer and the observed are one. Seeing a beautiful flower bloom, the sensuous person blooms with it, becomes a flower with it.

The sensuous person is liquid, flowing, fluid. Each experience, and he becomes it. Seeing a sunset, he is the sunset. Seeing a

night, a dark night, beautiful silent darkness, he becomes the
darkness. In the morning he becomes the light.

He is *all* that life is. He tastes life from every nook and corner.
Hence he becomes rich; this is real richness. Listening to music
he is music, listening to the sound of water he becomes that
sound. And when the wind passes through a bamboo grove,
and the cracking bamboos...he is not far away from them.
He is amidst them, one of them—he is a bamboo.

A Zen Master told one of his disciples who wanted to paint
bamboos, "Go and first become a bamboo."
He was an accomplished painter, he had passed all the art
examinations, and with distinction. His name had already
started becoming famous. And the Master said, "You go to
the forest, live with the bamboos for a few years, become a
bamboo. And the day you can become a bamboo come back
and paint, not before it. How can you paint a bamboo if you
have not known what a bamboo feels like from within? You
can paint a bamboo from the outside, but that is just a photograph."

And that is the difference between photography and painting.
A photograph can never be a painting. Howsoever skillfully,
artfully done, it remains only the reflection of the circumference of the bamboo. No camera can enter into the soul.

When for the first time photography was developed, a great
fear arose in the world of painting that maybe now painting
would lose its old beauty and its old pedestal; because photography would be developed more and more every day and
soon it would fulfill its requirement. That fear was absolutely
unbased. In fact after the invention of the camera, photography
has developed tremendously, but simultaneously painting has

learned new dimensions, new visions, new perceptions. Painting has become richer; it had to become. Before the invention of the camera the painter was functioning as a camera.

...The Master said, "You go to the forest." And the disciple went, and for three years he remained in the forest, being with the bamboos in all kinds of climates. Because when it is raining the bamboo has one joy, and when it is windy the bamboo has a different mood, and when it is sunny, of course everything changes in the being of the bamboo. And when a cuckoo comes into the bamboo grove and starts calling, the bamboos are silent and responsive. He had to be there for three years.

And then it happened, one day it happened: sitting by the side of the bamboos, he forgot who he was. And the wind started blowing and he started swaying—like a bamboo! Only later on did he remember that for a long time he had not been a man. He had entered into the soul of the bamboo, then he painted the bamboos.

Those bamboos certainly have a totally different quality which no photograph can ever have. Photographs can be beautiful, but dead. That painting is alive because it shows the soul of the bamboo in all its moods, in all its richness, in all its climates. Sadness is there, and joy is there, and agony is there, and ecstasy is there, and all that a bamboo knows, the whole biography of a bamboo is there.

To be sensuous is to be available to the mysteries of life. Become more and more sensuous, and drop all condemnation. Let your body become just a door. All your senses should become clear doors with no hindrances, so when you hear you become the music, and when you see you become the light, when you touch you become that which you have touched.

Tanmaya, you say, "I welcome and enjoy this growing sensitivity and 'orgasmic' affair with life. I cannot imagine God descending upon me but as the ultimate lover when I will be turned inside out, totally open and as readable as the glorious moon."

You have understood me rightly; this is my message in short: God comes always as a lover. God is the immediate and the ultimate Beloved. And if you know God in some other way, remember, that God is your mind creation, it is not the true God.

And because religions arose around untrue gods they have not been able to help humanity to become more loving. On the contrary, they have filled the whole world with hatred, with violence. The true religion can only conceive of God as the Beloved.

You are on the right track. Your past will pull you back: the priests, the parents, the conditionings in your mind, will pull you back. Beware. Drop all that. *Trust* this growing sensitivity, this orgasmic openness. This is the door to the divine. Trust it, and go headlong with it.

The second question:

When you say good, does it mean 'good' or does it sometimes mean 'don't bother me with your nonsense'?

Rudra, first meditate on this small anecdote:

I recall the time a man gave a speech at a Rotary Club on the subject of journalism and journalists. It is one of the tenets of the Rotarians that they may not swear or use cuss-words. But the speaker, not being a Rotarian himself, did not know this, and in his talk he used a profanity he should not have used in that particular hall to that particular audience.

At the end of the meeting a local minister in the audience approached the speaker and dressed him down for having used the language he did. The speaker apologized profusely, and the minister went on about how Rotarians, to say nothing of the church, strongly disapproved of bad language. He then walked away.

He got about ten feet down the corridor, then turned around and approached the speaker again.

"Off the record," he said, "and just between us, any time you want to call a journalist a sonofabitch, it is okay with me."

So on the record, 'good' simply means good. Off the record, it means 'don't bother me with your nonsense'.

The third question:

Watching the energy changes that are constantly happening in me, suddenly the question arises: What is that which is watching and in what sense is it different from the observed energy?

Kosha, this is a beautiful space to enter into, when the question arises for the first time: What is the observed and who is the observer? This is a beautiful space to enter into—when the question becomes relevant.

Now, on each step, you will start losing the duality of the observer and the observed. The observer and the observed, in the ultimate sense, in reality, are one. They are two only because we have not yet been capable of seeing the One.

Remember *The Secret of the Golden Flower*. It says: Tao is one; then it divides itself into two, yin and yang, darkness and light, life and death. But the reality is One. It looks like two; it looks like two because we see it through the prism of the mind. The twoness of it is a creation of our minds, it is not there.

It is just like when on a full moon night you look at the moon and then press your eyelid—and suddenly you see two moons. And you know the moon is one. But go on pressing the eye—and you know perfectly well the moon is one—and now you can see two moons.

That's exactly what is happening. Mind is creating duality, because mind cannot conceive the One. There is an intrinsic impossibility for the mind to conceive the One. Try to understand why the mind cannot conceive the One.

Mind needs distinctions; the One is distinctionless. The whole purpose of the mind is to demark things. The whole purpose of the mind is to particularize things—this is a woman and that is a man, this is a friend and that is an enemy, this is food and this is just stone, this is a chair and that is a table, this is the door and this is the wall. This is the function of the mind: the whole purpose of the mind is to make distinctions. It is very utilitarian; it has to be used.

But in the ultimate sense, it becomes the barrier. That which is a help on the circumference becomes a hindrance at the center.

Mind has no truth, but only utility; just as a child is born: no child brings a label with himself, a nameplate or anything. He simply comes. You don't ask him, "Who are you, and what is your name, and from where are you coming?" The child will simply look at you and will think you are stupid: "What nonsense you are talking!" You start giving him a name, an identity. And you know that name is false, although useful, but false; untrue, but utilitarian. He will need that name.

There are millions of people. If he falls in love with a woman and she wants to write a letter to him, how is she supposed to write a letter to a man who has no name? How can the letter be delivered to him?

It has utility in the world. We give him a name and slowly, slowly we completely forget that the name is just a utilitarian device, it has no truth about it. You can change the name. You can go to the court, declare that you drop your old name and you will be a new name. You can change as many times as you want.

Exactly like that, mind is a device, a natural device to help you function in the world, to find you things. If you drop the mind, all is blurred into one reality. Then it will not be possible to make any distinction between what is a marshmallow and what is a pillow. You may start sleeping with the marshmallow underneath your head and you may start eating the pillow.

So I am not saying mind is not useful. Mind is useful, but its very usefulness is based on creating distinctions.

But when you start moving in meditation, you are moving beyond mind. You are moving beyond utility into truth. Then you are trying to see that which is, not that which is useful. Then slowly, slowly the duality will disappear.

And, Kosha, this is just on the threshold—when the observer

and the observed disappear. And I have been watching you, Kosha; you have been growing so beautifully.

Kosha is a well-educated woman. She is a PH.D., although here she just cleans the toilets. But that has been of immense help; PH.D.s need that. Otherwise they remain hung-up in the head. It has been a device. Deliberately, I have put Kosha into cleaning work, and she has proved really beautiful. She has completely forgotten her PH.D., her education, her career, her name, et-cetera—completely forgotten. She has just become involved in the work that has been given to her utterly, totally.

And that utterness, that totalness, is bringing this great fruit into her being.

Now this is not a philosophical question that she is asking. Philosophy has disappeared from her mind. Now this is an experience, something existential. Now she is really faced with a problem: Who is the observer and who is the observed?

Now you will have to drop that idea also. Now the observer will be the observed. Now there will be no distinction bet-ween the two: the seer will be the seen and the knower will be the known and the lover will be the beloved. It is very strange when for the first time it starts happening—it blurs you, your whole mind structure simply shatters. It looks almost as if you are going mad—or what? Just think: seeing a bamboo, and you forget who is the bamboo and who is the seer—it will look insane. And when you come back into your normal, utilitarian world, you will become suspicious, distrustful, doubting: "What is happening? This is dangerous! How can I be the bamboo?" But this is true.

We are all part of one reality. I am in my right hand, I am in my left hand. I am in my body, but my body is joined with the earth and the sun and the moon. We are all joined together, interlinked. Nobody is independent, we are all interdependent.

When slowly, slowly the mind takes a leap from you—you say goodbye to the mind and the no-mind opens its infinity— then you are the bamboo, then you are in the bamboo, as the bamboo. The observer has become the observed. And the tremendous benediction of it! And the great transformation that comes through it!

And this will be happening, Kosha, more and more. You have earned it. Don't be afraid! It will appear like insanity and the mind will condemn it like insanity.

This is the point when you have to listen to the Master, not to the mind. I say to you: go ahead. You have risked a lot; now risk a little more. Let this distinction also disappear, and with its disappearance, the satori...

The fourth question:

Cannot the teaching of being herenow be sometimes dangerous— in the hands of fools, of course?

In the hands of the fools anything can be dangerous, anything whatever! The Koran is dangerous, the Bible is dangerous, the Gita is dangerous—and you know it. The whole history is full of proofs. Such beautiful statements, so crystal-clear, but in the hands of the fools something goes wrong—nectar becomes poison.

And just the reverse is the case: if you are intelligent, wise, even poison becomes medicine.

One day a man came to me. He was very worried because he had been following J. Krishnamurti for almost twenty years. Then he had a chance, accidentally, to fly with Krishnamurti from Delhi to Bombay.

And then he saw...and what he saw shocked him, shook him completely. He could not sleep. Why had he wasted time with this man for twenty years?

So he came to me and said, "What should I do now? My twenty years wasted!..."

I said, "What actually has happened?"

He said, "I saw him reading a detective novel!"

I said, "In the hands of J. Krishnamurti a detective novel becomes a Koran. And in your hands, a Koran becomes just a detective novel."

It depends. It all depends on you.

I have heard...

A man asked his psychoanalyst after many days of psychoanalysis...nothing was happening. The psychoanalyst was getting worried, the man was also getting worried. He was paying so much and nothing was coming out of it.

Finally he blurted out. He said, "I think the real problem is not my mind, the real problem is the people with whom I work— my manager, my treasurer, the clerks. The people with whom I work are the real problem. So just psychoanalyzing *my* mind is not going to help."

The psychoanalyst asked, "What exactly is the problem with the people you work with?"

He said, "They are all utterly lazy. Nobody wants to work, they all go on postponing."

The psychoanalyst said, "You do one thing: you make beautiful boards. Write on the boards in capital letters, 'Do it now! Tomorrow never comes! Tomorrow is death, life is today.' And put this board everywhere in your office, so wherever they look they will find it. This will have some impact on them." After the third day the psychiatrist phoned his patient. His wife was on the phone and she said, "He is in the hospital because he has been beaten badly by his people."

He said, "Why?"

The woman said, "I think it is because of your advice."

So he rushed to the hospital. The man was really in pain, fractured all over the body.

He asked, "What happened?"

The man said, "It is you and your stupid advice. The treasurer immediately escaped with all the cash—'Do it now! Tomorrow never comes! Tomorrow is death!' He simply wrote a note: 'I have been thinking of escaping with the cash for many years, but if it is so—tomorrow is death—then this is the time.' My manager has escaped, eloped with my typist. And the other workers just jumped upon me and started beating me. They said, 'We had always wanted to beat you, and we were postponing.'"

You ask me, "Cannot the teaching of being herenow sometimes be dangerous?"

It can be if you work in such an office, or if you have such people inside your head.

I have heard...

At the time of the Wilson government in England, George Brown—always drunk—is Foreign Secretary. A reception is held on the visit of the French President, Pompidou.

Madame Pompidou is seated next to Brown, who starts the conversation drunkenly. "What do you want out of life, Madame?"
Madame Pompidou replies, "All I want is 'a...ppin...ess.'" She added as she felt Brown's hand travelling up her thigh, "But not before the soup."

I teach you to be herenow, but you will have to take care of many things—'not before the soup'!

To be herenow needs great intelligence. It is not the message for the stupid, for the mediocre. When I say to you to be herenow I am giving great respect to your intelligence. This is my way of showing respect towards you. You have to be worthy of it.

To be herenow means to be very alert, aware, conscious, so that this moment is no more burdened with past, no more burdened with future; so this moment is unburdened of all garbage and is clear, pure, innocent. And in that innocence you will find the door into God.

But remember always: you can turn, change the meaning, impose your own ideas on the greatest of teachings and destroy them. All depends on you.

The fifth question:

Why is feminine energy the 'darkness' principle? Does this mean that there is supposed to be something sinister about it? The author of The Secret of the Golden Flower *seems a little male chauvinistic sometimes.*

The question is from Ma Ananda Prem.

Ananda Prem, you are a female chauvinist! Rather than thinking about the author of *The Secret of the Golden Flower*, think about yourself.

Master Lu-tsu is saying something just factual. Who has given you the idea that darkness symbolizes something sinister? That is your idea! Darkness is as beautiful as light, equally as beautiful and valuable as light. Do you think night has less value than the day? In fact, it may have more value than the day, but not less. It is the day that tires you, exhausts you; it is the night that rejuvenates you, replenishes you. It is the day that kills you, it is the night that refreshes you again, prepares you for tomorrow, keeps you young.

What is sinister in darkness? Darkness is vast. Light is never so vast. Light is always limited, darkness has no limitations. Light is shallow, darkness has depth.

That's why we have not painted Krishna as white but as black. One of his names is Shyam; 'shyam' means the black one. Why?—just to give a sense of depth. Whiteness is a little shallow.

Hence in the West, so much craze for a suntan, because the white face does not give the feeling of depth. Lying on the sun-beach under the sun, making it a little brown, and it starts having a depth and a beauty of its own.

And darkness is cool, and darkness makes you feel alone. It is very meditative. You cannot sleep in the light, you need darkness to sleep. And sleep and *samadhi* are very similar. In darkness you can enter into no-mind very easily.

Who has given you the idea, Ananda Prem, that darkness is

sinister? It must be your own female chauvinistic mind. Nothing is wrong in darkness. Darkness is the energy of the earth and light is the energy of the sky. And the meeting of the earth and the sky is the whole secret of existence.

Man is a meeting of the earth and the sky, and they both have to be in balance. If your light and darkness principle are balanced, if your male and female principles are in deep harmony, you will attain to One.

Lu-tsu is simply stating a fact. The woman is more restful than man. Light is the principle of restlessness. That's why in the morning as the sun rises you have to awake, you cannot rest anymore. As the sun sets you start feeling sleepy; now you are getting ready to rest, fall into tremendously deep oblivion.

Light will bring you back to the circumference, to the day-to-day affairs, the routine world. Darkness takes you far far away from this world. You forget all the turmoil and the anxiety and the worry and the hurry.

The woman has the same quality of giving you rest. If you love a woman, just being with her is restful.

Only a person who has come to meet with his inner woman can live without a woman. Then there is no necessity, because he is rested, he has found an inner shelter. But till you find an inner shelter, you will have to find an outer shelter; it is absolutely necessary. The woman gives you rest, hence Lu-tsu calls her dark.

The moment you are in the embrace of your woman or in her lap, you are again a child and she is your mother. She may be your wife, but she again becomes your mother. Again she overwhelms you like darkness. She makes you cool, she takes away all the heat that has been generated by the day. It is easier to fall in deep sleep with your woman. She is the principle of the dark. And the woman is as vast as darkness.

Man is very particular, woman is universal. That's why man is tired sooner; the woman has more capacity to resist. Women live longer than men. Women suffer less from illnesses than men. Women go mad less than men. Women commit suicide less than men. She is restful, cool, calm and collected, and she has that vastness.

The woman is always generous. She gives and does not ask in return. She protects, she nourishes not only the child: she nurses the child with her milk, she nurses her beloved with love —which is a higher-value food, which is a deeper food, a nourishment for the soul.

Who has given you, Ananda Prem, the idea that darkness is sinister? There is nothing sinister. But I can understand from where this idea must be coming.

The Western mind has lived on duality and has never been able to penetrate to the One. The Jewish heritage is of duality, and because of Judaism, Christianity and Islam also became dualistic. Ananda Prem carries a Jewish heritage.

The Jewish heritage is that God is good; but then where to put all the badness that you come across in the world? So as a scapegoat the Devil has been created. The Devil is all bad, God is all good—to protect God from badness. Otherwise you will have to put badness somewhere or other. And if there is only one God, that means good and bad both are contained in Him. Then He is both.

Jews have never been that courageous. They were afraid to put good and bad both in the same God, so the only possible way out was to create two Gods, a God of good and a God of bad. Hence the God-and-the-Devil duality.

Then God is light and the Devil is dark. Then the Devil is always painted as dark, animal-like, with horns and a tail and hooves, and with a dark color, like a dark night, sinister. That's from where Ananda Prem gets the idea of darkness being sinister.

And the same has penetrated into Christianity and into Islam. Both these religions are by-products of Judaism.

In the world, there have really been only two religions, Judaism and Hinduism. Christianity and Islam belong to the Judaic tradition. Jainism and Buddhism belong to the Hindu world, the Hindu vision.

The Hindu vision is totally different. And in the Hindu vision there is no Devil. It is non-dual; God is both. God *has* to be both. But both are so balanced in God that they cancel each other, and God is beyond. God is *both*; that's why God is beyond, because they cancel each other.

This is the Eastern concept of the transcendental, the non-dual. So you will see Eastern gods painted black and you will see Eastern goddesses looking very devilish. Just think of Kali, the Mother, with a garland of human skulls! No Jew can conceive that God is God with human skulls...and with a fresh head just recently cut, blood dripping, in her hand... and not only that, she is dancing on the chest of her husband... must be a real woman! And with all this, and a sword in hand, she is so beautiful, so utterly beautiful. Look into her eyes— the tremendous depth and beauty and compassion and love and warmth.

Now the Western mind is simply baffled: "What nonsense is

THE SECRET OF SECRETS

this? If this woman is God then who is the Devil?" They cannot understand, because we have been trying to bring both the polarities together. They have both been brought absolutely together in Mother Kali. 'Kali' means the black. And the word *kal* is very significant: it means three things. First, it means black; second, it means time; third, it means death. The Mother Kali represents all these three things. She is time, the eternal movement of time, this infinite movement, change, flux, and she is death too. And she is black.... And yet, look deep into her and see the beauty and the benediction and the compassion and the love and the warmth. She is life and she is death. She is black *and* she is white. She is the meeting of the polar opposites.

Lu-tsu is not a male chauvinist. Be a little more careful when you start talking about people like Lu-tsu. Be a little more alert. People like Lu-tsu or Lao Tzu or Chuang Tzu, or Buddha or Krishna or Christ are neither men nor women. They have gone, gone beyond. They have transcended all dualities. And still, both dualities are in them, but so balanced, in such harmony —sound and silence in such harmony—that great music is created; black and white in such harmony that the whole panorama of existence is created; life and death in such harmony, in such deep embrace, that eternity arises out of it.

The sixth question:

Bhagwan, do you believe in the Second Coming of Christ?

And who do you think I am?

Christ is not a person, Christ is a state of consciousness. There
have been Christs before Jesus, there have been Christs after
Jesus. Jesus is only one of the Christs. Buddha is a Christ,
Mahavir is a Christ, Lu-tsu is a Christ, Zarathustra is a Christ.
Christ simply means the ultimate state of consciousness; it
is equivalent to Buddha.

Buddha is not the name of any person, it is a happening. So
is Christ—it is not Jesus' name! His name was Jesus. One
day Jesus disappeared and the Christ-consciousness descended
in him. He was no more the ego, he became the vehicle of the
whole. He could say, "I and my Father in heaven are one."
This is Christ-consciousness; it has nothing to do with Jesus.

If you are waiting for Jesus' second coming, then you are
waiting in vain; but if you are waiting for Christ's coming,
Christ has always been coming. Christ is in front of you, you
are listening to him—not to Jesus, certainly, not to Gautama
Siddhartha, certainly. But you are facing a Buddha, just as
you are facing a Christ.

You remind me...

I have heard of an editor of an upstate small-town newspaper.
For years he had cherished a set of old-fashioned wooden
scarhead type of some sixty-point size. On more than one
occasion his assistants had tried to induce him to use it, but
he always firmly vetoed the idea.
One summer the old man went away for a short fishing trip.
In his absence a cyclone struck the town, tore the steeple off
the church, unroofed several houses, sucked a couple of wells
dry, and scattered a few barns around. No bigger catastrophe
had hit the town in years. So, figuring, "Now is our chance,"

his assistants got down the sixty-point type from the shelf and set up a sensational front-page headline with it.

Two days later the editor came storming into the office. "Great Jehosaphat!" he shouted. "What do you mean by taking down that type for a cyclone? All These Years I Have Been Saving That Type For The Second Coming Of Christ!"

Then you will be waiting in vain.

Don't think that Christ and Jesus are synonymous. That's where the error lies in two thousand years of the Christian Church. Many have come in this time—this has been a long period—many have come out of the Christian fold, and a few have come even in the Christian fold itself. Meister Eckhart was a Christ, so was Jakob Boehme, so was Saint Francis. These were in the same fold, but still Christianity missed them because they were waiting for Jesus—the same body, the same form. That is utter nonsense. It is not going to happen again. Jesus cannot be repeated.

To repeat Jesus you will have to repeat the whole history that preceded Jesus, and that is impossible. Jesus cannot be repeated, because for Jesus to be here you will need Mariam, you will need Joseph the Carpenter, you will need the two-thousand-year-old world of Jerusalem. You will need Herod the King, and Pontius Pilate the Governor General. You will need the whole structure, because Jesus came as part of it. No, Jesus cannot be repeated; there is no way. But Christ can descend, Christ can descend in anybody.

When John the Baptist baptized Jesus in the River Jordan, the story says a great white dove came from heaven, out of the blue—nobody had seen such whiteness, such purity—and he descended into Jesus and disappeared into Jesus.

This is just symbolic. This is symbolic of Christhood: Jesus became enlightened...something of the beyond.... As Master Lu-tsu would like to say, "Heaven penetrated the earth." These are just symbols, metaphors: a white dove descending from heaven, entering into Jesus and disappearing. And since that moment Jesus is no longer Jesus, he is Christ. The same happened to Buddha under the bodhi tree: something descended in him, and after that he was not Gautama Siddhartha, he was the Buddha.

Don't wait for Jesus' coming. And if you wait for Jesus' coming you will be wasting your time. He is not going to come, he cannot come. But if you are waiting for Christ's coming then there is no need to wait—Christ is already here! And those who have waited for Christ—not for the particular form, but the consciousness, the essence of it—have always found Christ somewhere or other. Thousands of Masters have existed in the same consciousness.

It is said...

A Christian missionary went to see a Zen Master. The old Zen Master had never heard of Christ. He lived in a faraway mountain cave. The missionary really took much trouble in reaching there; it was a hard and arduous journey, hazardous and dangerous too. He carried his Bible—he wanted to convert the old Master because his name was all over the country, and millions loved him and travelled to his cave.

So he went there and he told the Master, "I would like to read a few sentences to you." And he opened the Bible and started reading the Sermon on the Mount: "Blessed are the meek, for theirs is the Kingdom of God," and so on and so forth.

Only a few sentences, and the old Master said, "Wait! Whosoever said this was a Buddha! *Whosoever* said this was a Buddha. No need to read further. I have also experienced this. No need to read further. Yes, blessed are the meek for theirs is the Kingdom of God. Look at me! It has happened to me!"

Now this poor missionary had come to convert. He had come to convert this Christ into a Christian. He wanted to convert a Christ into a Christian! The utter stupidity of it! But he could not understand yet.

He said, "Let me read the whole thing. You will be very impressed."

But the old man said, "There is no need to read it. Whosoever said it is a Buddha. He knows, he knows as much as I know. We are the same. You look at me!"

But the Christian was too much of a Christian; he went back with his Bible thinking that this old man was crazy, "Calling himself Christ?" He was thinking in terms of Jesus; he does not know the meaning of Christ.

Christ is the Western equivalent of Buddha, the Awakened One, the Blessed One. That is actually the meaning of Christ. The meaning of Bhagwan is the meaning of Christ—the Blessed One.

And the last question:

I have fallen in love many times in my life, but it has always been very frustrating. What is the cause of it?

Love is almost an unknown phenomenon, so you must have fallen into something else.... And if you fall into something else, sooner or later you have to fall out of it. Love is a very rare experience; don't call it love. It is your desire, it is your fantasy that you call love. It is your need, it is your fear of being lonely. You feel lonely and empty and you want to fill yourself with somebody else. And nobody can fill himself with somebody else, so sooner or later, frustration.

Frustration is bound to happen to your so-called love. And then when you fall in love, what do you really start doing? You start fantasizing, expecting too much. Because you expect too much, too much frustration follows.

This is something new in this age, and more so in the West than in the East. The East has been very pragmatic about love, very realistic. Not much frustration happens in the East because people never expect much out of it—so what frustration? Marriage comes first in the East. And then living together with a woman or man, slowly slowly you start becoming friendly, you start liking each other, you start helping each other, and a kind of love grows. But there is no romance in it, hence no frustration.

In the West love has to happen first, and love drives you crazy. It is a hormonal disease that you call love; it is something chemical. And in that chemical impact, as if you are under a drug, stoned... Actually, it is that: the drug has been released by your own hormones so you don't know it. When you inject a drug, you know. It is a biological drug; nature has been using it to propagate. Otherwise, just think—if there were no intoxicant inside you...just think for a moment that there is no intoxication with love, no desire to propagate—who will propagate? for what? The world would stop. Nature has befooled you; it has put a built-in program in you, it triggers a process of hormones in you, and suddenly you start seeing dreams and small things start looking very great.

I have heard...

A lovely but rather flat-chested young woman visited a physician for her periodic physical examination.
"Please remove your blouse," the doctor told her.
"Oh no," the young lady protested. "I just couldn't!"
"Come, come," the doctor replied. "Let us not make mountains out of molehills."

But in love that is what happens—people start making mountains out of molehills. And then when frustration sets in, they start making molehills out of mountains.

Everything looks beautiful when you are in that drugged state. That's why in all the languages of the world the phrase is 'falling in'—you fall from your consciousness, you lose your consciousness, you are almost a drunkard. Then an ordinary woman looks so beautiful, so angelic. An ordinary man looks like Hercules. Everything looks so great and so big, and this is nothing but a projection of your desire.

And sooner or later it will clash with reality—and Hercules will come down, and Cleopatra will come down. And then you are sitting face to face with an ordinary man, an ordinary woman, wondering what you are doing there, wondering how you got there. And if there are a few children also playing around, then finished! Then just because of these children now you have to be together. Hercules is dead, Cleopatra is dead; just two ordinary, silly-looking people taking care of the children, because they have to be educated. And they will do the same, sooner or later.

Your expectations are so great, hence the frustration.

Meditate over this. Go very very slowly.

The lady of the house called down to her butler, "Smithers, come up to my bedroom, please."
When he came through the door, she said, "Now Smithers, the time has come. Take off my shoes." So Smithers took off her shoes.
"Now take off my stockings." So he took off her stockings.
"Now Smithers, take off my dress." So he took off her dress.
"Now Smithers, take off my brassiere." So off comes her bra.
"*Now* Smithers, take off my knickers, and if I ever catch you wearing my clothes again, you will have to find yourself another job!"

Now this is what happens—you were expecting, expecting, ex...and the frustration!

Chapter Fifteen

September 10th, 1978

THE FESTIVE DIMENSION

The first question:

One of the controversial issues about the Rajneesh Ashram concerns indulgence in sex and what are being condemned as sexual perversions or orgies. We would like Bhagwan Rajneesh to give us his views on sex and its role in transcendence.
—R.K. Karanjia, Editor, *Blitz*

My dear Karanjia, the way I teach is the way of life-affirmation. I teach life in its totality. In the past, religions have been life-negative. They have denied life, destroyed life; they have been antagonistic to life, their God was against life. To me, life and God are synonymous; there is no other God than life itself. I worship life.

And if life is God, then love is His temple. These three l's are the fundamentals of my teaching: *life* as God, *love* as the temple, *light* as the experience. If you have learned these three l's, you have learned all.

But because the religions have remained antagonistic to life and love, it is natural that a great controversy will arise around me. I cherish it. It is natural. I am not worried by the controversy. I would be worried if it didn't arise. It is absolutely expected; it is absolutely according to my plan of work.

Why have the religions been life-negative in the past? In the name of religion man has been exploited—exploited by the priest and by the politician. And the priest and the politician have been in deep conspiracy against man. The only way to exploit man is to make him afraid. Once a man is full of fear he is ready to submit. Once a man is trembling inside, he loses trust in himself. Then he is ready to believe in any stupid nonsense. You cannot make a man believe in nonsense if he has self trust.

Remember, that's how man has been exploited down the ages. This is the very trade secret of the so-called religions: make man afraid, make man feel unworthy, make man feel guilty, make man feel that he is just on the verge of hell.

How to make man so afraid? The only way is: condemn life, condemn whatsoever is natural. Condemn sex because it is the fundamental of life; condemn food because that is the second fundamental of life; condemn relationship, family, friendship, because that is the third fundamental of life—and go on condemning. Whatsoever is natural to man, condemn it, say it is wrong: "If you do it you will suffer for it. If you don't do it you will be rewarded. Hell is going to descend on you if you go on living naturally"—that is the message of the whole past—"and heaven will be given to you if you go against life."

That means if you are suicidal, only then will God accept you. If you slowly, slowly commit suicide in the senses, in the body, in the mind, in the heart, and you go on destroying yourself, the more you succeed in destroying yourself, the more you will become beloved to God. This has been the whole teaching of the religions in the past. This has contaminated man's being, poisoned man. These poisoners have exploited man tremendously out of it. These religions of the past were death-oriented, not life-oriented.

What I am heralding is a life-oriented vision: love life in its multidimensionality because that is the only way to reach closer and closer to the ultimate truth. The ultimate truth is not far away; it is hidden in the immediate. The immediate is the ultimate, the immanent is the transcendent. God is not there but here. God is not that but this. And you are not unworthy, and you are not a sinner.

I am here to help you unburden all your guilt feelings. I am here to help you to start trusting yourself again. Once you start trusting your own being, no politician, no priest can exploit you. Man is always exploited through fear.

I have heard...

Once Mulla Nasrudin got lost in a jungle. The whole day he tried to find a way out, but he could not—tired, hungry, exhausted, bleeding, his clothes torn apart because the jungle was really thick and thorny. And it was getting darker, the sun was setting and the night was just about to come.

He's an atheist, a confirmed atheist who had never prayed. But with the situation—the fear of the night and the wild animals—for the first time in his life he thought of God. He forgot all his arguments that he used to give against God. He knelt down on the ground and he said, "Dear Lord...." although he looked around, a little embarrassed, knowing perfectly well that there was nobody, but still embarrassed—the whole life's philosophy of atheism! But when fear knocks on the doors and when death is so close by, who bothers about logic, philosophies, isms? Who bothers about reason, argument? "Dear Lord," he said, "please help me get out of these woods, and I will always worship you. I will even start going to the mosque. I will follow all the rituals of Islam. I promise you! Just save me. Forgive me. I apologize for all the things that I have been saying against you. I was a fool, an utter fool. Now I know you are."

Just at that moment a bird passed overhead and dropped something right on his outspread hands. "Please Lord, don't give me any of that shit. I'm really lost!"

When a man is in fear, even though he has been a lifelong atheist, he starts turning into a theist. Priests came to know about it, and then they used it down the ages. The whole past of humanity is fear ridden.

And the greatest way to create fear is to make man feel guilty about natural things. He *cannot* drop them, and he cannot enjoy them because of the fear of hell, so he is in a double bind. That double bind is the base of man's exploitation. You cannot just drop your sexuality because some stupid priest is saying that it is wrong. It has nothing to do with your idea of right and wrong; it is something natural, something in the very being. You have come out of it, each of your cells is a sexual cell. Just by saying, you cannot drop it. Yes, you can start repressing it, and by repressing you can go on accumulating it in the unconscious, and that becomes a wound. And the more you repress, the more obsessed you become with it. And the more obsessed you become, the more guilty you feel. It is a vicious circle. Now you are caught in the trap of the priest.

And the priest himself has never believed in it, neither has the politician ever believed in it. These things were for the people, for the masses; the masses have been befooled.

The stories say that kings used to have hundreds of wives, and so was the case with priests. And it is a miracle: the people continued to believe in these charlatans.

Just in this century, just fifty years ago, the Nizam of Hyderabad had five hundred wives and was still thought to be a very religious man because he followed all the rituals. The priest and the politician have both been doing all that they have been telling the people not to do, sometimes openly, sometimes from the back door.

I have heard...

There is an old saying, "Fool me once, shame on you. Fool me twice, shame on me."

But the priests have been fooling you down the ages, and they have fooled you so long that it is now almost an accepted phenomenon. It has been so ancient that we take it for granted; nobody thinks that they are being fooled.

It reminds me of a church a friend of mine went to which

runs raffles. Once a year they get three automobiles, and they put them up in front of the church, and they sell the chances. Last year they raffled off a Cadillac, a Mercury, and a Plymouth. Three days after the raffle the pastor was walking down the street, and he bumped into my friend coming out of a thirst parlor.

My friend looked at him and said, "Can you tell me who won the automobiles? Who won the Cadillac?"

And the priest said, "Why, the Cardinal did. Wasn't he lucky?"

And my friend said, "Who won the Mercury?"

"Why, the Monsignor did. Wasn't he lucky?"

And my friend said, "Well, tell me, who won the Plymouth?"

And the priest said, "Why, Father Murphy. Wasn't he lucky?"

At that moment my friend started to go back in and get another drink. The priest grabbed him and said, "By the way, how many tickets did you buy?"

And my friend said, "I didn't buy a damned one! Wasn't I lucky?"

The priests have tremendously harmed the human heart, human consciousness. They have put this poisonous idea in man that life is something ugly. They have been teaching people how to get rid of life. I teach my people how to get deeper into it. They have been teaching how to be free of life. I teach how to make your life free. They have been teaching how to end this life, and I am teaching you how to move into it for eternity, on and on, how to live life abundantly. Hence the controversy; it is bound to be there. My vision is just the opposite to what has been taught in the name of religion.

I am bringing a new vision of religion to the world. This is the boldest attempt ever made: to accept life in its multi-dimensions, to enjoy it, to celebrate it, to rejoice in it. Renunciation is not my way, but rejoicing. Fasting is not my way, but feasting. And to be festive is to be religious. My definition of religion is the festive dimension.

No other animal can be festive; no other animal knows anything about festivals. Porpoises can play, chimpanzees can play; only man celebrates. Celebration is the highest growth of consciousness, expression, manifestation, flowering of the Golden Flower.

I teach you celebration. Celebration is my key.

And I teach you: celebrate your sex, it is a God-given gift. Celebrate your body, it is God's grace. Celebrate each moment that has been given to you, each breath, each heartbeat. It is such a benediction.

Live God right now! I don't give you God as a goal; I make God available to you right now, this very moment. Celebrate, and you are in God.

The old religions were sad. The old religions were serious. My religion is that of playfulness: everything has to be taken into the mood of playfulness. Don't take life seriously; it is fun.

And to take it as fun is to be prayerful. Then there is no complaint, then there is only gratefulness.

The question is important. A few things would be helpful.

There are people who are pathological, and the pathological mind has dominated in the past. Those people cannot enjoy; they don't know how to enjoy. Because they are incapable of enjoying, they make a great virtue out of it. Non-enjoyment becomes virtue.

Everybody is born with the capacity to enjoy, but not with

the art. People think just because they are alive and they breathe and they exist, they know how to enjoy. That is sheer stupidity. Enjoyment is a great art, it is a great discipline. It is as subtle a discipline as music or poetry or painting. It is the greatest creativity.

People are born and they start thinking that they are ready to enjoy life, and they cannot enjoy because they don't know how to enjoy it. They make a mess out of their lives, and sooner or later, when you are making a mess, there are only two possibilities. One is: think that you are being stupid with life; that hurts the ego. The other is: that life is worthless, that life is misery, that there is no joy in life—"That's why I am not enjoying it. Nothing is wrong with me; if there is something wrong, it is in the very structure of life itself." This has been the approach in the past: "If I cannot see light, then there is no light"—not that I am blind. "If I cannot hear sound, then there is no sound"—not that I am deaf.

This has been very, very helpful to the egoist. He tries, and then he finds he cannot enjoy; finding that he cannot enjoy, he starts condemning. He starts condemning those who can enjoy too. He feels jealous, he feels disturbed. Out of his jealousy, out of his disturbance, he poisons people's minds. If you are enjoying he says, "Look, you will suffer in hell. You are doing a crime!" Celebrating, dancing, singing, loving? Life is a punishment for him, and you are taking it as a reward? And these pathological people have dominated in the past.

Once, a friend of mine was alone on a dreary night in a lounge of an intercontinental hotel. Hoping to strike up a conversation with a distinguished-looking man sitting nearby, he said, "May I buy you a drink?" "No," said the man coolly. "Don't drink Tried it once and did not like it."

Nothing daunted my friend, so he offered him a cigar, saying he had just picked up a good one. "No, don't smoke. Tried it once and did not like it."

"Then how about a little game of rummy?"

"No. Don't play cards. Tried it once, but did not like it. But my son will be dropping by after a bit. He might want to play."

My friend settled back in his chair and said, "Your only child, I presume."

These are the potential priests. They tried once and they didn't enjoy—as if enjoyment is their birthright.

It has to be earned, it is an art. One has to imbibe it. It takes years of preparation, it takes years of cleansing. To hear classical music just for the first time, and think that you don't enjoy it so forget all about it, would be stupid. Your ears need a certain discipline, only then can they understand the subtle. The gross is available. It is easy to be with the gross because it is animal. But to move into the deeper realms of life one needs great discipline, great meditativeness, great prayerfulness, great gratitude.

And the basic thing to remember is: if life is not becoming a celebration, then something is wrong with you, not with life itself. The old religions said life is wrong. I make *you* responsible, not life. Life is God. And from there the whole process changes; then something has to be cleaned in you. Something that is hanging around you has to be cut. Chunks of conditioning have to be dropped. You have to go through a surgery.

That's what this Ashram is all about: it is a surgical place. It is no ordinary Ashram like the thousands there are in India. It is a great existential experiment: we are creating a future here, a new kind of man with a new responsibility. We are laying the foundation stones of a new day, of a new sunrise. We are opening new doors to possibilities which have remained closed in the past. And because of this, humanity has suffered in the past, suffered a lot, and unnecessarily suffered.

And the more people suffered, the more they thought, "The priests are right: life is wrong!" And the priests were creating more and more negative attitudes in people.

Moe went to a department store to buy himself a suit. He found the style he wanted, so he took the jacket off the hanger and tried it on.

A salesman came up to him. "Yes, sir. It looks wonderful on you."

"It may look wonderful," said Moe irritably, "But it fits terrible. The shoulders pinch."

The salesman did not bat an eye. "Put on the pants," he suggested. "They will be so tight, you will forget all about the shoulders."

That has been the common practice of the priest: if something hurts, he gives you an even more tight structure, more tight and dead and dull a character. If something hurts, he makes you hurt more so you forget all about the old hurt.

It always happens. If you have a headache and your house catches fire, you will forget about the headache. Who can afford to think about a headache when the house is on fire?

The priest goes on inventing more and more tortures for you. He has not allowed you to enjoy anything. Taste is wrong; you should eat food without tasting. If you taste you are committing a crime. Dance is wrong; why?—because it is bodily. The body is the enemy. Music is wrong because it is sensuous. *All* is wrong!

You have to go on cutting yourself. Rather than expanding, the priest has been trying to shrink you. In the modern age the psychoanalyst is called the 'shrink', but the priests have been doing that down the ages—they have been shrinking people. And when you have shrunk so much that it hurts all over, that you are almost in a prison cell, so small that you cannot move, that has been called character. Then naturally, one wants to get rid of life. One prays to God for only one thing: relieve me, redeem me.

Your priests have been against God! Let me say it that way, because God creates existence and your priests create only such structures around you so that you cannot live existence. Your *mahatmas* are against God.

I am all for God—and God means life.

You have asked, "One of the controversial issues about the Rajneesh Ashram concerns indulgence in sex...."

This is the only place where there is no indulgence in sex, but it will surprise you.

Indulgence needs repression; the more repressed a person is, the more he wants to indulge. It is like, if you have been fasting for a few days and then you relax; you start eating too much, you indulge. Indulgence is a by-product of repression. For thirty days you fasted, you repressed, you fought with yourself, you lived in a kind of hell. Then after thirty days you start moving to the opposite direction, to the opposite extreme: you start indulging. Indulgence is the opposite extreme of repression.

Because I am against repression, how is indulgence possible in my place? I cut the very root of it. If a man is healthily eating, he does not indulge in eating. If he is enjoying his food he does not indulge, he does not eat too much. In fact because he loves his body, he loves his food, he remains very careful. To stuff the body too much is not the sign of a lover of the body, it is a sign of the enemy. The body can be killed in two ways: either by starvation or by overstuffing it—but both are the ways of enmity. The lover of the body, one who respects his body as God's gift, cannot do either. He will neither fast nor will he indulge in food.

And the same is true about sex and about everything.

Indulgence is created by the priests because they create repression. Once you create repression people start indulging. The more a desire is repressed, the more it wants to assert. It becomes mad, it becomes aggressive!

When it is allowed its natural flow, when it is accepted, when there is no fight with it, there comes a balance.

So let me tell you, sir, that this is the only place—maybe the *only* place in the whole of the world—where indulgence is impossible.

Yes, when people come, in the beginning, for a few days they indulge—but *I* am not responsible for it. The priests, the politicians, the puritans, the moralists—Morarji Desai, etcetera —they are responsible for it. I have not been teaching people to repress; the people who have been teaching repression are responsible for it. And when people come to me they come with all those conditionings, so when I say relax, naturally they start indulging a little bit.

But how long can one indulge? When you really relax, sooner or later the balance is achieved. The moment balance is achieved there is no repression, no indulgence.

But I understand the question: for the so-called religious, my balanced, normal, natural people will look as if they are indulging. Just think of a man who is fasting, and you are taking your breakfast, and he passes by—and the aroma of the coffee and the smell of the bread and the butter, and the joy on your face—what do you think he thinks about you? He thinks you are indulging; you will suffer in hell: "You can go on indulging a few days more, then I will see. When you will suffer in hell, then you will know. You will have to pay very badly for what you are doing." These are the thoughts in his mind. These are the ways he protects himself, these are the ways he represses himself. It is out of his unnaturalness that he starts thinking you are unnatural. Now, enjoying one's breakfast is not unnatural at all!

And the man who enjoys his food never eats too much; he *cannot*, it is impossible. Have you ever come across wild animals who are fat? Now, nobody is teaching them naturopathy and nobody is teaching them dieting and nobody is teaching them fasting. You never come across a fat wild animal.

I am deliberately saying *wild* animal; I am not talking about the zoos, because it is different in zoos. Animals start imitating man. In zoos you can find fat animals, ugly, but not in the wild state. Why?—because an animal simply loves, enjoys his body, eats to the point where the body is satisfied, not a bit more.

And yes, sometimes it happens that the animal fasts too, but not according to Jainism. If he feels that the body is in such a state that it cannot take food, he is ill, and it is harmful to load the body—these are *natural* instincts—he does not eat. Sometimes even the animal may try to vomit, to unburden. A dog will go and eat grass; that helps him to vomit. And you cannot persuade him to eat till he becomes healthy again. These are natural instincts.

Priests have contaminated man so much that he has forgotten all his natural instincts. Now he lives by ideas. He has to fast because he follows a certain philosophy of fasting. He does not listen to the body; the body is hungry and he fasts. And then sometimes the body is not hungry at all and he eats. He goes on losing contact with his body.

I want you to come down from your mind to your senses. Enter back into your senses.

I teach you the body: the body is beautiful, divine. Come back to the body. Let the body become alive again, and it will take care; you need not worry about it. The body has a built-in program to keep you healthy, to keep you alive, to keep you vibrant, to keep you young, fresh. The body has a built-in program: you need not learn anything about it from books and teachings.

So when people come to me in the beginning, sometimes they may indulge—but I am not responsible for their indulgence. The priests, the people who have conditioned them, they are responsible. If these people can be here with me for a few days, sooner or later the balance is restored. And with balance comes tranquility, calmness, a subtle joy and a subtle naturalness.

Sex has four stages; those stages have to be understood. Only at the fourth stage does sex become the Golden Flower. Not to understand those four stages is dangerous, and the whole tradition has been keeping you unaware of those four stages.

The first stage is *autosexual*.

When the child is born he is a narcissist. He loves his body tremendously, and it is beautiful; he knows only *his* body. Just sucking his own thumb, and he is in such euphoria. You see the child sucking his own thumb—what euphoria is on his face, just playing with his own body, trying to take his toe into his mouth, making a circle of the energy. When the child takes his toe into the mouth a circle is created and the energy starts moving in a circle. The light circulates naturally in the child and he enjoys, because when the light circulates there is great joy inside.

The child plays with his own sexual organs not knowing they are sexual organs. He has not yet been conditioned; he knows his body as one whole. And certainly, the sexual organs are the most sensitive part of his body. He utterly enjoys touching them, playing with them.

And here is where the society, the poisonous society, enters into the psyche of the child: "Don't touch!" 'Don't' is the first dirty, four-letter word. And out of this one four-letter word, then many more come: can't, won't—these are all four-letter words. Once the child is told "Don't!" and the angry parent, mother or father, and those eyes...And the child's hand is taken away from his genital organs, which are naturally very enjoyable. He really enjoys it, and he is not being sexual or anything. It is just the most sensitive part of his body, the most alive part of his body, that's all.

But our conditioned minds.... He is touching a sexual organ; that is bad, we take his hand away. We create guilt in the child.

Now we have started destroying his natural sexuality. Now we have started poisoning the original source of his joy, of his being. Now we are creating hypocrisy in him; he will become a diplomat. When the parents are there he will not play with his sexual organs. Now the first lie has entered; he cannot be true. Now he knows that if he is true to himself, if he respects himself, if he respects his own joy, if he respects his own instinct, then the parents are angry. And he is helpless against them, he is dependent on them, his survival is with them. If they renounce him, he will be dead; so the question is of choosing whether you want to live. The condition is that if you want to live you have to be against yourself, and the child has to yield.

The child is the most exploited phenomenon in the world. No other class has been so exploited as the child. He cannot do anything: he cannot make unions to fight with the parents, he cannot go to the court, he cannot go to the government. He has no way to protect himself against the parental attack.

And when the parents stop him, they are stopping him because of their own conditioning; their parents had done the same to them. They are very much embarrassed by the child's touching his own genital organs and playing with them, and so unashamedly.

Now the child knows nothing of shame, he is innocent. The 'don't' has entered; the energy recoils. The first trauma has happened. Now the child will never be able to accept his sexuality naturally, joyously. Repression has happened and the child is divided in two; his body is no more whole. Some part of the body is not acceptable, some part of the body is ugly, some part of the body is unworthy to be part of his body; he rejects it. Deep down in his psychology he starts castrating himself, and the energy recoils. Energy will not be flowing as naturally as it used to flow before this 'don't' happened.

And the natural outcome of this stupidity that has been perpetually practiced on humanity is that first the child is no more a natural being, hypocrisy has entered. He has to hide something from the parents or he has to feel guilty.

This is the autosexual state: many people remain stuck there. That's why so much masturbation continues all over the world. It is a natural state. It would have passed on its own, it was a growing phase, but the parents disturbed the energy's growing phase.

The child becomes stuck: he wants to play with his genital organs and he cannot. Repressing, repressing, one day it is too much and he is *possessed* by the sexual energy. And once he has started masturbating, it may become a habit, a mechanical habit, and then he will never move to the second stage.

And the people who are responsible are the parents, the priest, the politicians—the whole social mind that has existed up to now.

Now this man may remain stuck at this stage, which is very childish. He will never attain to full grown-up sexuality. He will never come to know the blissfulness that can come only to a grown-up sexual being. And the irony is that these are the same people who condemn masturbation and make much fuss about it. And they make such statements which are very dangerous: they have been telling people that if you masturbate you will go blind, if you masturbate you will become a zombie, if you masturbate you will never be intelligent, you will remain stupid. Now all the scientific findings are agreed upon one point: that masturbation never harms anybody. But these suggestions harm. Now this is an absolute agreement; there are no two opinions about it. All the psychological researches agree that masturbation never harms anybody, it is a natural outlet of energy. But these ideas—that you will go blind—may make it dangerous to your eyes, because again and again you will think that you will go blind, that you will go blind, that you will go blind.... So many people are using glasses, and the reason may not be in the eyes; the reason may be just somewhere else. So many millions of people are stupid, and the reason may not be that they are stupid—because no child is born stupid, all children are born intelligent. The reason may be somewhere else: in these techniques. You will remain ill, you will lose self-confidence. And so many people are afraid, trembling continuously, have no trust, no self-confidence, are continuously afraid, because they know what they have been doing.

Now thousands of letters come to me: "We are caught up in this trap; how can we come out of it?"

And let me repeat: masturbation has never harmed anybody. But the moment when a person masturbates is a very sensitive and delicate moment; his whole being is open and flowing. In that moment if some suggestion is dropped in his mind—and he himself will drop the suggestion, "Now what if I go mad? if I go blind? if I remain always stupid?"—these constant autohypnotic suggestions are the cause of a thousand and one illnesses, of a thousand and one psychological problems, perversions.

Who is responsible for this?

And people who come to me come with all these perversions. And I try to help them, and *many* are helped and many grow beyond it. But the society thinks I am teaching people some perversions. This is just unbelievable. I am helping you to grow beyond your perversions; the society has given you perversions. You live in a perverted society!

If the child is allowed the natural phase of autosexuality, he moves on his own to the second phase, the homosexual—but very few people move to the second phase. The majority remain with the first phase. Even while making love to a woman or a man you may not be doing anything else but just a mutual masturbation. Because very few people attain to orgasmic states, very few people come to the glimpses that are bound to be there if your sexuality is mature. Very few people come to know about God through their lovemaking, which is a natural phenomenon. In lovemaking, meditation happens naturally.

But it doesn't happen, and the reason is that millions, the majority, are stuck at the first stage. Even if they have got married and they have children, their lovemaking is not more than mutual masturbation. It is not real lovemaking.

Lovemaking is an art, a great art; it needs great sensitivity, needs great awareness, meditativeness, it needs maturity.

The second phase is homosexual. Few people move to the second phase; it is a natural phase. The child loves his body. If the child is a boy, he loves a boy's body, *his* body. To jump to a woman's body, to a girl's body, would be too much of a big gap. Naturally, first he moves in love with other boys; or if the child is a girl, the first natural instinct is to love other girls because they have the same kind of body, the same kind of being. She can understand the girls better than the boys; boys are a world apart.

The homosexual phase is a natural phase. There society helps people to remain stuck again, because it creates barriers between man and woman, girls and boys. If those barriers are not there, then soon the homosexual phase fades away; the interest starts happening in the heterosex, the other sex. But for that, society does not give chances—a great China Wall exists between the boy and the girl. In the schools they have to sit apart or they have to be educated separately. In the colleges they have to live in separate hostels. Their meeting, their being together, is not accepted.

That is one of the problems that is happening to me and to my people in this so-called educated city. If this city is educated, then I wonder what city can be called uneducated. The only problem to the Poonaites is that my people are moving together, man, woman. It should be a natural phenomenon; people should be happy that men and women are moving together, creating a love-vibe around. But they have never moved together; they start feeling disturbed. They start feeling jealous, they start feeling angry, because who are these people to enjoy what has not been given to them? If it has not been their joy they will not allow anybody else to have it either. But they will not say it that way. They will talk great philosophy. They will hide their jealousies behind great words of morality, of religion, of culture—and they don't know anything of morality or religion or culture, because all culture, all religion, all morality has to be based on love. If it is not based on love it is not there at all. It is just a game, a pseudo-game that you go on playing on the surface. Deep down you remain just the opposite of it.

Homosexuality is perpetuated by the society and condemned by the same society. These strategies have to be understood. The same society condemns the homosexual, calls him perverted, criminal. There are still countries where homosexuality is punished, you can be sent to jail for ten years. There have been countries where a homosexual could have been sentenced to death! And it is the same society that creates it!

You divide man and woman apart so much, you create watertight compartments. And when the man wants to love he cannot find the woman, and the woman wants to love and she cannot find a man. Then, whatsoever is available...she starts falling in love with a woman, he starts falling in love with a man. And it is not satisfying either, but it is better than nothing. Nature has to find its way. If you don't allow the natural course, it will find some roundabout way. Otherwise homosexuality is a natural phase; it passes by itself.

And the third phase is heterosexual.

When a man is really out of autosex, homosex, then he is capable and mature to fall in love with a woman—which is a totally different world, a different chemistry, a different psychology, a different spirituality. Then he is able to play with this different world, this different organism. They are poles apart, but when they come close—and there are moments when they are really close and overlapping—first glimpses, lightning glimpses of *samadhi* are attained.

Because it does not happen, many people think that I am just talking something like poetry. It is not poetry! I am not talking fiction, I am talking reality. What I am saying is an existential phenomenon, but the need is that the man and the woman must be mature. They must have gone beyond the first two stages; only then can this happen. And very rarely, *very* rarely, are there people who are mature men and mature women. So nothing happens; they make love, but that love is only superficial. Deep down they are autosexual, or, at the most, homosexual.

To love a woman or to love a man, a new kind of being is needed which can accept the polar opposite. And only with the polar opposite—just as with negative and positive electricity meeting, electricity is born, just like that—when life electricities meet, man and woman, yin and yang, Shiva and Shakti, when that meeting happens, that merger, that total oblivion, that drunkenness, they have disappeared as separate entities, separate egos. They are no longer separately there, therefore they are throbbing as one, two bodies in one soul. That is the first experience of no-mind, no-ego, no-time, and that is the first experience of *samadhi*.

Once this has been experienced, then a desire arises: how to attain this *samadhi* so that it can become a naturâl state of affairs and you need not depend on a woman, you need not depend on a man?—because dependence brings slavery. Only out of the experience of heterosexual orgasm does a person start searching for ways, means, and methods—Yoga, Tantra, Tao— so that he can attain the same state on his own or on her own.

And yes, it can be attained, because deep inside each man is a man and a woman—half comes from his father, half comes from his mother—and each woman is half woman, half man. So once you have known it happening through the outside woman, you will have the first glimpse that it can happen within too. The outer woman simply triggered it, the outer man simply acted as a catalytic agent; now you start meditating.

Then the fourth phase, the ultimate phase comes, which is *brahmacharya*, which is *real* celibacy; not the celibacy of the monks —that is not celibacy at all—but the celibacy of the Buddhas. It is *brahmacharya*. Sex has disappeared; you don't need the outer woman, you don't need the outer man. Now your inner man and woman have fallen in a togetherness, and this together- ness is not momentary. This is real marriage; you are welded together. Now to be orgasmic is your natural state. A Buddha lives in orgasm continuously; he breathes in and out in orgasm.

These are the four stages of sex.

My effort here is to take you to the fourth, but people who

come to me come to me corrupted, crippled by the society, poisoned by the society. I have to take much poison out of them. I have to take much pus out of their beings. And only if they are courageous enough to be with me long enough, ready to risk, does this transformation become possible.

And the people who live on the outside and just hear rumors about what is happening here are bound to have stupid notions —that indulgence is happening, that orgies are happening, that violence is happening. It is as if in a surgery you come to know that that surgeon is very dangerous because he cuts people's parts, he opens their stomachs, much blood comes out—"That doctor is very dangerous; never go to him!"

I am a physician; or better, I am a surgeon. And this place is a place for spiritual surgery. It is an alchemical experiment in transforming your energies.

The ordinary masses *cannot understand it*, hence so much misunderstanding is bound to remain about me. It will go slowly, slowly; it may take centuries.

And the people who have so much repressed sexuality in their beings can't have understanding of what is happening here. Their repression makes their eyes blind; they start projecting their ideas.

For example, a man who has repressed all his sexuality for his whole life will go mad seeing a naked woman, because it will be like an explosion in his being. But a man who has not repressed any sexuality will not even take any note of seeing a naked woman; or he may simply think, "What a beautiful body!"—and that is that. He does not want to grab it, he does not want to possess it. Just as you look at a roseflower: the rose flower is naked, you don't put clothes on the rose flower. You don't put clothes on the animals.

There are a few ladies in England who try to put clothes on their dogs, because of 'naked' dogs. Now these old ladies must be dirty! What kind of mind is this?

So if in some of my groups nudity happens—which is a natural part of the group process—and some people, sly people, can sometimes take photographs with small, automatic cameras, and then those pictures are published all over the world and it is thought that orgies are happening here... Something totally different is happening here.

Twenty nuns were on a pilgrimage to Lourdes when their plane crashed. They all, of course, went to heaven where they were met by Saint Peter and the recording angel.
"Welcome ladies," he said. "Just a pure formality: will all those who are virgins take one step forward." There was an embarrassed silence as only nineteen stepped forward.
The recording angel put down his pen, turned to Peter and said, "Excuse me, but what shall we do with the deaf one?"

Whom do you think you are deceiving with your repressions? Your repressions are bound to take revenge on you from the back door.

The whole hypocrisy can disappear from the world if sex is accepted naturally. Ninety-nine percent of hypocrisy is dependent on sex-repression.

Now, religions go on giving you double-binds. They first say, "Be authentic, be true," and all that they teach makes you inauthentic, untrue, hypocrites. This is a double-bind. They say, "Believe in truth, believe in God"; now this is a double-bind. Belief simply means you don't know and still you are believing; it is untrue. If one has to be true, one has to seek and search and only then believe. But they say, "First believe in

God, and then you will be able to find Him." To begin with belief is to begin with a lie.

And God is truth, and you begin in lies. Life is truth, and you begin in hypocrisy. If you go on missing, it is no wonder. You are bound to miss all joy.

In the past, this antagonism towards sex has been exploited for one more reason. First, the priest exploited it to make you afraid, to make you tremble. Then he became very high, holier than you; he dominated you. And the politician exploited it in another way, for some other reason: if sex is repressed, man becomes violent. Now, again this is a scientific finding. If sex is repressed man becomes violent; violence is a perversion of sexual energy. Now, the politicians needed armies, violent people, murderers. The only way to get so many murderers was to repress sex.

If you don't repress sex, who wants to kill? For what? The sword, the dagger, the bayonet are nothing but phallic deep down. The man wanted to penetrate the woman's body and it would have been a beautiful phenomenon if it had happened in love; but it could not happen, it was not allowed. Now he is mad, he wants to enter anybody's body, in any way—with a dagger, with a sword, with a bayonet.

Sex has been repressed; the politician exploited it in his own way. He needed armies, he needed slaves ready to die or to kill. The person who has not lived his life in celebration is ready to die for anything. He is ready to become a martyr for any stupid idea, ideology, scripture, religion.

The man who has lived the joy and the blessings of a life will not be so easily ready to die. He will say, "Why? Life is so precious. I cannot sacrifice my life just for a piece of cloth called the national flag." "I cannot sacrifice my life," he will say, "just because somebody has burned the Koran. So what? Print another." "I cannot sacrifice my life because somebody has burned a temple. So what? My life is more precious than your temple, because it is the alive temple of God." But a man who has not loved and who has not lived is always ready.

I have heard: A great British politician went to see Adolf Hitler. They were standing on the fourth storey and talking to each other, and Adolf Hitler was bragging about his power and he was saying, "It is better that you yield without fighting. Otherwise we will destroy your whole country. You don't know what kind of men I have got." And to show, he just ordered a soldier who was standing on guard, "Jump!" And the soldier didn't say a thing, he simply jumped. He did not even hesitate for a single moment. The English politician was really impressed. And to impress him still more, he ordered the second soldier to jump, and he also jumped. By the time he ordered the third, the Englishman could not contain himself; he rushed and caught hold of the third. He said, "Are you mad? Why are you jumping like that?" The man said, "Leave me alone. Let me jump! It is better to die than to live with this man."

When life is misery it is better to die; any excuse is enough.

The politician needed violence; he exploited. The priest needed power; he exploited.

I am neither a priest nor a politician. I am just a human being, as you are. And I can see humanity—how *much* it has suffered. I feel for it because it is me, it is you, and I want to have a totally different future for humanity, for the children to come, for the people who will come on the earth. If we can create a different future for them, that will be the only revolution.

Up to now no revolution has happened, because ninety-nine percent of hypocrisy, untruth, exploitation, violence depends on sexual repression, and no sexual revolution has yet happened.

I am trying to create that situation. It is going to be against the society. It is going to be very controversial, but it is natural. I want the controversy to spread all over the world, because only through that controversy the people who have intelligence, the people who have any kind of understanding, are bound to come to me.

These repressed people cannot understand; their minds are full of holy cow dung.

I have heard about a Boston priest who had volunteered to work part-time in a peace group protesting the war in Vietnam. Doing some writing as well as organizing, he would scurry in and out of the storefront headquarters among the motley assembly of bearded students, jean-clad coeds, and young mothers with babies in papoose sacks or strollers. Once when he had to make an important phone call, he found all the phones taken. Knowing there was a pay-phone in the basement, he rushed downstairs. There at a table was a bare-breasted mother who had just finished giving lunch to her baby. In great embarrassment, the girl crossed her arms over her chest and said, "I beg your pardon, Father." The priest smiled, "Don't be embarrassed, young lady. We priests may be celibate, but in our work we grow accustomed to a great many things. I assure you your condition does not trouble me in the least. In fact, you can perhaps do me a favor: Could you give me a dime for two nipples?"

A repressed mind is an obsessed mind. He cannot see reality

as it is; it is impossible. Before he can see reality as it is, he will have to drop all kinds of repressions. A clean mind is needed, an innocent mind is needed.

The actor Charles Coburn told how his father warned him about the evils of certain types of theaters....
His father was a very, very religious man.
"What kind of theaters, Father?" he asked.
"Burlesque theaters, son. Don't ever go in one."
Immediately Coburn asked, "Why not?" And his father answered, "Because you will see things in a burlesque theater that you should not see."
That, of course, aroused his curiosity. Not many days passed before he took in his first burlesque. Coburn remarked, "And I found out my father was right. I did see something I should not have—I saw my father there."

Man has lived with hypocrisy.

I want you to be authentic human beings, true to nature, true to your being, respectful. Have some dignity. You have been chosen by God; it is a great gift, just this life. Make it a festival, celebrate it. Love deeply, and deep love will give you first glimpses of meditation and will release your prayer. Drop all the taboos.

You will have to risk much. That's what sannyas is all about: the art of risking—because you will be moving into the unknown. You will be moving into the unfamiliar, the unacquainted, the uncharted. The society gives you a map, a clear-cut style of life to live; I give you only freedom. The society gives you character, I give you only consciousness. The society teaches you to live a conformist life. Of course, if you live a conformist, conventional life you will be more secure, but more dead too. I give you an invitation to go on an adventure.

Live in insecurity! Live in revolution! Be a rebel, risk, because nothing is ever attained in life without risk. The more you risk, the closer you are to God. When you can risk all, all is yours.

And don't be a hypocrite, and don't compromise.

The situation recalls an incident around the turn of the century in a Baptist church. A young soprano in the choir loft got so carried away with her solo that she fell out. Breaking her fall, the singer caught herself in the chandelier—and there she was suspended upside-down. The fiery Baptist minister was equal to the occasion. He said, "Speaking on my very sermon subject of 'Hell and Damnation', I tell you that he who looks with lust in his heart shall be blinded."
An old codger in the front pew said, "Reverend, with such a great opportunity, is it all right to risk one eye?"

That's what people have been doing—risking one eye. I tell you, risk both! Don't compromise! Risk all! Let life be a play, a risk, a gamble, and when you can risk all you will attain to a sharpness in your being. Your soul will be born.

The Golden Flower can bloom in you only if you are courageous, daring. It blooms only in courage.

And remember, sex may look like mud, but it contains the lotus flower in it. This is one of my fundamentals: the lowest contains the highest, and the highest is nothing but the manifestation of the lowest. The seed contains the flowers and the flowers are nothing but expressions of the seed. Sex contains *samadhi*, because life contains God.

Move from sex to *samadhi*, from sex to superconsciousness; this is the only natural and rightful way. Don't get stuck anywhere in sex. I teach you sex and transcendence both, because the transcendence is possible only *through* it. And the people who are teaching repression are not teaching transcendence. In fact, they go on pouring more mud on you. They go on forcing you deeper in the mud because there is no possibility of transcendence if you have not moved through these sexual stages of autoeroticism, of homoeroticism, of heteroeroticism, and then to transcendence. And the lotus blooms, the one-thousand-petalled lotus. You are containing it in yourself. Avoid the priests and the politicians and you can achieve it. They are standing in the way.

But they always wanted it this way. It is good for them; it is not good for anybody else. They have diverted your love. They have taken its natural object from you; then love can be diverted. Now there are people who are in love with the motherland—what foolishness! What do you mean by 'motherland'? There are people who are in love with the fatherland —still more foolish. There are people who are in love with countries, ideologies—communism, fascism, Hinduism, Christianity.

Your natural object of love has been taken away; now your love is frantically searching for anything to become tethered to.

A great scientist was working on animals; he calls it 'imprinting'. He says when the animal comes out of the egg, whatsoever he comes across, he immediately becomes attached to it. He becomes attached to the mother because the mother is almost always there. Giving warmth, taking care of the egg, the mother is there. The moment the child opens his eyes, comes out of the egg, looks around at the world, the first thing he comes across is the mother. He becomes attached to the mother.

One scientist was trying to change the subject, and he succeeded. He removed the mother. When the child was coming out of the egg, he removed the mother; he sat there himself. Then he was in trouble, because the child would continuously follow him. And not only that, when the child became a grown-up, became sexually mature, he liked to make love to his feet. He would come to his feet and would try to make love to the feet—because that was the first thing he had seen.

Mother is your first love. It is because of the mother that you will fall in love with a woman some day. And, almost always, you will fall in love with a woman who looks in some way like your mother.

"Psychiatry is a lot of junk," said one man to another.
"Oh?" said his companion. "Why do you say that?"
"Well, today my psychiatrist told me that I am in love with my umbrella. Have you ever heard of anything so silly?"
"It does sound rather daft."
"I mean, me and my umbrella certainly have a sincere affection for each other. But *love?* That is just ridiculous!"

If your natural object of love is taken away, you will love money...you may even love your umbrella. You may start falling in love with things: you may start falling in love with flags, countries. All kinds of nonsense is possible once your natural love is distracted.

Bring your love to its natural object. Let it have a spontaneity

of its own, allow it to take possession of you, and you will
be transformed through it.

Love is the key, love is the secret.

The last question:

*Beloved Master, yesterday you so lovingly transmitted the
spirit of Tao. Throughout this series I have been bathing
rapturously in these waters. All that you have ever said is
coming true. I begin to feel surrender as the natural climate
of the flower growing toward the sun. The beauty is here, is
here. . . .*

Samarpan. . .

> The old pond,
> Samarpan jumps in,
> the sound.

BOOKS PUBLISHED BY
RAJNEESH FOUNDATION
INTERNATIONAL

For a complete catalog of all the books published by
Rajneesh Foundation International, contact:

Rajneesh Foundation International
P.O. Box 9
Rajneeshpuram, Oregon 97741 USA
(503) 489-3462 (or 3411)

EARLY DISCOURSES

A Cup of Tea
letters to disciples

From Sex to Superconsciousness

THE BAULS

The Beloved (2 volumes)

BUDDHA

The Book of the Books (volume 1)
the Dhammapada

The Diamond Sutra
the Vajrachchedika Prajnaparamita Sutra

The Discipline of Transcendence (4 volumes)
the Sutra of 42 Chapters

The Heart Sutra
the Prajnaparamita Hridayam Sutra

BUDDHIST MASTERS

The Book of Wisdom (volume 1)
Atisha's Seven Points of Mind Training

The White Lotus
the sayings of Bodhidharma

HASIDISM

The Art of Dying

The True Sage

JESUS

Come Follow Me (4 volumes)
the sayings of Jesus

I Say Unto You (2 volumes)
the sayings of Jesus

INITIATION TALKS
between Master and disciple

Hammer On The Rock
(December 10, 1975 - January 15, 1976)

Above All Don't Wobble
(January 16 - February 12, 1976)

Nothing To Lose But Your Head
(February 13 - March 12, 1976)

Be Realistic: Plan For a Miracle
(March 13 - April 6, 1976)

Get Out of Your Own Way
(April 7 - May 2, 1976)

Beloved of My Heart
(May 3 - 28, 1976)

The Cypress in the Courtyard
(May 29 - June 27, 1976)

A Rose is a Rose is a Rose
(June 28 - July 27, 1976)

Dance Your Way to God
(July 28 - August 20, 1976)

The Passion for the Impossible
(August 21 - September 18, 1976)

The Great Nothing
(September 19 - October 11, 1976)

God is Not for Sale
(October 12 - November 7, 1976)

The Shadow of the Whip
(November 8 - December 3, 1976)

Blessed are the Ignorant
(December 4 - 31, 1976)

The Buddha Disease
(January 1977)

What Is, Is, What Ain't Ain't
(February 1977)

The Zero Experience
(March 1977)

For Madmen Only (Price of Admission: Your Mind)
(April 1977)

This Is It
(May 1977)

The Further Shore
(June 1977)

Far Beyond the Stars
(July 1977)

The No Book (No Buddha, No Teaching, No Discipline)
(August 1977)

Don't Just Do Something, Sit There
(September 1977)

Only Losers Can Win in this Game
(October 1977)

The Open Secret
(November 1977)

The Open Door
(December 1977)

The Sun Behind the Sun Behind the Sun
(January 1978)

Believing the Impossible Before Breakfast
(February 1978)

Don't Bite My Finger, Look Where I am Pointing
(March 1978)

Let Go!
(April 1978)

The Ninety-Nine Names of Nothingness
(May 1978)

The Madman's Guide to Enlightenment
(June 1978)

Don't Look Before You Leap
(July 1978)

Hallelujah!
(August 1978)

God's Got a Thing About You
(September 1978)

The Tongue-Tip Taste of Tao
(October 1978)

The Sacred Yes
(November 1978)

Turn On, Tune In, and Drop the Lot
(December 1978)

Zorba the Buddha
(January 1979)

The Sound of One Hand Clapping
(March 1981)

OTHER TITLES

Rajneeshism
an introduction to Bhagwan Shree Rajneesh and His Religion

The Sound of Running Water
a photobiography of Bhagwan Shree Rajneesh and His work

The Orange Book
the meditation techniques of Bhagwan Shree Rajneesh

BOOKS FROM OTHER PUBLISHERS

ENGLISH EDITIONS
UNITED KINGDOM

The Art of Dying
(Sheldon Press)

The Book of the Secrets (volume 1)
(Thames & Hudson)

Dimensions Beyond the Known
(Sheldon Press)

The Hidden Harmony
(Sheldon Press)

Meditation: The Art of Ecstasy
(Sheldon Press)

The Mustard Seed
(Sheldon Press)

Neither This Nor That
(Sheldon Press)

No Water No Moon
(Sheldon Press)

Roots and Wings
(Routledge & Kegan Paul)

Straight to Freedom (Original title:
Until You Die)
(Sheldon Press

The Supreme Doctrine
(Routledge & Kegan Paul)

The Supreme Understanding (Original title:
Tantra: The Supreme Understanding)
(Sheldon Press)

Tao: The Three Treasures (volume 1)
(Wildwood House)

UNITED STATES OF AMERICA

The Book of the Secrets (volumes 1-3)
(Harper & Row)

The Great Challenge
(Grove Press)

Hammer on the Rock
(Grove Press)

I Am The Gate
(Harper & Row)

Journey Toward the Heart (Original title:
Until You Die)
(Harper & Row)

Meditation: The Art of Ecstasy
(Harper & Row)

The Mustard Seed
(Harper & Row)

My Way: The Way of the White Clouds
(Grove Press)

Only One Sky (Original title:
Tantra: The Supreme Understanding)
(Dutton)

The Psychology of the Esoteric
(Harper & Row)

Roots and Wings
(Routledge & Kegan Paul)

The Supreme Doctrine
(Routledge & Kegan Paul)

Words Like Fire (Original title:
Come Follow Me, volume 1)
(Harper & Row)

BOOKS ON BHAGWAN

The Awakened One: The Life and Work
of Bhagwan Shree Rajneesh
by Swami Satya Vedant
(Harper & Row)

Death Comes Dancing: Celebrating Life
with Bhagwan Shree Rajneesh
by Ma Satya Bharti
(Routledge & Kegan Paul)

Drunk On The Divine
by Ma Satya Bharti
(Grove Press)

The Ultimate Risk
by Ma Satya Bharti
(Routledge & Kegan Paul)

Dying For Enlightenment
by Bernard Gunther (Swami Deva Amitprem)
(Harper & Row)

Neo Tantra
by Bernard Gunther (Swami Deva Amitprem)
(Harper & Row)

FOREIGN LANGUAGE EDITIONS
DANISH

TRANSLATIONS

Hemmelighedernes Bog (volume 1)
(Borgens Forlag)

Hu-Meditation Og Kosmisk Orgasme
(Borgens Forlag)

BOOKS ON BHAGWAN

Sjælens Oprør
by Swami Deva Satyarthi
(Borgens Forlag)

DUTCH

TRANSLATIONS

Drink Mij
(Ankh-Hermes)

Het Boek Der Geheimen (volumes 1-4)
(Mirananda)

Geen Water, Geen Maan
(Mirananda)

Gezaaid In Goede Aarde
(Ankh-Hermes)

Ik Ben De Poort
(Ankh-Hermes)

Ik Ben De Zee Die Je Zoekt
(Ankh-Hermes)

Meditatie: De Kunst van Innerlijke Extase
(Mirananda)

Mijn Weg, De Weg van de Witte Wolk
(Arcanum)

Het Mosterdzaad (volumes 1 & 2)
(Mirananda)

Het Oranje Meditatieboek
(Ankh-Hermes)

Psychologie en Evolutie
(Ankh-Hermes)

Tantra: Het Allerhoogste Inzicht
(Ankh-Hermes)

Tantra, Spiritualiteit en Seks
(Ankh-Hermes)

De Tantra Visie (volume 1)
(Arcanum)

Tau
(Ankh-Hermes)

Totdat Je Sterft
(Ankh-Hermes)

De Verborgen Harmonie
(Mirananda)

Volg Mij
(Ankh-Hermes)

Zoeken naar de Stier
(Ankh-Hermes)

BOOKS ON BHAGWAN

Bhagwan: Notities van een Discipel
by Swami Deva Amrito (Jan Foudraine)
(Ankh-Hermes)

Bhagwan Shree Rajneesh: De Laatste Gok
by Ma Satya Bharti
(Mirananda)

Bhagwan Shree Rajneesh, Een Introductie
by Swami Deva Amrito (Jan Foudraine)
(Ankh-Hermes)

Oorspronkelijk Gezicht, Een Gang naar Huis
by Swami Deva Amrito (Jan Foudraine)
(Ambo)

FRENCH

TRANSLATIONS

L'éveil à la Conscience Cosmique
(Dangles)

Je Suis La Porte
(EPI)

Le Livre des Secrets (volume 1)
(Soleil Orange)

La Meditation Dynamique
(Dangles)

The Orange Book
(Soleil Orange)

GERMAN

TRANSLATIONS

Auf der Suche
(Sambuddha Verlag)

Das Buch der Geheimnisse (volume 1)
(Heyne Verlag)

Das Orangene Buch
(Sambuddha Verlag)

Der Freund
(Sannyas Verlag)

Dimension Jenseits
(Sannyas Verlag)

Ekstase: Die vergessene Sprache
(Herzschlag Verlag, formerly Ki-Buch)

Esoterische Pyschologie
(Sannyas Verlag)

Die Rebellion der Seele
(Sannyas Verlag)

Ich bin der Weg
(Sannyas Verlag)

Intelligenz des Herzens
(Herzschlag Verlag, formerly Ki-Buch)

Jesus aber Schwieg
(Sannyas Verlag)

Kein Wasser Kein Mond
(Herzschlag Verlag, formerly Ki-Buch)

Komm und folge mir
(Sannyas Verlag)

Meditation: Die Kunst zu sich selbst zu finden
(Heyne Verlag)

Mein Weg: Der Weg der weissen Wolke
(Herzschlag Verlag, formerly Ki-Buch)

Mit Wurzeln und mit Flügeln
(Edition Lotus)

Nicht bevor du stirbst
(Edition Gyandip, Switzerland)

Die Schuhe auf dem Kopf
(Edition Lotus)

Das Klatschen der einen Hand
(Edition Gyandip, Switzerland)

Spirituelle Entwicklung
(Fischer)

Sprengt den Fels der Unbewusstheit
(Fischer)

Tantra: Die höchste Einsicht
(Sambuddha Verlag)

Tantrische Liebeskunst
(Sannyas Verlag)

Die Alchemie der Verwandlung
(Edition Lotus)

Die verborgene Harmonie
(Sannyas Verlag)

Was ist Meditation?
(Sannyas Verlag)

BOOKS ON BHAGWAN

Begegnung mit Niemand
by Mascha Rabben (Ma Hari Chetana)
(Herzschlag Verlag)

Ganz entspannt im Hier und Jetzt
by Swami Satyananda
(Rowohlt)

Im Grunde ist alles ganz einfach
by Swami Satyananda
(Ullstein)

Wagnis Orange
by Ma Satya Bharti
(Fachbuchhandlung für Psychologie)

Wenn das Herz frei wird
by Ma Prem Gayan (Silvie Winter)
(Herbig)

GREEK

TRANSLATION

I Krifi Armonia (The Hidden Harmony)
(Emmanual Rassoulis)

HEBREW

TRANSLATION

Tantra: The Supreme Understanding
(Massada)

ITALIAN

TRANSLATIONS

L'Armonia Nascosta (volumes 1 & 2)
(Re Nudo)

Dieci Storie Zen di Bhagwan Shree Rajneesh
(Né Acqua, Né Luna)
(Il Fiore d'Oro)

La Dottrina Suprema
(Rizzoli)

Dimensioni Oltre il Conosciuto
(Mediterranee)

Io Sono La Soglia
(Mediterranee)

Il Libro Arancione
(Mediterranee)

Il Libro dei Segreti
(Bompiani)

Meditazione Dinamica: L'Arte dell'Estasi Interiore
(Mediterranee)

La Nuova Alchimia
(Psiche)

La Rivoluzione Interiore
(Mediterranee)

La Ricerca
(La Salamandra)

Il Seme della Ribellione (volumes 1-3)
(Re Nudo)

Tantra: La Comprensione Suprema
(Bompiani)

Tao: I Tre Tesori (volumes 1-3)
(Re Nudo)

Tecniche di Liberazione
(La Salamandra)

Semi di Saggezza
(SugarCo)

BOOKS ON BHAGWAN

Alla Ricerca del Dio Perduto
by Swami Deva Majid
(SugarCo)

Il Grande Esperimento: Meditazioni e Terapie nell'Ashram
Di Bhagwan Shree Rajneesh
by Ma Satya Bharti
(Armenia)

L'Incanto D'Arancio
by Swami Swatantra Sarjano
(Savelli)

JAPANESE

TRANSLATIONS

Dance Your Way to God
(Rajneesh Publications)

The Empty Boat (volumes 1 & 2)
(Rajneesh Publications)

From Sex to Superconsciousness
(Rajneesh Publications)

The Grass Grows by Itself
(Fumikura)

The Heart Sutra
(Merkmal)

Meditation: The Art of Ecstasy
(Merkmal)

The Mustard Seed
(Merkmal)

My Way: The Way of the White Clouds
(Rajneesh Publications)

The Orange Book
(Wholistic Therapy Institute)

The Search
(Merkmal)

The Secret
(Merkmal)

Take It Easy (volume 1)
(Merkmal)

Tantra: The Supreme Understanding
(Merkmal)

Tao: The Three Treasures (volumes 1-4)
(Merkmal)

Until You Due
(Fumikura)

PORTUGUESE (BRAZIL)

TRANSLATIONS

O Cipreste No Jardim
(Soma)

Dimensões Além do Conhecido
(Soma)

O Livro Dos Segredos (volume 1)
(Maha Lakshmi Editora)

Eu Sou A Porta
(Pensamento)

A Harmonia Oculta
(Pensamento)

Meditacão: A Arte Do Extase
(Cultrix)

Meu Caminho: O Comainho Das Nuvens Brancas
(Tao Livraria & Editora)

Nem Agua, Nem Lua
(Pensamento)

O Livro Orange
(Soma)

Palavras De Fogo
(Global/Ground)

A Psicologia Do Esotérico
(Tao Livraria & Editora)

A Semente De Mostarda (volumes 1 & 2)
(Tao Livraria & Editora)

Tantra: Sexo E Espiritualidade
(Agora)

Tantra: A Suprema Compreensão
(Cultrix)

Antes Que Você Morra
(Maha Lakshmi Editora)

SPANISH

TRANSLATIONS

Introducción al Mundo del Tantra
(Collección Tantra)

Meditación: El Arte del Extasis
(Collección Tantra)

Psicología de lo Esotérico:
La Nueva Evolución del Hombre
(Cuatro Vientos Editorial)

¿Qué Es Meditación?
(Koan/Roselló Impresions)

Yo Soy La Puerta
(Editorial Diana)

Sólo Un Cielo (volumes 1 & 2)
(Colección Tantra)

BOOKS ON BHAGWAN

Il Riesgo Supremo
by Ma Satya Bharti
(Martinez Roca)

SWEDISH

TRANSLATION

Den Väldiga Utmaningen
(Livskraft)

RAJNEESH MEDITATION CENTERS, ASHRAMS AND COMMUNES

There are hundreds of Rajneesh meditation centers throughout the world. These are some of the main ones, which can be contacted for the name and address of the center nearest you. They can also tell you about the availability of the books of Bhagwan Shree Rajneesh — in English or in foreign language editions. General information is available from Rajneesh Foundation International.

Meditation and inner growth programs are available at: RAJNEESH INSTITUTE FOR THERAPY and RAJNEESH INSTITUTE FOR MEDITATION AND INNER GROWTH at Rajneeshpuram. For further information, contact:

RAJNEESH INSTITUTE FOR THERAPY
P.O. Box 9, Rajneeshpuram, Oregon 97741
USA
Tel: (503) 489-3328 (or 3411)

USA

RAJNEESH FOUNDATION INTERNATIONAL
P.O. Box 9, Rajneeshpuram, Oregon 97741
Tel: (503) 489-3301

DEEPTA RAJNEESH MEDITATION CENTER
3024 Ashby Avenue, Berkeley, CA 94705
Tel: (415) 845-2515

SAMBODHI RAJNEESH SANNYAS ASHRAM
Conomo Point Road, Essex, MA 01929 Tel: (617) 768-7640

UTSAVA RAJNEESH MEDITATION CENTER
20062 Laguna Canyon, Laguna Beach, CA 92651
Tel: (714) 497-4877

ABHINAVA RAJNEESH MEDITATION CENTER
701 Mission Street, Santa Cruz, CA 95060
Tel: (408) 427-0188

DEVADEEP RAJNEESH SANNYAS ASHRAM
1403 Longfellow St., N.W., Washington, D.C. 20011
Tel: (202) 723-2186

CANADA

ARVIND RAJNEESH SANNYAS ASHRAM
2807 W. 16th Ave., Vancouver, B.C. V6K 3C5
Tel: (604) 734-4681

SHANTI SADAN RAJNEESH MEDITATION CENTER
1817 Rosemont, Montreal, Quebec H2G 1S5
Tel: (514) 272-4566

AUSTRALIA

PREMDWEEP RAJNEESH MEDITATION CENTER
64 Fullarton Rd., Norwood, S.A. 5067 Tel: 08-423388

SATPRAKASH RAJNEESH MEDITATION CENTER
108 Oxford Street, Darlinghurst 2010, N.S.W.
Tel: (02) 336570

SAHAJAM RAJNEESH SANNYAS ASHRAM
6 Collie Street, Fremantle 6160, W.A.
Tel: (09) 336-2422

SVARUP RAJNEESH MEDITATION CENTER
169 Elgin St., Carlton 3053, Victoria Tel: 347-6274

AUSTRIA

PRADEEP RAJNEESH MEDITATION CENTER
Siebenbrunnenfeldgasse 4, 1050 Vienna Tel: 542-860

BELGIUM

VADAN RAJNEESH MEDITATION CENTER
Platte-Lo-Straat 65, 3200 Leuven (Kessel-Lo)
Tel: 016/25-1487

BRAZIL

PRASTHAN RAJNEESH MEDITATION CENTER
R. Paulos Matos 121, Rio de Janeiro, R.J. 20251
Tel: 222-9476

PURNAM RAJNEESH MEDITATION CENTER
Caixa Postal 1946, Porto Alegre, RS 90000

CHILE

SAGARO RAJNEESH MEDITATION CENTER
Golfo de Darien 10217, Las Condas, Santiago
Tel: 472476

DENMARK

ANAND NIKETAN RAJNEESH MEDITATION CENTER
Strøget, Frederiksberggade 15, 1459 Copenhagen K
Tel: (01) 139940

EAST AFRICA

ANAND NEED RAJNEESH MEDITATION CENTER
Kitisuru Estate, P.O. Box 72424, Nairobi, Kenya
Tel: 582600

FRANCE

PRADIP RAJNEESH MEDITATION CENTER
23 Rue Cecile, Maisons Alfoet, 94700 Paris
Tel: 3531190

GREAT BRITAIN

KALPTARU RAJNEESH MEDITATION CENTER
28 Oak Village, London NW5 4QN Tel: (01) 267-8304

MEDINA RAJNEESH NEO-SANNYAS COMMUNE
Herringswell, Bury St. Edmunds, Suffolk 1P28 6SW
Tel: (0638) 750234

HOLLAND

DE STAD RAJNEESH NEO-SANNYAS COMMUNE
Kamperweg 80-86 8191 KC Heerde Tel: 05207-1261

GRADA RAJNEESH NEO-SANNYAS COMMUNE
Prins Hendrikstraat 64, 1931 BK Egmond aan Zee
Tel: 02206-4114

INDIA

RAJNEESHDHAM NEO-SANNYAS COMMUNE
17 Koregaon Park, Poona 411 001, MS Tel: 28127

RAJ YOGA RAJNEESH MEDITATION CENTER
C5/44 Safdarjang Development Area, New Delhi 100 016
Tel: 654533

ITALY

MIASTO RAJNEESH NEO-SANNYAS COMMUNE
Podere S. Giorgio, Cotorniano, 53010 Frosini (Siena)
Tel: 0577-960124

VIVEK RAJNEESH MEDITATION CENTER
Via San Marco 40/4, 20121 Milan Tel: 659-5632

JAPAN

SHANTIYUGA RAJNEESH MEDITATION CENTER
Sky Mansion 2F, 1-34-1 Ookayama, Meguro-ku, Tokyo
152
Tel: (03) 724-9631

UTSAVA RAJNEESH MEDITATION CENTER
2-9-8 Hattori-Motomachi, Toyonaki-shi, Osaka 561
Tel: 06-863-4246

NEW ZEALAND

SHANTI NIKETAN RAJNEESH MEDITATION CENTER
115 Symonds Street, Auckland Tel: 770-326

PUERTO RICO

BHAGWATAM RAJNEESH MEDITATION CENTER
Calle Sebastian 208 (Altos), Viejo San Juan, PR 00905
Tel: 725-0593

SPAIN

SARVOGEET RAJNEESH MEDITATION CENTER
C. Titania 55, Madrid, 33 Tel: 200-0313

SWEDEN

DEEVA RAJNEESH MEDITATION CENTER
Surbrunnsgatan 60, 11327 Stockholm. Tel: (08) 327788

SWITZERLAND

GYANDIP RAJNEESH MEDITATION CENTER
Baumackerstr. 42, 8050 Zurich Tel: (01) 312 1600

WEST GERMANY

ANAND SAGAR RAJNEESH MEDITATION CENTER
Lutticherstr. 33/35, 5000 Cologne 1 Tel: 0221-517199

BAILE RAJNEESH NEO-SANNYAS COMMUNE
Karolinenstr. 7-9, 2000 Hamburg 6 Tel: (040) 432140

RAJNEESHSTADT NEO-SANNYAS COMMUNE
Schloss Wolfsbrunnen, 3446 Meinhard-Schwebda
Tel: (05651) 70044

SATDHARMA RAJNEESH MEDITATION CENTER
Klenzestr. 41, 8000 Munich 5 Tel: (089) 269-077

DÖRFCHEN RAJNEESH NEO-SANNYAS COMMUNE
Urbanstr. 64, 1000 Berlin 61 Tel: (030) 691-7917